THE
HISTORY OF SPAIN

PART I

FROM THE VISIGOTHS TO THE DEATH OF PHILLIP II

LOUIS BERTRAND

OF THE ACADÉMIE FRANÇAISE

PART II

FROM THE DEATH OF PHILLIP II TO 1945

SIR CHARLES PETRIE BT.

M.A. (OXON), F.R.HIST.S.

CORRESPONDING MEMBER OF THE ROYAL
SPANISH ACADEMY OF HISTORY

SECOND EDITION

Revised and continued to the year 1945

COLLIER BOOKS, NEW YORK, NEW YORK

The Macmillan Company
866 Third Avenue, New York, N.Y. 10022

First Collier Books Edition 1971

This paperback edition is reprinted by arrangement
with Eyre & Spottiswoode (Publishers) Ltd., London.

Printed in the United States of America

CONTENTS

CONTENTS

§ V. THE RECONQUEST

§ VI. THE DISCOVERY AND CONQUEST OF AMERICA

§ VII. THE SPANISH HEGEMONY AND THE ESTABLISHMENT OF THE ABSOLUTE MONARCHY

CONTENTS

PART II

LIST OF MAPS

INTRODUCTION TO THE SECOND EDITION

IN this Second Edition no alterations have been made in Part I which was written by the late M. Louis Bertrand, but two chapters have been omitted in order to preserve the balance of the book. On the other hand, there have been a considerable number of additions to Part II: in the original edition it finished with the establishment of the Second Republic in 1931, but the narrative has now been extended to cover the Civil War, and the additional chapters carry the story of Spain down to the close of the Second World War. The documentation of the last years of this period is still incomplete, but it is hoped that the summary of the campaign, which left General Franco master of the country, and of Spanish foreign policy, will not, in the light of the information now available, be considered inadequate.

CHARLES PETRIE

April, 1951.

INTRODUCTION TO THE FIRST EDITION

THE subject of this book is the study of a great civilisation. It is the story of the influence which Spain has exerted in world history, first in mediæval Europe, when she drove the Moslem invader slowly back, and then both in Europe and America, when she colonised the greater part of a continent, without for a moment abandoning her traditional policy as the champion of Christendom against the infidel.

In the original French edition, of which the present English one is a translation, M. Louis Bertrand distinguishes four great periods in Spanish history: first of all, the contest with Islam in the Peninsula itself, which occupied eight centuries of Spain's existence, and is the capital fact of it; then her discovery and conquest of the New World; next the establishment of the absolute monarchy, and the struggle against the Reformation; and finally her effort to remain a Great Power.

The chapters which deal with this period are as M. Bertrand wrote them, but those which the French historian devoted to the centuries that have elapsed since the death of Philip II have been very considerably expanded by the present writer, and the events leading up to the establishment of the Second Republic in 1931 have been treated at length.

The common mistake made by British and American historians in dealing with Spain, in the mediæval period especially, is to regard her as a world apart. They fail to depict Spanish events against their European background, and thus miss their real significance. M. Bertrand has lived for some years in Africa with Spaniards and Moslems, in a setting, as he says: "somewhat analogous with what the Southern Spain of the Middle Ages must have been," and so he is peculiarly well equipped to present the history of the Spanish Middle Ages in its right light.

Much that he has to say may seem strange to the Anglo-Saxon reader, accustomed to regard Spain from the standpoint of his Elizabethan forefathers; but no one can follow M. Bertrand's brilliant analysis of the so-called Arab civilisation without reaching the conclusion that his interpretation is the correct one, and that many British workers in this field have gone seriously astray.

For two hundred and fifty years, that is to say from the death of Mary Tudor to the outbreak of the Peninsular War, England was intermittently at war with Spain, and the passions which were roused during that contest have unfortunately been only too faithfully reflected in the pages of English historians. The result has been that the ordinary educated Anglo-Saxon on both sides of the Atlantic still reads Spanish history with all the prejudice of his ancestors. The propaganda that attracted recruits to the colours in the days of the Armada still permeates the textbooks. The American is in an even worse plight, for he fought the Spaniards as recently as 1898, so that the older generation is still under the influence of the bitter feeling which that conflict engendered.

For millions of people, therefore, Spain in the days of her greatness was the embodiment of all that is evil; a Power which strove to suppress civil and religious liberty throughout the world, and was herself sunk in ignorance and superstition. The novelist has completed what the historian began, and the Spaniards portrayed by such writers as Charles Kingsley have been accepted as the normal type of their fellow-countrymen.

The decline of Spanish power was described as the inevitable consequence of the policy which had been pursued in the sixteenth and seventeenth centuries, and was generally treated as just retribution. It was not understood that what had exhausted the nation's strength was the simultaneous colonisation of America and the struggle against the Musulmans, and it was assumed, rather than proved, that a misguided people had met a fate to which they had been doomed from the beginning.

Nor was any allowance made for the economic difficulties of Spain at this period. The discovery of America, and the importation into Europe of precious metals in quantities previously unknown, caused a fall in the value of money, and a consequent rise in prices: Spain, the possessor of the Indies, was naturally the first and the most seriously affected by this development. If too much attention is perhaps paid to economic history to-day, too little was certainly given to it in the past, and for this reason, too, Spain has not received a fair deal at the hands of the Anglo-Saxon historians.

In her Golden Age she is shown as arrogant and intolerant, and when, in her decline, she was struggling to remain a Great Power, she is dismissed with a sneer as a beggar aping the state of his betters. As for her history since the Napoleonic invasion, it is invariably ignored, and nineteenth and twentieth century Spain is quoted as an excellent example of a nation that has had its day, and is scarcely worth a passing reference.

How those who adopted this standpoint reconciled it with the facts of Spanish civilisation it is difficult to say. The people who were steeped in ignorance and bestiality produced Velázquez, Murillo, and Goya; Lope de Vega, Cervantes, and Calderón. Their architects designed the cathedrals of Burgos, Toledo, and Seville, and covered the New World with buildings that are among its most treasured possessions at the present time. For a hundred and fifty years, from the time of Gonzalo de Cordova to the battle of Rocroy, the Spanish infantry were invincible, while Spanish sailors were revealing the secrets of the seven seas. Above all, America was being explored and colonised, and in the whole of recorded history there have been no feats to surpass those of the *conquistadores*. In the fuller knowledge and greater impartiality of to-day it must be admitted that the Anglo-Saxon presentation of Spanish history has too often been unjust.

The corollary of this persistent denigration of the Spaniard was the exaltation of his enemy, the Moor. The Musulman who had conquered the Peninsula became the very pattern of chivalry, and the civilisation of Cordova and Granada was contrasted with the savagery of the Christian Reconquest.

Those who took this line never stopped to enquire why, if this civilisation was purely Musulman, the Arab elsewhere should have remained sunk in the most profound ignorance. The overthrow of Spanish Islam was written down as a definite calamity, and one from which unhappy Spain has never recovered. The anarchy which was continually breaking out even in the heyday of Omayyad power, and the ferocity which marked the rule of the various Arab dynasties, were glossed over or altogether ignored, and a picture was painted which bore but a scanty resemblance to the truth. In the following pages M. Louis Bertrand sweeps away the misconceptions to which such treatment gave rise. He does not allow the romance of Musulman Spain to blind him to the reality, and he shows that such of it as is worthy of praise was in fact Spanish.

The work of the Spaniards in America has likewise been far too harshly judged, and the civilisation of such people as the Incas unduly praised. "The Inca," to quote M. Bertrand once more, "is represented sometimes as the type of good savage, full of innocence and virtue, dear to the heart of Jean Jacques Rousseau; sometimes as the heir of a high civilisation, hatefully blotted out by the barbarism of the *conquistadores*." What Spain set up was vastly superior to what she pulled down, and it is a mistake to allow our natural horror at the methods of the *conquistadores* (who were no more brutal than their English contemporaries) to blind us to their achievements, for they brought two-thirds of the American continent within the sphere of European culture.

Nor was Spanish rule in the New World the grinding tyranny that it is so often described in English and American textbooks; if such had been the case it would not have taken Bolivar and San Martin so many years to sever the connection with Madrid. The contest which resulted in the independence of Spanish America was a civil war, in which the side opposed to the continuance of Spanish government was victorious after a long struggle. Relatively few native Spaniards took part in the war, which was one between the colonists themselves.

In the pages which follow it has been the endeavour of M. Louis Bertrand and myself to place such events in their correct perspective, and in so doing not only to narrate the history of Spain, but to show how much that great country has contributed to the common stock of our civilisation.

CHARLES PETRIE

PART I

SPAIN FROM THE VISIGOTHS TO THE DEATH OF PHILIP II

§ I

MUSULMAN SPAIN

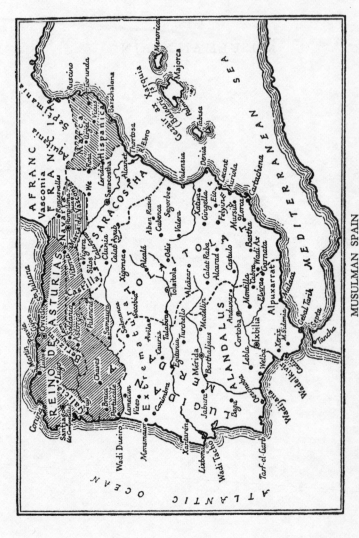

MUSULMAN SPAIN

From Abd-er-Rhaman (756) to Alfonso III (866), King of Asturias. The Kingdoms of Asturias and Navarre and the County of Barcelona (the shaded portions) were the only parts of the Peninsula in Christian hands.

CHAPTER I

Visigoth Spain on the Eve of the Arab Conquest

AFTER the battle of Algeciras, which handed Spain over to the Arabs, it was impossible, their annalists tell us, to find any trace of Rodrigo, the Visigoth king who was defeated in that battle. "The Musulmans," writes Ibn el Athir, "indeed found his white horse, which was mired in a slough, with its saddle of gilded buckskin adorned with rubies and emeralds. They found also his mantle of cloth of gold, adorned with pearls and rubies. . . ." A little farther away, stuck in the mire, was one of his half-boots, of cloth of silver.

But it was absolutely impossible to discover the body of the king, if he was killed in the battle or assassinated by one of his own side. If he fled, he escaped so completely from those who pursued him, and succeeded in hiding himself so well, that he was never heard of again.

That is all that remained in the imagination of the Musulmans, after this great event which delivered up to them, together with a great kingdom, the gates of Western Europe: a king who suddenly disappeared, who plunged into impenetrable darkness; with that disappearance, an empire which collapsed; and, as souvenirs of all this, a silver boot, a war-horse, a saddle spangled with rubies and emeralds, a mantle of cloth of gold embroidered with precious stones and pearls. . . .

The care with which the Arab annalists note these sumptuous relics clearly reveals their astonishment and admiration in the presence of the luxury of the Visigoth kings and their court. Spain all along appeared to them—especially to the uncivilised Berbers of the Moghreb—a country of enchantment.

The Roman cities into which they penetrated so easily surprised them no less than the fertility of the country. All their annalists recall the appearance at that time of Seville, Cordova, Merida, and Toledo, "the four capitals of Spain, founded," they tell us naïvely, "by Okteban the Cæsar." Among these capitals they forget, or they ignore, those of northern Spain: Tarragona, Barcelona, Pampeluna, León.

Seville, above all, seems to have struck them by its opulence and its illustriousness in various ways. "It was," writes Ibn Adhari, "among all the capitals of Spain the greatest, the most important, the best built and the richest in ancient monuments. Before its conquest by the Goths it had been the residence of the Roman governor. The Goth kings chose Toledo for their residence; but Seville remained the seat of the Roman adepts of sacred and profane science, and it was there that lived the nobility of the same origin." There is a similar eulogium of Merida: "This former capital possessed admirable ancient monuments, a bridge and magnificent palaces and churches."

When Mousa, after completing the conquest of Spain, went to Damascus to render account to the Caliph of his conquest and his administration, he proudly displayed the booty which he had taken from the Spaniards: "thirty thousand virgins, daughters of Goth kings and princes, and *an innumerable quantity of merchandise and precious stones*." Among these valuable objects there was one truly fabulous, which had been taken in a city near Guadalajara, and which the Arabs called the Table of Solomon. "The edges and the legs were of emeralds. . . . These, to the number of three hundred and sixty, were enriched with pearls and coral." Finally the invaders, after a raid as far as France, found in Saragossa "riches incalculable."

No doubt we must make allowance in all these marvels for Oriental exaggeration. Those who tell us about them are compilers writing in accordance with traditions already remote. But it is still certain that the spectacle of Roman Spain, even much diminished and much impoverished after the devastations of the Vandals, the Swabians, and the Goths, must have amazed, if not the Syrian Arabs, at least the Berbers of Africa, who made up the greater part of the conquering armies.

It was a country governed, administered, and organised on Roman lines, with a single head, a king hereditary at least in principle, at the apex of the hierarchy. Spain, thanks to the Visigoth kings, had ceased to be a province, or a group of provinces, and had become a kingdom. There was henceforth a King of Spain, as there had been a Cæsar in Rome, and as there still was an Emperor in Byzantium—a king who ruled over all the Spains: something that was not to be seen again until Charles V. It is from the date of this unification, superficial and artificial though it may have been, that, properly speaking, the history of Spain begins—that Spain has a history.

This Visigoth period, which runs from about 410 to 711, the date of the conquest of Spain by the Arabs, is a thankless and also, for lack of documentation, a somewhat obscure field of study. It is full of devastations, massacres, political assassinations, intestinal wars among the invading barbarians. Even after the triumph of the Visigoths and the coming of their monarchy disorder continued. It was only after the conversion of King Recaredo to Catholicism that one can recognise at least some progress in absolute power and, consequently, in internal pacification.

This absolute monarchy, like most of the barbarian institutions, was modelled upon that of the Roman Cæsars. The Visigoth kings adopted their sons as their eventual successors, by way of assuring at least the principle of heredity. But this principle was contested by that of election, which the nobles strove to maintain, and this led to disturbance at every succession.

For Spain the Visigoth monarchy was, in short, an aggravation of the Roman regime. Most of the land was in the possession of the Catholic clergy, who became all-powerful after the conversion of Recaredo. He was rich, cultured, and a lover of luxury. He made Seville and Toledo regular centres of study—what are rather pompously called universities.

This clerical culture of Visigoth times had its great man and its source of learning in the person of Saint Isidore of Seville, author of encyclopædic compilations, theological and philosophical works, and a history of the Visigoths, Vandals, and Swabians, which, despite its gaps and its defects, is a considerable achievement.

Side by side with the clergy, there was a military nobility, which shared with the clergy the ownership of the soil; and finally there was a whole administrative personnel, a whole army of officials, who were the same as those of the Roman administration, with their dukes and their counts, governing the cities and the provinces respectively.

But the class of small landowners had almost completely disappeared, and the condition of the serfs attached to the soil had become still worse since the end of the Empire. A whole part of the population, the Jews, very numerous then as they were in Spain throughout the Middle Ages, was the object of more and more rigorous repression. At the beginning of the seventh century, during the reign of Sisebut, there was open persecution: religious fanaticism no doubt, but also a political measure.

The Spaniards were always afraid of the intrigues of the Jews with their co-religionists of Barbary, who might influence the Africans among whom they lived to attempt fresh landings or fresh raids on the soil of the Peninsula. Let us not forget—and I shall have frequent occasion to recall this capital fact, which must never be lost to sight when one studies the history of Spain—that Spain lived for thousands of years in terror of African invasions or piracies.

Throughout the centuries the attitude of the Jews remained the same: they were the allies of the Africans against the Spaniards, of the Musulmans against the Christians, and of the Christians against the Musulmans, when the tide turned. They neutralised their enemies one with the other: it was a system of counterpoise.

In these first years of the seventh century, whether it was that their number and their wealth alarmed the government, or that they were suspected of being in negotiation with the Berbers or the Byzantines of Africa, drastic measures were taken against them. They were given a year to become converts to Christianity or leave the country.

It seems that 90,000 of them preferred baptism to expatriation, and there were pretended conversions by the swarm. Thanks to this expedient they remained. They continued even to practise their religion and live according to their law; but it was a wretched life of ceaseless anxiety that they led, with repression and tolerance alternating.

Towards the end of the century—that is to say, a few years before the Musulman invasion—they decided upon a general rising. Were they driven beyond endurance, as certain historians say, or did they judge the moment opportune and the circumstances particularly favourable? The two hypotheses are equally admissible, and it is very probable that the two motives operated at the same time. Carthage, the last foothold of the Byzantines in Africa, had just fallen (693). There were, so to speak, no Christians left on the other side of the Mediterranean. Islam was triumphant from one side of Africa to the other.

It was then that the Jews came to an understanding with their co-religionists of Barbary and with the Spanish Jews in exile in Africa in consequence of Sisebut's measures. The rising was to break out simultaneously with a descent by African Jews, no doubt supported by Berber tribesmen, on the coast of Andalusia. The plot was discovered, and its discovery led to a redoubling of repressive measures against the Spanish Jews. Once more they were confronted with the alternatives of becoming converts or leaving the country.

All this agitation profoundly disturbed the kingdom. It was ceaselessly distracted by the rivalries of the Grandees, and there were also other dissidents besides the Jews—namely, entire populations which had remained Arian or pagan in the midst of Christians and Catholics.

To all these causes of weakness was added laxity of morals, at least among the Grandees. Laity and clergy maintained regular harems of concubines, despite all ecclesiastical censures. It was not yet Musulman polygamy, but it was something that strongly resembled it. Ibn Adhari tells us that, when Mousa returned from Spain to Damascus, he was closely interrogated about that country by the Caliph Soleyman. The Caliph asked Mousa what had struck him most in it. "The effeminacy of the princes," replied that austere Musulman.

Spain, under the last Visigoth kings, was ripe for foreign invasion.

CHAPTER II

The Arab-Berber Conquest

AT Toledo, at the spot where the gorge of the Tagus closes in
and the bend of the river opens on to the plain, they still show
to-day a heap of shapeless ruins called the Baths of La Cava.
It was there, so the legend runs, that Rodrigo, the last Visigoth king,
seduced the daughter of Count Julian, the beautiful Florinda, whom
the poets of the *Romancero* call La Cava. It was to avenge the dis-
honouring of his daughter that the traitor Julian invited the Arabs
to Spain and handed over his fatherland to the infidels. As a matter
of fact, these ruins are the debris of an old bridge, and it is not certain
that La Cava ever existed.

So, from the very beginning of her history, Musulman Spain
possessed a romantic character, which she retained to the end.
When one emerges from the brief Visigoth annals, she conveys an
impression of fantasy and frivolity. It is another atmosphere; it is
the beginning of a new world, a world not made to our measure,
which attracts and shocks us, which disconcerts all our habits of
mind.

This world has scarcely been thought about or described by Latin
and European minds, so that it is difficult for us to represent it to
ourselves as it really was. A complete critical exegesis is required to
bring it in touch with us and subject it to the habitual conditions of
our point of view and the methods of our thought.

For the whole of this period, in fact, we have scarcely any documentation except in Arabic. Latin texts are rare, and the reasons for
this fact are only too easy to understand. The Musulman invasion
led to a decay, not to say a complete destruction, of Latin culture in
Spain, especially northern Spain, which remained Christian and
Roman. Perhaps it would not be paradoxical to say that this culture
was better preserved in southern or central Spain, at Cordova or at
Toledo, under the Musulman regime, than it was in Asturias or
Navarre, reduced by the invaders to a precarious and wretched
existence, and exposed to periodical devastations.

In any case, the Latin documents which we possess about Musulman Spain are few, and they do not tell us much. They are, in general,
the work of clerics or monks, who are interested only in their own
church or monastery and execrate the infidels. They speak of the
Musulmans and their princes only to revile them. What they see in
this lamentable story of Spain under the invader is a pretext for
teaching a lesson to their flocks. They see in it the finger of God and
the just punishment of the Christian people, in expiation of their
vices and their impiety. In any case it is an abominable story, and it
is much better not to talk about it.

It is, therefore, especially to Arabic texts that we must turn for this period of the early Middle Ages in Musulman Spain. But here every kind of precaution is called for on the part of foreign readers, especially those who are not Arabic scholars and have to resort to translations or content themselves with the commentaries of our historians. In the first place, it appears that the lack of precision in the Arabic language justifies the most disconcertingly wide interpretations of the same text. Who is to decide among the translators? We profane people are compelled to put up with what they offer us, though we may preserve a prudent scepticism.

We must, moreover, be on our guard against being deceived by words, which do not mean the same thing for us as for Orientals. The words "learning" and "scholar" have not the same sense for a Christian of the twentieth century as they had for a Musulman, or a Christian of the ninth century. When we are told about Musulman tolerance and about the cult of literature, science, and art at the court of the Caliphs, when the praises of the universities of Cordova, Seville, or Toledo are sung to us, it would be very naïve to judge them by our standards, and to see in these universities something like the Sorbonne, even that of the Middle Ages. The poetry of the Arabs is quite different from ours; and so also is their history.

The Arab "historians," as they are generously called, can only be regarded from our point of view as dry annalists or, in general, compilers without any critical faculty. As Gobineau has already remarked, in connection with the Persian writers, they do not possess the sense of what we understand by truth, or, more exactly, the sense of Yes and No. They have a hazy idea of the boundaries of history and poetry, properly so-called.

Thus their histories are strewn with long fragments of poetry, to which they attribute the value of historical evidence; they accept the most fabulous legends and traditions without interpreting them; they fall into all kinds of Oriental exaggeration; and, when they quote figures, they let themselves go to astronomical valuations. As for marshalling of narrative and methodical exposition, nothing could be further from their habits of mind. Everything is put on the same plane—trivial incidents and important events which led to changes of regime or the fall of empires.

The most annoying thing for us is that the narrative is cut up into annual sections and continually chopped off and interrupted by the obligation to respect the chronology. It is impossible to follow the development of an action: the plan of the annalist is opposed to it. This produces extraordinary complexity and intricacy, something like the inextricable labyrinth of lines in an arabesque: a torture to the mind, which finally gives up trying to make head or tail of it.

Along with this goes a lack of personality in the actors, a lack of relief in the characters, who repeat themselves indefinitely. These histories—if one dare give them that name—only too often leave us with the impression of an absurd and unintelligible chaos.

With regard to the Spanish historians who write in Arabic—especially those who write about the period with which I am concerned—Dozy remarks very pertinently that they have more common sense, or at least a more exact and realistic sense of things, than the Orientals. Ibn Kaldoun, the one among all these writers who approximates closest to our conception of an historian, was of Spanish origin. Yet these Spaniards themselves, these Islamised Spaniards, admit the fables of the Egyptians and the Persians as authentic documents for the ancient history of their own country.

Instead of investigating local traditions and Latin or Greek texts about Spanish antiquities, they prefer to rely upon the doctors of Cairo or Bagdad, who are regarded by them as the sources of all learning and the models of all orthodoxy, and therefore the sole repositories of truth. Hence arise the strangest fantasies. But, when it is a question of events of which they were witnesses and, in general, of Musulman Spain, even that of the early centuries, they rediscover their faculty of judgment and their realist and positivist mind.

In connection with the beginning of the Arab Conquest we have the good fortune to possess one of these Spanish documents, which is entitled the *Akbar Madjmoua*. According to the best judges, one can rely upon it without too much risk of error. The personalities and the facts, taken as a whole, seem to be quite authentic. We are as near as possible to the truth; but, even so, this history still preserves in places the air of a fairy-tale.

The governor of Africa for Rodrigo, King of Spain, Count Julian, had a daughter fair as the day, whose name was Florinda. In accordance with the custom of Spanish patricians, who sent their children to the court of the Visigoth king, there to learn the service of princes or the profession of arms, Julian sent his daughter to Toledo, where she was attached to the higher household ranks in the palace. As luck would have it, Rodrigo fell in love with the fair Florinda.

One day, when she was bathing in the Tagus, he surprised her treacherously and took his pleasure of her. Julian's daughter found means of informing her father of her dishonour. He swore to be avenged. A little later, Rodrigo asked him for falcons and hawks for his hunts. "I will send you," replied Julian, "a hawk such as you have never heard of before. . . ." It was a veiled allusion to the barbarian invader whom he contemplated launching against his master's kingdom.

He was, in fact, not slow in approaching Tarik, who was in command at Tangier in the name of Mousa, governor of Ifrikia, and showing him how easy the conquest of Spain would be for a leader of armies who was so close to her. Tarik responded to his overtures, and Julian sent over to Spain, in coasting boats and in small parties, lest the Spaniards should be put on the alert, a whole body of troops, who went to ground and awaited the arrival of their leader.

Tarik set off with the last contingent. He disembarked at Gibraltar, seized Algeciras, and, in order to terrorise the Spaniards, ordered his soldiers to cut a party of prisoners to pieces and boil their flesh in cauldrons. Then he set his other captives at liberty. Aghast at this horrible spectacle, they set off to spread the alarm throughout the country.

Tarik resumed his march, met Rodrigo on the banks of a river, and vanquished him in a battle which lasted from morning till night. After that he took possession, almost without striking a blow, of the principal cities of Andalusia, occupied Toledo, the capital of the kingdom, and, still pursuing his triumphal march, pressed on to Guadalajara and the pass of Buitrago. There he was overtaken by Mousa, his superior, who, jealous of his laurels, had come over to Spain himself. Mousa, after picking up many successes on his way, took Saragossa and, through the valley of the Ebro, penetrated even into France.

The whole of Spain was thus conquered in a very short time; and, when Mousa went to give his account of his conquest to the Caliph of Damascus, he laid at the feet of the Commander of the Faithful an immense booty, thousands of captives and inestimable riches. . . .

Such is the semi-legendary narrative which the Arab annalists all reproduce, with more or less important variations, but which is fundamentally identical in all of them. The *Akbar Madjmoua*, while it admits some fabulous features, nevertheless possesses a more seriously historical character. It offers the beginning of a genuine synthesis which modern critical methods can follow up to obtain at least an approximation very close to the truth.

In the first place, who was this Julian, this Count Julian, this traitor of melodrama, who was the cause of such a deplorable catastrophe: a catastrophe whose effects were to last more than seven centuries?

Was he in command at Ceuta or at Tangier, or, as others say, at Algeciras? Was he Visigoth by birth, Spanish, Greek, Roman, or Berber? All this is difficult enough to elucidate. At the same time, it seems reasonably certain that he was governor of Ceuta. Ibn Adhari tells us that, at the beginning of this eighth century, a certain number of "Christianities" still persisted, even after the Musulman invasion, on this part of the African coast.

"Tangier, Ceuta, Algeciras, and that region," he says, "belonged to the King of Spain, in the same way as almost all the coast of Southern Morocco and its neighbourhood were in the hands of the Roums. It was they who lived there, for the Berbers have no love for living in towns or villages, and seek only the mountains and the fields, on account of their camels and their flocks."

Dozy has found ingenious arguments for supposing that Julian was a Byzantine. His name certainly seems to indicate it.[1] Expelled from Tangier by Mousa, he took refuge in Ceuta, with the empty title of Exarch of Africa, and thence exercised purely nominal authority over all those "Christianities" which Islam was about to annihilate. Harassed by the Musulmans, and being able to base only the most precarious hopes on help from the Basilcus of Constantinople, he was driven to turn, as his natural ally, to the Visigoth king who reigned at Toledo, the Christian monarch nearest to his province.

Did he even declare himself Rodrigo's vassal, in order to obtain his protection against Mousa? Nothing is more likely. This would explain how Ceuta came to be regarded in the eyes of the Arab historians as a possession of the King of Spain.

What wrong did Rodrigo do Julian? The story of the seduction of La Cava and her father's vengeance seems difficult to accept. But Rodrigo certainly provided Julian with a pretext for betraying him. It is probable that Julian looked for this pretext himself. He had only the choice between two masters: Rodrigo or Mousa. The latter, the lieutenant of a prince who ruled over half the ancient Roman Empire, and whose armies were pressing him closely, was a more powerful protector for Julian than the King of Spain. Accordingly, to assure the goodwill of the Musulman, he facilitated his passage to the coast of Andalusia.

A number of other hypotheses are tenable. To multiply them gets us no further. The only certain thing is the invasion of Spain by the Musulman with the complicity of Julian. All the rest is darkness.

There is the same obscurity where Rodrigo is concerned. Was he of royal blood, or one of the great feudatories of the Crown? We know only that on the death of King Wamba, his predecessor, he was elected in preference to Wamba's sons. Henceforth the two ousted princes exerted themselves by all the means in their power to dethrone the man whom they regarded as a usurper. When the Musulman leader attacked Rodrigo, near Algeciras, they gave ground deliberately, and through this defection caused the loss of the battle and the death—or at least the downfall—of their enemy.

It required such treachery to compass the defeat of the Visigoth king. The anonymous author of the *Akbar Madjmoua* claims that he had assembled an army of about a hundred thousand men, whereas Tarik, his opponent, had only twelve thousand. Without discussing these figures, we may admit that the Visigoth troops were superior in numbers to the Musulman troops.

It may seem surprising that an army of invasion should be so small in numbers. The fact is that the Musulmans did not at the outset intend to invade Spain, or, if they were contemplating it more or less deliberately, they did not think that the opportune moment

[1] This name is disputed. The opinion now most favoured is that Julian, or rather Oulban, was a Berber.

had yet come. Mousa, the governor of Tangier, either as a sequel to Julian's advice and overtures, or spontaneously, had consulted the Caliph of Damascus on the subject. The Commander of the Faithful replied: "Make a *reconnaissance* into Spain with light troops, but be careful not to expose the Musulmans to the perils of a stormy sea." Was this "stormy sea" an Oriental metaphor, or should we take these words literally and read into them the Arabs' well-known fear of the sea and all its unknown dangers?

In any event the Caliph counselled prudence to his lieutenant. Accordingly, Mousa confined himself to having a preliminary *reconnaissance* made on the Andalusian coast by his freedman Tarif (not to be confused with Tarik, the first Musulman conqueror of Spain). This took place in 710 of our era. Tarif the freedman set off at the head of four hundred infantry and one hundred horsemen, transported in four ships. They landed opposite Tangier, at a port which has since been called Tarifa, in commemoration of Tarif. They pushed on as far as the outskirts of Algeciras, and made a fine raid there, laying hands on a quantity of money and bringing back into captivity women so beautiful that neither Mousa nor any of his comrades had ever seen anything like them.

Encouraged by this fortunate brigandage, Mousa decided to equip an expedition on a larger scale. The following year (711) he sent to Spain "another of his favourites, the leader of his bodyguard, who was called Tarik ibn Ziyad," according to some authorities a Persian by origin, and according to others a Berber. Tarik had at his disposal only seven thousand men and four ships to transport them. He assembled his troops on the Rock of Gibraltar (to which he gave its name: Djebel-Tarik), and lost no time in seizing Algeciras.

Meanwhile, having learned that Rodrigo, King of Spain, was marching against him with a strong army, he demanded reinforcements from Mousa, who sent him another five thousand men, thus raising the strength of his forces to twelve thousand men in all. Rodrigo was defeated as a result of the defection of the sons of Wamba. His numerically superior army disbanded and broke into flight before a handful of Berbers. Thereupon, thanks to all kinds of complicities, and especially to the advice of Julian, who revealed the weak points of the enemy to the Musulmans, Tarik, taking advantage of an unexpected opportunity, rapidly subjugated almost the whole country.

Apart from the treachery which prepared the path for him, and the facilities which were put at his disposal, it appears that the terror inspired by his barbarian hordes also worked to his advantage. Whether it was that the atrocities committed by his troops gave rise to the report, or that he judged it convenient to put it into circulation, he and his army advanced preceded by the reputation of cannibals. Let us note this significant detail: when the Musulmans penetrated into Spain, they were regarded not as representatives of a higher civilisation, but as absolute savages, who fed on human flesh.

After routing the remnant of Rodrigo's army in the neighbourhood of Ecija, Tarik, still relying on Julian's advice, decided to march on Toledo, the capital of the kingdom. He entrusted the siege of Cordova to his lieutenant Moghit, and dispatched different detachments against Elvira, Málaga, and Murcia. When Toledo opened its gates to him, Tarik pursued his march northwards, until he was overtaken by Mousa, jealous, as I have already said, of the laurels won by his lieutenant and attracted by the ease of the conquest.

Mousa lost no time in taking possession, if not of the whole country, at least of all the important strategic points of the Peninsula. Soon there was nothing left to the Christians but the mountains of Galicia and the coasts of the Basque territory. All along the line Islam had triumphed in the most glorious and the most unexpected way.

How is one to explain such a sudden collapse of the Visigoth autocracy? No doubt this monarchy, foreign in its origin, was not very deeply rooted in the old Iberian soil. I have just mentioned, moreover, the reasons which made it unpopular, and even unendurable, to a whole section of the population.

But all these reasons together do not suffice to explain this kind of triumphal progress of the Musulmans through a vast country, which seemed to accept their domination or to resign itself to it readily enough, even though there were some attempts at resistance here and there. Rodrigo, to all appearances, had superior forces at his disposal. Even after the loss of two battles, it was still possible for the Spaniards to cut the invaders' communications and throw them back to the other side of the sea.

But neither the nobility nor the population of the towns and the countryside seem even to have thought of it. Like the royal princes, the sons of Wamba and the enemies of Rodrigo, the Spaniards saw in Tarik's tribesmen only involuntary allies, who were going to rid them either of a detested rival and usurper or of a fiscal and clerical tyranny which was hateful to them. They imagined that these Africans, once they were gorged with booty, would turn their horses' heads around and re-embark for their Barbary, as Tarif had done the year before.

So far was this the case that almost everybody helped them on their way. They were regarded as liberators. It was Julian, a Christian, who had summoned the Musulmans to Spain; and it was Christian Spaniards who acted as guides to them and, on occasion, opened the gates of towns to them.

This incorrigible blindness was an error which was to repeat itself indefinitely in the course of the centuries. What Visigoth Spain had once done light-heartedly Musulman Spain was to do over and over again through a regular fatality of the conquest. At every turn the Caliphs and their successors, the little Moorish kings, called upon Africans to support them against a rival or a Christian prince, or simply to maintain their personal security.

They thought that they were finding in them merely momentary allies; they let them establish themselves in their towns; and, when they wanted to get rid of them, they had to fight and expel them at the cost of great effort, or else to submit themselves to the interlopers.

The Visigoth lords who had permitted the Berbers of Tarik and Mousa to penetrate into Andalusia were, therefore, cruelly deceived in their selfish calculations; and so, equally, were the rich inhabitants of the towns. When the enemy revealed their real designs, they had no option but to retreat to Toledo, and then to Galicia, or else submit to the conquerors.

Only the Jews and the serfs found some advantage in this change of regime, inasmuch as both of them were treated less harshly by their new masters than they had been by the Visigoth clerics and barons. In many districts the Jews acted as auxiliaries to the invaders. The captured towns were entrusted to Jewish garrisons, with a stiffening of Musulmans, to hold down the Christians.

The Spaniards were never to forget this treachery. Much later, during the reign of Ferdinand and Isabel, when the Jews were expelled from the Peninsula, resentment against this defection, strengthened by more recent grievances, was still alive.

The Spaniards, therefore, began by failing to realise the Arab conquest. They had already seen so many pillagers pass over their soil and disappear, like locusts after the harvest. The invaders themselves had not envisaged their expedition as anything more than a mere raid. They were the first to be surprised by the ease of their success.

But they felt very strongly that this success was not assured and that this great, unknown country, where chance had made them masters, contained all kinds of traps and dangers. They were afraid of it; they thought that at any moment they might have to pack up and decamp. When the whole country, from the Pyrenees to Gibraltar, was subject to them, the Caliph Omar ben Abd el Aziz still contemplated evacuating it.

"His purpose," says Ibn Adhari, "was to withdraw the Musulmans and let them evacuate this country, *for they were too widely separated from their brethren and too much in contact with the infidels and the enemies of God.* But he was informed that they were in great numbers and had spread themselves everywhere; and then he renounced this purpose."

Let us note, in passing, a curious resemblance between the motives of the Commander of the Faithful and those of the princes of the

Church and the theologians who advised the Catholic Sovereigns to expel the Moors and Moriscos. On both sides there was the same fear of seeing the true believers lose the purity of their faith through contact with the infidels.

But the fears of the Caliph were not solely of a religious order. He was afraid, above all, that the conquerors might be too few to occupy the country with complete security. It appears that Mousa himself, despite the rapidity of his conquest, shared these apprehensions. When he set off for Damascus, recalled by the Caliph, he chose Seville as the seat of government, no doubt because it was nearest to the sea, in case the Musulmans should be driven to take flight.

As a matter of fact, no great strength was needed to keep populations disarmed and abandoned by their leaders in their place. After the battles of Algeciras and Ecija, not very much can have been left of the Visigoth army. Besides, at that period, the occupying troops in conquered countries were always relatively few in numbers. Under the Emperors, Roman Africa was held by about twelve thousand men. Similarly the eighteen thousand soldiers of Tarik and Mousa, even if we concede that many of them returned to Barbary, were more than sufficient to assure order from one end of the Peninsula to the other.

Be that as it may, these conquerors despite themselves undoubtedly had the feeling that they were no more than encamped in this vast country which had so easily submitted to them. Thanks to a concatenation of improbable circumstances, they were to remain there for more than seven centuries; but this feeling of impermanency was never effaced among them, or at least among the princes and the nobles, who, in the midst even of Islamised Spaniards, always regarded themselves as being more or less in enemy country.

That was what had happened to the Visigoths. But the Visigoths, converted to Catholicism, professed the same religion as the Spaniards, and there was thus a prospect that they might end by fusing completely with the natives. In the case of the Musulmans, the difference in religion was to be an invincible obstacle to fusion. So they remained to the end foreigners in Spain.

CHAPTER III

The Establishment of the Musulmans in the Peninsula

THEY began by being nothing more than a handful of adventurers in the country, and they never succeeded in constituting a homogeneous people or establishing national unity there. In the brightest days of the Musulman hegemony Spain strongly resembled one of those countries of the Levant where, until modern times, a minority of Turks, garrisoned in a few important towns, held an amorphous mass of hybrid populations in check. Like Palestine, Syria, or Anatolia in our day—and no doubt also in antiquity—Musulman Spain at the period of the Caliphate was a medley of Jews, Berbers, Yemenite and Syrian Arabs, Christian and renegade Spaniards. The Musulmans, at the outset, were in a very small minority.

There were a number of reasons for this. The first was that Spain was separated from the rest of Islam by the sea—and the Musulmans were always very much afraid of the sea. The Arabs were never navigators. Mousa ibn Nosair, the governor of Ifrikia at the time of the invasion of Spain, had no fleet at his disposal. The first scouts whom he sent to raid Andalusia were transported there in four ships. The next year Tarik's seven thousand men had to make use of coasting vessels and passed over only in small detachments—no doubt lest the Spaniards should be put on the alert, but no doubt also because they had very few ships available.

The *Akbar Madjmoua* goes so far as to say that these seven thousand men were transported in the four ships of the first raid. But it adds that Mousa, realising the necessity of a fleet if he proposed to undertake expeditions into the Peninsula on a larger scale, had a number of other ships built.

In any case, the first expeditionary force commanded by the Berber Tarik numbered originally only seven thousand men, to whom five thousand reinforcements were then added, making a total of twelve thousand men. "Most of these soldiers," the *Akbar* tells us, "were Berbers and freedmen, and only a very small number were Arabs." Later Mousa crossed the straits with an army estimated at eighteen thousand men, who very probably were also Berbers for the most part.

This raised the numbers of the invaders to about thirty thousand men: a strength considerably inferior to that of the French army, which, in 1830–1, conquered no more than the city of Algiers and its neighbourhood. Out of this strength many were doubtless killed or went back to Africa with their booty, thus still further restricting the first Musulman population of Spain.

If we bear in mind that their domination extended from the marches of Septimania to the Strait of Gibraltar, it is obvious that these invaders must have been submerged in the native population. In any event, this small number of them certainly seems to have consisted mainly of African Berbers, stiffened by a few Arab leaders. Nothing, therefore, could be wider of the mark than to imagine Spain in the Middle Ages as occupied and peopled by the Arabs. No doubt there were many later infiltrations of Syrian and Palestinian Arabs, but these were small in numbers by comparison with the mass, which was Berber and, above all, Spanish.

The Caliphs frequently invoked the aid of African contingents, and finally there were two great Berber invasions in the time of the Almoravids and the Almohades. Despite this, the Musulman element never reached the point of being completely predominant in Spain, at least during the apogee of the Caliphate. According to the best authorities, only one-half of the population was Musulman. The remainder was composed of Christians and Jews; and, even among the Musulmans themselves, the majority of the population was of Berber or Spanish origin.

The expressions "Arab civilisation," "Arab art," as applied to the civilisation and art of Southern Spain in the Middle Ages, are, accordingly, as incorrect as they could possibly be—apart from the fact that the Arabs never had an art or a civilisation of their own.

These new-comers, small in number as they were, could not aspire to people a great country like Spain. They could not have lived there at all without the natives. For this reason they were compelled to treat them with consideration. Otherwise it meant famine and lack of commodities and primary necessities: no more means of livelihood, no more commerce, no more industry. In a country with a settled administration like Spain, extreme confusion and even complete anarchy would have resulted if the conquerors had failed to respect the old administrative framework. The population, mainly Christian, accordingly retained its counts, its governors, its bishops, its clergy, its judges and its courts, and its tax-collectors.

There remained the question of the division of the soil conquered by the invaders. Let us recall once more that at the outset they did not intend to remain in Spain. Like the true African nomads they were, they contemplated contenting themselves with taking booty and slaves, and then returning home. The leaders themselves, who were Arabs, had no desire to strike roots in Spain.

"When Mousa," says an anonymous text quoted by Dozy, "when Mousa and a number of his comrades in arms presented themselves before the Caliph Walid, *they asked him for permission to evacuate Spain and return to their homes*. The Caliph treated them with great consideration and kindness; *he gave them fiefs in the Peninsula*, but he refused to give them means of quitting the country, and would not allow that they should abandon it under any pretext whatever. Accordingly he sent them back there, after ordering them to communicate his reply to their comrades."

Elsewhere we read: "If Omar I, he said, had not given fiefs to his soldiers in India, the defence of that country would have been impossible. What was true in the case of India was even more true in the case of Spain. Please God that the Musulmans might not one day be forced to abandon this country!"

These words attributed to the Caliph Walid adequately interpret the feeling of instability which their over-rapid conquest inspired in the invaders of Spain. But for the occupation of the principal strategic points and the division of the soil it is unquestionable, as the Caliph said, that the Musulmans would have been unable to maintain themselves there.

Accordingly land was distributed among the soldiers. But it is important to distinguish between the territory that was conquered by force of arms and the territory that was surrendered in due form. The first was shared among the conquerors, with the exception of three districts, namely, that of Coimbra, that of Santarem, and another district in the East. A fifth part of these estates was reserved to the State, and was farmed by Christian peasants, who paid one-third of the proceeds to the treasury.

"Mousa," says the document quoted above, "left in the Khoms (that fifth part of the estates which had become State property) *the peasants and those children who were still young, so that they might cultivate it.*" Such was the system that was applied to the territory conquered by force of arms.

As for the other territory, that which was handed over to the Musulmans by capitulation, the Christians were left masters of it. They retained their estates, together with timber, dwellings, and all movable property; and they retained also the right of sale. This territory which was added to the domain of Islam by surrender was situated in the north of the Peninsula. "The whole country, with the exception of a small number of well-known localities, was annexed to the Empire. For, after the rout of Rodrigo, all the towns made terms with the Musulmans. Accordingly the Christians who lived there remained in possession of their lands and their other property and retained the right to sell them."

It would appear that this immunity applied only to landed estate. In accordance with the usages of war, the Christians who capitulated must have been subjected to a considerable indemnity and been freely plundered by the conquerors. This is proved, as a matter of fact, by the quantity of booty taken by Tarik and Mousa.

A regular Arab feudalism was established in the south of Spain, comprising the territory conquered by force of arms, the ecclesiastical property, and the estates of those patricians who took to flight. The soldiers of Mousa and Tarik were its first beneficiaries. Later the government of Spain was separated from that of Ifrikia, and the new governor, Saim ibn Malik, brought with him Syrian-Arab soldiers, who had to be provided for in their turn. Rivalry developed between the new-comers and Mousa's soldiery. Then the Caliph decided that the original occupiers should keep their lands and that the Arabs should have land taken from the Khoms, that is to say from the State territory. These Syrian-Arabs were called *Baladis*.

Later again a new governor, Baldj, brought with him a fresh contingent of Syrian-Arabs, who lost no time in coming to blows with the *Baladis*. It was a regular civil war, which lasted until the arrival in Spain of still another governor, who distributed the latest arrivals through the southern provinces and assigned to them for their subsistence one-third of the taxes paid by the Christians of the Khoms. All these immigrants were soldiers encamped in conquered territory, and lived on the native population.

The natives were divided into two categories: the Christians, who were called Mozarabs, and the converts to Islam, who were regarded as renegades in both camps.

The Christians, who had retained their own governors and their own tax-collectors, were subject to a head-tax. They were relieved of it if they embraced Islam, but they were not relieved of the Kharadj, the property duty, the tax on the produce of the soil. In general the Caliphal government did not want to see the Christians turn Musulman. The treasury lost too much if they did, inasmuch as it was they who paid the major part of the taxes.

It is difficult to find, as most of our historians do, an attitude of tolerance and broad-mindedness in this entirely self-interested line of conduct. The Caliph Omar declared frankly: "We must live on our Christians, and our descendants must live on theirs, as long as Islam endures."

That was what was really at the back of the conquerors' minds. At the outset, for reasons of prudence which can readily be understood, the Christians of Spain were not crushed with taxes. But soon, as Dozy admits himself, the domination of the Musulmans, "lenient and humane as it had been at the beginning, degenerated into an intolerable despotism." The Christians were bled white.

The least wretched of them were the serfs, who, in fact, found their condition better than it had been under the Visigoth regime. They could win their freedom by abjuring Christianity; and, despite the reluctance of the Arabs to accept converts, for the reasons of self-interest which I have just recalled, many of these unfortunates went over to Islam: for example, when they had not enough money to pay the head-tax, or when they were afraid of conviction by a Christian court. They only had to pronounce a brief formula, whereas being a Christian was a troublesome business.

But, whether they were Christian or Musulman, it was these Spanish peasants, these serfs attached to the soil, who continued to nourish the invaders, as they had nourished their former masters. It is necessary to insist upon this fact, because of the ineradicable

C

assumption, piously maintained even by serious historians, that it was the Arabs who introduced the art of cultivating and irrigating the soil into Spain.

We have only to reflect for a moment upon the desolation, the sterility, which the Arabs, like the Berbers, spread everywhere they went, to appreciate the absurdity of any such idea. Their historians admit it themselves and, in doing so, they pay tribute to the Spanish peasant. "Only the natives," writes Dozy, quoting one of these historians, "were familiar with the processes of agriculture (after the Arab Conquest), and in any case the conquerors were much too proud to engage in it."

We need not rely, however, upon the confessions of the Arabs. We know that these processes of agriculture and irrigation were familiar in Africa long before their arrival, since as far back as Roman and Carthaginian times. It was when Africa became Musulman, on the contrary, that these processes were abandoned, and that was the end of the legendary fertility of the country. The knowledge of the Roman or Carthaginian cultivator took refuge in the oases, where it persisted, in a paltry and bastardised form, down to our own time.

It is more than probable that these same Carthaginians and these same Romans, masters as they were of Spain, or at least of the coastal regions of the South and East, introduced their methods of cultivation there—always assuming that the Spaniards had any need of tutors in this direction; for, from the most remote times, the fertility of Betica was as famed as that of Numidia or the Proconsulate. But all these considerations do not suffice to prevent manuals of history from continuing to teach that the Arabs taught the Spaniards the art of cultivating and irrigating the soil.

It was not only the peasants, however, who became converts to Islam. Among the renegades there were many landowners and patricians. Taken as a whole they made up, together with the Jews, the majority of the population; and, like all fresh converts, they displayed great zeal in piety, real or pretended.

This did not make them any the more acceptable to the Old Musulmans, who were suspicious of them and jealously barred them from all lucrative employments. They were spoken of as "slaves" or "sons of slaves." Many of them, as a matter of fact, were freed serfs; but the same disrepute attached to the converted freedmen and patricians.

The fact is that there was not only rivalry of interest between the new converts and the Old Musulmans: there was also racial hostility. All these renegades were of Spanish origin, whereas the old believers were Arabs, Berbers, Syrians, or Egyptians. Nothing could prevail over this fundamental enmity. It was to continue to make itself felt throughout the domination of Spain in Islam, and, eight centuries later, it was to show itself still as much alive and as irreducible between Moriscos and Old Christians, between Musulman converts and Spanish Catholics.

Over against these renegades, these conquered people, Christian or Musulman, proudly stood the Arab aristocracy, some of whose representatives prided themselves upon belonging to the family of the Prophet or the families of his companions. Finally, there were the Berber lords, who were treated disdainfully enough by the Arabs, almost on the same footing as the renegades.

These warriors and horsemen, accustomed to nomadic life, lived for preference on their estates and in their strongholds, far from the towns and the seat of government. They were men of violence and uncompromising believers. In the course of centuries they might slough off their roughness and their fanaticism; but they could not get rid of their essentials of Asiatic and African barbarism. They might become more polished, but they lost nothing of their violence and their cruelty.

After the capture of Seville and Toledo, when Mousa met his lieutenant Tarik, whom he accused of peculation, he received him with blows of a whip and ordered his head to be shaved. He advanced across Spain himself, preceded by the reputation of a cannibal. Later, when booty was being divided, he wanted to deprive another of his lieutenants of an important prisoner, the Christian governor of Cordova. "It was I who made this man prisoner," cried this officer, who was called Moghit, flying into a passion; "they want to deprive me of him; very well, I will have his head cut off!" And so he did on the spot.

Never were these brutal habits to disappear completely from Musulman Spain. From one end to the other, the history of the Spanish Caliphate is strewn with severed heads and crucified corpses.

CHAPTER IV

The First Emirs Dependent on Damascus

THE conquest of Spanish soil was completed, or at least carried as far as possible, by the successors of Mousa. His son Abd el Aziz—who, so the Arab annalists tell us, hastened to marry a Christian, in the person of Egilona, widow of Rodrigo, the Visigoth king vanquished by Tarik—made an expedition into Portugal. His successor, El Horr, directed his efforts towards the northern frontier. The forward march of the Musulman armies crossed the Pyrenees, invaded France, and did not stop until 732, when Abd er Rhaman ben Abd Allah, one of El Horr's successors, was defeated in the battle of Poitiers by Charles-Martel.

A legend, reproduced by Ibn Adhari, has it that Mousa, the first conqueror of Spain, when he came to the limit of his campaign in the northern territory, found a statue, which had these words written on its breast: "Sons of Ishmael, here is your farthest point. If you ask whither you shall return, we tell you that it is to quarrels among yourselves—*such quarrels that you will cut off one another's heads.*"

This prophecy, clearly penned after the event, sums up in its few naïve words the whole history of the period which begins with the establishment of the Musulmans in the Peninsula, not only down to the arrival of the Omayyads in Spain, but even down to their definitive expulsion by the Catholic Sovereigns. In any case, the first part of this period, that of the Emirs dependent upon the Caliphate of Damascus, which lasted for more than forty years until the arrival of Abd er Rhaman in 755, is nothing but a long series of intestinal struggles, slaughterings, massacres, and assassinations.

It was anarchy in all its horror, fed by family hatreds and the rivalries of tribe against tribe—Arabs of the North against Arabs of the South, Yemenites against Kaishites, Syrians against Medinites. All these Asiatics had a common enemy in the nomad African, the Berber, the eternal spoiler of cities and the auxiliary of all invaders.

The Berbers of Africa, who in fact had been the real conquerors of Spain under Tarik's orders, were not content with their lot. When Mousa arrived after them with his Arabs, the hardest part of the job had been done. But, instead of treating the Berbers according to their deserts, the Arab chiefs, full of contempt for these new Musulmans, assigned them the most ungrateful share in the division of the soil.

While the Arabs laid hands themselves on the most fertile regions, those of the East and of Andalusia, "they relegated the companions of Tarik to the arid plains of La Mancha and Estremadura, and to the mountains of León, Galicia, and Asturias, where they had to skirmish ceaselessly with the unsubdued Christians." These dissatisfied Berbers were not long in coming to blows with the Arabs, who for their part were jealous among themselves and wantonly massacred one another.

Nothing emerges from this perpetual killing but the savagery, the brutality, and the cruelty of the new-comers. Under their domination poor Spain got used to being ridden over and devastated periodically, in a way that soon became as regular as the alternation of the seasons. It was the regime of the raid, to which northern Algeria was subjected for centuries down to the beginning of the French conquest in 1830.

In this chaos of meaningless little wars and atrocities there are no figures that stand out, unless it be by the violence of their unrestrained instincts, like those of Baldj or Somail. Baldj, who was a Syrian by origin and had gone to Africa to fight the Berbers, finally found himself besieged and being starved out by them in the town of Ceuta. Reduced to the last extremity, he appealed for supplies to the governor of Spain, the old Abd el Malik, who was a man of Medina and an inveterate enemy of the Syrians. Delighted to see the Syrians shut up in Ceuta in such an awkward position, he forbade the Spaniards to send them supplies.

Nevertheless, a noble of the tribe of Lakam, either through self-interest or out of compassion, had the audacity to send two shiploads of corn to Baldj's soldiers. The enraged Abd el Malik had the Lakmite arrested, and first condemned him to seven hundred lashes. Then, on the pretext that he was trying to foment disturbances, he ordered his eyes to be put out and his head to be cut off. His corpse was hung on a gibbet, with a crucified dog to the right of him.

The Berbers of Spain, however, became more and more menacing, and Abd el Malik found himself driven to invoke the aid of Baldj and his Syrians shut up in Ceuta. He had them transported across the straits under certain conditions. The Syrians defeated the Berbers in several engagements. But they had not forgotten Abd el Malik's earlier attitude and his ill-will towards them. Moreover, they were Yemenites, while the governor of Spain belonged to the hated tribe of the Kaishites.

Accordingly Baldj, though he was a Kaishite himself, allowed his soldiers to lay hands on the nonagenarian Abd el Malik. They beat him, slashed him with swords, and crucified him opposite the bridge of Cordova, between a dog and a pig also crucified.

After that Yemenites and Kaishites, delivered from the Berber danger, came to blows among themselves. The Kaishites, under the leadership of their chief, Somail, routed their adversaries in the plain of Secunda, the Roman town on the other side of the Guadalquivir opposite Cordova. The victorious Somail had the Yemenite chiefs beheaded in the square in front of the Cathedral of Saint Vincent, which as yet was only half turned into a mosque.

Seventy heads had already fallen when one of the chiefs in alliance with Somail protested against this horrible butchery, not in the name of humanity, but in the name of Musulman solidarity. Somail, nevertheless, went on with his executions until his ally, indignant at his excessive cruelty, threatened to turn against him.

These divisions among the Musulmans enabled the Christians who had taken refuge in the North to assume the offensive against the invaders.

Unhappily the history of this preliminary to the Reconquest is almost entirely obscure. The offensive was begun by a Visigoth chief, who afterwards became for the Spaniards a regular national hero: Pelayo, a semi-legendary figure, about whom we know nothing for certain, except that he defeated the Musulmans in 718 at the battle of Cavadonga. Even the date of this battle is disputed. We do not even know whether Pelayo was of royal blood, the successor of Rodrigo, or simply a chieftain who assembled some contingents of mountaineers.

However this may be, centres of resistance were gradually established in the north of the country, in the Basque provinces, in Navarre, and in the mountainous region of Aragón. In addition Pelayo's successors, notably King Alfonso I, known as the Catholic, succeeded in reconquering some towns in Galicia, in Cantabria, and in León. At this period the line of the Musulman frontier was drawn back slightly towards the South: it passed through Coimbra, Coria, Talavera, Toledo, Guadalajara, Tudela, and Pampeluna. Between it and the little Christian kingdom extended a neutral zone, which became a regular desert and was periodically invaded and raided by the two adversaries, who were ceaselessly on guard against one another.

Accordingly Musulman Spain, about the middle of the eighth century—only forty years, that is to say, after the Conquest—was already threatened in her very existence, not so much by the Christian armies as by her internal discord. It needed a man, a strong leader, to avert the inevitable catastrophe. The Musulmans of Spain were lucky enough to find him.

§ II

THE CALIPHATE OF CORDOVA

CHAPTER V

Abd er Rhaman, Emir of Spain

THERE is always an element of the romantic and the marvellous in Arab histories. The providential man who was to save the Musulman domination in Spain was cast for this great *rôle* by many prophecies. In any case it was good policy to make his soldiers and his subjects believe it, and Abd er Rhaman did not fail to do so. Perhaps he believed it himself.

In the whole history of the Arab peoples prophecy occupies a very important place. There is no event of any importance which was not predicted either by an old text, or by an astrologer or a "mathematician," as they were called. In the Arab world and at the court of the Caliphs these personages enjoyed the same reputation as they had formerly enjoyed in the Helleno-Latin world, and at the court of the Roman Emperors. They were fawned upon or persecuted, in accordance with whether their predictions were desired or feared. The soothsayers who foretold changes in succession were hunted out and put to death on the one hand, and flattered and loaded with presents on the other.

In the case of Abd er Rhaman, he related himself how his high destiny was announced to him in advance. "On my arrival in Spain," he said, "I was wholly possessed by the prediction made by my great-uncle, Maslama ben Abd el Malik, in the following circumstances. One day he came to see my grandfather, the Caliph Hisham, at a time when I was present, being then quite a child. When my grandfather proposed to send me away, 'Prince of Believers,' said Maslama, 'let the child be. For I see in him the man of the Omayyads, he who will revive this dynasty after its fall.' From that moment I observed that my grandfather always showed a marked predilection for me."

Later, when he was a fugitive in Africa and was arrested at Kairouan, he was proclaimed to the governor of Ifrikia by a Jew, an old servant of his great-uncle Maslama, "as destined to conquer Spain and no doubt Africa as well." This conqueror was to be called Abd er Rhaman, and would have two curls of hair on his forehead.

The governor Habib, having examined the new-comer and seen that he had two curls of hair, sent for the Jew and said to him: "Here, wretch, is the man of whom your prediction speaks. So I am going to have him put to death." "But," the Jew told him, "if it is indeed he, you cannot kill him, for Destiny does not permit you." Then Habib confined himself to putting to death the Omayyads who accompanied the fugitive and seizing their goods.

It is quite certain that these predictions, true or false, had a real influence upon the destiny of Abd er Rhaman. This future master of Spain was a Syrian, born in the territory of Damascus. He was of the

Imperial family, being a grandson of the Omayyad Caliph Hisham. When the Abbasids seized the throne and set about exterminating the numerous descendants of the fallen dynasty, young Abd er Rhaman succeeded in hiding for some time in a village near the Euphrates; but a party of Abbasid horsemen discovered his retreat. He fled with his brother, a boy of thirteen, flung himself into the river, and swam across it. The boy, who was not such a good swimmer as his elder brother, was captured by the soldiers. From the opposite bank Abd er Rhaman saw him beheaded by the Caliph's myrmidons.

This horrible spectacle was, no doubt, an excellent lesson in things for him. He who, perhaps, was already dreaming of empire learnt early at what price a throne is won and to what vicissitudes he who occupies it is exposed. Exile, a life of wandering, prison, torture, assassination—he must prepare himself for all these ordinary accidents of a royal destiny.

After succeeding in reaching Palestine, he traversed Egypt and finally arrived in Ifrikia by the long and dangerous caravan route. He stayed some time in Kairouan, where, as we have seen, he attracted the ill-will of the governor, Ibn Habib, who, having refused to recognise the Abbasid Caliph, contemplated carving out an independent kingdom in Africa and scented a possible rival in Abd er Rhaman. Fearing for his life, the descendant of the Omayyads escaped from Kairouan and resumed his wandering life. He crossed the whole of Morocco, and finally settled down among a Berber tribe near Ceuta—the tribe of Nafza, to which his mother, an African slave, belonged.

There he was bound to find support among the relatives and retainers of her family. There he was quite close to Spain, a country delivered up to anarchy and awaiting a master: Spain, the former fief of his ancestors. He had only to cross the Strait to win an empire, perhaps. Then he must have recalled the predictions which hailed in him the future conqueror of Spain. What a temptation to attempt such an adventure—the more so as he had no other prospect before him except either a wretched, always threatened life, or the adventure with all its risks!

In Spain, moreover, there were Omayyad partisans, who would perhaps be ready to declare for him. They were old soldiers, belonging to the divisions of Damascus and Kinnesrin, settled in the territories of Elvira and Jaen. Abd er Rhaman charged one of his freedmen, the faithful Badr, with the duty of going and sounding these veterans and coming to terms with them if they were favourably disposed.

The moment seemed as opportune as possible for this scion of kings. Spain at this time was tyrannised over by a kind of military duumvirate, consisting of the brutal and drunken Somail, the conqueror of the Yemenites, who had decimated them so cruelly in the square in front of the cathedral of Cordova, and the governor, Yousouf ben Abd er Rhaman, the Fihrite.

The Yemenites, who saw in the Omayyad's overtures an opportunity of taking their revenge on their mortal enemies, the Kaishites or Maadites—the partisans of Somail—finally declared for Abd er Rhaman. There followed long pourparlers with Somail, then governor of Saragossa, whom the wily Abd er Rhaman hoped to detach from his ally Yousouf. Finally, after much marching and counter-marching, Yousouf and Somail decided to join forces against this intriguer. They were defeated in a battle fought on the banks of the Guadalquivir, between Seville and Cordova, after which Abd er Rhaman was recognised as Emir of Spain by his two rivals (756).

He proceeded to make himself independent of the Caliph of Bagdad. It was the beginning of a new dynasty, a Syrian-Arab dynasty transplanted on to western soil. Almost the whole Peninsula was to have a single head, though one whose authority was ceaselessly disputed. This monarchical *façade* masked, in fact, an irreducible anarchy.

Abd er Rhaman spent himself in mastering it, and to a certain extent he succeeded. But after him everything had to be done all over again. It was to be the same in the case of those of his successors who were the most brilliant and the most jealous of their authority: so much so that the reign of Abd er Rhaman may be regarded as the prototype of the reigns that followed it. With minor variations, they were a monotonous repetition of it—the same internal dissensions, the same rising and harsh repressions, the same impotence to establish a durable authority and a unified empire.

So far as we can trust the Arab annalists, this is briefly what happened. Once he was in possession of the Emirate, Abd er Rhaman enjoyed barely a year of tranquillity. His two rivals, Somail and Yousouf the Fihrite, seemed at first to be resigned to their fate. Somail, sodden with drunkenness, was scarcely to be feared, though he was subject to frightful outbursts of rage. But Yousouf was not long in breaking openly with the Emir. He fled from Cordova and assembled an army of twenty thousand men, composed of all kinds of disaffected elements and especially of Berbers—those Africans who were always ready to engage in war, pillage, and massacre.

Abd er Rhaman, supported by the governor of Seville, routed his enemy, who took refuge in the region of Toledo. After wandering about there for some time he was taken prisoner and beheaded. His head was carried to Abd er Rhaman, who had it exposed on the bridge of Cordova, side by side with the head of his son, who had been held as a hostage and whom the Emir beheaded too.

There remained Somail, who was also imprisoned. He was strangled in prison. It was announced that he had died of apoplexy.

In any case Abd er Rhaman was henceforth disembarrassed of his two chief enemies.

His authority was none the more stable for that. This Syrian, after all, was a foreigner in the country. He had triumphed only thanks to the help of the Yemenites, who, moreover, had embraced his cause out of hatred of Somail and Yousouf. Judging themselves badly recompensed, they rose in revolt under the command of Ala ben Moghit, nominated Emir of Spain by the Abbasid Caliph El Mansour. Toledo, which had always been in rivalry with Cordova, rose at the same time.

Abd er Rhaman, though besieged for two months in Carmona, ended by routing the rebels. Their principal leaders were decapitated. Their heads were filled with salt and myrrh, they were packed in boxes, covered with the standard of the Caliph of Bagdad, who had been the instigator of the revolt, and Abd er Rhaman, with cruel irony, sent the Caliph this macabre present. El Mansour was at the time on pilgrimage to Mecca. Abd er Rhaman's emissaries deposited their boxes in front of the tent of the Caliph, who could do nothing but curse the butcher of his Spanish allies. "Allah be praised," he said with real piety, "that the sea divides us from this devil!"

As to the rebels of Toledo, they lost no time in surrendering. The leaders were brought to Cordova. Their heads were shaven, they were clothed in rags, and, in this grotesque guise, they were paraded on donkeys' backs through the streets of the city to the place where crosses had been made ready for them, and there they were crucified.

This was not the end of it. After the Yemenites, the Berbers rose in their turn, joining hands with the remnants of the Yemenite army defeated by the Emir. With their usual African perfidy, the Berbers betrayed their allies on the field of battle, where thirty thousand men are said to have been killed. The Berbers of Central Spain were still to be subdued, and it took ten years of warfare to do it.

This warfare was still in progress when a new and dangerous insurrection broke out in the North. The leaders of the coalition were the governor of Barcelona and the son and son-in-law of Yousouf the Fihrite. They called to their aid Charlemagne, Emperor of the Franks, who, with his nephew Roland, crossed the Pyrenees and laid siege to Saragossa.

Charlemagne, attacked in the North by the Saxons, had to raise the siege precipitately and retreat to France. This completed the disbandment of Abd er Rhaman's enemies. But Saragossa held out against him until finally the inhabitants of the town surrendered their defender, Hussein, to him. The Emir ordered his hands and feet to be cut off, after which he was killed with blows of an iron bar.

Abd er Rhaman had triumphed once more. But his enemies did not lay down their arms. Until his death (788) he had to crush conspiracies and revolts. His retainers, his associates, the members of his numerous family, all those Omayyads whom he had summoned from Damascus or who had hastened to Spain to profit by their relative's success—everybody conspired against him.

He had to exile to Africa one of his brothers, Walid, whose son had fomented a fresh plot against him. Walid, aghast at the execution of his son, burst into protestations of fidelity and obedience. But this servility on the part of his brother was far from allaying the suspicions of the Emir, who said to one of his confidants: "Let him not think to deceive me! I know him, and I know that, if he could assuage his thirst for vengeance in my blood, he would not hesitate for a moment."

The Omayyad turned into a tyrant. He who had once been popular no longer dared to walk about the streets of Cordova. Feeling safe no longer, he summoned Berbers from Africa for his bodyguard, and raised the strength of his personal army to forty thousand men.

His successors were compelled to follow his example. The Caliphate could maintain itself only on condition that it became a military despotism.

I have summed up in outline the principal events of the reign of Abd er Rhaman because, since as these events were to repeat themselves indefinitely during the reigns of his successors, the latter do not call for any detailed treatment. All these Arab sovereigns called in Berbers or other foreigners to maintain an always tottering authority; all of them had to suppress conspiracies hatched by members of their own family or by relatives of their victims; all of them had to fight against insurgent leaders or rivals; all of them, finally, made it a pious duty to raid the Christian territory at least twice a year.

I shall therefore confine myself to emphasising and commenting upon events that were new, and to isolating among all these figures —most of them as impersonal as the history of their reigns—those who were really significant.

Abd er Rhaman himself was a real character, an individual among this succession of princes who, in general, are all as like one another as the anonymous *stelæ* of Musulman cemeteries.

This exiled Omayyad, who escaped by a miracle from the massacre of his family and ended, by dint of strength and perseverance, in transplanting the dynasty of his ancestors to Spain—this Syrian of Damascus was in the first place a virile human animal: tall, fair, with a fairness bordering upon red, with a mole on one cheek and his two curls on his forehead; he was cut out to withstand the severest tests of his wandering adventurer's life. Despite his continual wars and the daily work of administration, with which he dealt himself, he found time to have twenty children: eleven boys and nine girls.

His successors, less busy or more sensual, had them by the dozen. This partly explains the troubles which multiplied in Cordova and in Caliphal Spain. The Emirs and the Caliphs, in ceaselessly increasing their progeniture, were preparing for themselves, or for the heirs designated by them, enemies and bitter rivals. The harem was one of the great causes of weakness of the Arabs in Spain, as it was, for that matter, everywhere they went.

Ibn el Athir tells us that Abd er Rhaman was a fluent and accomplished speaker and that, like all well-born Arabs, he took pride in composing verse. "Benignant, well-informed, resolute, prompt to crush rebellion, he never remained long in repose or given over to idleness; he never entrusted the care of his affairs to anybody, and relied upon no judgment but his own. Endowed with profound intelligence, he united bravery pushed to the point of daring with great prudence, and he showed himself broad-minded and generous. He usually wore white clothes. . . ."

Despite his recorded cruelties, we are asked to believe that this one-eyed man, clothed in white, was benignant. It is difficult for us to-day to pronounce upon the morality of his actions. They were no doubt imposed upon the Emir by circumstances and by the barbarous customs of his comrades and his enemies. Compelled to defend himself and, together with his person, the destiny of Islam in the West, he also found himself driven to be, like his adversaries, slippery, treacherous, and cruel.

At the same time there seems to have been in this red-haired colossus an inborn element of violence and savagery, brought from the Yemen by his nomad ancestors. He did not confine himself to ordering terrible executions; he carried them out himself. For example, he tried to stab with his own hand a Sevillian chieftain against whom he thought he had a grievance. The man defended himself vigorously, and he had to have him finished off by his guards.

Whatever one may say about him, it is certain that he had a highly developed sense of his greatness and that there were no limits to his ambition. He brought back from the East the Imperial idea, which, since the fall of Rome and of the Visigoth kingdom, had been almost completely eclipsed in Spain and throughout the Moghreb. He toyed with the dream of a new Empire of the West, or at least of a great monarchy, unified under an autocrat.

But the incessant wars which he had to wage prevented him from showing his worth as an administrator. He had not even time to build. He had work started on the Great Mosque, but the only other thing he found time to do was to adapt to his own convenience the old palace of Cordova, the *castellum* of the Roman and Visigoth governors. He had to leave the great bridge across the Guadalquivir, whose arches had been carried away by a flood, in ruins. Outside his capital, at the foot of the last spurs of the Sierra, he contrived to construct a country seat which he called Ruzafa, in memory of the Damascene Ruzafa, built by his grandfather, Hisham.

He was homesick for Damascus and for his Syria, at least towards the end of his life, after a long experience of bloody wars, conspiracies, assassinations, and betrayals, when he felt himself execrated by his own family. The Arab annalists have handed down two short poems of his, which give us a glimpse of all the melancholy of the exile, and perhaps also the disenchantment of the ambitious man disappointed by men and fate.

Traveller, you who go to my country, take with you there the salutation of half of myself to my other half. My body, as you know, is in one place, but my heart and its affections are in another. Marked out as it was by destiny, the separation has had to be accomplished, but it has chased sleep away from my lids. The Divine will that ordained this divorce will perhaps decree, some day, our reunion."

The other poem, inspired by the sight of a palm tree in the gardens of Ruzafa, makes one think of an epigram from the Greek Anthology.

In Ruzafa there has just appeared to me a palm tree, strayed into the soil of the West, far from the land where dwells its peers. There, I say to myself, is my image. I, too, live in a far-off exile, long separated from my children and my family. O palm tree, you have grown up in a foreign land, and, like you, I am distant and divided from mine own. . . . May the breasts of the morning dew give you to drink as much water as Arcturus and the Cluster pour!"

It is difficult for us to understand how that same hand of the rough adventurer, which made so many heads fall, could have written these graceful verses, so poetical and so tender in their sentiment.

CHAPTER VI

The Caliphate

ABD ER RHAMAN I, who at the outset did not dare to proclaim himself independent of the Caliph of Bagdad, did not himself take the title of Caliph. This title was not assumed until much later, in 929, by his seventh successor, Abd er Rhaman III. But the Caliphate was virtually established with the arrival of the first Omayyad in Spain. These Emirs of Cordova were true sovereigns, who regarded themselves as the masters not only of Spain, but also of all the African Moghreb. They were the Emperors of the West, or at least of the Mediterranean West.

They were at the beginning pure Arabs, who took a certain length of time to acclimatise themselves in Spain, and whose ruder traits were polished away but slowly. Their annalists are careful to note this fundamentally Arab character of theirs. But what does being profoundly Arab mean in their eyes?

According to Abou Mohammed ben Hazam, quoted by Ibn Adhari, "the Omayyad dynasty was truly Arab in the sense that none of its representatives made a capital for himself. Every one of them continued to live in the place and on the property where he had resided before becoming Caliph, *without troubling either to accumulate immense wealth or to build palaces*, without demanding of those who addressed him that they should call him 'Lord,' and without requiring demonstrations of servility, such as kissing the ground, the hand, or the foot."

This disdain for the ceremonial of courts, this contempt for luxury and, above all, for magnificent building, betray the nomad, accustomed to dwell in a tent, and also the devout Musulman. "Civilisation," says the historian, Ibn Khaldoun, "means sedentary life and luxury. . . . The character of men trained under the influence of sedentary life and luxury is, in itself, evil personified." To the pure Arab, therefore, *civilisation is synonymous with evil*. Nevertheless, the descendants of the Omayyads of Syria, those Puritans of Islam, transplanted into Spain, ended by admitting a certain measure of civilisation and even protecting and developing it.

The reason was, in the first place, that they were not slow to lose their racial purity. Abd er Rhaman I, the founder of the Spanish dynasty, was the son of a Berber slave. Abd el Aziz, the son of Mousa, the conqueror of Spain, had married Egilona, daughter of Rodrigo, the Visigoth king vanquished by the Arabs. This princess was followed into the Caliphal harem by a swarm of Christian captives or slaves, such as the Sultana Aurora and the favourite Romaiquia.

This perpetual intermarriage with women of Berber, Iberian, or Visigoth blood produced a race which had scarcely anything Arab

48

left about it, but, at the same time, was not altogether Spanish. Most of these Caliphs were ruddy men, or fair men with blue eyes: which would seem to indicate the predominance of Berber or Visigoth blood. But, since they took much pride in their origin, some of them dyed themselves dark, as though by way of asserting their Arab descent better.

The first Emirs, absorbed in their pillagings, their rivalries of clans and tribes, their wars of extermination, do not appear to have concerned themselves much about either the amenities or the refinements of civilised life. It was only during the reign of Abd er Rhaman II (822-852) that the Mussulmans of Spain began to imitate Oriental luxury.

"It was Abd er Rhaman II," we are told, "who first adopted the traditional usages of the Caliphs so far as concerned pomp, exterior form, the organisation of service, the use of the most luxurious clothes. He embellished the palaces and conducted water to them. . . . He built mosques throughout Spain, introduced embroidery for clothing and encouraged the making of it, established the Mint at Cordova, and, in a word, gave a setting of grandeur to his royalty. . . . It was during his reign that there entered into Spain rich carpets and all kinds of precious things, coming from Bagdad and elsewhere. After the murder of Haroun al Rashid and the plundering of his goods, there were imported into Spain rare and precious objects, as well as jewellery which had this origin: thither was brought, too, the necklace called 'the Scorpion's Sting,' which had belonged to Zobeyda, mother of Djafar."

This famous necklace of the Sultana Zobeyda, to which there seemed to be attached an influence fatal to anybody who touched it, we shall see making its appearance again, some centuries later, in equally tragic circumstances.

Abd er Rhaman II appears to have desired to rival, and then to eclipse, the court of Bagdad, where reigned his detested rivals, the murderers of his ancestors. This court of the Abbasids, affected by Persian influence, was at that time the model of all elegance for the Moslem world. Accordingly Abd er Rhaman II summoned the famous musician Ziryab from Bagdad to Cordova, to strike the right note for the Spaniards, not only in music and poetry, but also in deportment, style, and good manners. Nevertheless, despite all the efforts of these sovereigns to refine themselves, the old barbarian substratum still persisted in them.

The climate of Andalusia softened the sons of these rude horsemen. It soon made them sensual and voluptuous, lovers of wine, singers, and dancers, in short, of all the pleasures which had made Cadiz and the Gaditanes famous during the Roman period. Let us note that all this was forbidden by the law of the Prophet: wine, music, dancing, and even hunting.

The Emirs, no doubt, took up hunting in imitation of their predecessors, the Visigoth kings. We have seen that Rodrigo asked for falcons for his hunts from Count Julian, and probably also from his African vassals. But among the conquerors the love of wine degenerated into drunkenness. The feasts at the Caliphal court, and later at the little courts of the *Taifas*, were only too often nothing but gross orgies.

Here, for example, is a story which has much to tell us about the habits of these new masters of Spain. It happened during the reign of another Abd er Rhaman, the third of the name, the Victorious, the greatest of all the dynasty. This Caliph thought that he had a grievance against one of his officials, named Mohammed ben Said, whom he suspected of peculation. "One day, at one of his banquets, as Mohammed was pouring out wine for him, while he was himself cutting an apple with a knife, 'I should like,' he said, 'to cut off in the same way the head of him whom I know to have acquired an enormous fortune at my expense and to have paid none of it to the treasury.'

"Mohammed was quite taken aback, and, knowing that he was himself in question, he said: 'My fortune I acquired by saving. Please Allah that you do not lay hands on my goods, lest I reclaim against you! The souls of men are delivered up to avarice.'

"This reference to the sacred words of the Koran about avarice recalled the Caliph to himself, and, ashamed of his cupidity, he set himself to dispel Mahommed's fears in friendly fashion. Mohammed, still trembling, started drinking to drown his troubles.

"'Gently, Mohammed!' said the Caliph. 'Can you not see reason?'

"Mohammed went on drinking. He got drunk and started vomiting. Slaves hastened to bring him a basin and napkins, while the Caliph, holding his head, said to him: 'Get it off your stomach, and take it gently!'

"At first Mohammed did not distinguish his voice from that of the servants. But, turning his head, he saw that it was the Prince himself. Then, unable to restrain himself, he flung himself at his feet and kissed them crying: 'O son of Caliphs, is this the measure of your goodness to me?' And he began to address to him all kinds of vows and to manifest his gratitude very earnestly.

"'It is but just,' replied the Prince, 'that I should recompense you for my behaviour towards you this evening, by repaying you in attention for the fright I gave you, and in kindness for my harshness.' Then he had a cloak put about him, and the man went home" (*El Bayano' l-Mogrib*).

This story of the basin proves that tigers are capable of being tamed. Abd er Rhaman was not always so good-humoured, any more than his kindred. As I have already remarked, the customs of the time and their environment drove the governors to a certain degree of cruelty. They had to be cruel, or become cruel, in order to retain their power.

Not only did the Caliphs inflict atrocious punishments, but, in order to be sure that the guilty party or enemy had paid the penalty, they even saw it inflicted before their eyes. Sometimes they carried out executions with their own hands. Sometimes, too, the victim was their own son, or some member of their family. El Mansour, learning that one of his numerous sons was the accomplice of a gang of malefactors, had him brought to the hall of the *Chorta* and whipped to death. When another of his sons, Abd Allah, rebelled against him, he had him decapitated and sent his head to Cordova along with a bulletin of victory.

Under the regime of these Africans and Asiatics beheadings and crucifixions were continual. The custom of cutting off the heads of conquered enemies, dead or alive, and piling up these heads into a hideous trophy, persisted among the Moors down to their expulsion from Spain. After every campaign the number of cut-off heads was counted, and, to impress or terrorise the people, the heads were salted and sent in boxes to the principal towns of the empire, where they were exposed to the best advantage.

After some battles they made heaps so high, the annalists tell us, that horsemen could ride between them without being seen. El Mansour, having defeated the Christians of León, took thirty thousand prisoners, and by his order, so Ibn el Athir relates, the corpses were piled up and from the top of this bloody mass, as though it were from the height of a minaret, the call to evening prayer was sent forth by the muezzin.

Fundamentally these men were devout and even fanatical. It would be a naïve error to see in them easy-going sceptics, indifferent about religious matters and animated by the most broad-minded tolerance. We shall see later how much this alleged Musulman tolerance was worth. The utmost we can say is that some of these Caliphs, more sensual, more debauched than others, showed themselves very lax about the Islamic law. They drank wine, they gave themselves up to orgies in the midst of their dancers, their singers, their musicians, and their favourite pages—all things forbidden by their religion.

But to regard them as sceptics would be sheer madness. In most cases these debauchees ended by being converted, dying in the odour of sanctity, and giving every satisfaction to the faquis, those stern guardians of dogma and morals, those theologians of Islam who were as quarrelsome as our own scholiasts. In fact, all these Caliphs, without exception, were pious men, some of them as submissive to the faquis as certain Catholic kings later were to their confessors.

Under Abd er Rhaman II, the faqui Yahya ibn Yahya exercised the same influence over his sovereign as Cisneros did over Isabel and Ferdinand. Among these sovereigns there were some really religious men: for example, Hisham I, son of the first Abd er Rhaman, who sought to do good and live in accordance with the law of Allah, and Hakam II, who multiplied pious and charitable foundations.

It would equally be an error to represent these true believers as something like "intellectuals" born in advance of their time. It would even be rash to apply to them the traditional *cliché*: "They cultivated letters, science, and art." These deceptive words, these Western ideas, do not correspond to the reality of things where Eastern and Musulman culture is concerned. We must understand precisely what that culture really was.

Whatever it was, the Caliphs themselves had relatively little to do with it. They were too busy with the continual wars and rebellions that threatened their authority and they had to be on the look-out for treachery from all sides. They had at their disposal, it is true, secretaries and scribes who wrote a fine style and they were rather scrupulous in this matter, for fear lest they should be regarded as rude and illiterate in the eyes of the people of Bagdad and Cairo.

They had, moreover, poets in their pay, whom they maintained abroad and in the chief centres of their kingdom. These poets played a *rôle* analogous with that of our journalists of to-day: the *rôle* of jesters, but especially of political informers or agents. The Caliphs subsidised the poets just as our present ministries subsidise a newspaper.

As to their government and their administration, we do not know very much about them. When they established themselves in Spain, in any case, their task was very much simplified for them. They found there an administration which had been organised long ago. In this respect they had only to follow in the footsteps of their Roman or Visigoth predecessors. Whether it is a question of internal policing, of justice, of finance, or of the collection of taxes, their organisation, with its viziers, its walis, and its cadis, appears to have been of the most elementary kind.

Their greatest innovation in the sphere of government was the importance which they gave to the court and to the personal protection of their princes. The palace became a world of its own, with its servants, its officials, its eunuchs, its bodyguards, and its barracks of Prætorians. From the reign of Mohammed I onwards the eunuchs developed into an important power. In connivance with the harem, they distributed honours and jobs. Later the "Slavs" made themselves a regular party inside the framework of the State. Hakam I surrounded himself with Mamelukes and negroes.

But the worst scourge of this regime was its periodical appeal to the Berbers of Africa. Abd er Rhaman I, Abd er Rhaman III, and El Mansour all abused this expedient. They could not maintain their authority without the support of a foreign bodyguard and foreign armies. The consequences were inevitable. The Berbers, once they were installed on the soil, behaved themselves as though they were in a conquered country.

"They became its masters," says Ibn Adhari, dealing with the reign of El Mansour, "as a sequel to their notorious attack, which left the greater part of Spain uncultivated and desert, filled it with wolves and wild beasts, and left it for a time deprived of any security. . . ."

Still, undistinguished by personal features as the figures of these Caliphs may be, there are at least two who stand out with an air of grandeur and power. Seen from a distance, they assume the imposing appearance of autocrats who bent everything to their will and whose prestige spread far and wide. In this guise appear to us Abd er Rhaman III, who was the first to assume the official title of Caliph, and the usurper El Mansour, who was, as a matter of fact, the destroyer of the Caliphate.

During the long reign of Abd er Rhaman III (912–961) war was, practically speaking, continual—just as it was in Spain, for that matter, throughout the period of the Musulman domination. Struggles against the Arab aristocracy, against the renegade Spaniards, against the Christians at home and abroad, and finally against the Fatimides of the Moghreb—these more or less filled the half-century during which the reign of the new Caliph lasted.

By dint of cunning and, sometimes, of duplicity, of pitiless punishment, of cruelty, and, above all, by invincible determination and perseverance, Abd er Rhaman ended by putting most of his enemies in their place and establishing an almost absolute authority which extended throughout Musulman Spain. But these achievements were supremely fugitive: in the first place because reducing undisciplined and fundamentally refractory populations to obedience was a task all but impossible, and, in the next place, because these wars were never carried to a conclusion, either from lack of men or as a matter of tactical routine.

These annual, and sometimes biannual, expeditions were scarcely more than raids—the accustomed habits of ravaging and pillaging nomads—which came to an end as soon as enough booty had been assembled, enough prisoners taken, a few hundred heads cut off for exposure on the bridge of Cordova, and the back of the resistance broken at least for a season. As a result, everything had to be begun all over again. It sufficed to the Caliphs to weaken their adversaries and reduce them to famine, and to create a zone of desert between them and themselves by cutting down trees and crops, burning and sacking houses, and razing the ground to its very subsoil, after raiding it as completely as possible.

Under Abd er Rhaman's successors war broke out again as fiercely as ever, against the Christians of the North, and against the Berbers of the Riff. Conspiracies, rebellions, intestinal feuds recommenced in a cycle of struggles, in which the head of the central government often gained the upper hand only with the greatest difficulty. So the problem of national unity always remained in suspense. Nothing stable was created.

What was perhaps most solid in the achievement of Abd er Rahman III was his building. Like many men of war, he was a great builder, as though he wanted to make all the constructions which he had destroyed forgotten by his new ones. He embellished the old palace of Cordova and added to it. He raised a minaret above the Great Mosque and altered the *façade* of it, which must have resembled that of the former church of Saint Vincent, whose place the mosque had taken. Above all, he lavished his care upon the building of Medina az Zahara, at once a fortress and a country seat, which the Arab authors describe for us with evident admiration, but with no less obvious exaggeration.

He built this country seat, we are told, to please his favourite, Zahara (the Fair or the Golden), who had asked him to give her name to this palace of enchantment. He was certainly capable of such a piece of flattery, but it is more probable that he was guided in the matter by considerations of personal security. At Fez, as at Granada, Saragossa, or Cordova, the Musulman sovereigns constructed as their usual residences palace-fortresses, which dominated their capitals and held them in awe. They thought that they were thus better protected against conspiracies and insurrections.

There emerges from all this an unquestionable impression of greatness and magnificence. Threatened and baffled in his achievement though he was, the new Caliph sought to convey the idea that he was the real Emperor of the West. Cordova, his capital, was to eclipse Bagdad. The mosque of Cordova was to be the great sanctuary of Islam, throwing those of Damascus, Cairo, and Kairouan into the shade. It was his dream to extend his dominion over the whole of northern Africa, and this was why he finally occupied Ceuta and the coast of Barbary which faces Spain. But his Empire was nothing more than a brilliant *façade*.

Out of all this great effort, so long maintained by the first Caliph, there survived at least these two principles, which were handed on to the Catholic Sovereigns. The first was that Spain, ceaselessly threatened by the Berbers of Africa, could not be safe unless she occupied the points of embarkation on the African coast. Hence, in the case of the Caliphs, as in the case of the Kings of Spain, arose their anxiety to be masters of Tangier, Ceuta, and Melilla, and, later of Oran, Algiers, Bougie, and Tunis.

The Berber was the hereditary enemy, as Germany became for France. To the Spaniards the Riff frontier and the Barbary Coast assumed the same importance as the Rhine frontier did to the French. It was as important for them to hold the African ports as it was for the French to hold the bridge-heads over the great river. Abd er Rahman seems to have been the first Musulman sovereign who realised this necessity, though, perhaps, the Visigoth kings, when they occupied Ceuta, had already sensed it.

The second principle was that a country divided like Spain, inhabited by populations of a strongly particularist turn of mind, could only preserve its integrity and its independence with the help of a very powerful central authority. It is a significant fact that unity was never imposed upon Spain except by sovereigns of foreign origin: the Visigoth kings, the Musulman Caliphs, the Austro-Burgundians with Charles V and Philip II, the Bourbons of France with Philip V and his descendants.

Under Abd er Rhaman III this unity was extremely precarious; and it was, above all, artificial. This Caliphal Spain, made up of hybrid populations, in which Arabs and Berbers, Christians, Jews, and Musulmans, clashed with one another, could not have been anything but very difficult to govern, or even to pacify. The sovereign was so well aware that his authority was, so to speak, in the air, and that his person was always at the mercy of a conspiracy or a palace revolution, that he made up his mind, in order to maintain himself, to live outside his capital and rely upon a foreign guard and a foreign household administration.

These foreigners, who were erroneously called "Slavs," became not merely a party within the State, but even a regular population. During this reign, we are told, there were nearly fourteen thousand of them. As eunuchs they governed the harem and the palace. As scribes and officials they had the administration in their grip. As soldiers they controlled the army.

These "Slavs," detested by the Arabs, as well as by the Berbers and the Spaniards, came from all parts of the Mediterranean countries. Bought by Jews in the ports of the Black Sea and the Levant, they were re-sold to Spain, where they were subjected to a special training. Among them were Galicians, French, Germans, and Lombards. Certain towns of the South of France, it appears, fabricated eunuchs, who reinforced the strength of the "Slavs." Verdun also was reputed to be renowned for this kind of industry.

This army of Slavs, palatine officials and military chiefs, was the main instrument of the Caliph's authority. His power was a military dictatorship. He maintained himself only thanks to these foreigners, with the result that the unification of the empire was merely external. He was himself a foreigner in his own kingdom. After centuries of Musulman domination, he remained simply encamped in Spain as the Arabs and the Turks always were in every country they occupied.

Abd er Rhaman did not succeed in amalgamating the races of his empire. El Mansour, the other great man of the Caliphate, was no more successful. He was not even an authentic Caliph; he was only a usurper who tried in vain to found a new dynasty to take the place of that of the Omayyads. This adventurer, who, without assuming the Caliphal title, was the real ruler under the weak Hisham II, was a dicator in the fullest sense of the term.

He was, above all, even from his early youth, a man of great ambition, determined to seize power by all possible means. The following anecdote is told of him. One day, during one of the earliest years of the reign of Hakam II, Abd er Rhaman's son, he was dining in a garden in Cordova with four fellow-students. They were a gay party. Only the future El Mansour stayed silent, as though sunk in a deep meditation. Finally, emerging from his reverie, he cried suddenly: "Have no doubt about this—one day I shall be the master of this country!"

His friends burst out laughing. Not in the least disconcerted, he continued: "Let each one of you tell me what position he wants. I will give it him, when I am master."

"Well," said one of the students, "I find these fritters delicious, and, if it's all the same to you, I should like to be appointed inspector of markets. Then I could always have fritters in plenty, and without their costing me anything."

"I," said another, "am very fond of these figs, which come from Málaga, my native soil. So make me Cadi of that province!"

"The sight of all these beautiful gardens delights me," said the third. "I should like to be appointed Prefect of the Capital."

But the fourth kept silent, indignant at the presumptuous thoughts of his fellow-student.

"It's your turn," said El Mansour; "ask what you will."

The comrade whom he addressed got up and pulled him by the beard.

"When you govern Spain," he said, "wretched braggart that you are, order me to be smeared with honey, so that the flies and the bees may come and sting me, sit me backwards on a donkey, and have me driven thus through the streets of Cordova!"

El Mansour looked at him furiously, but he tried to restrain his wrath.

"Very well," he said, "each one of you shall be dealt with according to his desires. One day I shall remember all that you have said." And it appears that he kept his word.

This young man, so avid for power, was really named Abou Amir Mohammed. The Amirite dynasty which he tried to found could rival that of the Omayyads in nobility. El Mansour—let us give him the name which he did not assume until much later—prided himself upon his descent from an old Yemenite family and, even more, from one of the few Arab chiefs who formed part of the army of Tarik, the conqueror of Spain.

Despite this illustrious origin, the outset of his career was modest. At first a scribe in the service of the Cadi of Cordova, he contrived to have himself made steward of the estate of the young Abd er Rhaman, son of the Caliph Hakam II. This was the beginning of his good fortune. He lost no time in insinuating himself into the good graces of the Sultana Aurora, a Basque by birth and doubtless a Christian, who completely dominated the Caliph. He soon became her lover; and it was thanks to the fair Aurora that he was made overseer of the Mint, trustee of vacant inheritances, Cadi of Seville and Niebla, and finally commander of the *Chorta*, the regiment entrusted with police duties.

On the death of Hakam, he came to an agreement with the Grand Vizier to assassinate a pretender to the throne, who was supported by the all-powerful eunuchs of the palace, partisans of the "Slavs." After that his career was nothing but one long series of treacheries and assassinations, with the object of eliminating all his competitors one after the other. Hisham II, the new Caliph, shut up by him in the old palace of Cordova, let him reign in his stead.

El Mansour had a palace built for himself on the outskirts of the capital, thinking, no doubt, that residence in Cordova was not safe for him and that Medina az Zahara, the seat of Abd er Rhaman III, was too far away. Thence, amid perpetual struggles against rivals and rebels, he governed an empire more extensive than that of the great Abd er Rhaman had ever been.

To the South he reasserted Caliphal hegemony over maritime Barbary. To the North he pushed his conquests over the Christians almost as far as the Cantabrian Sea, seizing León and Santiago de Compostela. Never had the Christians found themselves in such a critical position. But, as always, these conquests were without a sequel. This Musulman Spain, which embraced almost the whole peninsula, which had the Kings of Castile and of Navarre for its vassals, was to fall to pieces once more.

Internally El Mansour's position, despite his cruel despotism, always remained equally unstable. As his predecessors had done, he had to rely upon an army of Prætorians and upon a following of foreigners. Whereas Abd er Rhaman III had organised the corps of the "Slavs" for his defence, El Mansour, following the traditional tactics of the Musulman princes, appealed to the Berbers of Africa.

A body of six hundred Africans began the process. But the dictator kept on summoning others, giving them an assurance "that they would be well and generously treated, so that they hastened to cross over to Spain and that all these warriors, arriving without intermission one after the other, came and grouped themselves around him. They disembarked with their garments in rags and mounted on sorry jades. But he soon clothed them in broidered silk and rich stuffs, gave them thoroughbred horses, and installed them in palaces such as they had never seen before, even in their dreams. Thus they ended by exceeding in numbers the soldiers of the Spanish *Djonds* (the standing army). It was they who enjoyed the confidence and the friendship of El Mansour, and it was they who flaunted it as the richest and the most influential" (*Ibn Adhari*).

This lucky lover of the Sultana Aurora, this assassin of his patrons and his allies, this despot who shrank from no cruelty and from no perfidy, became devout in his later years. Feeling himself to be suspect in the eyes of the faquis, those intolerant defenders of ortho-doxy, he satisfied them by increasing the mosque of Cordova to almost twice its former size, and by burning with his own hand "the materialist and philosophical works in the library assembled by Hakam II."

He punished "those who occupied themselves with philosophy or religious controversy." When an astrologer foretold the end of his power, he condemned him to crucifixion, after having his tongue cut out. He sentenced to be whipped, imprisoned, and finally exiled a poet who had spoken badly of him.

This real King of Spain had an ascetic side which foreshadowed that of Philip II. With the same hand that burnt the heretical books he made a copy of the whole of the Koran, which he carried about with him everywhere and over which he meditated endlessly. Taking a *sura* of the Prophet literally, he collected the dust which covered his boots and his clothes in the course of his campaigns against the Christians, inasmuch as this dust, according to the Book, was agreeable to Allah. "He thus collected a great coffer of it," which he ordered to be placed on his grave after his death. In a spirit of mortification, he travelled with the shroud in which he was to be buried: which reminds us of Philip II having his coffin placed in his room.

He asked Allah for the favour of dying in battle against the infidels. This favour was granted him. On his return from his last expedition against the Christians, after burning the monastery of Saint Æmilius, the patron saint of Castile, he died in the odour of sanctity at Medina Celi. Thither the dying El Mansour had been carried by his soldiers, as the dying Philip II was carried in a litter from Madrid to the Escorial, there to be interred.

CHAPTER VII

The Court of the Caliphs and Musulman Paganism

THIS Spanish civilisation reached its full bloom in the tenth century of our era, during the reigns of Abd er Rhaman the Great and under the usurper El Mansour. It was a century or even more in advance of the civilisation of the West and, in particular, of that of the little Christian kingdoms of Spain. This statement will fill with joy those historians who have a hatred of Christian Spain and see in Islam a civilising agency much superior to Christianity.

But these latter always choose to overlook the fact that Western Europe had been reduced to a condition of anarchy by the barbarian invasions which lasted until the tenth century, and especially that she had been cut off from the old centres of Mediterranean civilisation. Rome and Italy, ravaged by the same invaders, had lapsed into a state bordering upon barbarism, or at least into shameful degeneration. Constantinople was far away. The great eastern centres, Damascus, Alexandria, Bagdad, were closed to Christians.

If Western Europe as a whole was eclipsed, the plight of the little Pyrenean and Cantabrian kingdoms was worse. During the Roman period, as during the Visigoth period, this had always been the least rich, the least fertile, and the least civilised region of Spain. From the morrow of the Musulman conquest, this unhappy territory was subjected to raids at least once a year: devastation, burning, sacking of towns and monasteries, wasting of harvests, uprooting or cutting down of fruit trees. This went on for centuries. Every spring the armies of the Caliph started campaigning against the Christians. The Holy War was, so to speak, permanent, and for practical purposes remained declared all the time.

What country could have withstood such a regime? But this was not all. The population was continually decimated, when it was not exterminated. The objective of the Caliphal troops was to bring back to Cordova, together with plenty of booty, as many prisoners as possible, who became slaves—especially women and children; the others were massacred and decapitated. The more severed heads were piled up and brought back, the more the campaign was glorious and meritorious in the eyes of Allah.

In such conditions, we should admire the poor people of Navarre and Asturias for simply succeeding in carrying on their wretched and ceaselessly threatened life. They had neither the time nor the means to cultivate the fine arts and the flowers of literature. They had enough to do in hastily sowing their fields, burned by the enemy, and rebuilding their cottages.

Only a few monks in out-of-the-way monasteries, or clerics behind the walls of their towns, could pay some attention to the things of the mind, assemble a few books, and try to compose bad Latin verse or write dry-as-dust chronicles. That the Asturian and Basque peasants and even squires should not have been able to read or write is quite easy to understand. It would be surprising if the reverse had been the case.

Dozy, who feels uncomfortable in the presence of this illiteracy, tells us off-handedly that "in Andalusia almost everybody knew how to read and write." One may ask on what texts he bases this somewhat extraordinary statement. But knowing how to read and write constitutes at best an indifferent claim to superiority. Never have education and material well-being necessarily been marks of civilisation. One does not see, in any case, why the subjects of Alfonso or Ordoño should have minds more barbarous than those of Hakam or Abd er Rhaman. It was not on the Christian side that heaps of severed heads and rows of crucifixes were to be found.

Be that as it may, these poor lands of the North, ceaselessly invaded and devastated, could not dream of rivalling the favoured lands of the South and East, which enjoyed a peace less often disturbed. Western civilisation may have been asleep in the North for centuries; but it was thence that it was to set out to conquer the whole of Spain and yield such fruits as the Caliphal civilisation had never known.

That civilisation had the good fortune to find a ground eminently propitious for its development. Not only did the Musulmans possess themselves of the most fertile part of Spain, that part whose climate, like its sun, is the most blessed; they also found, when they arrived in Andalusia, the remains of a magnificent civilisation. The African barbarians who made up the greater part of their armies, coming from the half-savage regions of the Moghreb, had never seen anything in their own country to equal such capitals as Seville, Merida, or Cordova.

At the outset they confined themselves to following in the footsteps of their predecessors and picking up the Roman heritage, increased by the dowry of Byzantium and the Near East, which their Syrian horsemen brought at their horses' heels. Thanks to them, thanks to the efforts of their Walis and their Emirs to maintain the Latin order and preserve at least the material part of the old Mediterranean civilisation, that civilisation was able to live or at least to survive. It even had the beginning of a rebirth, foreshadowing the great Western Renaissance of the fifteenth and sixteenth centuries.

The chief merit of the conquerors was that they renewed the link, broken by the barbarians, between the East and the West. Henceforth the routes were reopened towards the great cities of Africa, Egypt, and the Levant: Tunis, Kairouan, Cairo, Alexandria, Damascus, Bagdad. The caravans resumed the Roman tracks which led towards the Moghreb through Cyrenaica and Libya. The Saracen ships found their way to the Spanish ports again. Carpets, silks, gold and silver ware and Oriental gems flowed to the courts of the Caliphs and into the bazaars of Cordova.

If, in the sphere of science, philosophy and letters the Spanish Musulmans did not add much to the old Greco-Latin heritage, they did increase it in the artistic, practical and utilitarian sphere. They added to the amenities of life—at least, of life as it had become in Spain and elsewhere after the decay or disappearance of the Roman culture.

In the field of art especially, their great originality was this: that they allied the delicate gracefulness and fancy of the Orient to Latin solidity and sense of rhythm. Fantasy of form, the charm of curved lines, the mysterious evocativeness of the arabesque—all this they taught to the Westerners; and, in doing so, they introduced into the world a new paganism, which doubtless was only a diminished and incomplete image of the old, but which, armed with new seductions, preserved an incomparable power of attraction.

The old paganism revived, paganism in turban and long robe— this was the aspect in which Islam first presented itself to the Spaniards. This, perhaps—apart from reasons of self-interest—explains why so many of them abandoned Christianity. These sensual Southerners saw only one thing: that Islam was indulgent towards pleasure. While the religion of Christ severely condemned all carnal delights, that of Mahomet authorised polygamy and promised to its faithful a paradise of houris and endless enjoyments.

This was the reason why, in the eyes of the Christians of the Middle Ages, the Musulmans were pagans, just as the Christians, in the eyes of the Musulmans, were polytheists. In the *Chanson de Roland* the Saracens are never called by any other name than "the pagans"— not exactly because they were reputed to worship a statue of Mahomet, as the author naïvely believed, but above all because they led a basely materialist and corrupt life. That was the chief complaint of the Spanish clerics and monks against the Musulmans.

Those of them who lived at Cordova under the Caliphs reproached them with wallowing in debauchery. Not only did they hold up to the contempt of the Catholics this Paradise which was nothing but a brothel, these harems which were haunts of all the vices, these pretended asceticisms of Ramadan which were nothing but an excuse for renewed revelries and fornications. They also denounced with horror this return of the Musulmans to all the pagan vices: the abuse of wine, torchlight orgies, dancers, and singers, musicians and poets who sang of carnal love and all the concupiscences of life; and finally luxury in building, the use of hot baths which softened the body, those *thermæ* which were places of illicit meetings and the refuge of every kind of vileness.

It is true that in all this they joined hands with the faquis and the Musulmans of strict observance. They, too, as we have already seen, proscribed dancing, music, hunting, and the usage of wine. But the influence of climate and environment was too strong.

Down to the very last day the Musulmans of Spain contrived to reconcile this paganism with the practice of their religion. As a result they lost their old warrior virtues; but they made it a kind of point of national honour to preserve their dancers, their singers, their musicians; and, on the eve of exile, they went on drinking, with their poets and their favourites, the heady, sweet wines of Andalusia.

This Musulman paganism exerted a regular fascination over the Spaniards. It was for this reason that the Christian priests regarded it as so dangerous for their flocks—not in the least from the doctrinal point of view, but because of the facilities which it accorded to the flesh. They might do what they liked and say what they liked, however: even the Christians who remained faithful to their ancestral religion allowed themselves to be contaminated by the pagan example.

The men of the North, the Franks especially, yielded at once to the attraction of these pagan pleasures. Many of them, who fought in the pay of Musulman princes, ended by living entirely in the Saracen way.

An Arab author tells us the strange adventure of a gallant Norman Count, who, after the taking of Barbastro by his co-religionists in 1064, installed himself in a house in the town and, not content with wearing the clothes of the former owner, started living *à la* Morisco. He was to be found sitting on a divan, in a room in which nothing—furniture or fittings—had been altered since the departure of the Musulman master, amid young slave-musicians. He had the lyre played for him and Arab songs sung to him. Around him silks and brocades were spread, jewel-caskets lay open, precious stones and metals were displayed. The hardy Norman had slid into the skin of the Saracen whose place he had taken.

It needed the virile virtues of a hero like the Cid to resist the pagan seduction of this decadent Islam. He joined hands in that with the faquis, who never ceased to reproach the Musulman princes with their laxity. To the Valencians who came to surrender to him he said sternly: "If you have urgent business, come to me and I will listen to you. For *I do not shut myself up with women to drink and sing*, as do your lords, of whom you can never have audience." These words of the Christian re-echo those of the Almoravid Youssouf ben Teshoufin, that unpolished African, that austere Musulman, who also reproached the Andalusian kinglings with being debauched and impious libertines.

Vain sermons! Neither the most edifying discourses, nor even the most vital reasons of dynastic or national interest, availed to convert the pagan soul of Andalusia. The sigh of the exiled Moor, when he looked back for the last time upon Granada, was one of regret for the Enchantress and her lost delights. . . .

At least, however, it cannot be denied that many of these Caliphs and these Musulman kinglings had a sense of beauty, and almost all of them a sense of magnificence. But unhappily these instincts of grandeur and luxury consorted ill with the poverty of the times. War and brigandage were continual, and droughts and famines frequent.

For more than a century the conquerors added little to Roman Cordova. It took more than two centuries to finish the construction and decoration of the Great Mosque. Nevertheless, there were periods of peace and prosperity, especially in the course of the tenth century. Commerce, in the hands of the Christians and the Jews, became considerable, and customs duties contributed much revenue to the State.

The most important source of revenue, however, appears to have been the booty taken at least once a year, and often twice a year, in Christian territory. The thousands of prisoners periodically brought back by the armies of the Caliph were employed as manual labourers, especially in the construction of mosques. Finally, the sale of Christian slaves, women, girls, and children, was also profitable to the treasury. To forestall criticisms which the magnificence of his buildings might arouse, El Mansour was careful to draw public attention to the fact that all this was paid for by the infidels. "The treasury," he said, "is well filled, thanks to the riches which I have won from the wretches."

Be that as it may, it is certain that all these sovereigns exerted themselves to invest their court, if not their capital, with an air of grandeur, and to introduce all kinds of embellishments into it.

They chose Cordova for their residence because Toledo, the former capital of the Visigoth kings, was too near the Christian frontier, and Seville, linked with the sea by its river, was at the mercy of an African fleet. The situation of Cordova, in Andalusia, was more or less central. Moreover, the ancient Colonia Patricia of the Romans, the old capital of Betica, still preserved a certain prestige in the eyes of the people.

Under the Roman and Visigoth domination the city, properly speaking, had about the same extent as it had under the Musulman domination. Its area embraced a number of suburbs, with farms, villas, monasteries, and churches. At the outset the Musulmans confined themselves to occupying the Roman enclosure and the suburbs, which must have been partly unpopulated and covered with ruins, especially after the sacking of the city by Moghit's Berbers.

The bridge across the Guadalquivir, in particular, was badly damaged. The restoration of this bridge was one of the first works of public utility undertaken by the Musulmans (719). Nothing else was undertaken until the reign of El Mansour—in other words, for nearly three centuries.

It is extremely probable that this Roman Cordova presented an appearance fairly close to that which we still see to-day. In any case the principal buildings—those which gave the city its character—even if they had not yet attained their full size and their full magnificence, were at least already in existence: the great bridge across the river; the monumental gate, which was called the Gate of the Statue because of the lion, probably in gilded bronze, which surmounted it; the *castellum*, which later became the Alcázar; and finally the Cathedral of Saint Vincent, which became the Great Mosque.

The city as a whole was small, like all the cities of antiquity and the Middle Ages. It is absolutely impossible to accept the fantastic figures which the Arab annalists give us and which Dozy blindly reproduces. According to them, Cordova had half a million inhabitants, three thousand mosques, a hundred and thirteen thousand houses, and three hundred public baths, without counting the twenty-eight suburbs. Under the Caliphs, as a matter of fact, the fortified area or *Medina* did not represent even half the extent of present-day Cordova, which has ninety thousand inhabitants at the most; and this area, we are told, included a number of spacious gardens!

Let us add to it the nearest suburb, which already existed in part during the Roman period and later was embraced within the area of the modern city, called by the Arabs the *Ajerquía:* let us add even the suburb of Secunda, another Roman foundation: we still cannot contrive to squeeze into this perimeter the half-million inhabitants, the hundred and thirteen thousand houses, and the three thousand mosques about which we are told.

We can only suppose that the Arab authors designated by the name of Cordova not only the present city and its suburbs, but also an immense area of environs which extended to the foothills of the Sierra, even as far as thirty-five kilometres from the present city. Even if we accepted a Cordova thus arbitrarily aggrandised, the figure of five hundred thousand inhabitants still seems remarkably exaggerated.

Of these environs, certainly more populous then than they are to-day, and of the Musulman city properly speaking, nothing remains apart from the mosque and some ruins of no great architectural interest. This seems to indicate that the buildings were not very substantially constructed, and that the Medina itself—like all Musulman towns to-day—possessed no monumental or even architectural character, at least in its exteriors.

It must have been a network of very narrow little streets, an agglomeration of little houses with few windows, whitewashed walls, and no external adornment. The houses of the rich, of course, were larger and comprised fairly extensive gardens; but from the outside there was nothing about them, any more than about the houses of the poor, to attract the attention of the passer-by.

They were the ancient Roman and Mediterranean houses, with

their interior patios and their gardens surrounded by high walls. A text of Aben Pascual tells us that there were to be seen in Cordova surviving buildings "Greek and Roman. . . . Statues of silver and gilded bronze within them poured water into receptacles, whence it flowed into ponds and into marble basins excellently carved." The Musulmans, in short, found ready-made in Roman Cordova not only the type of their dwellings and the lay-out of them, but also the principal themes of their interior decoration. They had merely to adapt all this to their personal tastes or convenience, or to new forms of Oriental style.

It is possible that the present city, despite so many successive revolutions and civilisations, has preserved the essential features of Musulman and even Roman Cordova. The houses have given themselves a little more air and light on the street side; but, in their coats of whitewash, they are still the same unsubstantial constructions of brick or clay-mortar, with the same bright, bare surfaces on which the smallest decorative accessory acquires an outstanding importance.

There are still the same street-corners, with low houses dominated by the square towers of churches, which were once minarets, after serving as Spanish or Visigoth watch-towers. There are still the same little squares, where a root of jessamine or plumbago assumes a fugitive aspect of the miraculous, and the red note of a pot of geraniums or carnations strikes with an intensity almost cruel in its sharpness against the blinding whiteness of the walls in the sun.

The Arabs, like the Berbers, had no love for residence in towns. That was why the Medina, the seat of the patrician families, scarcely exceeded the bounds of the Roman enclosure. The Musulman aristocracy, the higher officials, and the Court preferred the country and summer seats on the slopes of the Sierra.

In the case of the Caliphs themselves there were reasons of security in this choice. In their Cordovan Alcázar they were always at the mercy of a rising. These foreign sovereigns, encamped in conquered territory, felt themselves to be under observation by their subjects, with no goodwill towards them and ever ready to join hands with the disaffected. It was for this reason that they multiplied villas, pleasure resorts, and even fortified retreats in the environs of their capital.

Naturally the Arab authors speak of these villas in the most enthusiastic terms. Wonderful names are applied to them in their texts. There were the Perfect, the Flowery, the Amorous, the Magnificent, the Villa of Delights, the Villa of Felicity, the Villa of Prodigies. Unquestionably they were charming places, with water in abundance, shady patios, embowered retreats, and channels of marble or baked earth running between flower-beds. To understand the admiration of the Arabs for them, we have only to remember that their writers went into ecstasies in the presence of the merest clump of trees.

But, naïve or hyperbolical though these praises may have been, the homes of pleasance to which they were applied must at the very least have been extremely attractive, especially in the summer, in the harsh dryness and barrenness of the plain of Cordova. The Moorish villas, of which some survivals are still to be found in the environs of Algiers, may perhaps give us an approximate idea of them.

Among these Caliphal villas, however, some, it appears, were regular palaces: the Medina az Zahira, built by El Mansour; the Medina az Zahara, built by Abd er Rhaman III; and finally another, the Alamyria, which seems to have been an offshoot of the second. It is difficult to judge them, as we have little to go on except the descriptions of the Arab authors, which usually make up in dithyrambics what they lack in precision. Nothing of the Az Zahira is left to us. A few remains of the Alamyria survive. As to the famous Az Zahara, the excavations which have so far been made give us only a very inadequate idea of it. We are therefore driven back upon Arab testimony.

"Medina az Zahara," says Edrisi, "was a considerable town, built in an amphitheatre, in superimposed stages so that the ground of the upper town was on a level with the roofs of the middle town, and this on a level with the roofs of the lower town. All of them were surrounded by walls. In the upper town there were palaces of such beauty that it defies all description. The middle town comprised orchards and gardens. The lower town consisted of dwelling-houses and the mosque."

Here is what Ibn Adhari has to say about it. "It was begun under En Nasir (the surname of Abd er Rhaman III), at the commencement of the year 325 (936 of our era). Every day six thousand squared stones were placed in position, apart from the rubble employed in the foundations. The marble was imported from Carthage, Ifrikia, and Tunis by trusty agents. . . . The building required 4313 columns, of which 1013 came from Ifrikia and 140 were sent by the King of the Christians (the Basileus of Byzantium?). The remainder were derived from Spain herself.

"As for the magnificent basin, sculptured and adorned with gilded images, it was brought from Constantinople by the Bishop Rebi(?) . . . En Nasir had it placed in the chamber of repose in the Eastern hall, known by the name of Morines. It was adorned with twelve statues of red gold, inlaid with pearls of great price: statues fashioned in the workshops of the palace of Cordova. . . . Eight hundred loaves were used daily to feed the fish in the ponds. . . . It is said that the apartments comprised within the enclosure of the palace of Az Zahara, intended for the lodging of the Sultan, his family and his court, were of the number of four hundred; that the number of Slavonian eunuchs was three thousand seven hundred and fifty; that in the palace of Az Zahara the number of women, old and young, and slave-girls was six thousand three hundred; and that to feed everybody required thirteen thousand pounds of meat, without counting chickens, partridges, and birds and fish of all kinds."

Let us leave Ibn Adhari the responsibility for these figures, and note that this compiler was writing after the reconquest of Cordova by the Christians, at a time when Medina az Zahara was no more than a heap of ruins. Let us remark, moreover, that most of the columns were brought ready-made from Carthage and Constantinople or borrowed from the pagan temples and the churches of Spain, and that the decoration came in part from Byzantium: the basins, the gold and silverware, and probably also the mosaics.

There was, notably, "an extraordinary pearl, which figured in the marvellous hall. It came from the Greek Cæsar of Constantinople, who sent it to En Nasir *with a number of precious gifts*." I repeat once more: Islam, at least at the outset, adorned itself with the leavings of Latinity.

What has so far been cleared of the ruins of Medina az Zahara scarcely conveys the impression of a " considerable town." It is not larger—indeed, it is smaller—than the Alhambra of Granada. Rather than a town it is a fortress: the *Alcazaba* of all the Moorish or African kinglings, who, always afraid of insurrections or sudden attacks, lived outside their capitals, on a height whence they could command the city and the roads leading to it.

At the same time it is unquestionable that the excavated foundations and debris indicate a place of magnificence. Marble, onyx, alabaster, and the most precious substances are plentiful. The decorative themes are related to Byzantine sculpture, or the Roman African sculpture of the period of decadence; but, while they reveal Oriental influences, they possess an evident originality.

As a matter of fact what survives is so chaotic and so limited that it is absolutely impossible to come to any conclusion about this "marvellous" palace. It is probable that it was very luxuriously decorated and furnished, and it must have been a very pleasant and cool residence during the hot season. Medina az Zahara was abundantly supplied with water. It had plenty of shade in its gardens; and, from the height of its terraces, one must have enjoyed a delightful view over Cordova and its countryside, sown with villas, gardens, and orchards.

The luxury displayed in these buildings made the strict Musulmans murmur. It was not only a question of the scandal of statues, bas-reliefs, and perhaps paintings, which reproduced living or vegetable forms, all things forbidden by the law; it was also a question of the gold and the precious metals thus idly wasted. Ibn el Athir tells us that, after the construction of this Palace of Enchantment, Abd er Rhaman gave audience one day "in a pavilion inlaid with gold, whose marvellous architecture was beyond compare. The Prince, surrounded by great personages, asked them whether to their knowledge anyone had ever raised such a building. All of them replied, with high praises, that they knew of nothing like it.

"Only the Cadi Moudhir Ballouti remained silent, with downcast eyes. Questioned by the Caliph, he replied, with the tears running down to his beard: 'I call Allah to witness: I did not think that Satan (may he be confounded!) would win such power over you as to make you descend to the level of the Infidels!' And he quoted a text of the Koran, in which it is written that roofs of silver and ornaments of gold are made only for the wicked. Abd er Rhaman lowered his eyes without answering, and began to weep."

It is certain that nothing could have been more pagan than these voluptuous Andalusian villas. The nomad Arab or Berber, enemy of towns and of all dwellings built in stone, could not fail to condemn the impiety and the wantonness of these too magnificent palaces. To take pleasure in them men needed to be, like the Caliphs, sons of foreign concubines, men of mixed blood and suspect faith, who surrendered themselves to all the relaxing influences of a soil saturated with idolatry and of a climate and a sky only too beautiful.

It is paganism again, that ineradicable paganism whose subtle perfume still floats in the air of Andalusia—it is this again which we find in the most religious monument which the Caliphs have left us: that astonishing Mosque of Cordova, out of which the Christians vainly tried to make a cathedral.

Yet at the outset it was a church, placed under the patronage of the great Spanish martyr, Saint Vincent. During the Roman and Visigoth period it was the cathedral church of Cordova. It is well to recall this fact to the minds of literary tourists, who hasten to proclaim that Christianity is an intruder in this environment. No, the intruder was Islam, which ousted from it the Christ of the Gospels, Who, no doubt, had taken the place of some pagan god. From the earliest days of the Arab conquest, the Christians, after seeing all their churches demolished, had to share their cathedral with the Musulmans as well.

"The Musulmans," says the compiler, Ibn Adhari, "after their conquest of Spain, took as a precedent what Abu Obeyda and Khalid had done, with the consent of the Prince of Believers, Omat ben Khattab, touching the division by halves of Christian churches in territories which had surrendered on terms, for example, at Damascus and elsewhere. Accordingly the Musulmans came to an agreement with the barbarians [sic] of Cordova to take half of their greatest church, which was situated inside the city. Out of this half they made their principal mosque, while they left the other half to the Christians; but they destroyed all the other churches."

During the reign of Abd er Rhaman I this mosque, contiguous with the Christian church, became too small for the growing number of the faithful, and the Emir compelled the Christians to surrender the other half of their cathedral to him, in return for an indemnity and the right to restore churches which had been destroyed at the time of the Conquest *outside Cordova*. The edifice was completely rebuilt in 786 of our era. Most of the successors of this prince made a point of embellishing or extending this mosque, which ended by becoming the greatest sanctuary of Islam after the Kaaba of Mecca.

Abd er Rhaman II added new bays lengthwise. Then these bays were still further extended by Hakam II. Next El Mansour almost doubled the width of the edifice by adding eight lateral aisles to the eleven constructed by his predecessors. Finally, Abd er Rhaman III built the minaret which still stands to-day. In all its essential parts, therefore, the Mosque of Cordova was finished by the end of the tenth century.

It is extremely probable that this mosque, which took the place of an old Christian basilica, began by copying its arrangement and perhaps exactly reproducing its plan. That basilica, like the African basilicas with which we are familiar, had a courtyard in front of it, doubtless surrounded with porticos and provided with a basin for ablutions. This was what the Spaniards later called, in all the edifices of this kind, the "Court of Orange Blossom." The central nave must have been larger than the lateral aisles. It is possible that the Church of Saint Vincent itself had nine lateral aisles, like the mosque of Abd er Rhaman—in any case, the great basilica of Tipasa has nine aisles—and that the Musulmans only added one on each side of the building.

The *mirhab*—the niche which gives the orientation towards Mecca for prayer—simply took the place of the apse. This apse was progressively moved back with the outer wall, in proportion as the mosque was extended lengthwise. When El Mansour extended it crosswise, the sanctuary was thrown out of its axis, inasmuch as the *mirhab* remained on the axis of the old church. It is possible, in short, that until the reign of Abd er Rhaman III (912–961), who, we are told, regularised the *façade*, the mosque preserved the basilical form, that is to say, a central nave higher than the aisles.

Regarded as a whole, therefore, the Mosque of Cordova is merely a Christian basilica amplified in both directions. This amplification was limited to the alignment of columns and the prolongation and multiplication of their rows. These columns, moreover, were for the most part of pagan or Christian origin—whether they came from Africa or from Spain. The Roman civilisation had left the debris of an immense quantity of derelict material on the ground. The Arabs confined themselves to using all this over again, re-erecting the fallen columns and crowning them with their Roman or Byzantine capitals.

The only difficulty was that these fortuitous columns were not always high enough. Then it was necessary, as at Kairouan, to shore them up. Sometimes they were too high, and they had to be cut down. At Cordova the architects happily avoided the shorings of

Kairouan; but the second-hand columns, sometimes cut off above their pedestals, were still of inadequate height; and it was therefore necessary to surmount them with two superimposed arches in order to obtain a proper elevation of the ceiling.

We also know that the mosaics of the *mirhab*—in other words, the only feature that is properly speaking Oriental in the Mosque of Cordova—were executed by Byzantine workers lent to the Caliph Hakam II by the Emperor of Constantinople. Not only did the Basileus dispatch his workers, but he had also to send to Cordova even the material for the mosaics: "three hundred and twenty quintals of cubes," Ibn Adhari tells us.

For the masonry itself the workers were Christians. They were prisoners taken in the territories of the North and brought back to Cordova by the Caliphal armies. There has been found on a wall the form of a cross, rudely carved by one of these unfortunates. Finally, the building expenses were mostly met either by tribute imposed upon the Christian princes of the peninsula, or out of the proceeds of the raids made in their territory by the Caliph.

Accordingly in this great sanctuary of Islam, the first after that of Mecca, everything, or nearly everything, is Christian: the plan of the edifice, the material employed, and even the workmanship. We may know all this, all about these borrowings, these odds and ends assembled here and there; but still it must be admitted that the effect of the whole is as original as possible. The Mosque of Cordova resembles no other. It seems to be a product of Spanish soil, a unique plant which could have grown nowhere else.

Its fanatics lament the mutilations which the Christians of the Reconquest inflicted on it. They regret the old ceiling of painted and sculptured wood, and disparage the indifferent vaultings which have replaced it. They wax especially indignant over the Catholic cathedral, half flamboyant, half grotesque in style, which the Cordovan canons planted right in the middle of the Mosque.

These disturbances are, no doubt, very regrettable. But what may console us is, in the first place, that the *capilla mayor* and the nave of this cathedral make a magnificent whole; and, in the next place, that, without the high vaultings of this central part, the vaulting of the apse and the choir, and even the lower vaulting of the lateral aisles, the ceiling of this immense edifice, perched upon columns disproportionately small, would produce a crushing effect. One would feel as though he were walking through an endless mouse-trap. The vaultings of the aisles and, above all, the splendid sweep of the vaulting of the apse, in my opinion, relieve this too low ceiling very happily. They invest the building with a character of spirituality which the Musulman sanctuary never possessed.

But this character disappears as soon as one emerges from the Christian enclave. The canons may have done their best: there is no means of Christianising a place like that. The edifice remains pagan.

The architects who designed this marvel may have been Islamised Spaniards; they remained in their hearts Latins with the sense of voluptuousness and of the beauty of form. No religious idea possesses you as you sit in front of these rows of columns and these arches with their keystones painted purple. They make you think rather of series of flowery pergolas, with their green roofs, their trellises of climbing plants, their curves heavy with roses and convolvulus.

Or they make you think of the doorway of a *tepidarium*, or of a courtyard indefinitely multiplied, where you visualise at the end of the vista, in a flight of floating gauze, the harmonious outlines of ancient choirs and dances. Only the Oriental overloading and complexity of the intertwining and polylobed arcatures which surround the *mirhab* clash a little with this illusion. But to look aside and let your eyes stray among the beautiful columns of mauve or rose marble, with their Corinthian capitals, suffices to make the pagan vision continue.

The exterior of the edifice produces an effect no less striking. It should be seen from the left bank of the Guadalquivir, from that wretched suburb which is called the *Campo de la Verdad*. Surrounded by the neighbouring buildings, it acquires an accent of strange intensity. In summer, towards noon, when the architectural lines stand out with almost brutal precision against a dead blue sky, it forms part of an extraordinary whole, of the most vehemently Spanish character.

The old Roman bridge with its *castillo* of the Middle Ages; the Moorish battlements of the Alcázar; the quadrangular towers of the episcopal Palace, which, with the enclosing wall of the Mosque, recalls the stern nakedness of the Escorial; and finally, Philip II's monumental gate, at the other end of the bridge: these harsh, crude tones; these tones of ashes intermingled with the redness of live coals; these lilac and mauve tiles which look as though they were blazing away on the roofs in a silent fire—all this seems dried-up and dead, and yet burning. It is, as it were, a passion driven in upon itself, overwhelmed by the weight of the sun, which you expect to see burst forth and gush up with a cry of rage towards the sky of fire. . . .

CHAPTER VIII

What the Arab-Spanish Civilisation was

IT was in the tenth century, especially during the reigns of Abd er Rhaman the Great, of his son Hakam II, and even of the usurper El Mansour, that, despite the unpropitiousness of the time, despite perpetual wars and rebellions, what is called the Arab-Spanish civilisation developed.

It is here especially that we must be on our guard against being misled by words, which do not mean the same thing to us as they do to Orientals. To judge this civilisation reasonably, it is important not to let ourselves be carried away by the hyperbolical admiration, the preconceptions, and the prejudices of those who exalt Arab-Spanish culture to an exaggerated extent only in order to degrade Catholic Spain and, in general, medieval Christian culture in proportion.

The gravest error in this matter is to believe that the Arab-Spanish civilisation was the work of Arabs. The Arabs, who were very small in number in the Peninsula, were never anything for the Spaniards and for Western Europe but intermediaries, most of the time unconscious and involuntary, who reopened to them the roads of the great civilising centres of the East: Byzantium, Damascus, Cairo, Bagdad. The Arabs themselves brought nothing with them but their nomad poverty and roughness, their pride of race, their inveterate hatred of everything that we understand by the word civilisation. Even those historians who are most prejudiced in their favour are obliged to recognise their nullity as civilising elements and as factors of progress.

"They are the least inventive people in the world," writes Dozy. "Invention is so rare in their literature that, when one encounters an imaginative poem or story in it, one can almost always declare off-hand, without fear of being mistaken, that this production is not of Arab origin, but is a translation from a Hindu, Persian, Syrian, or Greek original." Elsewhere he writes: "They translated and commented upon the works of the ancients. They enriched certain specialised branches of study by patient, exact, and minute investigations. *But they invented nothing. We do not owe any great and fertilising idea to them.* As a result of contact with the peoples whom they conquered they cultivated learning and civilised themselves, so far as that was possible for them."

It should be added that, to be exact, it was above all the peoples conquered by them, the Syrians, the Persians, the Egyptians, the Spaniards, who, under their domination and through the medium of their language, went on cultivating and started popularising the ancient learning and philosophy, those of the East and of the old

Helleno-Latin world. If there was an Arab-Spanish civilisation, it was especially to the Spaniards—Christians, Jews, and renegades—that this civilisation was due.

Spanish Islam, in the first place, inherited all the material part of the Roman civilisation, as it subsisted after the Germanic invasions and the Visigoth attempts as restoration.

We have seen above that the administrative framework of the Roman and Visigoth period was adopted by the Arab conquerors. Similarly, so far as habitation, hygiene, and public works were concerned, they merely followed in the footsteps of their predecessors. They found comfortable houses, well suited to the climate, sometimes luxurious; towns planned by the military genius of the Romans, adorned with magnificent monuments, as their historians recognise; fortified areas, observation posts, roads, bridges, and aqueducts, which they had nothing to do but maintain or repair.

Doubtless the public fountains and baths still existed, if only, so far as the latter were concerned, in a state of ruin. These baths, abandoned by the Christians and condemned by the Church for reasons of morality and orthodoxy, because they were, so it was said, the sink of all iniquities and the last refuge of paganism—these baths did not need much reconstruction to become what the Catholic Spaniards called "Moorish Baths." They were merely less magnificent, more strictly utilitarian, than during the Roman period.

As for the fountains, we have only to look at those which survive at Timgad, at Djemila, at Dougga, or at Pompeii to recognise in them the prototypes of the Musulman fountains in Egypt, in Syria, in North Africa, or in Spain. There is the same arrangement in the form of a niche, and the same striking colours: colours made up of camletted stucco or mosaic inlay, which was later replaced by the enamelled faience of the *azulejos*.

The Arab and Berber chieftains, when they arrived in Spain, also found fields excellently tilled by the Andalusian peasants, who to this very day are first-class cultivators, worthy descendants of those who won Betica its reputation for fertility. It is probable that the heedlessness of the new masters produced the same results in Spain as in Roman and Byzantine Africa. The soil, less well cultivated, less well irrigated, became also less fertile. Some regions were allowed to lie fallow. In any case, from the date of the Musulman conquest droughts and famines—frightful famines which depopulated whole districts—tended to multiply.

We learn from the Arab historians that the first emigration of Andalusians to Morocco (749) was caused by a famine, which lasted nearly five years. In the course of the ninth century there were at least five great periods of dearth. Very frequently this formula recurs in these histories: "That year there was a great drought in Spain." It is a thing that cannot fail to surprise those who have read the dithyrambs of most modern historians about Spain and her wonderful irrigation by the Arabs.

Be that as it may, the new-comers had merely to set on its feet again a country formerly fertile and prosperous, which asked only to be reborn. But, without the aid of the conquered, in other words, the real sons of the soil, Arabs and Berbers would have achieved nothing. These Spaniards—Christians, Jews, or converts to Islam—had only to look around them to find models or stimulants in the vestiges of the old Hispano-Roman civilisation. The conquerors, moreover, by opening the roads to the great Oriental metropoles for them, presented them with new models, forms of art hitherto unknown; and they also brought with them in their train inventions and material refinements still novel in the West.

In addition to the old Helleno-Latin learning, Byzantine, Alexandrine, and Persian influences were put at the disposal of these aspirants to a new civilisation. Byzantium especially had much to teach to the architects, the sculptors, and the mosaic workers of Cordova and Medina az Zahara.

Undoubtedly under the Abd er Rhamans, in tne finest flower of the Caliphate, Musulman Spain aspired towards a renaissance. Given a good administration, in a country which was at peace and felt itself to be safe, and in which public spirit was exalted by a sense of national strength and greatness, such a renaissance might well have taken place. But the movement in this direction was thwarted by all kinds of unfavourable circumstances.

If a great civilising movement is to take place in a country, it is above all necessary that there should be a certain homogeneity of race, or at least a certain community of ideas and feelings. The Augustan age, or the age of Louis XIV, is comprehensible only in terms of a comparative unanimity of the nation. Musulman Spain, on the contrary, was an assembly of heteroclite populations. To get an idea of it we must hark back to the comparison which I have already made with the countries of the Levant as they were until quite recent times, before the enforced unification imposed by the Turks.

Spaniards, Visigoths, Berbers, Syrian Arabs, Arabs of the Hedjaz and the Yemen, Christians, Jews, Musulmans—all these peoples lived side by side, as best they could, most of the time without understanding one another. Unity of language did not exist. Literary Arabic, the official and religious language, was not understood or spoken except in educated circles and among the officials of the Caliphate. The lower-class Musulmans spoke a vulgarised Arabic, with a strong admixture of local idioms of Berber dialects. The Christians and the Jews commonly spoke "Roman," the first form of Spanish.

Nevertheless, by force of circumstances, conquerors and conquered were naturally driven to try and understand one another. A number of Mozarabs—that is to say, educated Christians—knew not only the vulgarised Arabic, but also literary Arabic. On the other hand, the Musulman magistrates and the Caliphs in person ended by familiarising themselves with Roman.

In general it was the degree of culture upon which the use of the two languages depended. Educated persons spoke Arabic, and the uneducated Roman. "We know," says Menéndez Pidal, "that about the year 1050 there were illiterate, but very devout, Musulmans in Toledo who could not speak Arabic."

Similarly four hundred years later in the kingdom of Granada, which had become the last refuge of Spanish Islam, and therefore was as Arabised or Berberised as possible, there were to be found Christians who could only speak Arabic. In some Christian villages, Marmol tells us, it was as much as one could expect if the priest and the beadle understood a few words of Spanish.

Can we believe that there was any mutual penetration among these juxtaposed ethnical elements? If so, it did not go very far. The habit of living side by side produced nothing more than a certain degree of reciprocal toleration, which readily turned into hostility at the least friction. To realise this we have only to look at what happens to this very day in Syria or in Palestine. Musulmans, Christians, and Jews live there side by side, use the same language, and often have the same way of life; but their minds remain profoundly different, even when they are not living in open strife.

Perhaps unity in teaching might have produced a public spirit favourable to a high state of culture and even a complete civilisation national in its character. But the schools remained, as they still do in the Levant, purely religious. Education was not organised and administered by the State; it depended entirely upon private initiative. There is quoted, it is true, the case of the pious Caliph Hakam II, who subsidised schools for the poor children of Cordova. There were three in the neighbourhood of the Great Mosque, and twenty-four in the suburbs. But this was an isolated act of charity and piety, a quite personal "good work" which does not appear to have been imitated by the successors of this Caliph.

It is true that schools of a sort were numerous, at least in the towns, as they had been during the Roman period. It was open to anybody to set up as a schoolmaster. These schools, however, were strictly sectarian, and the teaching was purely religious. Those which Hakam subsidised were intended to "teach the Koran" to the poor children of the capital. That did not even mean that the children were taught to read and write in Arabic. Teaching the Koran means teaching recitation of the *suras* of the Holy Book by heart. To affirm on the strength of this that everybody knew how to write in Musulman Andalusia seems to be a curious exhibition of credulity.

As for higher education, it did not exist, or at least it had no official existence. Like primary education, it was left to private initiative, and it was, moreover, strictly supervised by the Musulman theologians. Certain Caliphs, like Abd er Rhaman II, Abd er Rhaman en Nasir, and Hakam II, may have encouraged and patronised poets, writers, men of learning, and philosophers. That depended on their good humour. The masters taught at their own risk and peril. Besides, this teaching, if it were to be tolerated, had to restrict itself to the purely formal or utilitarian.

Grammar, rhetoric, prosody, for the training of scribes and versifiers; theology, exegesis, canon law, for the training of jurists and clerics—these were about all the subjects which were taught in these private schools, called "universities" by historians with vivid imaginations. If there were schools in Musulman Spain which remotely resembled our universities, they were schools of theology grouped around great mosques and maintained by pious foundations.

Learning, as we understand it, had only the most restricted place in them. It was regarded with suspicion by the religious intolerance of the faquis, which was often translated into very drastic prohibitions and persecutions. During periods of extreme rigour, all that was permitted to students of mathematics was to acquire the knowledge necessary to orientate the mosques in the direction of Mecca and determine the seasons, the phases of the moon, and the exact hour of prayer. Everything else was regarded as dangerous.

While the profane encouraged astrologers, soothsayers, horoscope-readers, and makers of amulets and talismans, astronomy properly so-called, scientific and rational astronomy, was frowned upon—though this did not prevent it from being cultivated clandestinely, or even openly, when circumstances permitted. What especially attracted pupils—even Christians from all parts of the Christian territory—around these Musulman and Jewish teachers was the occult sciences: demonology, magic, alchemy, when they were tolerated, or secretly favoured by powerful personages or by the Caliphs themselves.

Medicine and botany, by reason of their practical utility, escaped the severity of religious censorship. There were famous Spanish doctors and surgeons. The celebrated schools of Salerno and Montpellier owed part of their renown, it appears, to the influence or the presence of these Arabic-speaking Spanish doctors, who were mostly of Christian or Jewish origin. But, apart from certain altogether exceptional intuitions, this medicine makes us smile to-day. It was a formulary of incredible prescriptions. It sets one dreaming to think that these old wives' or negro sorcerers' remedies may once have cured.

All this so-called science had nothing in common with ours. It was the liquidation of the old Greco-Latin empiricism plus an Alexandrine and Oriental endowment. It was a farrago which the modern age had to abandon. The same thing applies to other branches of Arab erudition or "science."

Our historians invite us to marvel at the library assembled at Cordova by Hakam II, a library which contained four thousand volumes—others say six thousand. If the figures are correct, this obviously amounted to a considerable collection. But, if you eliminate from all this assembly the books of exegesis and of theology, of jurisprudence, of rhetoric, of grammar, of prosody—everything that is strictly Arab and Musulman—what remains that could really serve towards the progress of the human spirit?

Enemies of learning in general, the Musulman theologians were especially so in the case of philosophy. "It is only by a very deceptive equivocation," writes Renan, "that the name of 'Arab philosophy' is applied to the sum of works undertaken, through reaction against Arabism, in parts of the Musulman Empire as remote as possible from the Arabian Peninsula: Samarkand, Bokhara, Cordova, Morocco.

"This philosophy was written in Arabic, because that idiom had become the learned and sacred language of all the Musulman countries; but that was all. . . . *The origins of Arab philosophy derive, accordingly, from an opposition to Islam.* It is for this reason that philosophy always remained among the Musulmans an alien intrusion, a frustrated effort without effect upon the intellectual education of the peoples of the East."

I leave it to the learned to decide to what extent this severe judgment is justified in the case of the generality of philosophical writings in the Arabic language. So far as the Spaniards are concerned, it is in the first place to be noted that these philosophers were, for the most part, of Christian or Jewish origin. The most famous of them, Ibn Hazam and Averroés, were respectively of Jewish and Christian descent.

As Renan points out, their doctrines had no effect in Musulman circles. They were taken into consideration, studied and discussed only by the Christians. Moreover, the basis of these doctrines went back to the old Greco-Latin scholiasts, the neo-Platonism of the Alexandrines, or to Aristotelian peripateticism, more or less distorted by translators and commentators.

In any case these philosophers, who were in no sense regular professors, but masters who surrounded themselves with disciples, were constantly exposed to the suspicion and hatred of the orthodox theologians. So-called Musulman tolerance did not go the length of respect for other people's opinions. Ibn Masarra, the Cordovan philosopher, who was regarded as having renewed the pantheism of Empedocles, had to go into exile to avoid the accusation of atheism, with all its consequences, of which the gravest was the death penalty. He could not return to his country until after the accession to the throne of the great Abd er Rhaman III, who was able to moderate the fanatical zeal of the faquis. Even then he had to hide his opinions behind a display of strict piety and asceticism. But this did not disarm the clergy, who, justifiably alarmed by Ibn Masarra's doctrines, burnt his books, tainted with atheism and heresy, in default of the philosopher himself.

Ibn Hazam, who has been regarded as a critical historian of religions—though it takes an effort to do so—was subjected to similar persecution at the hands of the theologians. Driven by them to leave Majorca, where he had found a protector and even a partisan of his ideas in the governor of the island, he had to take refuge in Seville. The hatred of the faquis pursued him there. King Almotatid, yielding to their insistence, had his books publicly burned.

A century later Averroés found himself obliged to leave Cordova in his turn, after being deprived of his dignities and his property. He took refuge in Morocco, where he was imprisoned and constrained by the Almohade Caliph to retract his errors at the door of the Great Mosque. According to some accounts he had to stand there while the passers-by spat in his face.

In general, the Arab historians congratulate the Caliphs on the rigour with which they persecuted the heterodox. "El Mansour," writes Ibn Adhari, "was as ill-disposed as possible towards those who concerned themselves at all with philosophy or religious controversy, or discussed astrological matters and signs, or treated the prescriptions of the religious law lightly. He consigned the materialist and philosophical works comprised in the libraries of El Hakam to the flames, in the presence of the leading men of learning, *and it was with his own hand that he did this.*

"Among those whom he smote for reasons analogous with such detestable opinions figured Mohammed ben Abou Djoma, who professed to have learned of a danger foretold by the stars, threatening the end of his power. He ordered his tongue to be cut out, and then had him executed and crucified: which closed all mouths."

To close all mouths must have been, in fact, the main preoccupation of all these despots, whose authority was always precarious. Let us note that El Mansour was of Arab origin, and that he prided himself upon certain intellectual elegances. In the following century, under the regime of the fanatical Almoravids and Almohades, the theologians became even more powerful than before, so that free thought must have been more than ever persecuted and driven to conceal itself.

Whatever one may say of this philosophy and this "learning" in the Arabic language, it is nevertheless true that the Christians of the West owe a certain debt to them. For it was through these translations, these adaptations, and these commentaries that our schoolmen became acquainted with Aristotle, the doctors, the mathematicians and the geographers of Greco-Latin antiquity.

The influence of Arab literature and poetry appears to have been less deep, though some have sought to draw analogies between Arab poetry and Provençal and Catalan poetry. These are analogies purely of form, concerned solely with prosody.

The fact is that Arab poetry is almost all formal. It possesses a verbalism disconcerting to our Western minds. Let us leave the specialists to strain themselves in the effort to make us admire a poetry which consists entirely in plays upon words, in alliterations and metrical artifices and refinements, for it must be confessed that these beauties are foreign to our taste or beyond our understanding.

Whether we are examining martial, political, or satirical poetry, or bacchic songs and little erotic and gallant pieces, we find always the same gaudy and commonplace metaphors. Princes are compared with lions—and their enemies with tigers or leopards—or else with suns with their trains of moons, satellites, and stars. Women are invariably gazelles, doves, or sometimes camels ; and their cheeks and their breasts are only to be compared with lilies, roses, jessamine, hyacinth, myrtle, and narcissi. At the same time it is only fair to recognise that there may be in these poems, often obscure, deliberately enigmatic, or strangely far-fetched as they are, a verbal music which escapes us.

Among all these flowers of rhetoric I confess that I can find an interest in very few. Some of these pieces, such, for example, as the following, recommended themselves by real sincerity or real depth of feeling. This fragment is from the philosopher, Ibn Hazam, in whom one would scarcely expect to find a soul so sentimental.

"In the palace of my father there was a girl brought up with the other women. She counted sixteen years, and there was none to equal her in beauty, intelligence, modesty, reserve, shyness, and sweetness. . . . None dared to raise his desires to her, and yet her beauty made a conquest of all hearts. . . . She was serious, and had no taste for frivolous amusements, but she played the lyre divinely.

"I was very young then, and I thought only of her. I heard her speak sometimes, but always in the presence of other persons. For two years I had vainly sought to speak to her alone. Then, one day, there was held in our house one of those feasts such as often take place in the palaces of the great, to which the women of our house and of my brother's house, and of our retainers and our most respected servants, were invited. After spending part of the day in the palace, these ladies went on to the terrace, whence there was a magnificent view over Cordova and its environs, and they grouped themselves where the trees in our garden did not spoil the view.

"I was with them, and I approached the embrasure where *she* stood. But, as soon as she saw me beside her, she ran with graceful speed to another embrasure. I followed her; she escaped me again. Happily the other ladies did not notice; for, bent upon finding the finest view-points, they paid no attention to me.

"Then the ladies went down to the garden, and those who, by their rank and their age, had the most influence, begged the lady of my thoughts to sing. I supported their request. Then she took her lyre and started tuning it with a modesty which, to me, doubled her charms; after which she sang these verses:

"'*I think only of mine own sun, the lithe, graceful girl whom I saw disappear behind the dark walls of the palace. Is she a human creature? Is she a genie? She is but a woman: but, if she has all the beauty of a genie, she has none of its malice. Her face is a pearl, her form a narcissus, her breath a perfume, and all her body an emanation of light. When one sees her, clad in her robe the colour of saffron, walking with inconceivable lightness, one would say that she could set her foot on the most fragile things without breaking them.*'

"While she sang, it was not the strings of her lyre that she struck with her bow. It was my heart. Never has that day of delight left my memory, and, on my death-bed, I shall still remember it. . . .''

The Spaniard who caught this accent of quite platonic sentimentality anticipated by three centuries the sonnets of Petrarch. But it was only a sigh lost in a vain thrumming of guitars. Out of all this Arab poetry there is not a single piece which, so to speak, holds us: a cry of the soul or of the heart, a great lyrical outburst, a great work, in short, so widely human in its character that it takes its place quite naturally in universal literature.

There is nothing that resembles the *Divine Comedy*, just as, in the intellectual sphere, the Arabs of Spain produced nothing to compare with the *Summa* of Saint Thomas. Finally, so far as architecture and the plastic arts are concerned, there is nothing on the level of our cathedrals or the sculpture of our thirteenth century.

The civilisation of the Caliphate was rather an end than a beginning. It was the liquidation of the old Mediterranean civilisation—not without its unquestionable aspirations, first towards new forms of art, then towards new forms of thought. These aspirations were not to be realised until much later, in the great movement of our Renaissance. But it was neither from Musulman Spain, nor from Africa, nor from the Near East that was to blow the wind of resurrection.

§ III

THE AWAKENING OF NATIONAL AND CHRISTIAN SPIRIT

CHAPTER IX

The Day of the Ditch and the Revolt of the Suburb

AMONG the continual wars which these Musulman princes had to wage throughout the duration of the Caliphate, there were two which assume quite a special importance, by virtue of their national and religious significance : the war against the Spanish renegades, and the war against the Christians. Fundamentally, these were one and the same war, which went on for centuries; for the Spanish renegades, that is to say, the Spaniards converted to Islam, were of Christian origin and nurtured the same hatred of the Arabs and the Berbers as the Mozarabs, that is to say, the Christians who lived among the Musulmans, and the independent Christians of Castile and León.

The renegades, as we have seen, were treated with little consideration by the Old Musulmans. They were suspected of insincerity and kept aloof from the administration and from lucrative positions, and many of them regretted their apostasy. They regretted it the more inasmuch as it was impossible for them to return to their former religion. In this respect the Musulman law was rigid. Whoever denied Islam exposed himself to the death penalty. The renegades, therefore, were disaffected. The Christians were no less so.

If we bear in mind that these two groups, together with the Jews, who were very numerous in Spain, made up a majority of the population, we shall realise that they formed an element very dangerous to the Caliphate. Left to their own resources they could not do much; but, given the support of an Arab or Berber faction, they became a force to be considered very seriously. Agitators hostile to the government fully appreciated this fact. In order to overthrow the reigning Caliph, one of them made an alliance with the renegades, who in turn took advantage of the more or less declared complicity of the Christians.

This agitator was the Berber, Yahya ben Yahya, one of those faquis who, during the reign of Hisham I (788–796), acquired extraordinary importance and enjoyed extraordinary influence. These Musulman theologians were a regular power within the State. They not only controlled opinion and kept guard over orthodoxy, but also shared, in their own persons or through their nominees, in the exercise of authority. Never did the doctors of the Sorbonne exert such an influence under the French kings. They were not only inquisitors, but also political leaders.

When the pious Hisham died, the faqui Yahya declared against his successor Hakam I, whom he regarded as neither sufficiently deferential towards the doctors nor a good enough Musulman. The new prince, as a matter of fact, was far from being an unbeliever. But he was a man fond of pleasure, who had the fault, in the eyes of the faquis, of drinking wine and liking hunting. He was, in short, a *bon vivant*, who, in the course of his twenty-five years' reign, had fifty children, boys and girls, by his favourites.

The first conspiracy hatched against him by Yahya was discovered. The ringleaders, to the number of seventy-two, were arrested and crucified, and Yahya fled to Toledo.

This former capital of the Visigoth kings, still haloed by the prestige of an Imperial city and a city of learning, inhabited mostly by Christians and emigrants from the South, had never submitted to the yoke of the Caliphs with anything but repugnance. It was notorious throughout Islam for its spirit of independence and its rebelliousness. A Toledan poet, Gharbib, a renegade of Christian origin, maintained the effervescence of his compatriots, who were doubtless further stirred up by the refugee, Yahya.

The Caliph did not dare to attack the malcontents openly. He employed a subterfuge to checkmate the Toledans. He gave them as their governor a renegade from Huesca named Amrous, with whom he came to an understanding that the leading notabilities of the city, the heads of the Spanish party, should disappear. The Toledans, flattered by having one of their compatriots, and not an Arab, as their governor, received the newcomer more or less favourably. He persuaded them to construct an *alcázar*, for the purpose of housing the garrison troops as well as protecting themselves against a possible attack.

When the *alcázar* was built, the Caliph assembled an army on the pretext that it was to be employed against the Christians of Castile. He entrusted the command of it to one of his sons, who came and encamped not far from Toledo. The young prince, with Amrous's connivance, found a means of getting himself invited by the inhabitants to honour the city with his presence. Once he had introduced himself into the *alcázar* with his soldiers, he announced that he proposed to offer a great feast to the notabilities. They were admitted into the fortress one by one as they presented themselves.

In the courtyard was a trench, still full of chalk or clay-mortar, which had been used during the building operations. The Toledans had to walk alongside this trench, and, as they passed it one after the other, executioners posted on the spot decapitated them and threw their bodies into the chalk or clay-mortar. A great number died in this way: the Arab annalists declare that there were seven hundred victims. Some, with their usual exaggeration, assert that there were five thousand. This was what the annalists call "The Day of the Ditch" (806).

This drastic measure of repression daunted not only the Toledans, but also the Spaniards of Cordova. The clerical party of the faquis, however, did not lay down its arms. Yahya returned to the capital and continued to incite his students, as well as the renegades.

Insurrection simmered for a considerable time. Finally, it broke out in the month of May of the year 814. A soldier of the Caliphal guard killed an armourer who had taken the liberty of keeping him waiting to sharpen his sword for him, and the people rose—especially the population of artisans and theological students who lived in the suburb of Secunda, on the left bank of the Guadalquivir, opposite the bridge of Cordova.

The Caliph Hakam was in the greatest danger, but, having made up his mind to burn the suburb, he finally succeeded, not without difficulty, in quelling the insurrection. The repression was terrible and merciless. Three hundred notabilities were crucified, head downwards, along the river opposite the bridge and the Great Mosque.

It must have been a frightful spectacle for the people of the city. These three hundred wretches writhing in the convulsions of a slow agony ; these three hundred crosses aligned along the Guadalquivir— this surpassed in horror anything that they had hitherto seen in the way of punishment.   But that sinister spot—which is called to-day *El Campo de la Verdad*, "The Field of Truth," no doubt in testimony to all the cruelties which stained it with blood—that hideous bank was to witness many others.

Hakam, in his fury, ordered that all the inhabitants of the suburb should leave Spain within three days, and that the quarter where they lived should be entirely destroyed. It appears that fifteen thousand of them, after an exodus of great hardship across the Andalusian sierra, embarked for Barbary and thence for Egypt. After living some time in the suburbs of Alexandria they had to take refuge in Crete, where they finally installed themselves.

Perhaps the Candiote Theotocópuli, known as El Greco, who was the most Spanish of all the painters of the Renaissance and died at Toledo, was a descendant of one of these Spaniards exiled by the Musulmans. That would explain what it is fashionable to call "the secret of El Greco."

Another group of eighteen thousand families, also expelled from Cordova, went and established themselves in Fez, where they constituted the quarter of the Andalusians, which exists to this very day. These Spaniards, sons of Christians, never completely fused with the Musulman Arabs and Berbers, and they were undoubtedly a civilising influence in barbarous Morocco.

These mass expulsions aroused a violent hatred which lasted for centuries. When the Christians in their turn expelled the Moors from Spain, those Moors who were the sons of Berbers and Arabs, they were only avenging their brother Spaniards driven from their country by the Musulmans. There is no occasion to approve or excuse either of them. But it is astonishing that historians, who brand the expulsions ordered by the Catholic Sovereigns, should apparently regard those which were ordered *earlier* by the Musulman Caliphs as quite natural.

When Hakam I drove the Spanish renegades out of their fatherland, he was acting in obedience not only to political motives, but also to religious motives. These renegades were Spaniards and descendants of Christians. On both grounds they were incapable of assimilation by the Arabs and the Berbers.

From the beginning of the Musulman conquest war between the natives and the invaders had been more or less declared. It assumed a more and more bitter character in the course of the ninth century. From that period, one feels, one of the two peoples was bound to give way completely to the other. The duel between the African and the Spaniard, between the Christian and the Musulman—that duel which was to last seven centuries—had begun.

CHAPTER X

The Great Humiliation of the Christians

THE Christians of the interior were mastered. They had lost their leaders and their principal centres of resistance. The armies of the Caliph, the Arab and Berber chieftains, had massacred them, burned them out and pillaged them to the best of their ability. Thus decimated and humiliated, they nevertheless continued to exist, in a furtive and more or less precarious way of life, among the Jews and the Musulmans.

Like the Jews, they had their ghetto in order to spare true believers ·contact with their impure persons and also for reasons of prudence, in order to avoid brawling and plundering. They retained their counts, their special magistrates, their bishops, their metropolitans— often chosen by the government and suspect of treachery. Moreover, they were allowed to keep a certain number of churches. They were cultivators, merchants, scribes, office employees, and soldiers. Perhaps, on the whole, they did not think themselves too unfortunate and did not in the least envy their co-religionists of the North, free of Musulman domination, but subject to grasping and tyrannical clergy and feudal lords.

The Christians of the North scarcely knew the meaning of repose, security, or any of the amenities of life. They were continually at war with their Musulman neighbours. It was the fatality of that Arab conquest, a superficial and hasty conquest, never carried through to the end, that it had divided the country into two irreducible camps: that of the replete, and that of the hungry; those who held the best soil, and those who were relegated to the mountains or to desert plains.

Everything drove them to destroy one another—famine, rapacity, the mania for taking booty and cutting off heads, religious fanaticism or simply difference of belief, and, finally, the conviction among those of the North that they were the real masters of the country, and that they could not rest in peace so long as the invader was encamped on their soil. On the one side and the other, there were the same hatred and, after two centuries of oppression and carnage, the same thirst for vengeance.

Towards the Christians of the North the attitude of the Caliphs could not be anything but distrust and permanent hostility; first, because they were the natural allies of all rebels in the interior, especially along the Northern frontier—the people of Toledo and Saragossa; and next because at the first opportunity, as soon as the sultan was engaged in suppressing rebellion or repelling the Berbers of Africa, the Leonese, the Castilians, the Navarrese, and the Aragonese hastened to invade Musulman territory and make raids there, following the example of the Caliphal troops.

It was necessary, therefore, to remain constantly on a war footing. The sovereign of Cordova was hemmed in between the Musulmans of Africa and the Christians of the Pyrenean regions. He had to disarm or conciliate one in order to combat the other; with the result that, according to circumstances, the Berbers or the Christians were sometimes the enemies and sometimes the allies of the Caliph. It was true that he had the advantage over the Christians and the nomads of Africa of being at the head of a unified kingdom—though everything was far from being tranquil in his provinces, which were so often disturbed by racial or tribal rivalries—whereas the Christians of the North were split up into a number of little states, almost as torn by internal strife as those of southern Spain afterwards became.

There were at least three Christian States on the northern frontier: the kingdom of León, that of Navarre, and that of Aragón. These were further divided into sub-kingdoms: Galicia, Asturias, Castile, all more or less given over to feudal competition. Navarre and Aragón were bordered to the East by the Countship of Barcelona, itself sub-divided into the countships of Cerdagne and Besalu.

Of all these little States, the kingdom of León was, if not the most important, at least the most *national*, if one may say so: the one which had best preserved the Visigoth and Roman traditions, and whose head regarded himself as the representative and legitimate continuator of the Spanish monarchy. From the reign of Alfonso III (866–910) the Kings of León assumed the title of *Imperator*, *Basileus*, or *Rex magnus*.

So the Imperial dignity was restored by this little Pyrenean kingling even before the Emir of Cordova thought of taking the title of Commander of the Faithful. He was the Roman Emperor, the Emperor of the West, as the sovereign who reigned at Byzantium was the Emperor of the East. Theoretically he ruled over one-half of Christendom. Over against the Sultan of Cordova, he was the Commander of the Christians of the West.

León, his capital, was still the seat of the Roman *"imperium"*, as at the period when it had been a fortified camp, occupied by the Seventh Legion, the *Gemina Pia Felix*. It had preserved its walls and the powerful defensive system constructed by the military genius of Rome, which the Arabs, in Spain as in Africa, confined themselves to keeping in repair or copying. Behind the towers and battlements of the old Roman encampment the kingling could defy the Arab cavalry or the Berber hordes and protect the booty taken in Musulman territory.

This citadel of León was in the North the pendant of Bobastro in the South. Is it not a significant fact that, on the one side as on the other, for these Spaniards in revolt against Islam, the centre of resistance, and the starting-point of the Reconquest, should have been an old Roman fortress?

Were these little Christian kingdoms as poverty-stricken, as barbarous, as is generally believed? It is certain that these mountainous regions of the North could not be compared, either in fertility, or in wealth, or in degree of civilisation, with the more fortunate regions of the East and South. It is certain, moreover, that for centuries they were horribly overridden and devastated by the Musulmans.

But Galicia at least, and all the Cantabrian littoral, were generally spared this devastation. Thanks to the pilgrimage to Santiago de Compostela—that is to say, from the second half of the ninth century—all this Pyrenean territory was in constant relations with the rest of Christendom. Thousands of pilgrims maintained the sense of Christian strength and solidarity there. They reinforced and exalted the Christian faith there, and, at the same time, they brought there, together with their offerings, the products of their art and architecture and the models of their popular poetry.

In the following century these great religious manifestations were regularly organised. The Arab annalists themselves compare them with the pilgrimages to Mecca. In their eyes the tomb of Saint James had, for the Christians, the same importance and the same prestige as the Kaaba for the Musulmans.

If the tomb of the Apostle was inferior to the tomb of Christ, it is nevertheless true that Compostela rivalled Jerusalem in the number of its visitors. They went there not only from France, Germany, and all the countries of the North, but even from Ethiopia and Nubia. The Copts of Egypt united with the Auvergnats of Murat and Saint Flour to go and venerate the relics of the great Apostle, whom tradition represented to them in the guise of a celestial horseman leading the forces of Christ against those of Islam. So the Church, by creating this twofold current of migration among the Christian masses, taught them the way of struggle and resistance, by directing them towards the two most menaced points of Christendom, namely Spain and Asia Minor, Jerusalem and Santiago.

Compostela was a centre of both religious and martial faith. The treasury of the Apostle was rich, as a result of the perpetual war against the Musulmans. In accordance with "the vow of Saint James," it received every year the first-fruits of the harvest and a specified part of the booty taken in Musulman territory. The churches and monasteries strung out along the route of the pilgrimage were bursting with offerings and wealth. This is attested, not only by the ecclesiastical writers, who tell us of the treasures of the Church "accumulated for centuries," but also by the Arab authors, who frequently insist upon the rich booty taken by the troops of the Caliph at the expense of the Christians.

In any case, when they report these expeditions into Christian territory, they do not give us the impression of entering barbarous countries. Abd er Rhaman the Great, having led an expedition

against Aragón, defeated King Ordoño and his ally, Sancho of
Navarre, and then took possession of the fortress of Muez, which
was pillaged by his soldiers.

"In this fortress," writes Ibn Adhari, "and in the Christian camp,
which was close at hand, were found in innumerable quantity
merchandise, tents, *jewels artistically cut, vases* . . ." In other words,
the Musulmans found there precious stuffs, tents sumptuously
decorated like their own, and all kinds of jewellery. Later, when the
Musulmans penetrated for the first time into Compostela, the same
annalist, relating the sack of the holy city, is careful to note that "fine
palaces, *solidly constructed*, were reduced to dust."

This solidity of Roman construction always struck the Arabs,
accustomed as they were to their own buildings of brick or mud-
plaster. This architecture, made to last, secretly aroused their admiration, at the same time as their jealousy. What these "fine palaces" of
Compostela may have been we cannot attempt to guess—probably
remains of the Roman or Visigoth period. Let us be careful not to
exaggerate such splendours, which must have been rare and, in the
way of amenity, luxury and adornment, could not have rivalled the
palaces and the kiosks of the Cordovan Medina az Zahara. Nevertheless, about the same time as the taking of Compostela, an envoy of
El Mansour who was touring Biscay with Garcia, the lord of the
district, mentions, apart from the churches, "the pleasure pavilions"
which he was taken to visit.

Be that as it may, life cannot have been very gay, or very easy,
in the Biscay and the Cantabria of that time, least of all for the
peasant and the man-at-arms, who were ceaselessly on the alert.

Towards these little Christian kingdoms the tactics of the Emirs
and of the Caliphs of Cordova remained immutable throughout the
three centuries of their domination. Their watchword was to limit
themselves to the conquests of Tarik and Mousa, and above all to
make no further attempt to cross the Pyrenees and penetrate among
the Franks, into that vague region, full of terrors, which they called
"the Great Land." They had long memories of the battle of Poitiers
and the stout barons of Charles Martel.

But, far indeed from adventuring beyond the Pyrenees, they even
seemed decided not to go beyond the course of the Ebro and the
Duero. They interposed a desert between themselves and the
Christians, and made a waste of the region which lay on the left bank
of the latter river. This was what they called "the Great Desert."
When Abd er Rhaman wanted to transport his army from Clunia to
Tudela, it took him five days to cross a part of it. All those great
plains which lie between Salamanca and the Sierra de Guardarrama
were as bare as the steppes of the North of Africa.

To keep the Christians in their place it did not suffice to surround
them with a zone of famine and devastation. It was necessary also

to go and sow terror and massacre among them. Twice a year, in spring and autumn, an army sallied forth from Cordova to go and raid the Christians, destroy their villages, their fortified posts, their monasteries and their churches, except when it was a question of expeditions of larger scope, involving sieges and pitched battles. In cases of simply punitive expeditions, the soldiers of the Caliph confined themselves to destroying harvests and cutting down trees.

Most of the time they took the field to win booty. A district was allowed to repeople itself and be brought under cultivation; then it was suddenly fallen upon. Workers, harvesters, fruits and cattle were seized. It was a process of revictualling in Christian territory. As the Caliph Omar said, one "ate up the Christian," while waiting to be eaten up by him. The contemporaries of the Cid who went to eat and seek adventure at the expense of the Moors were following the example of the Moors themselves, who for centuries had eaten at the expense of the Christians.

If one bears in mind that this brigandage was almost continual, and that this fury of destruction and extermination was regarded as a work of piety—it was a holy war against the infidels—it is not surprising that whole regions of Spain should have been made irremediably sterile. This was one of the capital causes of the deforestation from which the Peninsula still suffers.

With what savage satisfaction and in what pious accents do the Arab annalists tell us of those at least bi-annual raids! A typical phrase for praising the devotion of a Caliph is this: "he penetrated into Christian territory, where he wrought devastation, devoted himself to pillage, and took prisoners. After that he brought the Musulmans back to Cordova safe and sound and laden with booty." Abd er Rhaman, in the course of a campaign in Navarre, "did not fail, whenever a Christian retreat was to be found in the neighbourhood, to carry destruction there and deliver the surrounding countryside to incendiarism, so that the Christian territory was ravaged by the flames to an extent of ten square miles."

The same Caliph, when he laid siege to Toledo, began by destroying everything in the rich plain which surrounded the town. "He commenced by doing the rebels unimaginable harm. He *remained there for thirty-seven days without ceasing his devastation*, cutting down the trees, pillaging and ruining the villages, destroying all the crops." And again: "the strongholds of this region were reduced to ruins. Not one stone was left upon another. . . . The suburbs were surrendered to the flames, the harvests and all the property in the neighbourhood were utterly ravaged and laid waste."

They did not content themselves with pillaging and devastating only Christian territory. They did the same thing in their own territory, where brigandage, revolts, and civil war were an endemic condition. Abd er Rhaman put to fire and sword a whole district of

Andalusia to starve out the rebels whom he was besieging. When he went to besiege Bobastro, "he cut down the fruit trees that still existed in the mountains." The next year he began over again: "he finished cutting down what remained of the fruit trees and the vines, and laying waste all the subsistence of the enemy. *He spent seven whole days in destroying and ravaging everything without mercy*, and he acted in the same way towards other fortresses of the rebels."

At the same time as they were devastated, whole regions were depopulated. The vanquished, the men in a condition to bear arms, were massacred pitilessly. Their heads were cut off: that was the great joy—triumph over the infidels in all its purity. To show that a good job had been made of it, these heads were stuffed into sacks or baskets and sent to Cordova to be exposed at the bridge-head or on the battlements of the Alcázar. Some were even dispatched to the cities of the African Moghreb for the purpose of "showing off."

But the really lucrative part of the operation was the booty and the sale of slaves. Thousands of women and children, whole populations, were sold by auction. Massacre, like slavery, did not threaten only the Christians. The Musulman population of Andalusia, as we have seen, was decimated in the same way.

How can one be surprised, after that, at the depopulation of Spain, above all when it is remembered that the Christians devoted themselves to similar extermination, as soon as they got the chance? Eye for eye, tooth for tooth—they replied to carnage with carnage, to executions with executions. Ordoño II, King of León, had the head of a Musulman general nailed to the walls of the castle of Saint Etienne de Gormaz, side by side with a boar's head. In both camps they spoke of each other mutually as "dogs" and "sons of dogs." They had nothing for which to reproach one another in the way of ferocity and destructive barbarism.

The prolonged presence of the Musulmans, therefore, was a calamity for this unhappy country of Spain. By their system of continual raids they kept her for centuries in a condition of brigandage and devastation. It was a state similar to, though much less lamentable than, that in which the French found Algeria when they arrived there in 1830. Northern Africa did not number two millions of inhabitants. It was the same thing in Spain. From the period of the Caliphs she had to be ceaselessly repeopled, either by slaves or serfs brought from the northern provinces, or by Berber immigrants.

What deceives us at a distance is the relative prosperity of certain great commercial and maritime towns, such as Seville or Málaga, or of a capital like Cordova, which was surrounded by a fertile countryside and was, moreover, protected against incursions and devastation by the presence of the Caliph and his armies. We forget also that in Musulman countries the greatest poverty often exists side by side with the greatest luxury and opulence. Somebody said of the Spaniards of the end of the eighteenth century: "they die of hunger beside Madonnas clustered with diamonds." That was equally true of Musulman Spain.

But not only did the Arabs make a desert there and introduce drought and sterility by their deforestation. What was worse was that they brought with them there, and maintained by their example, unpolished manners, cruelty in repression, in short, brutal and blood-thirsty habits of which the Spaniards were to have great difficulty in ridding themselves. Above all, by their atrocities they aroused among the vanquished an appetite for reprisals, a thirst for vengeance, of which they were later to be the victims.

Let us think of it for a moment—two expeditions a year; a perpetual holy war against the Christians! It must have been frightful. The greatest praise which the biographers of El Mansour bestow upon him is this: "he made war, summer and winter, against the Christians."

Among these expeditions there were some especially famous ones, which excited profound emotion both in the whole of Christendom and throughout the Musulman world: for example, that of Abd er Rhaman against Navarre, and that of El Mansour against Galicia.

The campaign against Pampeluna, in April 924, seems to have been provoked by the incursions of the Leonese and Navarrese. In the preceding years Ordoño II, King of León, had carried his raids as far as the neighbourhood of Cordova. A little later Sancho of Navarre took two fortresses on the Musulman frontier: Majera and Viguera. The taking of the latter especially was bitterly resented by the Moors. Then the Caliph swore that he would go and punish his imprudent aggressors. In the early days of spring he left Cordova at the head of his army, announcing that he was going "to avenge Allah and religion upon the impure race of miscreants."

After a feint towards Murcia and Valencia, he reached Toledo, destroyed a number of strongholds which belonged to the King of Navarre, and penetrated deep into Christian territory, spreading terror and desolation everywhere. By this means he succeeded in advancing as far as Pampeluna, which was abandoned by its inhabitants and emptied of everything it contained in the way of wealth and precious objects.

"The Prince in person entered it," says Ibn Adhari, "and, after going through it, gave the order to destroy all the houses and reduce to ruins the Christian church which stood there and served as a temple to the Infidels for the accomplishment of their religious practices. Not one stone of it was left upon another. Thence he transported himself to a place where stood a church built by the Christian prince, who had lavished his care upon it and delighted for a long time to adorn it and assure its defence.

"Our troops had arrived and were beginning to reduce it to ruins when this dog of an infidel appeared on a mountain which dominated the site, with the intention of defending it. But the servants of God, quicker than the twinkling of an eye, pursued him and forced him and his to show their heels. The church and the buildings that surrounded it were reduced to ruins, and the village became the prey of the flames."

After a whole series of burnings, destruction, and skirmishing of this kind, the Caliph made his entrance into Cordova in the month of August of the same year. The punitive expedition had lasted no less than four months. The Musulmans had penetrated into Christian territory much farther than they had ever done before. The worst feature, which especially dismayed the Navarrese and their neighbours, was the destruction of Pampeluna and its cathedral, not to speak of that other church, enriched and embellished by the King of Navarre, which seems to have been one of the principal sanctuaries of the region.

This pitiless proceeding made a great impression in the Pyrenean region and probably beyond. But, in these shadowed years approaching the year 1000, what most struck terror into Christendom was the sack of Santiago de Compostela by the armies of El Mansour. In Musulman annals also this expedition remained famous under the name of the "Campaign of San Yacoub."

The pretext for it was the refusal of King Bermudo II of Galicia to pay the tribute to which he was subject in accordance with a recent convention. The dictator left Cordova on July 3, 997, and invaded Galicia by way of Coria and Viseu. He was supported by a fleet which hugged the Atlantic coast, and at Viseu he found his army reinforced by the contingents of a certain number of Christian counts who recognised his authority.

The campaign appears to have been especially arduous owing to the difficulty which he had in forcing a way for himself through a mountainous region, traversed by rivers, water-courses, and arms of the sea. The Christians, following tactics which had become habitual to them, retired before the invader, leading him after them into defiled and desert districts.

Finally El Mansour, after having burned the highly venerated sanctuary of El Padrón, arrived with his troops at the walls of "the proud city of Saint James." It had been abandoned by its inhabitants, as in the case of Pampeluna at the time of Abd er Rhaman's campaign. The Caliphal army pillaged everything it could carry away, and the town was completely destroyed, including the church, "of which not a trace remained."

Nevertheless El Mansour, as a good Musulman, respectful towards a disciple of the Prophet Aïssa, mounted a guard of soldiers over the tomb of Saint James, which was thus spared. An old monk, it appears, was found sitting beside the sepulchre. Alone out of all the population that had taken to flight, he had regarded it as his duty not to abandon the relics of the great protector of Spain. The dictator asked him why he had stayed there. "To honour Saint James," he said simply. El Mansour ordered that he should be allowed to pray in peace, and so the old monk's life was spared.

El Mansour acted throughout this affair as a perfect Musulman. At the outset, in order to win the support of the Christian counts of the Portuguese marches, he gave them to understand that he had come solely for the purpose of punishing a rebel vassal, in the person of King Bermudo. In accordance with feudal custom, the counts who recognised him as their suzerain were in this case under an obligation to assist their lord.

But what was at the back of El Mansour's mind was in fact to inflict a deep humiliation on the Christians by laying waste one of their greatest centres of pilgrimage. It was to this end that he destroyed everything that was specifically Christian: basilicas, oratories, sanctuaries, and monasteries. He respected only what was honoured by Islam itself—namely, the tomb of a marabout who was a disciple of Aïssa, and the man of prayer who watched over that tomb.

Apart from this homage paid only indirectly to the religion of Christ, he did everything he could to give his triumph over the Infidels the appearance of a definitive victory. When he returned to Cordova, the Musulmans saw filing through the streets a throng of Christian prisoners, carrying on their shoulders the bells of Saint James's and the doors of his basilica. These doors, no doubt wrought and carved, were placed in the Great Mosque; and the bells, we are told, were turned into lamp-holders. Together with these trophies, the thousands of prisoners, who were employed on the work of extending the mosque, attested in the eyes of the faithful the irremediable defeat of the enemies of Islam.

For the Christians it was a disaster without precedent. An ecclesiastical writer, the monk de Silos, writes in his chronicle: "Divine worship was annihilated in Spain. The glory of the servants of Christ was utterly abased. The treasures of the Church, amassed in the course of centuries, were all pillaged."

There is here an obvious exaggeration. "Divine worship" was not annihilated throughout Spain, despite the sack of Santiago and that of the cathedral of Pampeluna. But it is true that never had Christendom been more humiliated, and that never had the Pyrenean kinglings, driven back into their mountains, found themselves in a more sorry situation. Nevertheless, despite all reverses and devastations, despite their ridiculous divisions in the face of the common enemy, salvation was to come to them from the fact which was momentarily their weakness: the fact that they were Spaniards and Christians.

In the first place, as ever, the Caliph did not know how to profit by his advantage. With their ineradicable nomadic habits, the Arabs were incapable of anything but pillage and destruction. They had no plans of conquest; they took no broad view of the situation as a whole. In the next place, the Arab theocracy was never anything more than encamped in any territory. It was a religious society, not attached to the soil, striking no deep roots.

On the other hand, over against the Caliph, the little King of León and Castile represented what was most profoundly Spanish. Despite all feudal rivalries, all divisions and all the narrownesses of the particularist spirit, the racial instinct, allied with the unifying tendencies of the old Visigoth monarchy, ended by gaining the upper hand. Moreover, behind the kings, the barons, and the middle classes were the monks: the inspirers and leaders of Crusades, who simply could not rest so long as the followers of Christ had not regained the mastery over those of Islam.

The monarchical idea, the Christian idea, merging in the idea of the Fatherland, was to end by expelling from Spanish soil the invaders who had trampled it underfoot and harrowed it for so long.

§ IV

THE REACTION OF THE ALMORAVIDS AND THE ALMOHADES

CHAPTER XI

The End of the Caliphate and the Little Musulman Kingdoms

EL MANSOUR, the usurper of the Caliphate, died in 1002 at Medina Celi, in the course of a further expedition against Castile: a fact which once more proves the fleeting effects of the Musulman victories and the uselessness, from the political point of view, of these biannual campaigns against the Christians.

Hisham II, the legitimate caliph whom he had set aside, was still alive. The sons of the usurper had to fight against his partisans to maintain themselves in power. But they were no better able than their father to establish an enduring regime. After terrible struggles, in which the old enemies took one another's measure once more—Arabs against Berbers, renegades and Christians against the central government and against the Musulmans—the Caliphate, which had ceased to serve any purpose, ended by collapsing. In 1031 the viziers declared it abolished, and Cordova became a republic.

Then the provinces broke the links which bound them to the capital. The Arab monarchy fell to pieces, and gave place to a swarm of little independent States, regular kingdoms in themselves, of which the most important were those of Seville, Granada, Almería, Badajoz, Valencia, and Saragossa. The Berbers were dominant in the South, the "Slavs" in the East, the Arabs in the South-west, and the renegades and Christians in the North of the Peninsula.

Thus, through the fault of the Arabs and Africans, as a result of their spirit of "sof," of rivalry and bickering, in short, their unbridled individualism, Spanish unity was more than ever compromised. There was no longer a great Musulman monarchy to act as a model and a stimulus to the Christian kingdoms of the North. The Arab anarchy could not fail to encourage them in their feudal anarchy.

This confusion was to last for centuries, despite the efforts made by certain Spanish sovereigns to re-establish a precarious unity. This was a great source of weakness to Spain. But, while she lost in power and political importance, perhaps she gained from it in culture, if not in civilisation. Between the death of El Mansour and the invasions of the Almoravids and the Almohades there was a period of about a century, during which the Arabs became almost completely Hispanised, their fanaticism waned, and they appeared to be won over to the ideal of luxurious and intellectual life. It was something like the Italy of the *podestas* and the little municipal republics.

These Musulman kinglings, softened by all the charms of the climate, lost their warrior virtues. So did their Arab and African soldiers. More and more, in order to defend themselves, they were obliged to appeal to Christian auxiliaries. The profession of *con-*

dottiero in Islamic territory became a means of existence for a swarm of Castilians, Basques, Navarrese, Aragonese, and Catalans.

The sovereigns whom they protected were in general dominated by their viziers, regular "mayors of the palace," ambitious intriguers who ended by making themselves omnipotent and often shared the luxurious and studious tastes of their masters. Among them may be mentioned Ibn Abbas, the vizier of Almería, who was a great glutton for money and a petty tyrant, but had a palace on a princely scale built for him; maintained five hundred singers in his harem; assembled a library containing thousands of volumes in rich bindings; and was a highly educated man who knew how to draft documents in the best diplomatic style and had the reputation of a master of the art of letter-writing.

Side by side with these all-powerful Ministers, however, there were some strong sovereigns, men of character, even if somewhat violent character, who were capable of commanding respect and making their will prevail. Among these princelings there stand out some figures who are worth studying a little more closely, if we desire to form an idea of Musulman Spain at this period. Musulman Spain showed more than one face. That with which we are now concerned differed noticeably from that of the Spain of the Caliphs.

The two most important—one can scarcely say the most powerful —of these little sovereigns appear to have been the princes of Granada and of Seville. These two capitals were in rivalry. Seville was Arab, Granada was Berber. El Mansour, although of Arab origin, had planted Berbers everywhere to maintain his tyranny as usurper and dictator. As a result he had bitterly incensed the Arabs and the Spaniards. It was their common interest to get rid of these foreigners and throw these African barbarians back across the Strait. The two hostile factions ended by finding two leaders equally implacable one against the other, in the persons of Badis, prince of Granada, and Motadid, prince of Seville.

They were two really extraordinary types. The first, Badis, was a bloodthirsty brute, the nomad of Africa in all his savage crudeness, a Berber without culture, speaking Arabic badly and glorying in his ignorance and roughness, and, along with that, a drunkard and a violent sensualist. Nevertheless he had been born in Spain and grown up in an atmosphere of opulence, and, indeed, on the steps of the throne. His father, Habous, was Sovereign Prince of Granada, which he fortified and surrounded with walls.

Badis himself constructed an *alcázar*, of which the Arab authors vaunt the magnificence. There he lived like a vulgar *parvenu*, surrendering power to a Jew, by the name of Samuel, who had dazzled him by his glibness of tongue and his knowledge of literary Arabic. The drunken Badis left his orgies only to put himself at the head of his troops and cut off heads; for he had at least physical courage.

Carried away by his attacks of blind rage and brutal cruelty, he often filled the office of executioner himself, and did his stabbing and beheading in person.

Very different was Motadid, his rival of Seville, though they resembled one another in their cruelty, their viciousness, and their drunkenness. In despite of the prescriptions of the Koran, Motadid of Seville was as fond of wine as the Berber of Granada. He spent days and nights together drinking with his companions in debauchery and his favourites. His harem was one of the best supplied of all Spain eight hundred girls, we are told, entered it in the course of his reign.

Naturally this lover of licence was a man of refined cruelty. Following the example of one of the last Caliphs of Cordova, he had flowers planted in the skulls of his enemies and adorned his terraces with these macabre pots. In order to refresh and nurture his hatreds, a label attached to each of these improvised flower-pots recalled the name of the decapitated. The skulls of conquered princes were treated with more consideration. The tyrant of Seville kept them in caskets like precious stones, and took them out from time to time to feast his eyes on them.

All this went comfortably hand-in-hand with a certain dilettantism. Like all Arabs, like any man in the street, Motadid composed verses. He had strings of poets in his pay and, by contrast with his rival, Badis of Granada, he prided himself upon fine language and fine style and turned his skill in letters to account. A diplomat and an arm-chair strategist, he scarcely ever appeared at the head of his armies. A man of guile and calculation, who never shrank from any treachery or any atrocity, he was the politician of his time in all its perfection.

Through divers traits in his character he maintained relationship with the rough conquerors of the early period, as he did with the Emirs and the Caliphs of Cordova. His son, Motamid, presents a newer and more varied psychology. He was a new type in Musulman Spain: the type of Arab refashioned by climate, by environment, by Spanish and Christian heredity. He requires to be studied in more detail, along with his friend Ben Ammar, who was also a striking and singularly representative personality.

In the life of Motamid there were, in the first place, a passionate friendship and a love story which invest him at once with a certain air of romantic poetry. When he was very young—he was barely twelve years of age—his father appointed him governor of Silves, capital of the province of Algarve. This province is one of the most picturesque in Portugal, and Silves, in the eyes of the Musulmans of that time, was regarded as a place of delight and enchantment. There the boy fell completely under the influence of a local poet, considerably older than himself, one Ben Ammar, an adventurer somewhat dubious, somewhat murky, somewhat shifty, but infinitely attractive.

This individual, though of low enough extraction, had nevertheless received a certain amount of education. He had studied first in Silves, his native town, and afterwards at Cordova. Then, as he had a real talent as a poet, he started wandering about Spain, peddling his verses in the best market. Poets at that time were paid panegyrists and polemists, or even newsmongers, filling something like the *rôle* of publicists to-day.

But Ben Ammar, badly served by his poor appearance and his beggarly attire, had no success with the powerful and highly-placed. Tired of a life of poverty, he decided to return to Silves, hoping that his compatriots would appreciate his talents better. He arrived there in the greatest destitution, having for all his belongings only the mule which served him as a mount. He had not even anything with which to feed it.

In his distress he remembered a rich merchant of the town who might be ready to help him out of his difficulties. He addressed to him a dithyrambic poem, in which, while flattering the merchant's vanity, he described the sad case of himself and his mount. The merchant, who liked his joke, confined himself to sending him a sack of barley for his mule.

It was in these circumstances that he made the acquaintance of the young prince Motamid. To what charm was it that he surrendered as soon as he saw Ben Ammar. It is certain that poetry played a great part in their relationship. Motamid, even more than his father, had literary pretensions. The verses of the poet of Silves captivated him to such a point that he appointed him his vizier and made him his favourite.

The friendship was a tyrannical one. Henceforth Motamid could not do without his new friend. Yet this extreme favour was not without its disquieting side for Ben Ammar. Perhaps he realised betimes that one had to reckon with the inconstancy of the great. One night, when Motamid had kept him with him, he dreamt that he heard a voice which said to him: "Unhappy man, Motamid will be your murderer!"

It was a prophetic dream, which frightened the favourite to such an extent that he got up at dead of night and tried to escape from the palace, in vain. The next day the two friends had an explanation, and Motamid lavished such words of affection on his poet and gave him such proofs of his attachment that everything was forgotten.

Their life of pleasure and intimacy went on with nothing to mar it. When Motamid returned to Seville, Ben Ammar accompanied him. He was the confidant of his love-affairs. One day, during a popular *fête* on the banks of the Guadalquivir at a place which was called the Meadow of Silver, the two friends, duly disguised and mingling with the crowd, were amusing themselves by improvising verses, as the

Sevillians do to this very day, and exchanging *saetas*. Motamid spoke a line; Ben Ammar, taken by surprise, was at a loss how to cap it, when a girl immediately provided the reply to the disguised prince. It was the famous Romaiquia, who was to become Motamid's mistress and soon rank as his wife and his regular consort.

Who was this Romaiquia, around whom the Christians themselves wove a legend? Was she one of them? It is very likely, given the fact that she was a slave and that she followed a profession quite unknown among Musulman women: she called herself a mule-driver. It is a profession which in Spain has always been at home with poetry. This plebeian and brazen creature therefore possessed enough natural genius to shine in the midst of fine wits. She appears, moreover, to have possessed all the charm and all the coquetry necessary to turn the head of a lover like Motamid.

The Infante Juan Manuel, in his curious book *Count Lúcanor*, tells a story about her which is as charming as it is poetical. Are we to see in it merely an imaginary piece of Spanish gallantry? It is quite possible; but the contrary is also possible.

The Infante tells us that one winter day, when she was at Cordova with Motamid, the beautiful Romaiquia, looking out of a window of the palace, marvelled at an extraordinary spectacle hitherto unknown to her: the Cordovan plain all white with snow. It seemed to her so lovely that she asked her husband to repeat this prodigy for her. She wanted to have snow before her eyes and go to countries which enjoy the privilege of this divine whiteness. To satisfy his sultana's caprice, Motamid had almond-trees planted in the plain of Cordova. So every year, when the winter was over, he was able to show her the Andalusian countryside covered with a white shroud of snowy blossom.

On another occasion the whimsical Romaiquia, seeing some women of the people trampling with their bare feet the red clay out of which bricks were made, declared that she was dying with desire to imitate these women. Motamid ordered all kinds of spices and aromatics to be poured out in the palace courtyard and mixed with rose-water, so that the courtyard became a regular perfume-vat. Then he invited Romaiquia and her women to come and trample with their bare feet in this perfumed paste.

Meanwhile, despite the sinister prediction, Motamid's friendship for Ben Ammar in no way diminished. Their intimacy, indeed, became so close that the prince's father, that terrible cutter-off of heads Motadid, took offence at it and perhaps became frightened of it. He exiled his son's confidant, who had to take refuge at the court of Saragossa.

But the old tyrant was no sooner dead than Motamid hastened to recall his friend and appoint him governor of Algarve. The poor boy of Silves, who had once had to beg a sack of barley for his mount, returned to his native town with all the trappings of a sovereign. He did not stay there long. His master, who could not do without him, soon recalled him to Seville and made him his prime minister.

It was, no doubt, at his instigation that Motamid undertook an expedition against Cordova, which he finally succeeded in seizing, after alternating reverses and successes, and after crucifying the leader of the resistance to him. Even at the Alcázar of Seville life could not be a perpetual pleasure-party. Surrounded by fierce enemies and competitors, these Moorish kinglings, lovers of enjoyment though they might be, were compelled to concern themselves with serious affairs.

Doubtless it was also on Ben Ammar's advice that Motamid undertook another expedition against Murcia. The prime minister was certainly an ambitious man, and besides, despite all his protestations of affection, he was afraid of his master. To put himself out of reach of his anger and treachery, it is extremely probable that he sought to possess himself of a principality where he could make himself independent. In any case, once master of Murcia, installed in the town and with all the resources of the province at his disposal, he severed relations with his sovereign, to such a point that Motamid, egged on by his counsellors, regarded him as a traitor and a rebel.

Ben Ammar, fearing the worst in the way of revenge from the friend whom he had deceived, fled to Saragossa. The crowned poet and his former favourite mutually loaded one another with epigrams in verse and satirical pieces, until the day came when Ben Ammar, betrayed by his allies, finally fell into the hands of the tyrant of Seville.

He was put in irons and spent some time in prison. But, poet as he still was, he contrived to soften Motamid by his flattery, by his invocation of the past, and by all the artifices of his prosody. There was a kind of reconciliation between them. In the end the prince, exasperated by an imprudent boast on the part of the prisoner, seized an axe and pursued him up the palace stairs to his room. There it was in vain that the unhappy Ben Ammar threw himself at his feet, once more appealing to their past friendship. Motamid, brandishing his axe, nerved himself to strike him until the corpse lay in a pool of blood. Perhaps the prince had just left his singers and was drunken with wine.

Such was what they were. Soft living did not destroy the instinctive savagery which they brought with them from Africa and Asia. They were rhetoricians of decadence. Their rhetoric masked the persistence in them of the old barbarian strain. They were bloodthirsty, readily cruel, and atrocious in their cruelty, drunkards, and sensualists. They were prodigal, but they were also greedy and miserly, and they became so more and more. The hunt for gold became the main object of all their raids. They were to communicate this lust for gold to the Spaniards, who were to intoxicate themselves with it to the point of madness, of launching themselves into the wildest enterprises to satisfy their rapacity.

But they had also the qualities of their vices. These voluptuaries were more intellectual than their predecessors. If they lost their warrior virtues, they became wily diplomats and sometimes clever politicians. The fanaticism of their ancestral faith weakened in them. Without being sceptics, they practised a less rigid and perhaps more human religion. They displayed a laxity of morality and observance which scandalised the puritans of Islam.

Bastardised by mixture of blood, corrupted by the delights of Andalusian life, captives of that only too charming soil, they were in process of forgetting their fatherland, their ancestors, their religion itself. Like the last Visigoth kings, who preceded them in the Peninsula, they were ripe for a new invasion.

CHAPTER XII

The Advance of Ferdinand and Alfonso

IN fact, as early as that second half of the eleventh century Spanish Islam was in a very awkward position. While Motamid and Ben Ammar were amusing themselves by rhyming erotic poems, and spending their nights in drinking or listening to the story-telling of Romaiquia and the singers of the harem, the Christians were encamped on the frontier and threatening the gates of Seville.

Their advance became so menacing that one is driven to ask why they did not press it to the end, and why Spain had to wait another four centuries for her definitive liberation. In any case, from this period the military superiority of the Christians over the Musulmans of Spain asserted itself in a striking and unquestionable way.

Ferdinand I, King of Galicia and Castile, reconquered extensive Portuguese territory from the Prince of Badajoz. He made incursions into the domains of the King of Saragossa, and recovered from him a certain number of fortresses south of the Duero. Mamoun, King of Toledo, became his vassal. So did Motadid, King of Seville, who came to his camp in person to implore his clemency. Finally he led an expedition against the kingdom of Valencia. The city was in a critical situation when illness compelled Ferdinand to raise the siege.

His son, Alfonso VI, took up the struggle with renewed vigour and bitterness. He knew the Musulmans well. Driven by his brother to go into exile at Toledo, he offered his services to Mamoun. Living on the spot, he had leisure to observe the weak points of the defence and study the character of his host, as well as those of the Toledans and the principal personages of the court.

No sooner had he assumed power than he laid hands on the weak Cadir, son of Mamoun, his former protector, who, like his father, remained tributary to the Kings of Castile and León. To satisfy Alfonso's demands, Cadir had to impose extraordinary taxes. These aroused protests from his subjects, who finally revolted and demanded aid from the Musulman prince of Badajoz. Under pretext of defending Cadir, his ally, Alfonso proceeded to lay siege to Toledo. He ended by compelling it to surrender and restoring Cadir.

But, by way of payment for this service, he exacted—obviously with intention—such an exorbitant price that the unhappy prince preferred to abandon his kingdom, in return for an almost illusory compensation. Cadir signed a capitulation by whose terms he ceded the city of Toledo and its territories to Alfonso, Emperor of the Christians.

The lives of the Musulmans were to be respected. The Christians took them and their property under their protection. They were free to leave the country or to remain there, and, if they remained, they were to be constrained to pay no more than a tax fixed in advance, roughly equal to that paid by the Christians in Musulman territory. They preserved also the free practice of their religion and possession of the Great Mosque, which had formerly been a basilica consecrated to the Virgin, and was not much later to become the Cathedral of Toledo. Finally Alfonso undertook to support Cadir's pretensions to the kingdom of Valencia.

On May 25, 1085, the King of Castile and León made his solemn entrance into the old capital of the Visigoth kings, in other words the old capital of the Kingdom of Spain. It was a great date in the history of the Peninsula. Henceforth the monarchical idea had resumed embodiment for the Spaniards and the effort towards unity had begun.

But, while Spain awaited this still distant realisation, a most important result had been achieved for Castile. Henceforth her security was assured on that one of her frontiers which hitherto had been the most threatened. From the banks of the Duero she had extended to the other side of the Tagus. On the Musulman side, however, she still had two troublesome neighbours: the kingdoms of Saragossa and Valencia, which constituted a menacing enclave, a salient thrust forward into Christian territory.

Alfonso had sworn to take Saragossa. He laid siege to the city, and, still under pretext of defending Cadir, now in Valencia, imposed upon him the protection of Castilian troops under the command of the famous Alvar Fáñez. These troops, which pillaged and massacred allies and enemies without distinction, conducted themselves in their protégé's territory as though they were on conquered soil. In fact, Alfonso was master in Valencia.

One of his lieutenants, Garcia Xímenes, threatened Murcia. Alfonso himself, having occasion to complain of Motamid, his vassal, who was trying to defraud him of his tribute by unloading base money on him, blockaded Seville. Thence he raided the surrounding territory, took slaves and booty, and reached as far as the beach of Tarifa: as far as those Pillars of Hercules which the Christians had had to abandon almost four centuries earlier. Exulting in this thought, he drove his horse into the foam of the ocean, and, mad with joy and pride, cried aloud: "Here is the uttermost limit of Spain. I have touched it!"

If all Spain was not reconquered, he had traversed her from one end to the other. All the little Musulman sovereigns were either his tributaries or else he had reduced them to impotence. It remained for him to subdue only the extreme South: Málaga, Granada, Almería. Why, then, were four centuries more to pass before the Peninsula was completely freed from the yoke of Islam?

In the first place, the case was the same with these expeditions of the Christians as with those of the Caliphs. There was never a definitive victory, never an advantage exploited to the full. It sufficed to put the enemy temporarily out of condition to do any damage.

In the next place, these little kingdoms of the North were severely limited in their resources. They were short of men and short of money. It was difficult for them to maintain regular campaigns, or even expeditions of any considerable duration. Finally the Christian princes were divided among themselves: Castile against León and against Navarre, Aragón against Catalonia. They had to reckon, besides, with feudal rebellions and all kinds of internal divisions.

Above all, what retarded the Reconquest, what indefinitely prolonged the *status quo*, the condition of stagnation and partition which threatened to become eternal in Spain, was the difficulty of peopling the vast regions which would have become almost desert if the Musulmans had been expelled. The Christians of the South had been decimated by the Caliphs, and the Pyrenean regions had been bled white, to such an extent that the kings of Castile found themselves faced with the impossibility of repeopling the territories which they reconquered.

Accordingly they preferred to adopt the system practised by the Arabs and by the government of Cordova: to make the infidel territories a zone of raids and contributions. Castilians and Aragonese found it convenient to go and live at the expense of the Moorish lands—*"ir a tierra de moros"*—as the Musulmans had long lived at the expense of the Christians. One went to prey upon his neighbours —the more respectable said to "make a living" among them. The ordinary means of making a living was marauding and pillaging by force of arms.

Alternatively, enormous contributions were imposed on the little Musulman sovereigns which reduced them to impotence. This was what was called the system of *parias*. It was something like a rough sketch of our "protectorates" of to-day. The Christian prince who levied the *paria* upon a Musulman prince owed him aid and protection against all his enemies, whoever they might be, Christian or Musulman. But most of the time this aid was illusory. In reality the tributary was at the mercy of his protector, who, thanks to this system, had all the advantage of sovereignty in occupied territory without any of its expenses.

Accordingly Islam was able to maintain itself indefinitely in Spain. The Christian princes either yielded to the necessities of a period of impoverishment, or else let themselves be infected by the contagion of Arab customs and spirit. This was what delayed the Reconquest so long.

Northern Spain acquired the habits and the vices of the Musulmans of the South, or rather of the Arab, and especially the Berber, bands which had installed themselves in Andalusia. Living by pillage, eating at the expense of one's neighbour, cutting off heads, taking booty—all these deplorable practices were unhappily to enter into the Spanish character. Wars as a rule were to be nothing more than raids.

Alfonso VI, who had lived at Toledo in the service of King Mamoun, became too Arabised, or too Africanised, to be able to react vigorously against such habits and such a state of affairs. To do so would have required a man of great strength of character, of original and really superior turn of mind, a man of new ideas, capable of thinking along Roman and European lines. Such a man Spain nearly found in him whom she was later to make a national hero—in Rodrigo de Vivar, surnamed the Cid Campeador.

CHAPTER XIII

The Cid Campeador

HERE, indeed, was a man—a man Spanish and Christian, standing as sharply opposed as possible to the men of Islam, Arabs or Berbers—with a mind capable of prevision and of conceiving great designs, of fashioning order and unity and organising on lasting lines, and with a strength of will capable of resisting events and compelling them to yield to his law.

This Castilian small squire, whom the Musulmans as well as the Christians called "Lord," had an extraordinary, a paradoxical fortune, if one bears in mind the modesty of his beginning. The imagination of posterity has played so much around him and his adventurers that it is difficult to recover his true physiognomy. History has distorted him as much as legend. This obvious distortion has inspired such doubts that some critics, such as the Spanish Jesuit Masdeu, have ended by denying his existence and regarding him as a fabulous personage. The Cid, according to this point of view, is as legendary as the heroes of Greek or Germanic epic.

The *Romancero* represents him as a turbulent and undisciplined vassal, more or less a rebel against his king, a Moor-killer whom nothing can withstand. Modern poetry depicts him as a fiery youth, the slave of his lady and his honour, or as a knight-errant, defender of the poor and the oppressed, a conqueror who crosses a dazzled and dominated world in a clamour of apotheosis.

> "So, it is you, who have but to take the field
> And say 'Forward!' to sound through Spain,
> From Avis to Gibraltar, from Algarve to Cadafal,
> O great Cid, the thrill of trumpets triumphant,
> And to draw hastening over your tents,
> Beating their wings, the swarm of singing victories."

On the other hand some historians, such as Dozy, have exerted themselves to deprive him of his halo. Prejudiced against the Cid by the fact that they are Arabophiles, interpreting texts badly, and as ignorant of states of mind as they are of environment and customs, they refuse to see in him anything but a bloodthirsty brute, a cruel veteran, without faith or loyalty, a mercenary without a fatherland who sells his sword to the highest bidder.

The real Cid was very different from all this, so far at least as the definite data of history allow us to visualise or guess him. These data are neither so few nor so suspect as is sometimes believed. Apart from annals of Arab origin and Latin chronicles close enough in time to the facts, we also possess authentic documents bearing the Cid's signature, which in the first place assure us of his existence, and in the next place give us information as substantial as it is suggestive about his life, and even about his character. The traces which he has left behind him are numerous enough to enable us to reconstruct from them a type of medieval man magnificent in his originality.

Rodrigo de Vivar was in the first place, as much as a man could be, the man of his country, the Spaniard of the North, the Castilian, he who ransomed Spain from Islam and refashioned her unity. He resembled his native soil, which has nothing either poetic or striking about it, is the very negation of all fantasy, and represents prose in its severest and most strictly practical form.

Vivar is a little village, even to-day backward and grim in its appearance, a few kilometres away from Burgos. Neither the proximity of the city nor the sierra which displays its outline in the distance avails to diminish the impression of poverty-stricken barrenness that is conveyed by the wide, desolate and stony plain in which it lies. Burgos itself is poor; it possesses nothing but its magnificent cathedral. The defiles of Pancorbo and the high summits which bound the horizon in the other direction are sinister in their ruggedness. The plain of Vivar, which extends to the foothills of the mountains, is a tawny desert, in which are to be seen only a few clumps of trees, a few rows of slender poplars, along the chilly watercourses which turn two or three mill-wheels.

But this sterility is only apparent. The countryside is agricultural, fertile in corn despite the climate, which is rigorous in the extreme, glacial in winter and torrid in summer—violent contrasts which are similarly to be found in the character of the Cid. Its dominant feature is its severe utilitarianism. This soil, burning and icy, produces only at the cost of the most persevering and the most praiseworthy efforts. Its flatness and its harshness are overcome only by dint of asceticism and self-discipline.

At the period of the Cid, Vivar was also a frontier district, marching with Navarre, which was often at war with Castile, and traversed by hostile armies and bands of partisans. This circumstance doubtless played its part in the training of a future leader who was to spend his whole life waging war and, in the memory of Spaniards, was to remain the frontiersman: he who defended the marches of the kingdom against the eternal African invader.

Was he born in the castle of Vivar, or did he see the light in Burgos, as an old tradition would have it? Nothing of this is verifiable, any more than the date of his birth. It is to be presumed, however, that the Cid was born about the year 1043, and what is certain is that he was given the name of Rodrigo: a name predestined in the eyes of the Arab historians themselves.

It was that of the last Visigoth king, whose defeat delivered Spain over to the Musulmans. Ibn Bassam claims that the Cid one day declared to somebody, who repeated it to him: "This Peninsula was conquered under a Rodrigo. It is another Rodrigo who will deliver it!" It was a saying which most probably, like so many others, has nothing historical about it except the truth of fact which it recalls.

The child's mother belonged to a great Asturian family. But the lineage of his father, Diego Leíñez, descendant of Laín Calvo, one of the great judges of Castile, was nothing more than respectable. Later, it appears, the Cid had occasion to regret the inadequate lustre of his origin. I shall endeavour in a moment to show how this came about.

In any case, there seems to have been a little bitterness or something of the insolent pride of the upstart in the following sentences, which the Campeador is said to have spoken in the presence of the notables of Valencia, on the morrow of the surrender of their city: "I am a man who has never possessed a kingdom, and nobody in my lineage has ever had one. But, from the day when I saw this city, I found it to my liking and I desired it, and I asked God to make me master of it!" There came a time, in short, when it would have been useful to the Cid to be a king, or at least of royal blood.

Having lost his father at an early age—probably when he was about fifteen—he was brought up at the court of the Infante Don Sancho, where he doubtless received the education which was then given to royal princes. This teaching, as in all the schools of the Middle Ages, comprised the liberal arts—namely, grammar, rhetoric, logic, perhaps a little mathematics, and finally law. The Cid, as we shall see, was a good jurist. It was, in short, in Latin guise, the very same education as he would have received at Cordova if he had been a Musulman.

Accordingly those who imagine him as a rough soldier, completely illiterate, not knowing how to read or write, or even how to sign his name at the foot of a contract, are utterly mistaken. Several signatures of his have been handed down to us, together with this Latin sentence written in his own handwriting on the charter of a donation made to the cathedral of Valencia: "*Ego Ruderico, simul cum conjuge mea, afirmo oc quod superius scriptum est;* I, Rodrigo, in agreement with my wife, affirm what is written above." Doubtless he was sufficiently familiar with Latin not only to write a formula such as this, but also to understand the meaning of a document drawn up in Latin.

At the same time it would be childish to exaggerate the culture of the Campeador. It is certain that he was never a fine wit, or a poet, like those kinglings of Seville and Granada who rhymed gallant madrigals—or even a man of erudition, a connoisseur of fine bindings, or a collector of rare books, like such-and-such a vizier or caliph. But, without being a great reader himself, he encouraged men of learning and had Arab stories read to him.

Inasmuch as he spent almost the whole of his life among Musulmans, he was acquainted with their language. This is attested by the following passage from Ibn Bassam: "Books were studied in his presence. The doings and deeds of the paladins of Arabia of old were read to him, and, when one came to the story of Mohallab, he was enchanted to the point of ecstasy, and showed himself full of admiration for that hero." From this it emerges that this untutored man delighted to listen to fine heroic tales, and that this Christian, not content with knowing the language of Islam, did not withhold his admiration from the enemies of his race and his faith.

That he held this intellectual culture in small enough estimation himself is extremely probable. At that period the essential thing for a man of his quality, together with physical strength, was excellence in all bodily exercises and knowledge of the profession of arms. Rodrigo's robustness and power of endurance are sufficiently proved to us by the harassing and perilous life which he led for such a long time. The same applies to the single combats, or rather the judicial duels, which he had to fight as Constable of Castile and from which he emerged victorious, thus demonstrating that he was a jouster to be feared.

As to the soldier's profession, he learnt it at an early age. When he was barely twenty he fought his first campaign with the Infante Sancho and took part in the battle of Graus, in which Ramiro, King of Aragón, was defeated by the Castilians and the Moors of Saragossa in alliance.

What was the appearance, what was the exterior of this fine soldier, of this youth whom poetry has made the sigher after Jimena? The chroniclers of the time paid no attention to this detail. Perhaps we may find a memory of oral tradition, and something like a reflection of reality, in those verses of the *Romancero* which represent the Cid to us as a sturdy man, very tall and very hairy, a rough warrior in a leather jerkin, but, like an Arab chieftain, a lover of magnificence, of arms and horses of price, of trappings embroidered with gold, of sumptuous tents, flinging over his rude war harness the folds of a great mantle dyed purple.

Yet, during the earlier part of his life, this future leader of raiders, this heroic adventurer, presents himself to us as a man of sedentary habit, a country gentleman, above all careful to protect and increase his property. He does not appear to have done anything different from what his fathers had done before him: occupy himself with his estates and the men on his estates; protect his vassals, his retainers, his servants, "those of his table and his bread," as the old Castilian poem says; and finally support his suzerain, fight for him as a good vassal ought to do, and obtain the due recompense of his services.

He began by being *Alférez* of Castile under King Sancho: a dignity comparable with that of *Connétable* in France. In this capacity he was not only the king's master of the horse, but also the supreme head of the army. He watched over the interests of the kingdom. Moreover, he was chief justice; he defended the widow and the orphan, and prosecuted lords who were rebellious or false to their obligations. In short, he was entrusted with a judicial function, which from time to time carried military duties with it.

We find, in fact, that Rodrigo Díaz de Vivar had frequently to fight for his sovereign in the struggles which he carried on either with his neighbours or with his brother Alfonso. Finally, when Alfonso had Sancho assassinated, or was privy to his assassination, Rodrigo, evidently suspect by the new sovereign, had to resign his office as *Alférez*. Henceforth he was no more than a vassal of Alfonso, who, for political reasons, did not wish to break with him openly.

Alfonso carried his policy to the point of marrying Rodrigo to a relation of his, Jimena Díaz, daughter of the Count of Oviedo and of the niece of Alfonso V, King of León. It was a brilliant match, which seems to have been arranged solely for the purpose of reconciling the nobility of Castile with the Leonese, and in which sentiment appears to have played a very small part.

Rodrigo accepted Jimena because she was offered to him, and perhaps imposed upon him, by his suzerain. All that we know of their relations clearly indicates that it was a marriage of convenience and interest, performed in accordance with the usual formulæ of the period. As a matter of custom, the lord of Vivar settled a marriage-portion on his wife, and, also as a matter of custom, he justified his donation, in the document which has been handed down to us, in the time-honoured formula: "*por decoro de su hermosura y por el virginal connubio*: in consideration of her beauty and of her virginity as a spouse." It has been sought to read an avowal of affection into these few words; but they were nothing more than a conventional phrase which is to be found in all matrimonial contracts of the period.

We are far, therefore, from the lover immortalised by the tragedy of Corneille, and even from the brutal boy of the *Romancero*, who shot down Jimena's doves with arrows and bespattered his future fiancée's pinafore with blood. Nor did he fight any duel with her father. Jimena was not the passionate and practical daughter who fell in love with her father's slayer on account of his strength and his brutality—just because he would be capable of defending her. It was a perfectly quiet and, if one may venture to say so, a perfectly middle-class marriage. Rodrigo, we may assume, saw nothing in his wife but the head of his household and the perpetuator of his line.

Deprived of his dignity as *Alférez*, he installed himself in his castle of Vivar, a sombre feudal stronghold in a still more sombre countryside, from which he emerged only to accompany his suzerain in some of his progresses and form part of his escort of honour. This life of retirement embraced no more than two or three events of some importance: a mission to Seville to the court of Motamid to receive the annual tribute which he owed to Alfonso VI; a victorious engagement with his rival, Count Garcia Ordóñez, who had taken the liberty of attacking Motamid, Alfonso's ally; and finally a punitive raid in Moorish territory in the kingdom of Toledo.

He spent nearly ten years in this comparative inaction, in this leisure without glory; and he was in the flower of his youth—not yet thirty years of age! During these years of his full development, we imagine him bursting with sap and desire, drunk with ambition, dreaming only of battles and victories. Instead of all that, he was a squire living among his peasants and servants, concerning himself with lawsuits, boundaries and party-walls, and saddling his great war-horse only to go and raid his neighbour's cows and sheep.

Let us try and see what lay hidden behind this unstriking *façade:* what passions, what feelings, in short, what character were maturing slowly during these years preparatory to so resounding a destiny.

What we know definitely about Rodrigo de Vivar does not indicate a nature spontaneously precocious. He was rather a man of tardy development, of solid and serious genius which, to give its full measure, required in the first place favourable circumstances, an opportunity to point the way to it, and, in the next place, reflection, consideration, a whole course of education. Solidity, seriousness—these were his most obvious characteristics. He was also a strong-willed and obstinate man who followed his path without deviating from it.

Fundamentally tempestuous and violent by nature, he learnt how to hold himself in check. He got the better of his competitors and his enemies by a perfect mastery over himself, even though he was sometimes subject to terrible gusts of passion. He restrained them almost immediately. This violent man was able to pass himself off as a man temperamentally moderate.

He went farther: he was chivalrous towards his adversaries, even the most embittered. When he took prisoner Count Berenguer of Barcelona, who had sworn to destroy him, he treated him honourably and let him go without ransom, though this was contrary to the usages of war. No doubt he had his reasons for doing so; for the Cid, a man prudent above all things, did nothing haphazard.

Unquestionably he showed himself stern in repression, and he regarded this sternness as necessary to keep fierce and merciless enemies in awe. Such repression, or reprisal, was in accordance with the habits and customs of the time. Modern historians have taken it as a text to represent him as a monster of cruelty.

This allegation is either based solely upon Arab documents, whose partiality is only too obvious, or it is a generalisation from isolated instances. In short, the reputation for cruelty attributed to the Cid comes from the Musulmans, and it can only be justified by some drastic proceedings which he took during the two sieges of Valencia.

It is alleged that he had his prisoners torn to pieces by dogs or burned alive. This did happen, in fact, at Valencia, and in very special circumstances. The Cid had been besieging the city for some time, and he was afraid that armies from Africa might force him to raise the siege. At the outset he allowed starving Valencians to enter his camp. Finally, in order to hasten surrender through famine, he decided that henceforth he would drive back any further refugees into the city, under threat of the direst punishment. The besieged were warned to the sound of trumpets of the penalties to which they would be exposed if they continued to try and escape.

As the exodus continued, the Cid carried his threats into execution. The refugees were thrown into bivouac fires or chased back towards the gates by the camp dogs. Obviously this treatment was not merciful; but at least it had the justification of exceptional circumstances and also of the example set by the Musulmans themselves, who treated their prisoners in the most barbarous way.

Another grievance against the Cid is the punishment which he inflicted upon the cadi of Valencia, Ibn Djahaf, who had betrayed him by intriguing with the Almoravids and had previously instigated the assassination of his sovereign King Cadir, *protégé* of the Campeador and ally of Alfonso VI of Castile. In having him burned alive, the Cid considered that he was acting judicially; he was punishing an assassin—the assassin of a prince who was his friend—and he was avenging himself upon a many times perjured traitor.

Let me repeat: these were unquestionably cruel proceedings. We can only accept the fact—and at the same time the fact that they were in accordance with the customs of the period. We are not judges of the necessities or the circumstances which imposed atrocious measures of repression and terrifying measures of prevention upon the men of war of that time. How do we know whether the Cid was not like Marshal de Saint-Arnaud, who, in the heroic days of the conquest of Algeria, gave orders, sick at heart, that the cruelties of the Bedouin should be met by similar cruelties, and grieved over the trees cut down and the homes reduced to ashes by his own troops?

Rodrigo de Vivar was certainly a hard man, and, in the environment in which he lived, it was essential that he should be. But he knew how to be merciful when he believed it opportune, and sometimes simply from instinctive pity and natural kind-heartedness. After threatening the Moors of Murviedo with putting them to fire and sword if they did not surrender within a stated period, he ended by granting them a reprieve and letting them depart with their belongings. Most of them took advantage of this permission. Those who stayed behind entrusted their hoards of money to the refugees to put them in safety, and even handed over to them subsidies intended for the Almoravid armies which were marching against the Cid.

Very justly, he punished the guilty parties by imposing upon them a contribution equal to the sums which they had hypothecated from the war indemnity or treacherously sent to his enemies. Thereupon prejudiced historians, who always find a Spaniard and a Christian in the wrong, but slur over all the Musulman atrocities, accuse the Cid of perfidy and inhumanity.

But not only was this stern man capable of unbending on occasion; he was also kind and courteous towards the humble. Popular poetry so represents him, and, if it has given him this reputation, he must certainly have provided some reason for it.

An incident which illustrates one of the most pleasant aspects of his natural kindliness has been handed down to us by a Spanish annalist. The Cid, exiled with his men and his servants, was wandering in the region of the marches of Castile and Saragossa. Suddenly he gave the order to strike camp. The baggage was already being loaded when he overheard some of his men remarking that his cook's wife had just given birth to a child. At once the thoughtful Cid asked them: "How long do Castilian ladies usually remain in bed after childbirth?" The men told him. "Well," said the Cid, "we shall stay here for that length of time. Set the tents up again!" Despite the fact that the countryside was swarming with enemies, he did not budge until the good woman, intensely proud of being thus treated by her lord as a great lady, was on her feet again.

It is extremely probable that the charge of perfidy is no better founded than that of inhumanity. The bad faith of the Cid could not have been worse than that of the Arabs and the Berbers, who at all times have been past-masters of it. Unquestionable proof of the charge, moreover, is lacking. All the examples which have been adduced are subject to reserve, when they are not flagrant errors due to a hasty and also prejudiced interpretation of texts.

The same thing applies to the Cid's rapacity, which has been enormously exaggerated. No doubt, like all the Musulman and Christian princes of that time, he went after treasure and continually made raids in enemy territory. But we must bear in mind the obligations of a guerrilla or army leader who had nothing but the booty taken from the enemy with which to pay and feed his men. If the Cid raided and hoarded, it was in the first place for the maintenance of his troops.

At the same time, it certainly seems as though, like the Moors of Granada and Seville, he, too, yielded to the fascination of gold, and that his imagination was haunted by the idea of buried treasure. When he took the castle of Polop from the Lord of Denia, he found dug in the mountain-side a regular Ali Baba's cave, where the Moorish prince had accumulated enormous wealth in gold, silver, and precious stones and stuffs.

It is very probable that the Cid was a great connoisseur of all such things. At Valencia Ibn Djahaf had seized the treasure of King Cadir. When the Cid made him disgorge it, he kept for himself the famous necklace of the Sultana Zobeyda: that necklace of fabulous value which was called "the Scorpion's Sting," and was said to bring misfortune upon its possessor. It is a fact that the Cid died shortly afterwards, after being present at the defeat of his army.

The most specious accusation which has been formulated against him is that he was a mere mercenary without faith or fatherland, fighting for or against his king, passing over from one camp to the other without the least scruple, and, in short, as much of a Musulman as a Christian, as much of an Arab as a Spaniard. This charge is now rebutted, thanks to searching critical studies[1] which have reduced all such prejudices and misunderstandings to nothingness.

It is proved, on the contrary, by the most ample evidence that Rodrigo de Vivar was not merely a good Christian, but even a devotee, and that he was so throughout the whole of his life, in Castile no less than in Saragossa and Valencia, scrupulous about celebrating religious festivals, observing Lent as a Musulman observes Ramadan, and making donations to monasteries and churches. It is no less certain that he conducted himself always as a good vassal, no matter what wrongs his sovereign did him.

He fought for Musulman princes, as did at that time all the Christian princes of the peninsula, who had allies and vassals among the Moors and vice versa. It is to be noted that he never fought against the allies of his suzerain, Alfonso VI, whether those allies were Musulmans or Christians. When he finally conquered the king-dom of Valencia, he reserved the suzerainty of Alfonso over and above his own rights. Finally this exile, kept in disgrace by his king, always remembered his native Castile with a kind of tenderness; and —as we shall see in a moment—this alleged *sans-patrie* respected the quality of Spaniard even in the case of those of the Musulmans who were his enemies or the allies of his enemies.

All this contradicts the preconceived idea of the medieval squire who recognised only the right and the law of force. The Cid was respectful of all written laws. This man, who was a regular jurist, presided over trials, discussed the authenticity of documents, and was as familiar with the Musulman code as with the *fueros* of León or Castile, always put reason before violence. If he was terrible in repression, he was concerned above all to be just and scrupulously to observe contracts or customs.

I insist upon this point, as upon certain traits of his character, solely for the purpose of defining this outstanding figure. It is essential not to make a plaster saint out of him, but to discover the reason for his immense popularity and the nature of the great ser-vices which raised him to the rank of a national hero. If he became so when he was nearly forty, after spending a dozen years in semi-obscurity, are we to see in that only the result of chance or of favour-able opportunity? For men of this stamp chance is never more than apparent and opportunity is always providential.

Rodrigo de Vivar, suspect in the eyes of Alfonso of Castile from their very first meeting, became embroiled with his king. Alfonso exiled him, though without depriving him of his property. This exile

---

[1] See, in particular, the masterly study by Menéndez Pidal: *La España del Cid*, Madrid, 1929.

nevertheless condemned him and his retainers to a life of wandering and to poverty. It was the point of departure of his extraordinary career.

On which side did the wrongs lie? It seems that the gravest were on the side of the king. If Alfonso could reproach Rodrigo with having raided among his Moorish allies of the kingdom of Toledo, and perhaps with having taken money from Motamid of Seville, all this served as scarcely more than a pretext for paying off old scores. Alfonso's bitterest grievance was the memory of the oath which the Cid had made him take at Burgos, in the church of Santa Gadea, before an assembly of Castilian nobles, to the effect that he had not been his brother's assassin. For Alfonso was, at least, privy to the assassination.

But that, too, scarcely mattered: the real reason of their rupture was that the suzerain was secretly jealous of his vassal. After all, a man like the Cid could not live in the background, relegated to the life of a country gentleman. The exile to which he was condemned meant liberation for him, and at the same time the revelation of him as a hero.

Rodrigo left Jimena at Vivar with their children. The separation was to be a long one; but it was only prudent. Somebody had to stay and take charge of the old family manor and look after the abandoned fiefs.

Moreover, one can hardly imagine the Cid's wife living in the promiscuity of a band of adventurers, following her husband's hard road, exposed to all kinds of dangers. For it was a perilous and painful existence which the exile was henceforth to lead. In his own words, he had to "win his bread" and that of his men. There was only one means of winning it—the means employed at that time by all needy squires: fighting and marauding in Moorish territory.

He offered his services first to Berenguer of Barcelona, expecting that he would engage him to fight against his neighbours, the Musulmans of Saragossa and Lerida. Finding himself cold-shouldered by the Barcelonan, he turned to Moctadir, the Moorish King of Saragossa. It is such *volte-faces* which have made the Cid regarded as a mere mercenary, who sold his sword indifferently to Musulmans or Christians. What is forgotten is that the Musulman princes of that time were almost all allies or vassals of Christian kings, and that the protecting prince, in return for the tribute which they paid him, owed them aid and support.

As a matter of fact, Moctadir was the tributary and ally of Alfonso VI, the suzerain of the Lord of Vivar. Rodrigo, in putting himself at his service, was doing nothing more than defend the *protégé* of his prince. Moreover, he was acting as a good Castilian in keeping Saragossa in subjection to Castile, and in preparing by his presence and his influence for the annexation of this great principality to the Kingdom of León and Castile. This had long been the objective of Ferdinand and Alfonso.

He was able to make himself indispensable to Moctadir, and then to his successors, Moutamin and Mostain. He defeated their Christian or Musulman enemies on several occasions and returned to Saragossa in triumph. It was at this period that he acquired the reputation of invincibility throughout Spain and was hailed as the great *Campeador*: a vague term, about which there has been much discussion, that seems to mean simply "the victorious." He became a regular power side by side with the prince, who, inasmuch as he needed him, treated him tactfully and loaded him with honours.

These sovereign princes of Saragossa, the Beni Houd, were of Arab origin, but they had long been under the protection of Castile. This was perhaps one of the reasons why the Cid got on so well with Moctadir. Once installed at his court, he lived there for several years. Doubtless it suited his purposes. In any case, it may be said that his stay there coincided with a decisive evolution in his character and ideas. Saragossa opened horizons to him.

The ancient Cæsarea Augusta was not exactly a great city. All these cities of the Middle Ages, especially the ancient colonial cities enclosed within the boundaries of an old Roman camp, were in general quite small. But all the same it was something different from Burgos or León. Apart from its strategic importance, Saragossa, proudly established on the banks of its river, enjoyed a quite special prestige among the cities of Spanish Islam.

It was called "the white city" on account of its tufa-stone walls and its houses whitened with chalk, which, it appears, rose in an amphitheatre above the ramparts and shone in the sun like an enormous snowy cupola. At night, it was claimed, this whiteness illuminated the darkness, no doubt miraculously. The Christian Mozarabs of the district explained this nocturnal splendour by the presence of the famous Virgin of Pilar. It was the supernatural purity of the Immaculate which appeared through the white walls of her cherished city.

Despite its strong Roman and Christian stamp, Saragossa was perhaps the most Islamised city in Spain. It owed this, no doubt, to its quality as a frontier-city. It is always on the marches of a country that the colonising effort of conquering peoples is most intensely brought to bear. Even to-day traces of Islam are to be found everywhere in Saragossa. Its church towers are minarets, its churches and its cathedral are former mosques. Its venerable sanctuary of Pilar itself, with its domes encrusted with glazed porcelain, reminds one of the Great Mosque of Cordova. Its *Aljaferia*, the old palace of the Moorish kings, still preserves some excellent remains of "half-orange" ceilings, and above all a little oratory, blossoming with arabesques, which is a gem of Arab-Spanish art.

When the Cid arrived there, Saragossa was still in all its glory as a

Musulman capital. Moctadir, a man of letters, surrounded himself with a court of poets, philosophers and learned men, for the most part of Jewish or Christian origin. As he talked with this prince, who appears to have been a man as intellectual as he was cultivated, the great Castilian soldier must have been persuaded that it was possible to reach an understanding, at least on certain points, between all Spaniards, Musulman and Christian. He familiarised himself more with the Moors who surrounded him.

Doubtless it was from this time that he adopted a line of conduct towards them from which he departed only when he was constrained by circumstances or by the attitude of the Moors themselves: that of treating them, in short, as compatriots, respecting their possessions, their estates, their language and their religion, and bringing them little by little to accept life in common with the Christians.

It was obviously an ideal difficult to attain, upon which reality was not slow to inflict cruel disillusions. But it is certain that the Cid was haunted by the idea, not indeed of fusion, but of reciprocal tolerance. It is extremely probable that this idea would have led him nowhere owing to the irreducible hostility of the two opposed civilisations; but as a political expedient, a means of arranging things provisionally, it proved to have its advantages.

Among the distinguished Musulmans whom the Cid met at Saragossa I should perhaps mention one who may have exercised a certain influence upon his projects: the famous Ben Ammar, the minister and friend of Motamid of Seville, who had tried to seize the kingdom of Murcia at the expense of his master, and to escape his anger had been driven to take refuge with Moctadir.

Undoubtedly the Lord of Vivar was equally possessed for some time past by the idea of carving out an independent principality for himself somewhere in Musulman territory. Alfonso's injustice towards him seemed to counsel such a measure of precaution. The vain attempts which he repeatedly made to effect a reconciliation with his suzerain showed him quite unmistakably that he had nothing to expect from him but bad treatment, and that he must provide for his own security as soon as possible. Why should not he, too, be a king, like so many Musulman and Christian princelings who had been nothing but squires or lucky soldiers?

Still, the example of Ben Ammar, who had just failed in such a fine scheme, constrained him to be prudent. There was an example even more outstanding: that of the famous El Mansour, who, though he had usurped the sovereign authority, had never gone so far as to assume the Caliphal title. If the Lord of Vivar dared to proclaim himself king, he would have against him not only his suzerain, but also all the Musulman princes, including Moctadir, his ally and his *protégé*.

In these circumstances, he must arrange matters so that he would be the master of a territory which he could hold strongly, but without breaking the link of vassalage with Alfonso of Castile. While pretending to be acting in his interests, he could make himself powerful enough not to be afraid of him. In case of misfortune, of extreme danger, he could always call upon the help of a suzerain towards whom he had always showed himself a good vassal. It was, no doubt, for similar reasons of prudence that he never quarrelled with his friend the prince of Saragossa: he might need him some day.

But upon what "kingdom" was he to cast his choice? The easiest to conquer was that of Valencia, where reigned the weak Cadir, former King of Toledo and *protégé* of Alfonso VI. Surrounded by rivals, he maintained himself there only thanks to Castilian mercenaries under the orders of the Cid's own nephew, the famous Alvar Fáñez. The delicate part of the affair was to oust the competitors, or at least to put them in their place. The cleverness of the Campeador consisted in presenting himself not as a conqueror or a usurper, but as the defender of Cadir, the *protégé* of his suzerain. Thus he continued to conduct himself as a good vassal, zealous for the interests of his lord.

The most formidable obstacle, however, was the threatening advance of the African hordes which, under the leadership of the Almoravid Caliph, Yousouf ben Teshoufin, seemed on the eve of regaining all the territory lost by Islam. The Cid realised the gravity of the situation immediately. While King Alfonso of Castile withstood the pressure of the Almoravid armies in the South-west, his own *rôle* was to bar their way in the East, and prevent them from reaching Saragossa and joining hands with the Musulman princes who still held the valley of the Ebro, the south of Catalonia, and the kingdom of Valencia.

So the personal ambitions of the Cid were subordinated to the national interest. It was a question of preventing a second invasion of Spain by Islam. His great merit was that he appreciated that the Spanish efforts must be concentrated upon the East and a solid barrier be established there against the Moorish invaders.

For this purpose, it no longer sufficed to make raids in Moorish territory, or even to inflict serious defeats on the enemy, or, again, to impose tribute upon Musulman kinglings. It was essential for him to establish himself strongly and definitively in the conquered territory, and, if necessary, found a new dynasty there. So it was that the Cid was brought to undertake the conquest of Valencia and the neighbouring region in the East, and that Valencia became for some time "Valencia of the Cid."

This conquest was slow and arduous. The Campeador bent his whole soul to the task. "He fastened upon that city," says an Arab author, "as a creditor fastens upon his debtor. He loved it as lovers love the places where they have tasted the delights of love." One might say more: he loved it like a mistress. The great love of the Cid was not Jimena; it was Valencia.

He did not possess it for very long—four or five years at the most. But he made a point of acting there as a master, a sovereign, who was taking possession of a territory for ever. He gave the city a new statue. The first thing he did was to convert the Great Mosque into a cathedral and enthrone an archbishop there.

This warrior proposed to be a founder. He administered and he legislated. He established his residence in the Musulman Alcázar and summoned his wife and his daughters there. But the Berber hordes were at the gates. He had to go on fighting to his last breath. Undermined by fever, weakened by old wounds, he died at the age of fifty-six, in the month of July 1099.

After him his wife succeeded in holding out for a few years more. Finally she had to abandon beloved Valencia and take to flight, carrying with her the bones of her husband, which she had exhumed lest they should be profaned by the Musulmans. Such profanation was the great dread of the Christian leaders of that time. "If by chance I should die on Moorish soil," says one of them in his testament, "may my soul be with Christ and may my body be carried to my own land and buried with those of my ancestors. And if I die there, and my vassals do not bring me back here, may they be stamped with infamy as traitors to their lord!"

Jimena, therefore, regarded it as a matter of conscience to bear the remains of her husband back to Castile. This exodus of the vanquished must have been a pitiful business. We may imagine it from a miniature in the Escorial which represents a similar scene: a little box, containing the bones of the hero, tied on the back of a mule, jolting along the paths and the rocky roads of the Valencian sierra; and, behind the funereal burden, in the middle of an escort of retainers, Jimena in her widow's veil, drooping upon her palfrey and following for days and days, threatened by all kinds of dangers, that poor little coffin which holds a whole world of poetry.

The long victorious ride of the Cid across Moorish and Christian territory ended, then, in this lamentable progress. The invincible was vanquished; nothing was left of his work; and his beloved Valencia, the Valencia of the Cid, was again to become the Valencia of Islam.

But the defeat of the Campeador was only apparent. He had blazed the trail for the conquerors of Spanish soil and shown them the tactics which they must pursue. Nothing would be done so long as they did not renounce the sterile system of raids and protectorates imposed upon Musulman princes. They must first take Saragossa and Valencia, cut Islam's road to the North, and replace the little kingdoms of the Moors by a great Christian kingdom.

It is, indeed, impossible that this great Castilian, who remained faithful to the end to the King of Castile, to him who proudly called himself "Emperor of the two religions," should not have conceived the future unification of Spain as an absolute necessity. In any case, his example and the memory of his deeds were to confer upon the name "Christian" an incomparable prestige, before which the Musulmans themselves bowed down.

CHAPTER XIV

The Invasion of the Almoravids and the Almohades

WHAT momentarily made the work of the Cid sterile and arrested the Christian advance for more than a century was the double invasion of the Almoravids and the Almohades—the return of the Berbers *en masse* on to the soil of the Peninsula.

As always, they were summoned by the Spaniards, who never schooled themselves—whether they were Christians or Musulmans —out of periodical appeal to the barbarian, regarded as a saviour. To deliver themselves from one oppressor, they threw themselves into the arms of another, who proved worse. Accordingly the Andalusians and all the Musulmans of Spain, frightened by the progress of Alfonso VI, resigned themselves to demanding help from Yousouf ben Teshoufin, the Almoravid Sultan of Morocco.

They saw the time coming when they would be obliged to submit to the Emperor of the Christians, or, if they were not ready to bow to the yoke of the Infidel, emigrate to Islamic lands. "Be on your way, O Andalusian," sang one of their poets, "for to stay here is madness!" Those of them who knew the Africans were afraid in advance of having them as allies. They realised that these so-called protectors would behave among them as though they were in conquered territory. Perhaps it would be better to accept the domination of the Christians, who at least were Spaniards, men of their own country and even of their own race.

But religious considerations prevailed over those of politics and prudence. Motamid of Seville, sick at heart, decided with some of his neighbours to implore the aid of the Almoravid. "I do not wish," he said, "that my name should be accursed in all the Musulman pulpits, and if I must choose, I would rather be a camel-driver in Africa than a pig-driver in Castile."

Accordingly he allowed the Moroccan troops to disembark at Algeciras. Soon afterwards Yousouf ben Teshoufin came to take command of his army. Alfonso VI of Castile, who had hastened to the Andalusian frontier to bar his way, was defeated in a great battle on October 23, 1086, which the Musulmans called the battle of Zallaca and the Christians the battle of Sacralias. But, as usual, the Berber did not press his advantage over the Castilians. He judged it more opportune to subdue the whole of Southern Spain to himself. After that he marched against Saragossa.

So the Moorish kinglings who had called him to their aid were dethroned, their treasures were pillaged, and those of them who were not killed found themselves, like Motamid, carried away into captivity. Soon the tyranny of the Almoravids became so unendurable to the Spaniards that they began to turn their eyes again towards

Africa. A new dynasty, that of the Almohades, more fanatical still than that of the Almoravids, had replaced them in Morocco.

In 1146 the Caliph Abd el Moumin began the invasion of Spain, where, little by little, the Almoravid leaders were ousted. In 1195 the Caliph Yacoub el Mansour defeated Alfonso VIII of Castile in the battle of Alarcos. Thence he advanced towards the North, and took possession of Madrid, Ucles, and Guadalajara.

Almost all Musulman Spain was once more reunited under a single master. This new advance of Islam became a great danger to Christendom, the more so as at the other end of Europe, over against the feeble Empire of the East, the young power of the Turks was rising as a terrible threat.

This double invasion had as its result the further Africanisation of southern Spain. The Musulman Spaniards were once more decimated by the Berbers of Africa, and this went on throughout this lamentable twelfth century. Their cities were taken, and their princes massacred or expelled.

The fate of the Christians and the Jews, still numerous in Andalusia, was even worse. During the reign of Yousouf ben Teshoufin the Jews were compelled to become converted, on the ground that, according to a tradition, they had entered into an agreement with Mahomet to turn Musulmans at the end of the fifth century of the Hegira. They escaped this cruel necessity only at the cost of paying an enormous sum to the Caliphal treasury. Later, under the Almohades, they were compelled to wear a special costume and were deprived of their synagogues.

"Among us," writes Marrakeshi, "no security is accorded either to Jews or Christians since the establishment of the Masmoudite (Almohade) power, *and there exists neither synagogue nor church in all the Musulman territory of the Moghreb.* . . . The Jews profess Islamism externally; they pray in the mosques and teach the Koran to their children. God alone knows what they hide in their hearts and what their houses conceal."

From the outset of the Almoravid invasion the destruction of Christian churches had begun. Among them was destroyed a very old and very curious basilica in the neighbourhood of Granada, the church of Gudila. The faquis commenced to persecute the Christian Mozarabs so intolerably that they begged the King of Aragón, Alfonso the Warrior, to come and deliver them. The Aragonese did not succeed in taking Granada. When they retreated, the faquis avenged themselves on the Mozarabs in the most merciless fashion.

Already ten thousand of them had been compelled to emigrate into the territory of Alfonso to escape their enemies' repression. The remainder were deprived of their property, imprisoned, or put to death. Many of them were deported to Africa. They were established in the neighbourhood of Salé and Meknes, where oppression of all kinds compelled them to embrace Islam. Ten years later there was a fresh expulsion. The Christians were again deported to Morocco *en masse*.

Here, then, were cities and whole districts depopulated by massacres and proscriptions. This corresponded with a plan drawn upon in advance, a systematic course of action. "Sultan Yousouf," writes Marrakeshi, "never failed to repeat at every one of his audiences: 'To rid the Peninsula of the Christians—that is our sole purpose; since we have seen, on the one hand, that they have become entirely its masters, and, on the other hand, how great is the carelessness of the Musulman princes, their lack of zeal in making war, their internal dissensions and their love of repose. None of them has any other thought but to empty goblets, to listen to singers, and to spend his life in amusing himself. If I live, I shall not fail to restore to the Musulmans all the provinces that the Christians have taken from them.'"

Accordingly, after having expelled the Christians, he replaced them by Berbers. "To combat our enemies," said Yousouf himself, "I shall fill Spain with horsemen and footmen who think nothing of repose, who do not know what it is to live softly, whose sole thought is to groom and train their horses, take care of their arms, and hasten to obey their orders."

The Almohades devoted themselves no less ardently to repopulating the South of Spain by filling it with Africans and Arabs. "When Abd el Moumin left the Peninsula," says the author quoted above, "he installed Arabs there, some in the neighbourhood of Cordova, others in the direction of Seville and in the direction of Jerez and its territory. They are still there in the present year (621 of the Hegira), and constitute an important group. For they have increased in number through births and through the new recruits sent there by Abou Yacoub and Abou Yousouf."

Spain, therefore, was submerged by a whole influx of foreign invaders, whom the natives, Christian and Musulman, no longer counterbalanced, as during the first period of the conquest. So any hope of fusion between victors and vanquished, the dream of unity cherished or played with by the great Caliphs, and especially by Spaniards such as the Cid and some of the Kings of Castile—this dream was henceforth made impossible of fulfilment.

While the national element predominated, it was possible to hope that the spirit of the race would end by absorbing Berber and Arab. Now, after so many massacres and expulsions, after this new flood of barbarous and fanatical invaders, understanding between Christian and Musulman became absolutely unrealisable. Religious passions and hatreds, which had certainly died down under the regime of the little Moorish kingdoms, acquired intensified vigour and virulence. Once more the fatal dilemma which had hung over Spain for more than four centuries presented itself to the Spaniards: expel the foreigner, or be expelled by him!

What rendered contact with these Africans the more unpleasant to them was the lack of culture of these soldiers who thought of nothing but their arms and their horses. The little Moorish courts of Andalusia, as we have seen, prided themselves upon their high degree of refinement. They were very proud of their poets, their rhetoricians and their grammarians. The Berbers themselves were considerably dazzled by the Spanish civilisation.

"Spain," said Marrakeshi, "is the true capital and centre of the Moghreb el Aksa, *the source of its merits*. All talents of all kinds derive their origin from her and are regarded as belonging to her. It is in this country that the suns and the moons of learning rise; it is the centre and the pivot of talents."

Jealous of their brilliant neighbours, though they affected to despise them, the Almoravid and Almohade Caliphs tried to make their own original roughness and barbarism forgotten by attracting to them men of letters, fine orators and penmen, and even philosophers. It was said to be in accordance with a desire expressed one day by Abou Yacoub El Mansour, one of the Almohade Caliphs, that Averroés undertook his commentary on Aristotle. But this zeal for philosophy seems to have been nothing but a passing whim, the "gesture" of an upstart. This same El Mansour, no doubt under the influence of the Musulman theologians, soon changed his tastes.

"Having convoked the principal personages of Cordova," writes Renan, "he summoned Averroés before him and, after having anathematised his doctrines, condemned him to exile. At the same time the Emir had edicts dispatched to the provinces prohibiting dangerous doctrines, and ordering all books dealing with them to be burned. Exception was made only in favour of medicine, arithmetic and elementary astronomy."

One of his predecessors had already condemned to the flames the books of the celebrated Ghazzali, author of *The Vivification of Religious Knowledge*. At Bougie the founder of the Almohade sect, Ibn Toumert, in a fit of puritan zeal, had set an example by breaking amphoræ and musical instruments.

Fundamentally all these Berber sovereigns were fanatical devotees. Never did the faquis enjoy a greater influence than during their reigns. It was the theologians who were consulted about affairs of State. No important decision was taken without their advice.

Philip II is the object of mockery because he submitted his cases of conscience to his confessors. Apparently it is regarded as quite natural that Yousouf ben Teshoufin should have thought fit to ask the approbation of his faquis before undertaking a military operation or deposing a traitorous prince. The founder of the Escorial considered public prayers and processions the surest means of winning victory. The Almohade El Mansour, when he took the field, surrounded himself with pious personages whose intercession he sought, and he said to his officers: "There is my real army!"

These men, rude and full of faith, might have arrested the Spanish Reconquest completely. In any case they held it back for nearly a century. Their lack of a sense of continuity, their incapacity for taking a broad view, and finally their perpetual divisions, enabled the Christians to gain the upper hand again.

After the terror inspired throughout the West by the defeat of Alfonso VIII at Alarcos, the Spaniards succeeded in reorganising themselves and stimulating a kind of crusade in the neighbouring countries. On July 16, 1212, the victory of Las Navas de Tolosa, in which the Africans were overwhelmed, marked the beginning of the deliverance.

§ V

THE RECONQUEST

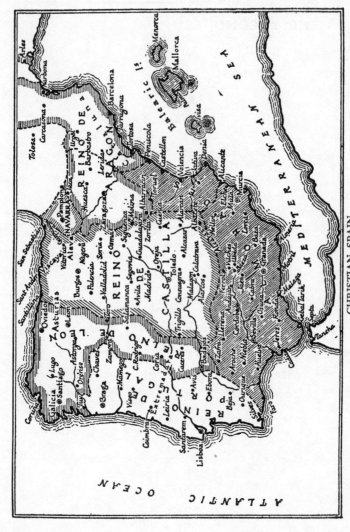

CHRISTIAN SPAIN

Before the union of the Kingdoms of Castile and Aragón (1157–1230). The area of the Moorish (Almohade) sovereignty is now reduced to Andalusia, Murcia and Valencia (the shaded portions).

CHAPTER XV

The Stages of the Reconquest

IT would be very simple-minded to imagine Christian Spain as sighing, during eight hundred years after her defeat under Rodrigo, for revenge and the reconquest of her lost provinces. In the first place, there was at that time no such thing as Spain, but merely a swarm of little states more or less divided one against the other.

Unity is a Roman conception, which was instinctively repugnant to the Arabs, and no doubt also to the Arabised Spaniards. Fundamentally, it was only the clergy—and even so only the regular clergy, obedient to the Cluniac discipline and subject to Rome—together with the monks, and a few ambitious and intelligent princes, who favoured a return to the unity of the kingdom.

On the other hand, the *status quo* undoubtedly presented many advantages, though we are no longer in a position to judge them to-day. Peoples, or the soundest sections of them, tend to prefer the conditions they know to the risks of revolution or of a change of regime. Disturbances are never welcomed except by a turbulent minority. The masses submit, willy-nilly, to events which they cannot control.

I have already pointed out why the reconquest was so slow. But in the thirteenth century new factors emerged, which for a time hastened the march of events. The power of the Almohades was overthrown in Africa by that of the Merinides. That was the end of the African strangle-hold on Spain, even though there were still some attempts at Berber invasion of Andalusia under the Merinide princes.

At about the same period, Spain was fortunate enough to produce certain energetic and enterprising sovereigns, who regained some important fragments of the national patrimony and began the process of throwing the hereditary enemy back to the other side of the Strait: for example Ferdinand III, Alfonso X, and Alfonso XI of Castile; and Alfonso the Warrior and James I of Aragón.

Victorious over the Africans in the battle of Las Navas de Tolosa, Alfonso VIII of Castile was no more capable of profiting by his success than any Caliph of Cordova or Marrakesh. After a few raids in Andalusia he recrossed the Sierra Morena and retired towards the North. It was only under his successors that the reconquest accelerated its tempo and acquired a scope hitherto unaccustomed.

In 1236 Ferdinand III, whom the Church made a Saint, obtained the capitulation of Cordova on unexpectedly favourable terms. Some years later, in 1241, he advanced as far as Málaga and finally, in 1248, to Seville. Southern Spain was beginning to recover her natural frontiers. His son, Alfonso X the Wise, retook Carthagena, Cádiz, San Lucar, Niebla, and some towns in Algarve.

Meanwhile, in 1118, the King of Aragón, Alfonso the Warrior, had taken possession of Saragossa, which the Almohades vainly endeavoured to reoccupy. In the course of the thirteenth century—which was decidedly the great century of the reconquest—his successors made progress throughout the region of the East. James I the Conqueror drove the Moors out of the Balearic Islands (1229), and recovered Valencia (1238), which had been evacuated by the Christians after the death of the Cid, and finally Elche and Alicante.

In the following century, Alfonso XI of Castile stopped a final offensive of the Africans at Rio-Salado. This was after the Merinide Sultan of Fez, summoned to Andalusia by the King of Granada—in accordance with the deplorable custom of the Musulman kinglings—had crossed the Strait with the intention of recovering Andalusia from the Christians. Alfonso reconquered Algeciras, an important strategic point as the disembarkation place of Berber invaders. Only illness prevented him from recovering Gibraltar as well.

In short, by the second half of the fourteenth century almost the whole of Spain was in the hands of the Christian princes. One cannot say that the reconquest came to a complete standstill at that date, for it continued to progress slowly up to the end of the following century. But it slowed down in a fashion which at first sight appears incomprehensible, inasmuch as the Christians had nothing left in front of them except the little kingdom of Granada. It seemed that, after forcing one after another—and at the cost of what efforts!—all the mountain ramparts which divided the Peninsula, they became immobilised at the one which protected the last Musulman state, in front of the last of the Andalusian sierras, as though the final obstacle were the most difficult to surmount.

This stagnation is to be explained in the first place by the dissensions and civil wars which tore Spain during all the second half of the fourteenth century and the first half of the fifteenth century, and also by the rivalry between Castile and Aragón. But perhaps the main reason was the habit which the Spanish princes had acquired of living at the expense of the Musulmans. It was so convenient to go and raid in the territory of the Moors—who for that matter did the same thing to the Christians. There was no reason why this deplorable system should come to an end so long as the two adversaries found it to their advantage.

Only religious or monarchical motives could dictate the complete and definitive expulsion of the Moors. But for that purpose a regular campaign, a great military effort, was necessary. The kingdom of Granada was not only excellently defended by nature, but also, with the progress of the reconquest, it had become peopled by all the elements which were most refractory to Spain and to Christianity in the whole of the evacuated area of the Peninsula. Apart from the fact that the population had grown very dense, it was conspicuous for its fanaticism and its hatred of the Christians. Finally these Moors, descendants of the African Berbers, could always count upon their brothers of Africa in case of attack by the Spaniards. Their ports were open to all the tribesmen of Barbary.

For this final assault upon Islam, therefore, there were required great strength and a unified Spain. This was why nothing serious was attempted before the union of Castile and Aragón under Ferdinand and Isabel. Then the King of Granada, Abou Hassan, made the mistake of provoking the Queen of Castile by taking Zahara from her in 1478.

Isabel, occupied elsewhere, deferred her revenge for four years. But in 1482 she inspired a regular crusade against the Moors, assembled a considerable army, and decided her husband to act vigorously against the Granadines. It was a great undertaking: it took ten years to reduce the little kingdom and plant the Cross on the walls of the Alhambra.

CHAPTER XVI

The Kingdom of Granada

WHAT was this kingdom of Granada which so intensely aroused the desire of the Catholic Sovereigns, of the Spanish nobility, and of all adventurers in quest of booty?

To inform ourselves on this subject we can scarcely count on the Arab writers, or even upon some Spanish writers, who have described it without moderation or common sense. Both of them let themselves go in laudatory exaggeration, in the most extravagant hyperbole, the Spaniards in order to emphasise the value of their conquest, the Arabs in order to stress their regret for the lost province.

In the case of the latter, especially, the rigmarole and grandiloquence of the wildest rhetoric are equalled only by the vagueness and banality of their descriptions. The faults of decadence make themselves sadly conspicuous among these writers of Oriental prose. The most important of them, Al Khatib, the Granadine historian, disappoints us the more in proportion to the great hopes which we base upon the exactitude and sanity of a Moor of Granada in describing his city and his native soil to us.

This rhetorician—who, at the same time, was a very shrewd and clever politician—boldly entitles his history of Granada: *Splendour of the Full Moon upon the Kingdom of the Nasserites*. To him the city and the court of Granada, as sublime as they are magnificent, defy all praise and all judgment. They exhaust and reduce to impotence any genius of language which would seek to describe and exalt them. The beauty of the city is without rival, the desirableness of its situation beyond compare. Its throne is resplendent with glory. The two rivers which enclose it are as a necklace of pearls.

Let me not seek to stop this windmill of words. Let me say merely that out of all this beating of wings not very much emerges. Yet these Arab word-mongers are less deceptive for us than the modern historians, romancers and æsthetes, who have buried poor Granada under such a mass of prejudices, naïve or clumsy errors, ready-made phrases, in short under so much "literature," that its true appearance has ended by becoming unrecognisable. The case of certain historians is the most lamentable. These professionals of criticism, whom elementary prudence ought to put on their guard, have accepted the vaguest dithyrambs of the Arab authors with their eyes shut and as "scientific" evidence.

Attempting to derive from these authors what residue of definite information they nevertheless provide, and taking as my guide the Spaniard who was best acquainted with the Musulmans of Africa and Spain—namely, Luis del Marmol Cárvajal—I shall endeavour to present here a more faithful picture of Moorish Granada and the Granadine kingdom.

This little kingdom was in its decadence at the period of Ferdinand and Isabel: in the first place on account of the palace intrigues and revolutions and the wars of partisans which had weakened the central authority; and in the next place, and especially, because it was ceaselessly threatened and attacked by the Christians.

Going back to the worst traditions of the caliphs and the Moorish kings, the Christians raided the frontiers of Granada several times a year. Despite truces, tributes paid by the Musulman princes, and treaties of vassalage concluded by them, the Granadines within reach of Castilian territory found themselves periodically invaded by armed bands which cut down fruit trees, carried off crops and cattle, made prisoners and seized all possible booty.

There was no security except in the city of Granada itself, which was defended by the sovereign's mercenaries—and, even so, Al Khatib admits that it was sometimes alarmed by the incursions of the enemy. The maritime regions and towns were probably more peaceful than the inland. They had not very much to fear from the Christians, although Castilian squadrons practised piracy there from time to time. They remained in touch with Barbary, which could defend them in case of extreme necessity, at their own risk and peril.

The best protected part of the population was undoubtedly the mountaineers of the Alpujarras, that region of the Andalusian sierras where the peasant was more or less his own master, and soldiers and police only ventured with precaution in view of the difficulty of access.

The country was certainly fertile and prosperous. The Arab and Spanish authors excel one another in admiration of so much richness and fecundity. One would like to know precisely what justified these eulogies and what exactly this terrestrial paradise was like. But they tell us nothing that we could not guess in advance from a little reading of the Arab geographers.

We may take it for granted. In all the towns there were excellent baths and mosques, and bazaars bursting with merchandise. Here the local figs were noted for their exquisite taste. There was to be found cool water, even in summer—and this water was sweet as honey. Such-and-such a locality was renowned for its almonds and raisins. Such another was noted for the excellence of its milk and the perfumed breath of its women. A third—Málaga—"smelt sweet as an uncorked phial of musk."

All this is charming, but it does not tell us much. At all times this region of Andalusia was fertile; it still is, despite the heat of a more than African climate. It is naturally watered by the very abundant streams of its mountains. During the last centuries of the Musulman domination, when the population was considerably increased as a result of the exodus of the Moors expelled from the reconquered provinces, the soil must have been intensively cultivated to a quite exceptional extent.

At the same time, we should not exaggerate the fertility of the land. In general the district is of quite African aridity—an aridity tempered by oases of cultivation. Wherever there is water, fruits and crops grow as well as could be wished. These water-points, these *vegas* and these *huertas*, abound in Andalusia. Moreover, at the period with which we are concerned the cultivable soil of all this region was in the hands of those admirable Spanish peasants who, in the distant days of the Roman hegemony, gave Betica its reputation, and who nowadays have succeeded in restoring in French Algeria the fertility destroyed by the carelessness and barbarism of the Arabs.

These peasants are agricultural workers of extraordinary endurance and application. It is they who have cleared the bush of the Algerian Sahel and Tell, planted vines and sown corn, act as harvesters every year in the province of Oran, created zones of kitchen-gardens around Algiers, and fill the French markets with early vegetables. Under the Arab domination, these serfs, attached to the soil by the Romans and the Visigoths, became converts to Islam in large numbers, owing to the facilities of affranchisement which were offered them. It was they who nourished their new masters, ignorant of agriculture and, in addition, too proud and too lazy to engage in it.

When the Christians regained the upper hand, these Spanish peasants regarded it as a point of honour to remain faithful to Islam. It was necessary to expel them, or attempt to convert them. After they had gone, it was a hard job repopulating the soil, which for a long time remained uncultivated. Hence arises the tenacious and deep-rooted idea of modern historians that it was the Arabs who gave Andalusia its fertility. In fact, these alleged Arabs were Spanish peasants converted to Islam, when they were not Christians.

While the native element predominated in the country, in the towns the bulk of the population was composed of Berbers and a small number of Arabs, whose ancestors generally came from Syria. In Granada itself, notably, the majority of the inhabitants were Berbers, in other words Africans—hence the hatred of them by the Spaniards. On their side, all the Musulman Granadines, of whatever origin, cordially execrated the Spaniards, "the barbarians who," as Al Khatib puts it, "worship the wood of the Cross."

In this little state, the most fertile and undoubtedly the best cultivated in all Spain, wealth was above all agricultural. The Granadine *vega*, dotted with farms and country-houses, full of gardens and orchards, aroused the admiration of the Venetian ambassador, Andrea Navagero, as late as the reign of Charles V. The abundance of water, of fountains, of irrigation canals, the plentifulness of flowers in spring and of fruits almost all the year round, were another source of marvelling for foreigners.

The figs of Málaga enjoyed a special reputation throughout the Mediterranean. It appears that they were exported not only to Egypt and Syria, but even, according to Al Macari, as far as China and India. A similar reputation was enjoyed by the Malagan raisins and wines—especially the wines, with which the good Musulmans regaled themselves, whether they were fermented or not. There was a saying current among them which was attributed to one of these connoisseurs, a hardened drunkard. When he was at the point of death and was exhorted to repentance, he found only this prayer: "Lord, I ask but one thing of Thee in Thy Paradise: to drink the wine of Málaga and the *zebibi*[1] of Seville!"

The kingdom of Granada also produced a wheat which was highly esteemed. Nowhere, it was said, was the bread better than at Granada. It was that very compact and very white bread which is still made in the eastern Spanish countryside, and of which the fugitive Moors carried the recipe to Africa.

Apart from this agricultural wealth, the Granadines also enjoyed commercial wealth and even, up to a certain point, industrial wealth. The capital had some luxury industries: jewellers' work, embroidery, business in stuffs of all kinds. But the two really rich towns were the maritime towns, Almería and Málaga. Both of them maintained close relations with the ports of Barbary—Oran, Algiers, Boné, Tunis —and even with the Italian, Catalan, Levantine, and Turkish ports.

It was especially in the eleventh and twelfth centuries, under its independent emirs, that Almería witnessed a great prosperity. It carried on active trade with all the countries of the Mediterranean. It had silk factories which, we are told, occupied as many as eight hundred looms. It also wove brocades and precious stuffs as well as manufacturing cheap cotton stuffs. It produced pottery, glass-ware, and all kinds of utensils in iron and bronze. If the Arab authors are to be believed, its countryside was an enchantment, a paradise of shade and greenery.

Most of these advantages and these beauties were no more than a memory at the time of the conquest of Granada by the Christians. On the other hand, Málaga had preserved all its importance and all its wealth. It was still the rendezvous of the Barbary ships. It was thither that flowed the alms collected throughout African Islam to carry on the holy war against the Christians of Spain. Musulman fraternities, analagous with the French fraternities *de la Merci* or *de la Trinité*, were established there to ransom Musulman prisoners and slaves in Christian territory. Finally, it was at Málaga that were unladen the ships bringing arms, munitions and even troops sent to the support of the sovereigns of Granada by the Sultan of Morocco.

On account of this great strategic importance of Málaga, and of its famous citadel of Gibralfaro, which was regarded as impregnable, Ferdinand began his campaign by laying siege to this rich and strong city, and ended by capturing it. Its customs dues were to be an important source of revenue to the treasury of Castile, apart from its

[1] *Zebibi* appears to have been a wine manufactured out of dried grapes.

still considerable commerce: its figs, its raisins, and its famous wines, whose manufacture was increased by the Christians. I may also mention its gilt porcelain, which at that time enjoyed a Mediterranean reputation.

But all these places were eclipsed by Granada, of which the Spaniards, like the Arabs, speak with a kind of amorous exaltation. It must be admitted that this city, so loved and so celebrated, possesses a charm to which we are still subject to-day, and which the Spaniards of the sixteenth century must have felt more intensely than we do, despite the presence of an execrated race and the almost intact environment of a civilisation which they would have liked to destroy—a charm which is at first sight enigmatic; for Granada is not what is called a fine city, nor is it a comfortable or agreeable place in which to live.

Marmol says that it resembled Fez, and that the citadel of the Alhambra resembles that of Fez Djedid. He adds this illuminating comment: "The Kings of Granada always imitated those of Fez; and their cities, in site, appearance, buildings, administration and the rest of it, much resemble Moroccan cities." The analogy is certainly striking. When you contemplate Granada from the heights of the Albaycin, this city built in tiers, with its terraces descending sharply towards the steeply banked bed of the Darro, you are in fact reminded of the Moroccan capital as it is seen from that belvedere where are the tombs of the Merinides.

But it is especially the colour, the atmosphere, which are the same: the tawny, bare mountains in the distance, quite African in their ruggedness and nakedness; and, sloping down the ridge in which the river is swallowed up, the white and mauve tones of the buildings, the burning red of the roofs, and the pale green of the porcelain which armours the campaniles of the churches and the *koubas* of the old Moorish pavilions. One thinks also of Tlemcen, whose countryside, however, is greener and better watered than the *vega* of Granada. One thinks of it especially because of Sidi Bou Medine, which strangely recalls the Generalife, quite white in its belt of cypresses.

The landscape remains African. But the city of to-day is not in the least like what it must have been under the Moorish kings. If we wish to get an idea of it, we must deliberately close our ears to the extravagances which the Arab authors tell us about it. They tell us that it numbered more than two hundred thousand inhabitants, that its fortified area was flanked by thirteen thousand towers, that it contained more than sixty thousand houses, and all the rest of it. Marmol, who interrogated Musulmans contemporary with Moorish Granada, and may have seen the city very much like what it was at the time of the conquest, gives us much more modest figures.

"When the Moors possessed it," he says, " and especially under

Abou Hassan, about the year 1476 of the Christian era, Granada had thirty thousand inhabitants. There were, besides, eight thousand horse, more than twenty-five thousand crossbowmen, and three days sufficed to assemble there fifty thousand men at arms, come from the Alpujarra, from the Sierra, and from the Granadine valleys and countryside." Marmol, moreover, reduces to thirteen hundred the number of towers that flanked the enclosure—which remains a respectable figure.

It follows that the Moorish city, if we add the soldiers of the permanent garrison to the civil population, had scarcely more than sixty-three thousand inhabitants: a total decidedly less than that of the present population, which is about one hundred thousand.

But one has only to follow the line of the old ramparts, of which important remains subsist, to realise that the area of the Moorish city, like that of Caliphal Cordova, was much less than that of the modern city. The old city appears to have been divided and subdivided into a network of quarters or islets, enclosed within walls, such as is still to be seen in the Moroccan cities and as was to be seen also in Europe in the cities of the Middle Ages.

The chief quarter, to begin with the oldest, was that of the Albaycin, built on the slope of a hill which runs down very steeply to the rocky bed of the torrent and forms, in conjunction with the closely neighbouring hill of the Alhambra, a regular rocky gorge. This quarter was the true heart of the Moorish city. The first emirs of Granada constructed there a fortress which was called the Alcazaba Kadima, or the Old Citadel.

Another quarter, contiguous with this, comprised the Alcazaba Djedid, or New Citadel; and finally there was the Albaycin properly so-called, which occupied the highest part of the hill. Opposite, on the ground with a gentle slope which runs down to the *vega*, are the more modern quarters of Zenete, Bibarambla, and Antequeruela.

As to the Alhambra, which dominates both the upper city and the lower city, it was very early—from the end of the ninth century—a fortified place. The Granadine princes, following the example of the Cordovan emirs, who did not feel very safe in their capital, preferred to establish themselves outside its walls, in a strong castle, whence they could keep their subjects under surveillance and defend themselves against them in case of insurrection. But the Alhambra did not reach its full development and attain its full splendour until the dynasty of the Nasserites, that is to say at the end of the thirteenth century and especially in the fourteenth.

Granada, like all Musulman cities, had no monumental character. "The streets," says Marmol, "were so narrow that from a window one could touch the one opposite by stretching out his arm. There were quarters where men on horseback and carrying lances in their hands simply could not pass." The houses were small and narrow, with very thick walls and no exterior ornamentation. The principal public buildings were the mosques, which were very numerous, the Koranic schools, the *medersas*, and the hospitals.

Marmol adds that these buildings were constructed along African lines—"*a la usanza africana.*" It seems more correct to say that they were African houses built in the Spanish style, inasmuch as the Berbers, especially the Moroccans, did nothing but imitate their co-religionists of Spain: that Spain which was regarded, in their eyes, as the fatherland of art and enlightenment. Marmol, contemporary with a Spain already re-Christianised, who had travelled in Africa, may well have made the error of confusing the imitation with the original: he was not acquainted with Musulman houses other than those of Africa.

It does not appear, in any case, that these buildings were anything out of the way. Otherwise, despite all vandalism and all religious or æsthetic prejudices, they would have been preserved, as were the Mosque of Cordova, the Alcázar of Seville, and the Alhambra itself.

The *souks*, for reasons of public utility, were preserved longer. As in all the cities of Barbary, they were surrounded by high walls and closed with heavy gates, strongly bolted and barred with iron. There was what was called the *Alcaicería*, the great silk market, whose remains subsisted until modern times: narrow booths like those of the old Roman markets, of which the *souks* are only a survival, a maze of lanes, often covered by vaulting, in which the merchants grouped themselves together in accordance with the nature of their commerce.

Everything which is still sold in such places was sold there. But there were Granadine specialities in the way of stuffs and jewellery, necklaces, ear-rings, and silks and brocades of gold which were especially renowned. The women, it appears, were very elegant, and fond of rich and striking stuffs and of all the adornments of luxury.

One of the obstacles to the conversion of the Moriscos was the obligation which was imposed upon them to change their Moorish costume for the sober and severe Castilian costume. The Spanish Moors clothed themselves in a way which foreshadowed that of the Algerian Moors of to-day. The women, veiled in white and with their faces completely covered, except for the eyes, wore trousers and plaited stockings which made their legs inordinately fat.

According to Andrea Navagero, the Venetian ambassador, who visited Granada in 1526, they were shod in little shoes very neatly worn, like our Algerian Moorish ladies. Finally, according to the same witness, they wore in their hair high combs, whose shape could be seen through their veils: a detail of fashion which has been preserved by the Andalusian women, and of which something is to be found even to-day in the coiffure of the women of Tlemcen.

Places of business on small lines and modest shops, the *souks* are only exceptionally great commercial centres. At Granada wealth and government revenue were derived from other sources. Much has been made of the weaving of silk, which still persisted there at the time of the conquest. These looms must have been beginning to vegetate, threatened as they were by Italian competition ; but they made shift to live for some time longer. The silk industry had existed for centuries in Spain, where it was not introduced by the Arabs, as is continually repeated, but was already flourishing in Roman and Visigoth times, when it was the subject of special regulation.

The major part of private fortunes, as of national wealth, was derived in Granada, as elsewhere in the kingdom, from the fruits of the soil. It is unquestionable that at that period the *vega* was excellently cultivated, and covered with gardens and orchards, watermills and windmills, farms and villages, villas and country houses.

These retreats of shade and verdure, these oases bursting with flowers and fruits, the abundance of water in a region of intense heat and general aridity, at all times aroused passionate admiration and recognition on the part of travellers. Still, neither these beauties of the countryside, nor the natural amenities, nor the dazzling sunshine, nor the sublimity of the sierras—none of these things would suffice to explain the charm of Granada, where one might pass by carelessly enough, were it not that, along with all these advantages, it possesses something unique : namely, the astonishing perfection of its Alhambra.

There is, nevertheless, something else to be seen at Granada : there is a magnificent cathedral, which is one of the masterpieces of the Spanish architecture of the Renaissance. Alongside this cathedral there is also a sacrarium, occupying the site of the principal mosque of the Moors (a fact which at least proves that this mosque was not very large) : a chapel-royal in which is the mausoleum of Ferdinand and Isabel. Finally there are the Lonja and the old Chapter House, which in their way are little masterpieces too.

But all these pale into insignificance beside the outstanding grace of the Alhambra and of its satellite, the Generalife. The marvellous cathedral of Granada has its counterparts in Spain herself, to begin with in its nearest neighbour, that of Seville. The Alhambra and the Generalife have no analogies. There is nothing that resembles them. They are as extraordinary in their perfection, measure for measure, as the Parthenon or the little temple of the Wingless Victory.

It must be recognised that chance has its part to play in this perfection : it is the fortuitous meeting of an accomplished work of art and a great, or a charming, setting. The Alhambra, in short, is no more than a *kasbah*, an *alcázar*, such as are to be found throughout the lands of Islam : like Medina az Zahara, like Fez Djedid. But these sumptuous edifices lack a pedestal.

Dismount the Parthenon from its Acropolis, and it is diminished down to, if not below, the level of the temple of Paestum. Dismount the Alhambra from its hill, deprive it of the altitude of its towers and its walls falling sheer to the gorges of the Darro, rob it of its view of the Albaycin as a background—and it is reduced to the same level as the Alcázar of Seville, which is larger, richer, is in parts as fine, and opens upon splendid gardens.

The Alhambra and the Generalife are masterpieces made out of nothing, whose charm depends upon the intimate collaboration of all kinds of external influences and circumstances, which unite with the resources of an art bordering upon perfection. As to this art itself, in what does it consist? It is an affair of plaster, wood, brick, arrayed in mouldings. It is a fragile setting which has no pretensions to lasting, and has had to be restored over and over again. This gallery, or that belvedere, stands all awry.

Yet the architects who grouped these effects, who arranged these vistas, have made mediocre material and cheapness yield the maximum of advantage in the way of amenity and beauty. These plasters crumble away, they are coloured in crude or common tones—which are not always modern restorations. But the artists in stucco who worked upon them were endowed with a startling and never equalled imaginativeness.

These so much vaunted gardens and courtyards are little flowerbeds and squares. Only the Court of Myrtles, with its mirror of water, satisfies the demands of our eyes. The Court of Lions strikes us as congested and crowded; it lacks proportion. These stuccos seem cut out of cardboard, these columns all in a row seem mean and flat as wood-carvings. These little rose-jets of water which scatter a scanty shower; these little water-channels; these little basins; these pigeon-baths; these lawns on which a meagre verdure withers; these few roses, these few jessamines; these pots of flowers here and there; these glazed pantiles and porcelain—all this is utterly simple and puerile; it is the very infancy of art. The greenery itself is restricted to a few shrubs.

To create some shade around the Alhambra, it was necessary for the English to come along and plant some elms—the English know what they are doing where trees are concerned. But this fine British park, which serves as a vestibule to the palace of Boabdil, and which tourists take to be a Moorish creation, is regarded as extremely commonplace by comparison with the little courtyard of Lindaraja, where there is nothing to be seen but a fountain inside four walls and half a dozen cypresses.

One can understand the contempt of the architects of Charles V for these dolls' gardens, these kiosks in plaster and brick, all this mediocre material. It was in fine marble that they preferred to build—and build edifices which defied the centuries. They started their own masterpiece opposite the Moorish rubbish-heap—a heavy barracks, which in some of its proportions is nevertheless admirable. But this colossal palace, with its pretensions to overwhelm everything, cannot stand up for a moment against the fragile miracles of the Granadine stucco-workers, gardeners, and architects.

Who were these artists and architects? Whence did they come? The Alhambra is a unique creation, whose antecedents and themes of inspiration may indeed be found elsewhere, which itself served as a model; but it is of such clean-cut originality that it could not have arisen anywhere but where it stands. It is a product of the soil. Those who summoned this piece of fairyland out of the ground, like those who raised the mosque of Cordova, could not have been anything but Spaniards, sons of a country of delight, a country of sculptors and builders.

We know for a fact that a number of Christian captives worked on the Alhambra, either as decorators or as simple artisans. Some critics profess to see in it, or at least in certain parts of the edifice, the achievement of Christian artists.[1] The arabesques of the Barka and those of the Court of Lions admit floral elements, notably corols of jessamine, which are contrary to the canons of Musulman art. It is quite possible. But it is equally admissible that the authors of these marvellous embroideries of stucco were Musulman Spaniards influenced by the ornamental sculpture of the Visigoth artists.

The Visigoth sculptors and ornamenters in Spain appear to have rivalled the Musulman stucco-workers: the former did with stone and marble what the latter did with stucco. It was a question who could push decorative exuberance and complexity furthest. In any case, the influence of Gothic seems obvious in the Alhambra, in the paintings of the Hall of Justice as well as in the arabesques of the Barka and the Court of Lions.

Yet the two arts, the Gothic and the Moorish, appear to be mutually exclusive. They proceed from opposed principles. The first is wholly penetrated with life and intellect. Not only does it strive to reproduce all living forms; it also speaks to the mind. It desires to instruct It suggests a conception of the world and of life. It is human and serious.

The second lays claim to nothing but an appeal to the eye. It is an art which is extremely sensual. It seeks voluptuousness much more than beauty. That is why one stands disarmed in the presence of it. It conquers you with the minimum of effort. It is the courtesan who has only to present herself naked before her judges to make them yield.

Contemplate the Court of Myrtles one evening, at the hour of twilight. I know no enchantment comparable with it. You have around you nothing but bare walls framing a mirror of water. At the two ends of the courtyard two galleries extend their arcature under a lacework of stucco. In the background the battlements of the Tower of Comares stand out against the sheen of the sky—a powerful, war-like masonry which contrasts with the fragility and grace of the

[1] Cf. Georges Marçais: *Manuel d'Art Musulman*, Vol. II, p. 640.

arabesques, with the wide, warm orange surfaces still tinged with the splendour of the setting sun.

At your feet lies the shining surface of the quadrangular basin, which reflects all these reposeful, magnificent forms. There is the pearly tinkle of a fountain or a jet of water dropping into a vase. A fresh breeze, coming from the snowy mountains, adds its caress to the perfume of myrtle and jessamine still burning with the heat of the day. In the distance, beyond the shady halls with their stalactite cupolas, is the double arch of a single window, whose middle column stands out divinely against the background of an aery landscape bathed in all the lights of Paradise.

One does not say for a moment: "How fine this is! How uplifting this is!" but "How delicious this is! How charming it is here! I wish I could stay here always!"

On January 2 of the year of grace 1492, in the morning, the Catholic Sovereigns made their solemn entrance into the Alhambra. They had just planted the silver Cross and the standard of Castile on the Watch Tower. On the threshold of the Citadel, the *alcaide* Youssef Aben Comija had handed over the keys to Their Highnesses.

But these grave personages had no eyes either for the wonderful landscape or the miracles of art which surrounded them. Perhaps they were only half sure of themselves when they penetrated into this last retreat of their vanquished enemy. In any case serious anxieties must have absorbed their thoughts. They entrusted the keys of the fortress to the Count de Tendilla, whom they appointed their Captain-General of the Kingdom of Granada. They had the ramparts and the towers occupied by their infantry. Then, after receiving a delegation of notables, they spent their first night in that unknown palace, above a city silent, secret, and seemingly deserted.

CHAPTER XVII

The Surrender of Granada and the Expulsion of the Moors

THIS surrender did not make an end of anything. In history as in life, there is no such thing as an end: everything begins all over again. It would be a mistake to suppose that, after the taking of Granada, Spanish Islam was decisively vanquished—that there was nothing left except, on the one side, faithful subjects of the Catholic Sovereigns, honest Musulmans who asked only to be allowed to live in peace, and, on the other side, fanatical Christians, intent upon persecuting them.

In reality there was still in Spain a foreign people, once victorious and conquering, now momentarily beaten, but awaiting a revenge foretold by prophecies, as its defeat had been. This people was not confined to the narrow limits of the kingdom of Granada. Its ramifications extended throughout all Spain. It maintained constant relations and contact with its co-religionists in Africa. It was restless and still to be feared.

Outside the Peninsula it was not understood in the first place why the Christian reconquest had been so slow, and, above all, why the Spaniards, now that they were masters of the country again, did not exterminate or expel the Moors once and for all. As far back as the thirteenth century, at the time of the great Almohade peril, when contingents from beyond the Pyrenees came to the help of the Castilians, these allies of theirs were indignant at the comparative leniency of the Spaniards towards Moors who were defeated or compelled to surrender.

After the victory of Las Navas, the Archbishop of Narbonne, who was among the combatants, openly complained about the capitulation proposed by the inhabitants of Ubeda, which guaranteed them possession of their city and the surrounding territory, together with their property. According to the archbishop, this was "an arrangement made against God," a veritable sacrilege. Later, when François I was a prisoner of Charles V, and the story of the conquest of Granada was read to him, it appears that he exclaimed: "And these Musulmans? They were not driven out? Then everything is still to be done!"

Events more and more justified the view of the King of France, who was reasoning here as a political realist. But neither the French nor any other foreigners could understand the practical motives which dictated the conduct of the Castilian and Aragonese princes. In maintaining the Moors in Spanish territory, in granting them what was called "the share of the Mudéjares"—that is to say, the convention specifically made with the Musulmans living on Christian soil—they were solely concerned with avoiding the depopulation of the reconquered territories. They did not want to ruin either the commerce or the agriculture of their new domains.

Besides, it was a long-standing custom among the Christian princes to prefer protectorate, with payment of tribute, to complete conquest and expulsion or extermination. For centuries they had lived on tribute paid by the Moors. In the same way as the Moors for centuries had "consumed the Christians," so, since they had become the stronger, they had started consuming their enemies. There were thus created and maintained supporting territories, tributaries which cost nothing and paid handsomely. Indeed, it seemed quite natural and even quite just to take the conquered enemy's money and sell him for hard cash the right to live and possess. Given this system, it was no wonder that the reconquest dragged on so long.

It must be recognised, moreover, that this system did not involve too much inconvenience so long as the Catholic Sovereigns found themselves confronted by an Islam divided into a swarm of little states, which they could always play off one against the other. The situation changed when, in opposition to a unified Spanish Christianity, there remained only a confused mass of Musulmans united only by religious belief, hatred of the conqueror, and desire for independence.

Superficially the territories formerly occupied by the Moors were all reconquered. They were so only on paper. Parchments, covered with signatures and duly sealed with leaden seals hanging by silk threads, recognised the Spanish sovereigns' possession of the towns and fortresses which had surrendered to them. As much by guile and diplomacy as by force of arms, they were the victors. Then they had to accept the consequences of conquest: either assimilate the vanquished, or else eliminate them.

The greatest error of all is to suppose that, for the Spaniards, the maintenance of the Moors in their national territory reduced itself to a question of liberty of conscience. Liberty of conscience is never more than a pretext, which always covers material interests of the most tangible character. If motives of a religious kind were advanced to justify the expulsion or conversion of the Moors, the real motives, or at least the most pressing, were of a political kind.

In default of forming a clear idea of the political side of the problem, most modern historians have judged it in the most unreasonable way. They speak of this tragic affair as though it were solely a matter of principle, as though it all resolved itself for the Spaniards into a question of showing tolerance and Christian charity. They refuse to see that after the taking of Granada, as before it, Spain was partly occupied by a foreign people, with whom the Spaniards could have nothing in common: a people fixed in their religion, their language, and their customs, who proposed to go on living there as though they were at home, detested their rulers and neighbours, and maintained relations with peoples which were enemies of Spain and Christianity—the Berbers, the Moroccans, the Egyptians, the Turks—and plotted with them.

One must be completely blinded by prejudice, or have no sense of historical realities, to fail to see how dangerous the presence of the Moors in the territory of Spain was to the Spaniards. Imagine the situation if, say, the French had, not only on their marches, in Lorraine, in Champagne, and in Franche-Comté, but even in Provence and Languedoc, whole populations of Germans, installed in their towns and their countryside, proposing to remain German and learning nothing of French language or French usages, continuing to live as a separate "nation," and finally trafficking and intriguing with their compatriots on the other side of the Rhine.

The answer is supplied by facts. When they recovered Alsace and Lorraine, which the Germans had annexed, the French began by expelling a number of Germans whose presence in French territory seemed to them dangerous. Everybody found this measure quite natural and perfectly legitimate. Similarly nobody took exception when the government of Mustapha Kemal expelled a million and a quarter of Greeks from Asia Minor.

It is true that the reasons invoked were political reasons. Nevertheless, in the case of the Turks, the real and fundamental reasons were of a religious kind. It is a wretched business to mix up religion with these brutal measures of national security. That is what has aroused so much hatred against the Spaniards. But in the sixteenth century, as in the Middle Ages, political measures were masked by religious pretexts, just as to-day they are masked by racial, social or humanitarian considerations. It is in the name of humanity that millions of Russians have been exterminated or driven to take flight by the Soviets.

Fundamentally, it is always a question of suppressing the adversary, of taking his property or his purse. But we require an ideal to veil or colour human weaknesses. Humanity does not dare to be frankly frightened or nakedly ferocious. It was, alas! in the name of Heaven that the Spaniards exterminated and expelled the Moors; but it must be recognised that in doing so they had the best of worldly reasons.

I may add that they had, above all, the example of the Moors themselves, and, in addition, an appetite for vengeance and reprisal which had been awaiting its satisfaction for centuries. We have seen that, under the Emirs of Cordova, as under the Almohades, whole populations of Spaniards, Christians and Musulmans, had been massacred, deported or exiled, forced to abjure or die. It was this violence, these bloodthirsty proceedings, which provoked the reprisals of the Spaniards and made them, in their turn, fanatical and merciless.

Finally we should not forget that, at the time of the war of Granada, Barbary piracy was more than ever afflicting the coasts of Andalusia and the East of Spain; that thousands of Spaniards were regularly being reduced to slavery by the Moors of Africa; that the Christians in their turn were bent upon capturing Barbaresques; and that it was a war without mercy, in which each side tried to do the other the utmost possible harm.

But, I repeat, we are not concerned to justify or condemn either the one side or the other. History is not a special pleader. It seeks to explain, to understand, to discover the causes of events and disclose the motives of human actions. Let us see, then, how the situation presented itself to the Catholic Sovereigns, on the morrow of the taking of Granada.

The Moors were very far from being crushed. The proof that they had not ceased to be formidable was that fighting against them had been going on for ten years, and no longer in a little war of skirmishes and raids, but in a regular campaign involving large numbers of men, an imposing amount of artillery, and a whole field train. Despite this great effort, the Spaniards had succeeded in taking only the principal fortresses. Moreover, they had obtained surrenders such as those of Málaga and Baza only after more or less dubious dealings which strongly resembled treachery on the other side.

Granada itself would have been very difficult to take by force of arms. The Spaniards confined themselves to besieging it on the side of the *vega*. But this blockade was quite inadequate, as the communications of the besieged on the side of the mountains remained entirely free.

Finally, in despair of anything else, Isabel caused a rival city to be constructed opposite Granada, Santa-Fé, where her army would remain indefinitely until Granada capitulated. It was the Arab system, employed notably by El Mansour to reduce Tlemcen. The prospect of an interminable siege, maintained by a numerous army, alone decided the notables and King Abou Abdilehi (Boabdil) to surrender.

Conscious of their strength and their number, they proposed their own terms to the Spaniards. They treated with them as equals with equals. In short, there were neither victors nor vanquished. This was why the Moors thought that they could show themselves exacting, while the Catholic Sovereigns, realising how insecure their opportunity was, gave proof in the matter of really extraordinary generosity and spirit of conciliation. This capitulation, which comprised no less than fifty-five articles, is worth studying in detail. It shows in how much of a hurry Ferdinand and Isabel were to end the war, and, accordingly, how ready they were to make any concessions.

On the Spanish side the dominant idea was to persuade the Granadines that, in capitulating, they were merely passing under the protection of masters much gentler than their Musulman princes.

Instead of being ground down by greedy tyrants who loaded them with taxes and were incapable of defending them, they were to become the faithful vassals of powerful lords, who would treat them 'with kindness and consideration.

One point to which the contracting parties revert repeatedly is this: "It is established and agreed that the governors and officers of justice appointed by Their Highnesses shall be such as will be capable of respecting the Moors, and treating them well."

The Christian soldiers were forbidden to enter the mosques without the permission of the faquis, to go into Moorish houses, steal fowl or beasts, or give balls and feasts against the wishes of the inhabitants. Further, on the day of Their Highnesses' entrance into the Alhambra, the Christian troops did not march through the city. They took a roundabout route, outside the walls, in order to avoid any provocation. Finally, the Spanish soldiers were not allowed to set foot on the ramparts which separated the Alcazaba from the Albaycin, whence they could have cast indiscreet eyes upon Moorish dwellings. It would have been impossible to be more respectful towards the vanquished and their usages and susceptibilities.

They were, of course, granted complete liberty of conscience and freedom of public worship. They preserved their mosques, their minarets, and their muezzins. Conversions to Christianity were to be unforced. "The Moors shall be judged by their own laws, in accordance with the decisions of their cadis. They shall maintain, and be maintained in, their usages and good customs."

They were to retain their property, movable and immovable. In regard to taxes, "they shall not give and pay others to Their Highnesses than those which they give and pay to the Moorish kings." A capital clause was that they owed no military service. "It is established and agreed that the Moors shall not be summoned or constrained to any service of war against their will."

If they did not wish to be subjects of the Catholic Sovereigns, they had the option of emigrating to "the other side of the sea," in other words, to Africa. Ships chartered by Their Highnesses would transport them there in all security. They could pass freely to Barbary or Morocco with their property and their merchandise, their gold, their silver, their jewels, and even their arms, fire-arms excepted.

If they were not satisfied "on the other side of the sea," if they found themselves molested—as was to be foreseen—by their co-religionists there, they had the right to return to the kingdom of Granada within a period of three years, and they would then enjoy all the advantages contained in the capitulation.

Merchants could come and go freely and in all security to transact their business "on the other side of the sea," in other words anywhere in Africa. "They may travel and traffic in all the provinces subject to Their Highnesses, without paying more excise dues than the Christians pay."

The markets and the slaughterhouses of the Christians were to be separated from the markets and slaughterhouses of the Moors. Their merchandise and provisions were not to be intermingled with those of the Christians. They were to conserve their aqueducts and their fountains. They were to drink their own water. The Christians were forbidden to drink it or wash clothes in it.

All this was summed up in the preliminary formula: "The Moors shall be favoured and well treated by Their Highnesses and their honourable officers as good vassals and servants."

It was too good to be true for the Moors, and it was disastrous for the Catholic Sovereigns. Such a treaty amounted purely and simply to recognition of a "Moorish nation" maintained in Spanish territory in a privileged position—no military service, right to be judged by a special jurisdiction, right to travel in Barbary and traffic there with other Musulmans.

One is driven to ask how Ferdinand and Isabel could have put their signatures at the foot of such conditions, and done so in the most strictly and solemnly binding formulæ: "We assure, promise and swear by our faith and royal word that we will observe, and make observed, everything herein contained, everything and every part, now and hereafter, now and forever."

Did they sign this capitulation only for the purpose of bringing to an end a costly war, which had been going on for ten years, and with the secret intention of breaking their engagements? It is quite possible in the case of Ferdinand. It is less admissible in the case of a Christian as pious as Isabel. Perhaps she really believed, at the outset, that everything could be settled in a friendly way, given plenty of goodwill on both sides.

Certain members of the clergy themselves, such as the first Archbishop of Granada, Don Fernando de Talavera, were in favour of the broadest tolerance. "They are children," this prelate said of the Moors; "they must be nourished with milk." This missionary spirit was convinced that, by dint of charity, it was possible to educate and convert them. Perhaps, too, the victorious sovereigns were subject to that common and always reborn illusion, which consists in believing that the vanquished may stretch out his hand to the victor, because it suits the latter to forget the harm they have done one another.

If Ferdinand and Isabel began by sharing this illusion, they were not to keep it long. To know where they stood, they had only to cast an eye over their new conquest, and take stock of the position in which they had themselves placed the Moors in their respective states.

The situation was far from being reassuring to them. They occupied, in fact, only Granada, the surrounding cities, and the maritime towns. Apart from these, the coasts were not safe: they were infested by Barbaresque pirates and spies. The inhabitants of the little ports and the coastal villages concerted plans with the Africans for descents and raids inland. The whole mountainous centre, and notably the region of the Alpujarras, was peopled almost exclusively by rebels, declared or secret. A mistake had been made in allowing these warlike mountaineers, like the rest of the population, to retain their arms.

These Moors of Andalusia were mostly of Berber origin, in other words, Africans who could not fail to detest the Spaniards and be detested by them. It is generally forgotten that racial hatreds are at the bottom of all fanaticisms and all religious hatreds.

Another piece of imprudence was the permission granted to the Moors to cross over to Africa, where they went to swell the number of pirates and enemies of Spain and Christendom. Still worse, those who stayed behind were permitted to travel in Barbary and do business there—in other words, maintain relations with the worst enemies of the Spanish Sovereigns. Spies were thus benevolently provided for future invaders or for the ordinary pirates who perpetually made clandestine descents on the Andalusian coast. Realisation of these grave errors came quickly. Later, instead of the expelled Moors being directed towards Barbary, they were compelled to proceed to Biscay and Catalonia.

The worst danger was that not only was the kingdom of Granada mainly peopled by Moors, but also they were established throughout the Peninsula. There were *Mudéjares*, as they were called, in Castile, in Aragón, in the old kingdom of Valencia, and even in León. Those of Granada were now authorised to circulate freely in all the Spanish provinces. It was obvious that an intolerable situation was being created and that the Musulmans were being positively encouraged to form a dangerous solidarity.

Side by side with this internal danger there was the external danger, which, at that moment, was even worse. If Barbary was divided and its sovereigns no longer had anything more than a nominal authority, the Barbaresque corsairs, protected by the Turks, were increasing all the time. Since the taking of Constantinople, the Ottoman menace had become a nightmare for Europe. The Moors of Andalusia went on repeating that at any moment the fleets of the Sultan, in alliance with those of the Barbaresque pirates, would once more invade Spain.

This popular belief kept the Musulman masses in a more or less latent state of effervescence and rebellion. In fact they relied quite openly upon these protectors of Islam. Some years after the capitulation, when the Catholic Sovereigns compelled the Moors to become converts or cross over to Barbary, those of the Albaycin dispatched emissaries to the Sultan of Egypt to demand his intervention. He threatened the Spanish Sovereigns with reprisals against the Christians of Asia, and they were reduced to sending the first prior of the

Cathedral of Granada, Pedro Martir, to furnish him with explanations and put before him letters signed by the authorities of the maritime towns of Barbary, attesting that the expelled were being treated by the Spaniards with all possible consideration.

All this was sufficiently humiliating for Ferdinand and Isabel, and the position of the Moors established in Spain became a more and more disquieting problem. They might present the appearance of the most peaceful submission, they might even become converts; they remained nevertheless fundamentally Musulmans, watching for a favourable opportunity and patiently awaiting the hour of revenge, promised by their prophecies.

So the taking of Granada, so much celebrated by the Castilians and by the whole of Christendom, did not seem at first sight to be more than a decorative event, which masked a very serious situation and a future full of menace. At the same time, the mere fact that there was no longer a single Musulman state in Spain was in itself a considerable result. But it was only the beginning of a long process of unification which was to last more than a century.

For Ferdinand and Isabel the most pressing task was that of preventing the cohesion of all the Moors scattered about the soil of the Peninsula. Their obviously designated intermediary was the Jew—the travelling, trafficking Jew.

The Spaniards still remembered the *rôle* which the Jews had played at the time of the invasion of Spain by the Musulmans. They had made a pact with the invaders, and provided garrisons to watch over the Christian cities and keep them in subjection. The Christians regarded them as traitors and as the natural allies of the Moors. Now that the whole of Spain had become Christian again, the Jews had no other resource but to lean upon the Musulmans, their sometime enemies.

This certainly seems to have been the reasoning which decided Isabel and Ferdinand to expel them from Spain, less than three months after the surrender of Granada. Besides, their money was wanted to defray the expenses of the war. Once again religious motives lent cover to a brutally cynical proceeding. On March 30, 1492, the decree of expulsion was signed.

After this preventive measure, the line of conduct adopted by the Spanish Government towards the Moors appears to have been this: to induce them to leave by an underhand system of oppression and by pressure aimed at bringing them to baptism. The illusion prevailed for a time that mass conversions might yield good results. It was reckoned that, failing the parents themselves, at least the sons of converts might make good Spaniards and good Christians.

This illusion was dispelled. Despite the most severe supervision, despite the terrible rigours of the Inquisition, the converted Moors, the *Moriscos* as they were called, remained obstinately Musulman.

They were a permanent danger to the Spanish state, especially when war or European politics provided them with favourable opportunities for trying to shake off the yoke.

At the end of the reign of Philip II, the Moriscos of Aragón made an offer to Henri IV of France to put at his disposal an army of eighty thousand men. It was not treason, inasmuch as these Moriscos regarded themselves as foreigners in Spain and were treated there as pariahs. But it is understandable that these malcontents and secret rebels should have remained a continual object of suspicion and anxiety on the part of the Spaniards.

So, after the expulsion of the Moors, the logic of the reconquest led the conquerors to expel the Moriscos as well. That this drastic procedure was disastrous for Spain there is not the shadow of a doubt. If a swarm of people profited by it, the country as a whole was impoverished, and above all it was depopulated.

It is idle to attempt hypocritically to disguise the fact that every conquest, like every revolution, is always an expropriation, more or less disguised. While the constables and the officers of justice had filled their pockets with the fines to which repressive regulations exposed the poor Moriscos, Christian merchants and landlords bought at bargain prices the houses and the lands which they abandoned when they were expelled. But the nobles who employed Moorish or Morisco peasants on their estates to till their land were furious at these expulsions, and they opposed them as far as they could, making themselves responsible for the peacefulness and submission of the suspects.

Indeed, the government of Madrid itself was dismayed at the thought of depopulating whole regions and ruining the commerce of towns. Philip II, despite his religious convictions, only very reluctantly brought himself to sign the edict which, in 1565, gave the Moriscos the choice between exile and sincere and complete conversion.

One can easily realise, therefore, what Spain lost through these radical measures of protection. But the truth is that there was an absolute incompatibility of temperament between her nationals and these foreigners, descendants of Africans. She could not keep them on her soil except at the price of subjecting them to armed force and constraining them to perpetual surveillance, as in colonial territory.

The Peninsula, with its unassimilable Moors and Jews, would have been nothing more than a transit territory, as the countries of the Levant still are to-day: a hybrid country, without unity, without character. Europe would have had its "Levantines" like Asia. Spain would have become one of those bastard countries which live only by letting themselves be shared and exploited by foreigners, and have no art, or thought, or civilisation proper to themselves.

As though they realised this, her rulers sacrificed everything to the task of political and religious unification. It is a surprising thing that, despite their terrible hecatombs, they diminished neither the military power of their country nor its capacity for expansion. After rudely rejecting all the foreign elements which might adulterate its strength of character, the Spanish genius, as though it had been contracted and driven in upon itself, acquired a unique originality.

Never did it give more abundant and more magnificent fruits than in that period of nearly a hundred and fifty years which followed the conquest of Granada, and which the Spaniards called their "Golden Century." Finally, and above all, thanks to this pitiless policy, Europe, threatened in the East throughout the sixteenth century and even in the seventeenth century by the advance of the Turks, was delivered in the West from the Musulman peril.

CHAPTER XVIII

The Balance-Sheet of the Arab Conquest

WHEN you travel in Greece of to-day, you are surprised at the fewness of the traces which the Turkish domination has left. At most in some little town, entirely European in appearance, you will find, if you look for it carefully, a minaret or the wall of a mosque which the Greeks forgot to demolish.

Similarly in Spain, though there the Musulman domination lasted very much longer, you must have good eyes to find Arab remains. Certainly many more exist than the uninformed tourist or traveller realises; but you have to look for them. The three most important monuments which have survived, namely the Alhambra of Granada, the Alcázar of Seville, and the Great Mosque of Cordova, clash so sharply with the buildings which surround them that they have the air of exotic edifices. So the spontaneous feeling of the passer-by is that Spain, like Greece, did everything she could to rid herself of Islamism.

It requires very little reflection to realize the utterly contradictory factors which separated the Christians from the Musulmans of Spain. Externally there was nothing in common between these two species of men inhabiting the same country: nothing either in costume or in manner of life. The miniatures of the Middle Ages show us the Andalusian Musulmans clothed in the Asiatic way, with turban and long robe, whereas the Castilians wear the helm and breeches of the men of the North. I have also insisted earlier upon the horror of the Christians for the dissolute life of the "pagans" of Andalusia.

Yet, though the external influence of the Arabs is but little to be seen in Spain, their moral influence, their action upon character and mentality, were more profound than is generally believed. At this point in our study, it is appropriate to ask ourselves in what this influence consisted and what the Spaniards owed to the Arab conquest.

What they certainly owed to the schools of Cordova, Seville and Saragossa was a variety of scholasticism, similar enough, for that matter, to that of our own universities of the Middle Ages. The scholasticism of the Arabs was in itself only a shadowy derivative of Greco-Latin scholasticism. The bulk of this teaching—terrible in its verbalism and almost entirely theological—reduced itself to some idea of medicine, mathematics, and astronomy, but especially of astrology, alchemy, and demonology. The occult part of the Judeo-Arab learning was what most attracted the Christians not only of Spain, but also of the whole of medieval Europe.

Let us recall, in this connection, that the basis of this scientific teaching was of Greek, Latin, or Persian origin. It was the philosophy of Aristotle which came back to the Latins of the West through the medium of the more or less faithful interpretation of Averroés.

In the way of art, the influence of the Arabs was certainly considerable. It was this art, invented and practised by Spaniards, that was the most original thing they produced. Mudéjar art was adopted, in the thirteenth, fourteenth, and fifteenth centuries, by the whole Christian community. If it acted upon Gothic, Gothic in its turn reacted upon it. It must be admitted that this action of the Mudéjar was not always very happy. It led the Spaniards to rival it in decorative overloading and complexity.

For example, the doorway of the cathedral of Salamanca clearly reveals how anxiety to rival arabesque led the Christian sculptors to work marble as the Moors worked plaster, in such a way as not to leave upon a wall the smallest surface empty of ornamentation. The same anxiety is apparent in a still more striking manner at the Audiencia of Barcelona, in the sculptures which decorate the entrance to the little chapel of Saint George. In this case there is even, in the Gothic forms, an evident imitation of the Mudéjar.

It is especially in the forms of Spanish poetry that one feels the Arab influence. The short poems of the *Romancero* recall the poetry of Andalusia through the character of their inspiration, which is either historical and warlike, or romantic and gallant. It is obvious that the refinements of style of Góngora are a throw-back to the Arab rhetoricians and versifiers, and that the popular improvisations of the modern Sevillians, in their famous *saetas*, is a traditional survival from the popular poetry of the Moorish improvisers of the time of Motamid and Ben Ammar.

But all this, after all, is very superficial. The influence of the Arabs and Berbers of Africa upon the Spanish character was radical in quite a different way. It may even be maintained that through contact with them the Spaniards became half Arabised or Africanised.

This Islamic impress is very visible among the contemporaries of the Cid, or among those of Isabel and Ferdinand. It is still evident among the subjects of Philip II. Later it may have diminished, or even become effaced on the surface; but it always reveals itself to a close observer as more or less latent.

In the first place there is an excessive individualism—that habit of indiscipline and anarchy, as a result of which two Arab chieftains could never get on together, and Musulman Spain was parcelled out into a swarm of little states, delivered up to political rivalries, torn by the warfare of tribe against tribe. It was the same individualism, the same jealous particularism, which so long prevented the unification of Christian Spain and, even after the establishment of the absolute monarchy, was to maintain in face of it vice-royalties very much attached to their privileges and a provincial autonomy that refused to abdicate.

It was the same spirit of indiscipline and anarchy which was to array against one another the conquerors of the New World, to such a point that half a dozen Spaniards could not find themselves together in a fort or a caravel without at once forming two or three parties bent upon destroying one another. These defects may always have existed among the Spaniards; but it must be conceded that the example set by the Arabs and the Berbers could not fail to intensify them.

Another bad example was the sinuosity of these Africans and Asiatics, their shifty ruses, their duplicity in the keeping of contracts. The historians who accuse the Spaniards of bad faith in their conventions with the Moors forget to tell us that the Moors were at least equally perfidious: it was merely a question who should outwit the other.

Habits of this kind are not easily lost. Given favourable circumstances, they tend rather to develop and perfect themselves. In the sixteenth century, Spanish diplomacy was notorious for its hidden traps and, in general, for its excessive craftiness. Louis XIV, in his *Memoirs*, still had to complain that the Spaniards could not sign a treaty without the idea of breaking their engagement at the back of their minds.

Lust for gold, bloodthirsty rapacity, the feverish pursuit of hidden treasure, application of torture to the vanquished to wrest the secret of their hiding-places from them—all these barbarous proceedings and all these vices, which the conquistadors were to take to America, they learnt at the school of the caliphs, the emirs, and the Moorish kings.

When the Almoravid Yousouf ben Teshoufin seized Granada, he opened the treasury of Abdallah, the prince whom he had dethroned: a prodigious treasury in which, in addition to great quantities of gold and silver, he found heaps of precious stones, among them a necklace of four hundred pearls of fabulous value. But, as Yousouf suspected Abdallah's mother of having hidden other riches, he subjected her to torture to make her reveal her hiding-places. That was not enough: fearing that she had not told him everything, the Almoravid ransacked even the foundations and the drains of the palace. The companions of Cortés and Pizarro acted no differently towards the Aztecs and the Incas.

Like the Moors, the Spaniards were to keep their women jealously sequestered and veiled. Gratings and duennas were to replace the harem and the eunuchs. There was the same secret and often bloodstained lust, the same habit of taking foreign concubines. The caliphs and the Moorish kinglings had Catalan and Basque slave-girls as their favourites. The Christian princes chose to imitate them. If they did not dare to install harems openly in their palaces, they had Musulman concubines. Alfonso VI, the suzerain of the Cid, had five wives, among whom was the Moorish Zaida, daughter of Motamid, King of Seville.

The worst characteristic which the Spaniards acquired was the parasitism of the Arabs and the nomad Africans: the custom of living off one's neighbour's territory, the raid raised to the level of an institution, marauding and brigandage recognised as the sole means of existence for the man-at-arms. In the same way as they went to win their bread in Moorish territory, so the Spaniards later went to win gold and territory in Mexico and Peru.

They were to introduce there, too, the barbarous, summary practices of the Arabs: putting everything to fire and sword, cutting down fruit-trees, razing crops, devastating whole districts to starve out the enemy and bring them to terms; making slaves everywhere, condemning the population of the conquered countries to forced labour. All these detestable ways the conquistadors learnt from the Arabs.

For several centuries slavery maintained itself in Christian Spain, as in the Islamic lands. Very certainly, also, it was to the Arabs that the Spaniards owed the intransigence of their fanaticism, the pretension to be, if not the people chosen of God, at least the most Catholic nation in Christendom. Philip II, like Abd er Rhaman or El Mansour, was Defender of the Faith.

Finally, it was not without contagion that the Spaniards lived for centuries in contact with a race of men who crucified their enemies and gloried in piling up thousands of severed heads by way of trophies. The cruelty of the Arabs and the Berbers also founded a school in the Peninsula. The ferocity of the emirs and the caliphs who killed their brothers or their sons with their own hands was to be handed on to Pedro the Cruel and Henry of Trastamare, those stranglers under canvas, no better than common assassins.

But the most lamentable thing of all was the permanent state of division and anarchy in which the Arabs kept Spain for centuries. Through their discords, their racial and tribal wars, their systematic and continual ravaging, their massacres and their deportations, they rendered her sterile and depopulated. They made a desert of her as of Northern Africa. Even to-day this country, only too largely arid and under-populated, bears the stigmata of the foreign conquest in the aspect of its soil as well as in the character of its inhabitants. The traveller through the mournful solitudes of La Mancha feels only too intensely that the Berbers of Africa have passed that way.

On balance, it can fairly be said that the Musulman domination was a great misfortune for Spain.

§ VI

THE DISCOVERY AND CONQUEST OF AMERICA

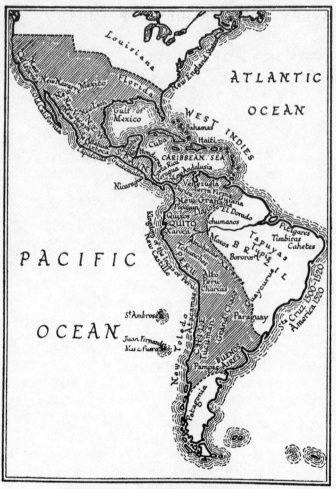

THE SPANISH POSSESSIONS IN AMERICA
From the sixteenth to the nineteenth centuries.

CHAPTER XIX

The Conquest of the New World, or the Last Crusade

GRANADA had no sooner opened its gates to the Catholic Sovereigns (January 2, 1492) than, after protracted discussion and prolonged hesitation, they decided to provide the funds for the expedition, long advocated by Christopher Columbus, which was to end in the discovery of the New World.

Its avowed object was to reach the East Indies, so as to take Islam in the rear, and to effect an alliance with the Great Khan—a mythical personage who was believed to be the sovereign of all that region, and favourable to the Christian religion—and finally, after the sectaries of Mahomet had been reduced to impotence, to diffuse Christianity throughout that unknown continent and trade with the traditional source of gold and spices.

These chimerical ideas and these very definite aspirations were in the air of that "*fin de siècle.*" All the hotheads, all the ardent or ambitious souls of that time, monks, soldiers, and adventurers, were obsessed by them. In short, it was the Crusade against the Moors which was to be continued by a new and surer route. It was by way of the Indies that Islam was to be dealt a mortal blow.

There are three facts which leave no room for doubt on this subject. The connection between them is so evident that Columbus himself noted it in his *Journal*, in a passage whose religious inspiration is obvious and whose substance—since the original is lost—Las Casas, the historian of the Indies, has preserved for us in the following terms:

"In the name of the Lord Jesus Christ, the Most Christian, the most high, the most excellent and most powerful princes, King and Queen of the Spains. . . . In this present year 1492, after Your Highnesses had brought to an end the war against the Moors who reigned in Europe, and *after Your Highnesses had terminated this war in the very great city of Granada*, where, in this present year, on the 2nd of the month of January, I saw, by force of arms, the royal banners of Your Highnesses planted on the towers of the Alhambra, the citadel of the said city, and where I saw the Moorish king come out of his gates and kiss the royal hands of Your Highnesses;

"And *immediately afterwards, in this same month*, in consequence of information which I had given Your Highnesses on the subject of India, and of the Prince who is called the 'Great Khan,' which, in our Roman, means 'the King of Kings'—namely, that many times he and his predecessors had sent ambassadors to Rome to seek doctors of our holy faith, to the end that they should teach it in India, and that never has the Holy Father been able so to do, so that accordingly so many peoples were being lost, through falling into idolatry and receiving sects of perdition among them;

163

"Your Highnesses, as good Christian and Catholic princes, devout and propagators of the Christian faith, as well as enemies of the sect of Mahomet and of all idolatries and heresies, *conceived the plan of sending me, Christopher Columbus, to this country of the Indies,* there to see the princes, the peoples, the territory, their disposition and all things else, and the way in which one might proceed to convert these regions to our holy faith.

"And Your Highnesses have ordered that I should go, not by land, towards the East, which is the accustomed route, but by the way of the West, whereby hitherto nobody to our knowledge has ever been. *And so, after having expelled all the Jews from all your kingdoms and lordships,* in this same month of January, Your Highnesses ordered me to set out, with a sufficient fleet, for the said country of India, and, to this end, Your Highnesses have shown me great favour. . . ."

It is of little importance that Columbus, writing after the event, should approximate his facts rather arbitrarily. It is nevertheless true that within the period of three months three great events occurred, which certainly seem to have a close connection among them. Probably, indeed, Columbus's impressions are more exact than chronology. If the capitulation of Granada occurred on January 2, 1492, the expulsion of the Jews on March 30, and the convention granted to the Discoverer on April 17, it is unquestionable that, as early as January of that same year, the Catholic Sovereigns had made up their minds to expel the Jews and to support the enterprise of the Genoese at the cost of the treasury.

As long as Granada had not surrendered, Ferdinand and Isabel were afraid of committing themselves to a maritime adventure which might prove very expensive—in fact they lacked the money for even the most modest expedition. Now that they were relieved of this anxiety, they were more inclined to lend ear to the wonderful promises of Columbus.

If they made up their minds in his favour, they would have to find the money. Well, it would be the Jews who would pay both for the expenses of the war against the Moors and for those of the Armada which was to discover the New World—that is to say, those chimerical Indies in which popular imagination saw the land of gold and spices.

But these mercenary motives were not the only ones. There were political and religious reasons as well. Inasmuch as the capitulation of Granada licensed the existence in Spanish territory of a Musulman population—no attempt had yet been made to convert it—it became a dangerous matter to allow the subsistence side by side with it of another dissident population, which, in case of persecution, had always tended to make common cause with it.

Besides, the mercantile Jews maintained relations of all kinds with the Musulmans of Africa, who already were in only too close contact with their co-religionists in Andalusia. Finally, the surrender of Granada had not eliminated the Islamic and African threat to Spain. Revolt was simmering not only in the region of the Alpujarras, but even in the heart of Granada, in the Moorish quarter of the Albaycin. If the Barbaresques, exasperated by the defeat of the Andalusian Moors, aided by the Ottoman fleet, and profiting by all kinds of connivance, should attempt a descent upon the Spanish coasts, the danger for the Catholic Sovereigns might become great.

It was especially the Ottoman menace which was to be feared. The Catholic Sovereigns realised that they had not finished with Islam. The Crusade, organised for the conquest of Granada, must be continued. For this last campaign had been a real crusade, for which the Pope had promulgated Bulls, accorded indulgences, and offered a massive silver Cross—the one which was planted on one of the towers of the Alhambra at the time of the entrance of Ferdinand and Isabel. The Spanish clergy and the Cardinal Archbishop of Toledo had contributed subsidies towards it.

Columbus's shrewdness consisted in dazzling the eyes of Isabel with the possibilities of a last Crusade, which, after all, would not be very costly and would definitely reduce Islam to impotence. The very terms of the text which I have just quoted proved conclusively that the Genoese had conceived his discovery as a pious enterprise of mass conversion. So it was that the discovery of America was the last Crusade against Islam.

To understand this properly, we must bear in mind the terror which the Turks had inspired throughout Europe since they had set foot there, and especially since the taking of Constantinople. As early as 1442, Pope Eugene IV issued an encyclical calling the Christians to arms against the Infidels, who were increasingly threatening the Empire and Italy. In 1459 Pius II, the learned Sylvius Aeneas Piccolomini, convoked an assembly of the Christian nations. at Mantua to concert means of combating the new barbarians. In the following year he proclaimed a holy war against the Turks.

But the Christian nations, at war with one another, made no response to the appeal of the Sovereign Pontiff. He refused to be discouraged. In November 1463, Pius II set himself at the head of a crusade against the Turks, and once more conjured the Christian world to unite against the common enemy. It was a fruitless effort. Europe took no interest in what was happening on the banks of the Danube.

In 1477, Mahomet II penetrated into Carniola, Styria, and Carinthia, and invaded Salzburg and Friuli. In the following year he occupied Albania. There he was at the gates of Italy. In 1480 he launched a fleet of a hundred sail against the town of Otranto and seized it. Now he was at the gates of Naples and of Rome.

The startled Pope addressed the most pressing adjurations to

Christendom. "The conquerors," said Sixtus IV, "spread themselves with insatiable avidity over the towns and the neighbouring country-sides. Nardi, Lecci, Castro, Brindisi, Bari are exposed to their out-rages or have already fallen into their power. Soon they will be masters of Sicily, of the Neapolitan kingdom, of the whole Penin-sula, if we remain plunged in the same inertia, if the princes and the peoples do not rise incontinent, hasten to arms, and lend one another mutual support, *to defend their fields and their homes, their children and their wives, their religion and their liberty.*

"Let them not think that they are protected against invasion, those who are at a distance from the theatre of war! They, too, will bow the neck beneath the yoke, and be mowed down by the sword, unless they come forward to meet the invader. The Turks have sworn the extinction of Christianity. A truce to sophistries! It is the moment not to talk, but to act and to fight!"

This, no doubt, was why this same Sixtus IV encouraged the Spanish crusade against Granada and sent the Catholic Sovereigns, by way of a standard, the famous massive Cross of silver which was finally planted on the Watch Tower of the Alhambra. To fight Islam in Andalusia was equivalent to depriving the Turks of ports of disembarkation and lessening the chances of invasion.

Accustomed as we are to-day to regarding the Turks as mere catspaws, or seeing them only through the spectacles of Loti's idyllic descriptions, we cannot imagine what terror the Ottoman fleets and Barbaresque corsairs inspired in the men of the fifteenth and sixteenth centuries, as much in Italy as in Spain and even in Provence.

The danger seemed so menacing that, in the very year which preceded the capitulation of Granada, Innocent VIII organised, once more, a Crusade to attack the Turks by land and sea. This time it was to be an operation of great scope, in which a dozen states were to take part. This ambitious project failed like all the others, and for the same reason: the indifference or the selfishness of the European peoples and potentates. Happily the Turks, like the Arabs and the Barbaresques, never exploited an advantage to the uttermost. They confined themselves to taking booty; and, when they had raided and pillaged a district or a town sufficiently, they disappeared, to begin over again at the first favourable opportunity.

It is nevertheless true that the Church, by playing the part of an alarmist, rendered a very great service to the Christendom of that time. The Popes, engaged like the princes in temporal interests and petty wars, had not always, perhaps, a very keen sense of the danger. On the other hand, the religious Orders, especially the Dominicans and the Franciscans, redoubled their vigilance against the old enemy of Christendom, that Islam which not only did not cease to menace it, but also appeared to close all avenues to its apostolate, by blockading against it the two extremities of the ancient world.

The monks may have believed for a time in the possibilities of a pacific or clandestine penetration. In the thirteenth and fourteenth centuries, they tried to make catechists in Morocco and in India. India especially attracted them, because they believed that it had already been evangelised by Saint Thomas. The audacity, the heroic intrepidity of the Franciscans was something almost inconceivable.

But, perpetually in contact with the Musulmans as they were— in the first place, in their capacity as guardians of the Holy Places— they were not slow to recognise that an apostolate, to be really efficacious, must lean upon armed force, or at least upon the power of a great nation capable of making itself respected at a distance.

Inasmuch as the European nations did not seem to understand the Islamic peril, could one not find, in Africa or even in the depths of Asia, peoples capable of counterbalancing the influence of Islam and even, if need be, of uniting against it? The Franciscans must have penetrated into Abyssinia as early as the thirteenth century. Now the Abyssinians were Christians. It was no doubt at the instigation of the Friars Minor that the Negus, at the end of the fourteenth century, sent emissaries to Europe to propose to the Christian princes an alliance against the Musulmans.

In 1391 a Franciscan, who had lived for several years in the country of the Negus, was presented by the Count de Foix to John I of Aragón. In 1427, Alfonso V received at Valencia, in the presence of the Cardinal-Archbishop of Foix, two Abyssinian ambassadors, who renewed this offer of alliance. In 1452 the presence of an Ethiopian ambassador in Lisbon was on record.

Two years later, in 1454, Pope Nicholas V dispatched a Bull to the King of Portugal, on the occasion of the discoveries and conquests made in Africa by the Infante Dom Henry, with the object of regularising the titles of possession of the Portuguese Crown in connection with the newly acquired African territories.

"The Infante," wrote the Pope, "bearing in mind that never within the memory of man has anyone been able to navigate this oceanic sea (the Atlantic Ocean), in order to proceed to the distant harbours of the Orient, that this was utterly unknown to the peoples of the West, and that the knowledge of these countries was nil, believed, accordingly, that he would give God the greatest testimony of submission if, through his agency, *one could render this oceanic sea navigable as far as the Indies, which are said to be subject to Christ. If he should enter into relations with these peoples, he would arouse them to come to the help of the Christians of the West against the Saracens and the enemies of the faith. At the same time, he would, with the royal permission, subject the pagans of those countries, not as yet infected by the Mahometan plague, by making known to them the name of Christ.*"

So here is sketched, twenty years in advance, the great idea of Christopher Columbus. It was of Portuguese origin. It is what was known as "the Plan of the Indies."[1] Let me add that the inspiration of it was entirely clerical. The idea was hatched, and perhaps launched, in Portugal by the monks. It was the missionaries of Abyssinia who elaborated it. The plan consisted, in the eyes of the Christians, in making alliance with the Negus and the fabulous Great Khan, King of India—India which was supposed to be Christian—in order to take Islam in the rear and begin, in the first place, by ruining its commerce in the Red Sea.

But how was one to approach the Negus and the Great Khan? Would it not be possible to reach the Indies by the route of the East, by following the coast of Africa? This was the *rôle* assigned to the Portuguese navigators in the development of the Plan of the Indies —whose object, let us remember, was to outflank Islam in order to make sure of beating it.

In proportion as the Portuguese discoveries multiplied along the African coast, this plan became more definite and its execution became easier. So it was that in 1487, five years before the discovery of America, Bartholomeu Diaz reached the Cape of Good Hope—in other words, the threshold of a world hitherto unknown. Henceforth it became possible to reach the Indies by the route of the East.

Columbus's great idea was that of reaching there by the route of the West. The Genoese was merely synthetising all the more or less chimerical ideas which had been in the air for the last half century at least, adding to them his own peculiar genius. It was to realise the dream so long cherished by pious imaginations—the dream of a final and definite Crusade against Islam by way of the Indies—that he asked the Catholic Sovereigns for the three poor little caravels which were to lead to the immense discovery.

[1] See, in this connection, the novel and most interesting study by Senhor Joaquim Bensuade: *Origin of the Plan of the Indies*, Coimbra, 1930, from which I have drawn the most penetrating suggestions.

CHAPTER XX

Christopher Columbus, Propagator of the Faith

IT has been denied that Columbus, in his first voyage, proposed to go to the Indies. His objective, so it is said, was simply unknown islands and lands whose existence had been revealed to him either at Lisbon, by his father-in-law Perestrello, or at Palos, by the brothers Pinzón, or, again, at Huelva, by Alonso Sánchez, that mysterious pilot whose strange story Garcilaso de la Vega has told us, and who was reported to have touched at San Domingo, about the year 1484, after a storm which lasted twenty-nine days. It was only later that the Genoese conceived his grandiose idea.

The argument on which this theory is based is that, in the agreement with Columbus signed in the month of April, 1492, by the Catholic Sovereigns, there is no precise mention of the Indies but only of lands to be discovered. This is easily explicable. Although it was possible that islands might be discovered in the oceanic sea, it was much less probable that one could reach the Indies by this route of the West. To the scientists of the period the idea was Utopian, and to the theologians it was a heretical and damnable proposition.

To count upon this problematical discovery was therefore a decidedly delicate and dangerous matter. In case of failure such an enterprise ran the risk of exposing its backers to ridicule. For all these reasons, it is likely that the sovereigns confined themselves to banking upon what seemed humanly possible.

It may be, for that matter, that Columbus had given them formal assurances on the subject of these unknown lands, in accordance with the information, true or false, which he had obtained at Lisbon, at Palos, or at Huelva. We know nothing about what was said at the private interviews which he had with them, and the most elementary prudence bound them to keep the secret.

But the proof that he undoubtedly had the intention of going to the Indies, and was sure of getting there, is that the Catholic Sovereigns furnished him with a letter of credentials to the unknown, and therefore anonymous, sovereign of these distant lands: a letter which has been discovered in the archives of the Kingdom of Aragón, and in which diplomatic subtlety went hand in hand with the most naïve simplicity. Here is the translation of this documetn, drafted in Latin, the universal language, which the Castilian chancellery naturally assumed would be understood by the Hindus:

"To the Most Serene Prince, our very dear friend. . . . According to reports which have been made to us by many of our subjects, and also other travellers come from your kingdom and the neighbouring regions, We have had the satisfaction of learning of your good disposition and your excellent intentions towards us and towards our State, and at the same time of your keen desire to be informed about our recent success. . . . In consequence whereof We have decided to send you as ambassador our Captain, the noble Christopher Columbus, bearer of these presents, from whom you may learn of our good health and our fortunate estate, as of other matters which we have ordered him to report to you on our behalf."

Certain historians have claimed that this open letter was addressed to the Negus of Abyssinia. That is quite possible. But it could equally have been addressed to that Great Khan of the Indies, whom people talked about without knowing him, and who was assumed to be a neighbour of the Negus. We have seen that the Pope counted upon him to ally himself with the Negus and the Christians of the West against the Saracens.

Let us admit, however, that no great importance is to be attached to this document. But why was it necessary to assemble a commission of learned men and theologians to examine Columbus's project, if it was a question only of islands to be discovered and of ordinary commercial interests? To explain this intervention of men of learning and the excitement aroused in scientific and religious circles by the ideas of Columbus, we must recognise that these ideas were in contradiction with official theories, and that they interested learning and religion alike in the highest degree.

At the beginning of the year 1488 Columbus betook himself to Cordova to present his project to the Catholic Sovereigns. They were away, with the result that he could not obtain audience of them until four months later. Sympathetically received by the sovereigns, he was sent by them before a commission presided over by the Queen's confessor, Hernando de Talavera, Prior of Our Lady of the Prado at Valladolid, and future Archbishop of Granada.

What happened at this *junta*? We do not know. In any case Columbus's son, Ferdinand, later complained that this *junta* was composed of incompetent persons, or at least of persons insufficiently informed to pass judgment upon his father's propositions.

These propositions must therefore have been very bold and very technical to demand such a high degree of competency. Did the *junta*, realising this, refer them to the University of Salamanca, which condemned them? Did the Dominicans of the monastery of San Esteban at Salamanca, on the other hand, take up arms on behalf of Columbus against the university theologians? All this is the subject of controversy. Be it as it may, it seems certain that the discussions aroused by the theories of the navigator were of the first importance, inasmuch as they excited so many learned personages and set them at loggerheads.

Some years later further conferences took place at Santa Fé, that is in the fortified camp of Isabel, who was then besieging Granada.

They lasted from the month of July, 1491, to the month of January, 1492, just after the surrender of the city. According to Las Casas, this new *junta* was composed of a number of persons, philosophers, astrologers, and cosmographers, of the highest repute in all Castile, as well as navigators and pilots.

The Italian Geraldini, who was present at some of these conferences, tells us that "a great number of the bishops of the kingdom found the ideas of Colombus manifestly tainted with heresy, because, they said, Nicholas of Lyra professed that there was no inhabited land in the part of the globe lower than our own, which extends from the Fortunate Islands, by sea, as far as the coasts of the Orient. Moreover, Saint Augustine affirms that the antipodes are not inhabited."

What emerges from this text, as from several others, is that the ideas of Columbus were not entirely original, since the theologians themselves admitted that beyond the Fortunate Islands, in other words the Canaries, extended a sea which touched the Indies. The great point in dispute was whether by this sea, by this route of the West, one could reach the Indies.

The theologians affirmed that it was impossible, given, as they claimed, that no inhabited land existed in that part of the globe. Columbus's project was therefore chimerical, by reason of the length of the voyage and the difficulties of navigation. To adventure into these unknown seas was to expose oneself to shipwreck and to death by starvation.

For the future Admiral of the Oceanic Seas to be able to triumph over these *a priori* arguments, he must have provided the two sovereigns with the most reassuring information about the mysterious lands, known only to himself, which he was sure he would find on his way to the Indies. But that he proposed to go to the Indies there is no shadow of doubt. As Henry Harris writes in his book *Ferdinand Columbus*, "the admiral was convinced that he was going to make a landfall, in a direct line, in China or Japan; and he died persuaded that he had discovered what he went to seek, the East coast of Asia, nothing else and nothing more."

When he reached Cuba, he imagined that he was in the kingdom of the Great Khan, and he sent two ambassadors to find him in order to deliver his letter of credentials from the Catholic Sovereigns to him. If Columbus had been told, before he started, that he was going to discover a new continent and not reach the Indies, it is probable that he would never have set out.

So much for the geographical and scientific character of the enterprise. Its religious character is no less striking.

If it had not been so, it would be difficult to explain the really passionate interest which the Franciscans and the Dominicans took in Columbus's projects. We do not know up to what point he was supported by the Dominicans against the theologians and the universitarians of Salamanca, or whether he really was sheltered and protected by them against possible prosecution by the Inquisition. What is certain is that he was encouraged and taken under his wing by Diego de Deza, the former prior of the monastery of San Estabán, who probably received him when he stayed at Salamanca.

This Dominican, who was to become Archbishop of Seville and Toledo, was at this time tutor to Prince John, the son of Ferdinand and Isabel. He was at Santa Fé with the royal family when Columbus met with a second refusal at the hands of the sovereigns. Deza, who had great influence with the Queen, is said to have contributed towards making her change her mind. Las Casas affirms that Deza and Cabrera, King Ferdinand's groom of the bed-chamber, "vaunted themselves as having been the cause of the Sovereigns' subscribing to the enterprise and the discovery of the Indies."

The *rôle* of the Franciscans appears to have been still more active and decisive. They intervened on two occasions, in the persons of two of them, Father de Marchena and Father Juan Pérez, one a monk, the other prior of the monastery of La Rábida, near Palos, where Columbus, after his first disappointment, took refuge with his young son. It was Juan Pérez who facilitated his first meeting with the sovereigns and recommended him to Talavera, the Queen's confessor.

Later, when Columbus, disappointed a second time, had made up his mind to go and offer his services to the King of France, and was threatening to set out at once for Marseilles, the prior of La Rábida persuaded him to defer his departure. Immediately, in the middle of the night, with a haste which was really very strange, the prior set off to Santa Fé to plead the navigator's cause once more with Isabel.

If it had been a question merely of islands to discover and of commercial interests, such zeal on the part of men at least theoretically aloof from this world's goods would seem remarkable, if not reprehensible. What is more likely is that Columbus's religious exaltation impressed the prior of La Rábida very strongly. This visionary promised to open an immense field to evangelisation.

The Franciscans were the great missionary Order of the Middle Ages. It was they, as we have seen, who contributed the most to the elaboration of the Plan of the Indies in Portugal. Here was this plan revised by Columbus with a boldness which dazzled the imagination. He promised to realise all that the disciples of Saint Francis had so long dreamed: reach the Indies directly; come to an understanding there with the Great Khan and the Negus to attack Islam in its commerce and in the very centre of its propaganda, in Arabia and Mecca—in short, take the Musulmans in the rear, while a new Crusade, paid for out of the treasures of the Indies, wrested Palestine and the Holy Sepulchre from them.

It was certainly chimeras such as these which made the monks such warm partisans of the Discoverer. At the same time as their ardour for apostolic conquest had been fired by the taking of Granada, those of them who knew the Musulman world well could cherish no illusions about the danger which still threatened Spain and Christendom, as much from the Barbaresques as from the Turks. A diversion must be made to ward off this danger. Many other reasons of a practical kind militated, in their eyes, in favour of the enterprise.

Besides Cardinal de Mendoza, the Archbishop of Toledo, who also supported it with the Queen, two somewhat mysterious persons intervened with the King: namely, his groom of the chamber, Juan Cabrera, and the Controller-General of Aragón, Luis de Santangel. Both them were of Jewish origin and were in high favour with the King. He had so much confidence in Cabrera that he chose him as one of the executors of his will. As to Luis de Santangel, we know that he was a member of the royal council, treasurer of the Holy Brotherhood, and chancellor and controller-general of Aragón. He was at the head of an important business house, and belonged to a rich family of converted Israelites.

Such conversion, incidentally, did not prevent these *Marranos* from being persecuted by the Inquisition. Between 1486 and 1496, more than ten of them perished at the stake. In the following year, 1497, Santangel obtained from Ferdinand an ordinance which guaranteed him against any accusation of apostasy on the part of the Inquisition—a guarantee which extended to his descendants. This converted Jew was one of the warmest protectors of Christopher Columbus. On the other hand, in a letter to Ferdinand, which Las Casas claims to have seen, Columbus himself recognised that the discovery of the Indies was due to the intervention of the *Marrano* Cabrera and the Dominican Deza.

There is an intriguing factor here, more especially if one associates it with that other claim made by many historians of the Conquest—namely, that the mariner in Columbus's caravel who first sighted the *terra firma* of the New World was also a Jew. Israel thus collaborated, in a more or less direct way, in this great enterprise which was to change the face of the world. When the American continent was opened to modern civilisation, the Jews had something to do with it.

Similarly, when a whole part of the African continent was opened to French influence, it was the Jewish credit of Busnach and Bacry that was a contributory cause. Without this credit, the French would never have gone to Algeria, and France's colonial Empire might have been limited to her old possessions overseas at the time of the monarchy. Religious minds may see in this a Providential intention towards the People of the Promise, which, if it is not the principal actor, must play a part in all great human events.

What, on the other hand, were the particular reasons which

induced Cabrera and Luis de Santangel to embrace the cause of Columbus? Was it only a case of that "wanderlust" which drives Jews into the most risky adventures? Did these two men, under the influence of their ancestral dream of world domination, foresee how widely Columbus's enterprise was going to enlarge the Old World? Did Santangel, head of a business house, simply count upon new markets for his merchandise?

It is more probable that religious zeal had much to do with it. Some members of the Santangel family had just been burned for secret apostasy; and the expulsion of the Jews was imminent. For these two *Marranos*, certainly suspect, it was a fine opportunity of proving the ardour and integrity of their faith, by associating themselves with an expedition which had for its object the propagation of Catholicism throughout an unknown world.

But what purpose does it serve to pile up unverifiable hypotheses? Let us stick to what is certain: the most ardent supporters of Columbus were monks and Jews.

Over and above all personal schemes and reckonings, as over and above all plans of conquest, we must set the Pontifical instruction, which was formulated in two famous Bulls promulgated in 1493, on the morrow of Columbus's first voyage, by Pope Alexander VI.

The Portuguese were alarmed at the Spanish discoveries in the oceanic sea, and the two nations decided to resort to the arbitrage of the Sovereign Pontiff. For him it was an opportunity of defining Pontifical sovereignty in the temporal sphere once more. As the vicar of Jesus Christ he was, by Divine delegation, the master of the world, and he had the right to divide it up and distribute kingdoms to the greater glory of God and the greater good of religion.

In the particular case of the dispute between Castile and Portugal, the Pope decided that the Catholic Sovereigns were to be the legitimate sovereigns of all the territories discovered *or to be discovered* in the Western Ocean, in the same way as Nicholas V had earlier attributed to Portugal the countries washed by the seas of Africa. A line drawn from one Pole to the other, and passing a hundred leagues to the west of the Azores and Cape Verde, separated the Portuguese possessions from the Spanish zone. As to the route of the Indies—for the objective was still to reach the Indies in order to take Islam in the rear—it was agreed that the Spaniards should follow the route of the West and the Portuguese that of the East.

Here, then, was a whole continent given to the Spaniards by the grace of God, but on the condition of making His name known there and spreading His worship there. As His representative on earth, the Pope dared to do this extraordinary thing: make a present of a world to a Christian prince, and confer upon him absolute authority over millions of human beings and over immense territories, which he did not know and of whose very names he was ignorant. This extraordinary thing was not only respected by the whole of Christendom, but was even admitted by the conquered peoples. In return for such a favour, the beneficiaries were under the obligation of converting these peoples and propagating the faith in their new Empire.

From this point of view, which was that of the Papacy and the Catholic Sovereigns, as it was that of Christopher Columbus, the conquest of the Indies accordingly had as its object to combat Islam and convert idolatrous peoples to Christianity.

In practice, as we know, the Spaniards were not to be slow in straying from this programme. The winning of gold was to end by supplanting the winning of souls. But this was the initial object, or at least the pretext which covered the enterprise. The colonisation of America was profoundly stamped with this religious character. The spirit which animated and inspired the ordinances of the Spanish Sovereigns, like the conduct of the viceroys, was the same as that which maintained the crusade against the Moors and drove Columbus to the conquest of the Indies. The essential thing was the propagation of the Christian faith.

We must take this as our point of departure if we wish to understand the Spanish colonisation of America at all. If one does not keep this idea constantly present in his mind, he is exposed to unfair judgment of the colossal work accomplished in the New World by the conquistadors.

CHAPTER XXI

What the Conquest Meant

COLUMBUS set out to find the Indies by the route of the West. That implies, incidentally, that he certainly counted upon finding islands where he could replenish supplies on his way. Otherwise this long navigation would have been impossible. Although he was widely mistaken about the distance which separated the Indies from Spain by way of the Atlantic, and imagined it to be much shorter than it really was, he quite certainly expected to make a call at islands more or less close to the Asiatic coast.

But that these lands were a new continent—here was something of which he had no idea, and which he never admitted. There has been seen in this an ironical denial given by facts to the imagination of the Discoverer. Yet it was, after all, this visionary of genius who was right. Others after him were to reach the Indies by the route of the West, as he had foreseen.

There was another denial given by reality to the projects of Columbus. He had set out with the intention, more or less official, more or less expressed, of starting a new crusade against Islam and conquering pagan nations for Christ. But there were no Musulmans in the countries which he reached. If, on the other hand, there were plenty of pagans to convert, it soon happened that anxiety to win them for Christ vanished in the presence of that of winning plenty of gold. It was claimed, indeed, that the gold brought back from the Indies would be used to deliver the Holy Sepulchre. This fiction was soon abandoned. The conquerors concerned themselves above all with making fortunes as quickly as possible, acquiring vast estates, and, to this end, expropriating and exploiting the natives.

Yet the evangelical ideal maintained itself strongly in the presence of the most materialist and the most mercenary motives. Never did Catholic Spain renounce her programme of evangelisation, any more than she ever renounced her system of colonial exploitation. In fact, the rapacity of the Spaniards and the apostolic zeal of their missionaries were the two great crow-bars of the conquest. Without this twofold passion for the winning of gold and the winning of souls, America would never have been colonised.

Let us try to imagine the extraordinary difficulties of such an enterprise, the almost superhuman courage which was required to confront its dangers—and we shall realise that those who dared to throw themselves into such an adventure must have been moved by appeal to the emotions or the instincts, at one and the same time the most selfish and the most sublime, which divided between them the Spanish souls of that time: the lust for gold, and the most extreme self-sacrifice.

Without the least hypocrisy, these two motives could co-exist in one and the same person. Colombus was two things together, a converter and an exploiter of the natives. He wanted gold, not only to satisfy his real avarice, but also to maintain those who had followed him, to justify the promises of Paradise which he had lavished upon the Spanish Sovereigns, and finally to plant the Cross and build chapels and churches on pagan soil.

As a matter of fact, the reality was far from the dream. In the first place the voyage itself was a terrible enterprise, even for professional sailors. Although it has been disputed—but what has not been disputed in the story of Columbus?—it seems clear that the admiral had all the difficulty in the world in assembling a crew for his first expedition.

To sail far from the coasts, to distances which were regarded as prodigious; to brave that great unknown Ocean, that sea of horrors —here was something to daunt the stoutest heart. Let us bear in mind what the ships of that time were like, and how little security they offered, and also what the art of navigation was at the end of the fifteenth century, despite the progress recently made by the Portuguese.

Alternatively, the three caravels which made the first known crossing of the Atlantic have been underestimated and, probably, overestimated. Some, with the intention of exalting the audacity of the navigators, speak of wretched barques scarcely decked, mere coasting vessels. Others, on the contrary, represent them to be ships as good as anybody could want, of a reasonable tonnage, fine sailing craft and well armed. According to this version it was Columbus who was a poor navigator.

But, despite its hundred and twenty tons and its length of thirty-four metres overall, the *Santa Maria*, the admiral's caravel, must have felt an insecure shelter enough to the men who had to traverse seven hundred leagues of sea before making a problematical harbour. If the admiral's outward voyage lasted only a month, not counting the crossing to the Canaries and the stay there, his homeward voyage took twice as long, and he was overtaken by a terrible storm, in the course of which his ship nearly foundered.

During these long months of navigation any number of risks were run, with shipwreck as only the worst of them. Apart from other inconveniences, the crew suffered from thirst, hunger, malaria, and all kinds of diseases. When the admiral, after a second expedition to the Antilles, disembarked at Cádiz, in the month of June, 1496, the inhabitants were startled at the sight of the voyagers, who seemed, according to an eye-witness, "more dead than alive." It was a lamentable procession of sick and starving men who could hardly stand on their feet.

The crew of the first expedition, badly fed, anxious through being out of sight of land, and feeling themselves lost in the midst of this marine immensity, mutinied. In fact, there were times when they were completely lost. The admiral himself did not know where he was. He steered at random. If the pilot, Alonso Sánchez of Huelva, really had given him information about an island where he had touched, driven by storm, after twenty-nine days of navigation, this information must have been extremely vague.

"He (Sánchez) was constrained," relates Garcilaso de la Vega, the historian of the Incas, "to lower his canvas and abandon his ship to the violence of the gale. It was so tempestuous that it made him run before it for twenty-nine days, *not knowing where he was or what course he ought to steer*, inasmuch as throughout this time it was impossible for him to take elevations either by the sun or by the North." This pilot may have had a confused idea of the direction to be followed, but not of the length of the voyage. To this very day, the caravaners of the desert count neither time nor distance. They know confusedly that the end of the journey is "that way," as they say, and this vague orientation suffices for them.

When, after all these anxieties of the voyage, the adventurers finally touched land—generally at random—new and terrible experiences awaited them: hardships of soil and climate, scarcity of food, endemic diseases, hostility of the inhabitants. If the first natives whom they met seemed as pacific as they were defenceless, they were not slow in running up against warlike peoples provided with formidable weapons, against which their rudimentary artillery was often a poor advantage.

In any case, the conquerors were only a handful against thousands of enemies. That a few hundred Spaniards, who were not even always professional soldiers, should have been able little by little to conquer a whole continent, is a prodigious fact which still remains insufficiently explained. They must have had extraordinary boldness, courage, and endurance, and, along with them, heroism and faith. The most remarkable thing is that almost all this was due to private enterprise.

Sometimes a royal governor organised an expedition, which he entrusted to the command of a man of his choice, who took the pompous title of Captain-General of the Armada. This was the procedure in the case of the conquest of Mexico. Diego Velázquez, governor of the Antilles, appointed Hernán Cortés captain-general of the little army which he sent to Yucatan.

But most ships were fitted out by business men, landowners, or the conquistadors themselves. Apart from professional soldiers, anybody who liked could join the expedition, so long as he equipped and fed himself. A captain had to do the same for his men. Stores consisted of bacon and manioc bread. "It was on bacon and manioc," Señor Carlos Pereyra tells us, "that America was conquered."

Apart from firearms and cold steel, beasts for killing and beasts of burden, provision was also made of glassware, Castile cloth, shirts, bonnets and caps for exchange with uncivilised tribes or for presents to chiefs. All this, in fact, did not amount to much weight or make very heavy packs.

Before embarking for Mexico, Bernal Díaz, the admirable chronicler of the conquest, tells us, Cortés "took tally of his soldiers, to see how many he was leading. He found after the count that we were five hundred and eight, without counting the master-pilots and mariners, who numbered one hundred and nine, sixteen horses and mules (all war and racing mules), and eleven ships, great and small. There were thirty-two crossbowmen and thirteen blunder-busses, and ten cannons of bronze and four falconets, and a quantity of powder and shot."

Apart from the cannon and falconets—difficult to handle and better suited for parade purposes than for attack or defence—let us note the small number of firearms: thirteen blunderbusses against thirty-two crossbows. The armament was still almost entirely that of the Middle Ages.

Nevertheless this was an armada of considerable proportions. The size of these expeditions was, in general, much more modest. Pizarro set out for the conquest of Peru with a single ship, which did not even belong to him. It was Hernán Ponce de Léon who fitted it out. "He embarked in it," says Agustín de Zarate, "with his four brothers and the largest number of foot and horse he could assemble." But it was a very small number, by comparison with that of the enemy whom they had to fight. In the first battle, in which the native king Ataliba was taken prisoner, the soldiers of Pizarro were one against a hundred—some say even two hundred.

They set out in the assurance that nobody could resist good and faithful subjects of His Majesty of Spain. They encountered both peaceful peoples who brought them chickens and maize and warlike tribes who resisted them stoutly. In either case, the first thing the captain-general did was solemnly to take possession of the country in the name of the Catholic King. A royal notary, brought expressly for the purpose, drew up documentary evidence during the proceedings.

It was a piece of high comedy, this bureaucratic red-tape displaying itself pedantically in the midst of barbarism. They might be short of food, or clothes, they might march with sandals on their feet; but they took along with them a notary provided with good ink, sealing-wax and parchment.

When Cortés disembarked at Tabasco, says Bernal Díaz, "he took possession of this country for His Majesty and for himself in his royal name. And it was after this fashion: drawing his sword, he smote three times, in sign of possession, against a great tree called ceiba, and he declared that, if there was anyone who contested it, he would defend his right with his sword and the shield he bore. And all the soldiers who were present on this occasion said that royal possession had been duly taken in the name of His Majesty, and that we were ready to aid him, if anyone dared to contradict him. *This proceeding was registered in the presence of a notary of the King.*"

In the eyes of the conquerors, however, this taking of possession was legitimatised only on the condition of observing scrupulously the obligations of conscience imposed upon the possessors by the Pontifical Bulls. Let us not forget: the Pope, the absolute master of new lands to be discovered, had granted them to the Spanish and Portuguese sovereigns only to win them to the Christian faith. This was why, after the Catholic King had been proclaimed master of the country, it was added that he held his rights from the Pontiff who dwelt in Rome, and benignantly called upon the new subjects of His Majesty to renounce their idols and become converts.

They were preached a little sermon on the subject. After that, no time was lost in raising crosses and building a chapel, in which was placed the image of Our Lady. When one reads the history of the conquest of Mexico in Bernal Díaz, one finds that this edifying ceremony was repeated at every stage by the conquerors.

Some of the natives listened to these pious exhortations without moving a muscle. Fifteen Mexican Indians of an important village came to salute Cortés and do homage to him, and he "showed them much affection and told them many things touching our holy Faith, *as we were in the habit of doing everywhere we went*, saying that we were vassals of our great Emperor Don Carlos, and he gave them some glass trinkets and other bagatelles of Castile."

At other times the audience was less receptive. When Cortés himself endeavoured on several occasions to make Montezuma, the Mexican emperor, "see reason," that "savage" very politely put him in his place. The Spanish captain had begun by telling him "that we are vassals and servants of a great lord called the Emperor Don Carlos, who has for his subjects numerous and powerful princes; that having been informed of him (Montezuma) and his greatness, he had sent us to these countries to see him and beg him to make himself a Christian, with all his people, like our Emperor and ourselves, and to save his soul and the souls of all his vassals—and many other good things."

Some days later, the self-made catechist besought Montezuma "to be attentive to the words which he wished to say to him at this time. And immediately he told him, and all very well explained, about the creation of the world and how we were all brothers, sons of a single father and a single mother who were called Adam and Eve; that our great Emperor, in this quality of brother, grieved at the perdition of the great number of souls which idols were leading to Hell, had sent us to the Indians to bring them the remedy of our counsel and the exhortation no longer to adore the said idols." To which Montezuma replied: "We have here our gods whom we have long worshipped, holding them to be good. Yours may be good, too. For the moment, do not concern yourselves to speak to us of them!"

The fact is that Cortés, in his zeal as a converter, went a little too far, to such a point that the chaplain of the armada, Fray Bartolomé de Olmedo, thought fit to recall him to a sense of the opportune, and also of the ridiculous. The monk jeered gently at the warrior and his overdone sermonisings. The "Padre" himself employed more tact and discretion. But this did not prevent the conquistadors as soon as they arrived in a Mexican town from hastening to have Mass said, planting their crosses, and purifying a temple of idols, stained with human blood, in order to install a statue of the Virgin in it.

Later, in Peru, they were less ceremonious about seizing territory. Nevertheless Pizarro himself, despite his expeditious brutality, made it a point to preserve the forms, at least at the outset of his campaign. He sent two emissaries, one after the other, to King Ataliba, in order to inform him "that he approached him on behalf of His Majesty the King of Spain, with the object of assuring him of the good will of his master, in pursuance whereof he desired to meet him, adding that he desired to be regarded as among his friends."

That was the first summons in the name of the Spanish sovereign, appointed by the Pontifical Bulls absolute and legitimate master of Peru. The second summons, in the name of the Pope himself, followed it immediately. Ataliba, determined upon resistance, marched against the Spaniards at the head of a powerful army—so powerful that Pizarro's soldiers were aghast at it and regarded themselves as lost, failing supernatural aid.

When the combatants were face to face, there was witnessed a sight dumbfounding in its audacity, if not its madness. The chaplain of the conquistadors, Bishop Francisco de Valverde, advanced to King Ataliba's litter, holding his breviary in his hand, and said to him in substance: "that there was one God in three Persons, who had created Heaven and earth . . . that, through the disobedience of our first parents, Adam and Eve, we were all become sinners, in no condition, accordingly, to enter the Kingdom of Heaven, until Jesus Christ, our Redeemer, suffered death to win us salvation and life; that this Jesus, after dying upon a Cross, left Saint Peter in His place to be His vicar.

"He added that *it was the successors of Saint Peter who had divided all the countries of the world among the Christian kings and princes*, giving every one of them the charge to conquer some part of it; that this Kingdom of Peru had fallen to his Imperial Majesty the King Don Carlos, and that this great monarch had sent in his place the governor Don Francisco Pizarro, to make known to Ataliba, on behalf of God and on his own behalf, all that he had just said; that, if Ataliba was ready to believe what he had said, receive baptism and obey the Emperor, this prince would protect him and defend him; that, if he did otherwise, the governor declared to him that he would attack him and put everything to fire and sword."

So it went on at great length: the discourse of the good bishop was a regular sermon duly divided into three parts. Ataliba replied spiritedly enough "that this country and all that it contained had been handed down to him by his ancestors; and that he did not know how Saint Peter should have been able to give it to anybody else . . . that, in regard to Jesus Christ, Who had created Heaven and earth, he knew nothing whatever about all this, or that anybody had created anything . . . that, in regard to the King of Spain, he knew nothing about him, and had never seen him."

Thereupon battle was engaged, and, after a desperate struggle, the unfortunate Ataliba was captured by the Spaniards. Peru was virtually conquered. In the eyes of Pizarro and his companions, it was also conquered legitimately, inasmuch as the Sovereign Pontiff, master of the whole world, had given this country to the Emperor their master. He had given it to him on the condition of converting it. Accordingly, to keep in line with the Pontifical Bulls, every campaign must begin with a sermon. If the sermon did not take effect, the conquistador regarded himself as entitled to obtain conversion by other means.

These men, lost in the immensity of a hostile continent, must have had the conviction that they were the masters of it by Divine right to enable them to endure all that they suffered there. The lust for gold could not have sufficed. Without all this religious ideology which, in their eyes, legitimatised their violence, they would have been nothing more than mere brigands, murderers, and highwaymen. The invaders brandished Bulls and theological texts, a whole rubbish-heap of documents, by way of justifying their invasion.

But the invaded peoples did not let themselves be thus talked over. The Spanish adventurers were met by thousands of Indians, often very well armed, who discharged a hail of poisoned arrows against them. They had to make their way through unknown regions, in perpetual dread of ambush or sudden attack, under a burning sun or, on the other hand, in mountainous districts where they died of cold.

The soldier advanced painfully, streaming with sweat and suffocating under his quilted armour—padded with cotton to deaden the effect of arrow strokes—and with his feet bleeding in his tattered sandals. Higher up, he froze and his teeth chattered in the cold of the sierras, where he had nothing with which to cover himself.

He lacked the most elementary surgery. He was driven to dress his wounds—those frightful wounds inflicted by cold steel—with boiling fat taken from the corpses of the Indians. Then there were the attacks by wild beasts, the danger from reptiles, the exasperating swarms of mosquitoes which made sleep impossible to men dying with fatigue.

The most demoralising thing was their small number—which we should always bear in mind—against a host of enemies. The advance of Cortés upon Mexico and the occupation of that great city by a handful of adventurers was a *coup de main* of reckless heroism. Despite their contempt for danger and their habit of not being surprised at anything, some of them ended by feeling the extravagance of such enterprises.

But it was still more the pride of having dared the impossible which dominated these hidalgos. Bernal Díaz, who was, as I have said, the Xenophon of this prodigious Anabasis, cannot restrain himself from remarking upon this, after telling us about the entrance of his comrades into the capital of the Aztecs, the capture of Montezuma, and the execution of his captains.

"In the whole world," he says, "what men has one ever seen who dared to enter, to the number of four hundred and fifty soldiers—and we did not even reach that muster—into a city as strong as Mexico, greater than Venice, and so far, at more than one thousand five hundred leagues, from our Castile, arrest such a powerful lord and do justice upon his captains under his own eyes? Certainly there is here much to be praised, and by no means so soberly as I have done it."

At night they trembled with dread in their beds at the thought of the great city which offered them such a suspect hospitality, and might rise against them and crush them. "Their blood," says Bernal Díaz, "turned into poison in their veins." It was to rid themselves of this terror that they conceived the desperate remedy, the plan insensate in its boldness, of taking prisoner in his own palace the sovereign—venerated and obeyed as a god—whose guests they were.

No doubt they realised that seizing the person of the king was equivalent to striking terror into the Indians and paralysing any idea of resistance among them. The facility of the conquest is explained not only by these tactics, but also by the advantage of armament, by all the superiority that European civilisation put into the hands of the Spaniards, and by all the extent to which it was in advance of rudimentary civilisations.

The war-horses and the war-dogs employed by the conquistadors sowed terror in the ranks of the Indians—especially the horses, unknown at that time in America, which the Indians regarded as animals as fearful as they were fantastic. The sight of sailing ships, and artillery, and musketry, in their infancy though they were, were a great source of astonishment and dread to them.

But all these inventions of European enterprise would have ended by succumbing to the omnipotence of numbers, if it had not been for the fact that a powerful element of mysticism mingled with the fear inspired by the arms and the military science of the invaders. These white men, coming from regions where the sun rose, had been announced to the Indians by prophecies. The Indians bowed down before the masters foreseen by their divines and imposed upon them by their gods. They regarded as foreign gods these fearful beings who could release the thunder when they would. They were slow to realise that the Spaniards were not immortal, as they had thought at first. How could they resist these omnipotent demons?

On the side of the Spaniards, an element of mysticism of another kind was essential to give scope to such a rapid conquest. Not only did they believe themselves to be the masters and apostles of the New World; they were also persuaded that the hand of God led all this fabulous adventure. There were times when Cortés and Bernal Díaz stood in astonishment before the results of their victories, those unexpected results so disproportionate to their deeds, heroic as they were, and asked themselves whether they were not the phantasmagoria of a dream.

Once installed in the conquered countries, they had to live and support themselves there. It was no small matter. These Castilians and Andalusians who disembarked in the Antilles or in Mexico had to change all their habits of hygiene, comfort and diet. There was no wheat or oats, or any butcher's meat. They were obliged to introduce pigs, goats, sheep and fowl from Castile.

The first American wheat was regarded as a miraculous growth, which soon had its legend. This legend is so charming that it is worth preserving. It was said that the introduction of wheat into Peru was due to Inés Múñoz, the wife of Francisco Martín Alcantara, brother of Pizarro. It was she, too, who created the gardens and orchards on the outskirts of Lima.

One day, when she was winnowing some rice which had recently arrived from Spain in a barrel, she found among the rice some grains of wheat, "and she put them aside, with the intention of sowing them and seeing whether one could cultivate wheat in that country. She sowed them in a flower-pot, with as much care as though she were planting shoots of mignonnette or basil; and, thanks to the solicitude with which she watched over her little seed-bed, watering it as she should, the grains grew, and the plant developed strongly and gave numerous and large ears." So, through a happy chance, the Peruvian harvests of the future emerged from the flower-pot of Inés Múñoz.

There was a lack also of draught and riding beasts. There were no horses or mules. As Señor Carlos Pereyra remarks very truly, "without the cattle from the islands, and especially the horses, pigs, goats, sheep and fowl, not a single step could have been made in the continent."[1] At the outset horses were a rarity. They were worth their weight in gold. Bernal Díaz relates that Hérnan Cortés,

[1] Cf. Carlos Pereyra: *La obra de España en América*, p. 77.

when he set out on the Mexican expedition, had to sell the shoulder-knots off his fine velvet doublet to buy a mare. As we have seen, he was not able to assemble more than sixteen horses for his armada.

These beasts, which terrified the Indians so much, were better cared for than the men. Their lives seemed so precious that Bernal Díaz himself describes them with more care and in greater detail than his comrades in arms. The sixteen horses which carried Cortés and some of his companions are piously catalogued and characterised more exactly than Ortiz the musician and Juan de Escalante who rode them. We are told the colour of their blankets, whereas we are not told the colour of the beards or the hair of these gallant conquistadors.

After they had assured themselves food and shelter, as well as means of transport, they had to exploit the immense territories of which they had boldly proclaimed themselves the lords and masters. If they had expatriated themselves, if they had undergone the trials and torments of a long and perilous journey, it was not to live worse than in a village in Castile or Estremadura. They had come to find gold and precious stones, to acquire great estates.

All this necessitated considerable manual labour. Where was it to be found? One could not think of deriving it from Spain. Like the earlier Arab invader of the Peninsula, the conquistador was much too grand a gentleman to work with his hands. Besides, Spain, emptied of her Moors, was in great need of manual labour herself. So, quite naturally, the conquistadors fell back upon the natives, upon whom work in the mines and plantations was imposed.

Like the expropriation of the soil, the forced labour and the slavery of the natives claimed as its justification fine theological reasons and relied upon famous Pontifical Bulls, to which we must always return in studying the history of the conquest of the Indies. The Spaniards had come to America to convert the Indians. The best means of doing so was to reduce them to slavery. So there was established the notorious regime of *encomiendas* or "commanderies of Indians."

The concession of an estate or a district was officially obtained, together with all the natives in it, but always on the condition of converting them to the Christian faith. The Spanish colonist had the same titles as the Emperor and King: titles of proprietorship and rights of sovereignty were legitimatised only by apostolate. There was here—as we must admit—a very lofty and noble idea, which it was, unfortunately, only too easy to distort and falsify in practice. The colonists mocked at their apostolic duties, made a convenience of Christian charity, and refused to see in their Indians anything but slaves and beasts of burden, from whom they extorted the utmost possible profit.

The first slaves made in the Gulf of Mexico belonged to degenerate, weak and lazy races. The excessive labour to which they were constrained was not slow in decimating them, in such proportions that the home government became alarmed about it. The missionaries, scandalised and indignant at the rapacious cruelty of the colonists, constituted themselves protectors of the oppressed, and denounced their oppressors to the Catholic Sovereigns. Bartolomé de Las Casas and Fray Louis Bertrand, who evangelised New Granada, distinguished themselves especially by their zeal in favour of the Indians.

Las Casas in particular became their advocate and apologist. He made several voyages to Castile and carried on controversies with the theologians, including a famous one with the learned Ginés de Sepulveda, with the object of securing royal assent to the abolition of the *encomiendas*. He recalled the great religious principles upon which the right of colonisation had been based. The Christians could not be regarded as the legitimate masters of a territory except on the condition of establishing the religion of Christ there.

On the contrary, the Spanish colonists of the New World, by their barbarous behaviour towards the natives, could not fail to arouse hatred of that religion. Moreover, conversion ought not to be obtained by violence. Finally the Indians, converted or not, once they ceased to be prisoners of war, could only be regarded as good and loyal subjects of the Catholic Sovereigns. In these circumstances, it was a regular crime of treason to reduce them to slavery.

The partisans of the commanderies claimed to justify this slavery by the moral decadence of the natives. They were an inferior race, marred by all kinds of physical blemishes and infected by all imaginable vices. It was necessary to treat them sternly if obedience was to be secured from them. But Las Casas replied that these accusations were pure calumnies; that the Indians were "gentle sheep," who asked nothing better than to serve their masters well, on condition that they were humanely treated; that the vices with which they were reproached were exceptional; and, finally, that they were not morally or intellectually inferior to the Spaniards, any more than the Berbers or the Moors.

One may imagine the scandal which these propositions aroused in Spain, where passion was still hot from the struggle against the Musulmans. With self-interest and ideological pedantry added to it, the monk who made himself protector of the Indians raised a storm against him.

Las Casas compromised a generous cause by the very intensity which he brought to it. There was at once suspected in his arguments the rivalry of cleric and layman. He claimed to know better than the governors of His Majesty, and he was impatient at being restrained, in his often chimerical proposals, by the civil power. It is only too certain that he wanted to be master and carry out the evangelisation of the Indians in his own way.

This excellent man, who appears to have been good, if simple-minded, as utopian as he was obstinate, imagined that he had only to take a cross and present himself to the Indians with words of love to bring them to baptism *en masse*. Sepulveda retorted quite fairly that, wherever the missionaries had gone without the support of soldiers, they had either been killed or their preaching had no effect. Apart from the stupidity, the perfidy, the laziness, the drunkenness and the sodomy of the natives, he instanced their barbarism and their cruelty; the human sacrifices which stained the temples of their idols with blood and made them regular slaughter-houses; their markets of human flesh, their revolting cannibalism.

Their protector, carried away by his apostolic zeal, then resorted to regular sophistries to excuse those whom he called "gentle sheep." According to his argument, human sacrifices, abominable in themselves, did not constitute a sin on the part of those who offered them in good faith, piously, to do homage to their gods. Such quibblings bordered upon the ridiculous.

A still graver matter was that Las Casas turned appearances against himself, and made the purity of his motives suspect, by his advocacy of replacing the slavery of the Indians by that of negroes. It was insinuated that, if he favoured the introduction of negroes into the New World it was because he was interested in the Portuguese companies which organised traffic in them. He discouraged Spanish colonists by his activities on behalf of the Indians. He was, therefore, a bad citizen and a dishonest man.

The honesty and charity of the good Las Casas are unquestionable. It is equally unquestionable that, if in all good faith he exaggerated the cruelties and the devastations which he reported, these cruelties and devastations were nevertheless only too true. But how can one pronounce at this distance of time, after more than four centuries have elapsed, upon what ought to have been done at that period?

The quarrel between Las Casas and the viceroys, or the Spanish colonists, was the quarrel which is constantly renewed in colonial countries between people from home who visit there and the administrators and landowners who live there; between the humanitarians or the sentimentalists and the hard-headed men or the merely businesslike. If colonists, through rapacity and brutality, sometimes run the risk of provoking the natives to revolt and compromising the authority of the motherland, ideologues, through weakness and ignorance of environment and states of mind, run the risk of losing the colonies.

Without the veterans of Diego Velázquez, Cortés and Pizarro, Las Casas and his missionaries would have been massacred or ignominiously driven out by the Indians. On the other hand, it is obvious that the affairs of the Spaniards themselves would have been all the better for a little more justice and humanity.

For by now the problem was no less than that of the colonisation of the New World. Once they set out to conquer it, they had to accept the consequences of the conquest to the full, or else evacuate the country. The Indians must be held in subjection, or else the Spaniards must pack up and go. Which was better—to make a whole continent enter the community of civilised peoples, or to leave it isolated and shut up in its barbarism, with its cannibal peoples, its temples which reeked of the slaughter-house, and its gods thirsty for human blood?

The means employed to secure more or less superficial civilisation were harsh—often as barbarous as the barbarians whom it was sought to enlighten and evangelise. The sovereigns, like the Spanish missionaries, exerted themselves to soften these means as much as they could. Could they have succeeded completely? To answer this question fairly one would require to have lived in the America of that period. It must have been a frightful business.

Most of the time the colonists were subject to the cruel necessities of climate and environment. There was no choice of means. The Catholic Sovereigns, who by their ordinances abolished slavery and recommended kindness towards the Indians, nevertheless demanded that the "royal fifth" should be paid by these same Indians to their tax-collectors or be levied on the galleons. So, through a contradiction doubtless unconscious, they maintained work in the mines and perpetuated slavery and the cruelties which they sought to abolish.

At that period, moreover, and in a barbarous country like America, it was impossible to dispense with servile manual labour. Las Casas himself proposed to substitute negro slavery for Indian slavery. There remained, perhaps, the possibility of introducing agricultural workers, colonists or serfs, brought from Europe into these new countries—for example, the Moors and Moriscos whom, for reasons of security, it was decided to expel from Andalusia; or, as in modern times, immigrants from all the European nations, North as well as South.

But this was contrary to the religious ideas of the period. Historians profess surprise that the Spaniards should not have thrown their colonies open to the workers and the merchants of the whole world. They forget the very principles which governed the Spanish colonisation, and which we must once more recall. It had, theoretically, no other object but that of winning the New World for the Christian and Catholic faith. Accordingly, apart from commercial and self-interested reasons, these propagators of the Faith could not admit there either Musulmans or Lutherans, or any kind of pagans or heretics.

CHAPTER XXII

The Psychology of the Conquistador

WHAT were they like, these extraordinary men who had only to appear, so to speak, in order to bring the whole of an immense continent into subjection to the crown of Castile—a subjection which, as a matter of fact, was quite superficial, for the pacification took a long time, was interrupted by terrible wars and revolts, and may indeed be said to be not yet ended?

For such an adventure, undertaken so far from the motherland, with the primitive ships and armament of the period, there were required, as I cannot repeat too often, exceptional courage and endurance. For these were civilised men, who voluntarily accepted a return to uncivilised life, and resigned themselves to hunger, thirst, loss of sleep, and all the hostilities and all the cruelties of a tropical climate and of wild men and beasts.

Nor were they insensitive brutes. They suffered cruelly. They realised their wretchedness and their isolation. "What a terrible thing it is," writes Bernal Díaz, "to go and discover new lands, and in such a way as we adventured there! Nobody can imagine our estate, unless he has himself endured these excessive toils."

The worst risk was the perpetual one of shipwreck or, for those who escaped it, slow death on some desert island. Garcilaso de la Vega tells the story of one of these shipwrecked men who, reduced to living like the beasts, assumed the appearance of one, becoming so covered with hair that he looked scarcely human. When another shipwrecked man was cast away on the same island, the first occupant was afraid lest he should take him for some diabolical animal, half-man and half-beast. To reassure the new arrival, he had the touching inspiration of reciting the *Credo* as he advanced towards him. Other castaways, obliged to live naked, changed their skins, we are told, "twice a year, like snakes."

It has been remarked that the majority of these heroic adventurers were natives of Andalusia and Estremadura, in other words of the more southerly provinces of Spain, and also those where the struggle against the Moors lasted for centuries. They were hardened against the most burning suns of the Equator and tempered to endure anything, and at the same time they were already experienced in the kind of warfare which was to be imposed upon them.

They had practised their hands in guerrilla warfare. It was the same kind of war that they had to wage against the Indians: raiding and marauding, burnings and devastations to starve or scatter the enemy. Those who had cut down fruit-trees in the orchards of Baza, or burned farms in the Granadine *vega*, had something on which to exercise their talents in Peru and Chile. In the school of those pillagers, seekers after treasure, and cutters-off of heads, the Arabs, they had learned useful lessons in rapacity and cruelty.

They were hard, merciless, bold and enterprising, as befitted conquerors and founders who had to battle ceaselessly against the most unfavourable conditions and against fierce enemies, and were compelled to exact the maximum of effort from themselves and from their auxiliaries. They were destined to perpetual guerrilla war. Of war on a large scale, as it was beginning to be understood in Europe, there could be no question in the New World, and those whose experience of warfare was confined to the campaigns against the French, the Swiss, or the Germans, found themselves hopelessly at a loss.

Some newly disembarked recruits, full of the glory of having campaigned under Gonzalo de Cordova or taken part in battles such as Marignano or Cerignola, presumed to give advice to the adventurers in sandals who fought against Indians armed with bows and arrows and armoured in cotton-wool. Rude misadventures were not slow in undeceiving them. It was another type of warfare which they had to learn.

It has been pointed out elsewhere[1] that most of the great leaders of the Conquest were not professional soldiers: they were merchants, business men, shipbuilders, navigators, gold-seekers, whose principal advantage was that they knew the natives well and had adapted themselves to the climate, as to the customs, of the country. These Spaniards, or these foreigners—for there were Europeans of all origins among them, and even Africans—needed a regular process of *Americanisation,* in other words years of acclimatisation and apprenticeship, before the Conquest, properly speaking, could be undertaken with any chance of success.

This preliminary adaptation has to take place at all periods in all colonial environments. In Algeria the French soldiers and the great military leaders found themselves immobilised for years before they learnt how to fight against the Arabs and were in a position to advance into the interior.

For the conquistadors Americanisation was a very rapid process. Historians have noted, indeed, how readily the Spaniards let themselves be contaminated by the natives. They explain this contamination by the influence of women and the multiplication of half-breeds. As Spanish women were very few, at least at the outset of the conquest, the conquerors had to take Indian women as wives or concubines. Those who lived in isolation, in remote regions, or again certain prisoners of war, by dint of living with the Indians ended by resembling them. The degraded civilised man let himself go and became a regular savage.

Bernal Díaz tells us the story of a man, a native of Palos, who was captured by the Indians and became one of their chiefs. An

[1] Cf. Carlos Pereyra: *Las huellas de los Conquistadores,* p. 108 *et seq.*

emissary of Cortés tried vainly to win him back to the Christians. "I am married here," this man replied to the envoy, "I have three children, and I am regarded as chief and leader in time of war. So leave me alone! I have my face tattooed and my ears pierced. What would the Spaniards say of me if they saw me decked out like this? Besides, look at my three little ones—how pretty they are! As you live, give me those green glass beads you have with you, and I will say that my brothers have sent me them from my country."

Despite the most pathetic entreaties, there was no doing anything with him. The new savage did not want to become a civilised man again at any price.

In general, however, they reacted harshly against being mastered by their environment. As always happens in colonial countries, the character of the colonist was strengthened by the contradiction, or the hostility, of his surroundings. When he was subjected to the influence of foreign customs and new environment, some of his racial feelings and prejudices, some of his ideas, acquired fresh vigour. It happened also that, as the colonist was no longer in contact with the motherland, where national characteristics were in course of evolution, his own remained stationary.

The feelings, the instincts, the prejudices which he had brought with him from his native environment became intensified or exaggerated without being transformed. Ancestral character mummified in him. The hidalgo, cousin of the Cid or the Great Captain, became the Argentinian or Peruvian *estanciero* who, under the outward appearance of the most up-to-date business man, hides the hardened, set soul of a conquistador.

The two mainsprings of this soul, at the time of the conquest as still, perhaps, to-day, were pride of race and the instinct of domination. The Spaniard of pure blood, not crossed with Jew or Moor, regarded himself as an individual of higher quality, and could feel nothing but contempt for other peoples. It was he who had fought for centuries against Islam, and ended by throwing it back into Africa—who had, in fact, inherited the Empire of the West, and looked forward to European and world hegemony.

By virtue of Pontifical Bulls, he was the sovereign master of the New World, the conqueror to whom everybody must bow the knee, the apostle designated by the Vicar of Jesus Christ to win millions of souls to the Christian faith. Subject of His August Cæsarian and Catholic Majesty, he was, in his own eyes, the perfect type of Catholic and Christian. In warrior virtue, in purity of blood, as in purity of faith, he was without rival. He had all the pretensions, as he had all the rights.

Such feelings could only develop a bellicose and irreducible individualism. The conquistador was a superb individual. He had a high idea of his own worth, as also of the worth of his comrades.

In proportion as he and they felt themselves to be a small number, in short an *élite*, lost amid barbarian hordes, this sense of individual worth became exalted in them. They were human beings of value, inasmuch as they were almost unique examples of humanity. They considered themselves superior even to their compatriots of the motherland, because their adventurous and perilous life developed in them aptitudes unknown to the civilised man.

Personality affirmed itself in characteristics sometimes excessive and brutal. That is what always happens in colonial countries. Because of their small number, of the isolation in which they live, Europeans attribute an extreme importance to the personality of another European. They all know one another by their names, or, what is more significant, by their nicknames. In America they knew one another's birth-places, and were proud of the fact: Hernando López came from Ávila, Juan Velázquez from León. Often the name of origin ended by effacing the family name. One became Juan the Castilian, or Miguel the Valencian. Spanish waggoners whom I have met in the South of Algeria carry on the tradition of the con-quistadors in this respect.

Together with pride in their birth-place, they had an almost aristocratic sense of the worth of the individual. In their eyes, as in the eyes of Bernal Díaz, Alonso the one-armed, or Ortiz the musician, simple manual labourers or porters, were persons on a level with Captain-General Hernán Cortés.

The horses themselves and the war-dogs, on account of their small number, assumed importance and inspired a touching con-sideration. A kind of personality was acquired by these precious animals through their contact with men. Their names have been piously preserved for us, together with their traits of character, and even their deeds, carefully noted and even celebrated in the heroic fashion.

Such highly individualised people could not be very well dis-ciplined, or very obedient. The old Spanish particularism, still more strengthened by the example of the Berbers and the Arabs, led directly to anarchy through personal rivalries and quarrels. The conquistadors made the mistake of their ancestors in the presence of Islam: they split up into fiercely contending factions and exter-minated one another in the presence of the enemy.

Little by little, the instinct of independence led them to open rebellion against the motherland. For a long time loyalty to the King was, in America as in Spain, the only link between these individualists at odds with one another. After fighting with one another, they ended by turning against the King and the motherland itself—and the ancestral separatism had its way.

It would be a mistake to regard these violent men as rough veterans, adventurers without education and without culture.

Their leaders and those among them who were successful, who conquered or populated countries, were in general hidalgos.

By way of proving their ignorant and destructive barbarism, it is often recalled that, for example, Pizarro, the conqueror of Peru himself, did not know how to read or write, and could barely sign his name. On the other hand, Hernán Cortés, the conqueror of Mexico, was a former student of Salamanca, and had at least a certain literary culture which made him a clever and fluent orator, who adorned his discourses with allusions and examples borrowed from classical antiquity. One even feels in him, as in Bernal Díaz, an anxiety to imitate, if not to eclipse, the illustrious captains of Greek and Roman history.

Together with that, this fine speaker prided himself on being a man of good manners, a model of courtesy and elegance, as careful to observe all the rules of etiquette towards Aztec sovereigns and *caciques* as towards a Grandee of Spain. He was, moreover, as magnificent as he could be in his dress and his retinue.

But these refinements of civilisation, and intellectual culture itself, are things altogether secondary in colonial countries. The inborn intelligence of Pizarro, absolutely illiterate, that intelligence so perfectly adapted to a barbarous environment, was worth more than any diplomas. Firmness, endurance, strength of will, gift of command, perfect knowledge of the country, a spirit of initiative united with all the resources of guile and ingeniousness—all this put Pizarro high above all the present-day products of our Staff colleges, still more above our universitarian *Diafoiri*.

These conquerors have also been accused of destroying, through ignorance and barbarism, precious civilisations like those of the Aztecs and the Incas. This is making civilisation a laughing-stock. Let me repeat once more: those rudimentary civilisations have been overestimated in the most ridiculous way, with the object of lowering and defaming the Spaniards and Catholicism, held as responsible for this alleged destruction.

Can one regard as civilised the Peruvians, who did not know how to write, and who reckoned years and centuries by knots tied in cords; or the Mexicans who used infantile hieroglyphics for history and chronology; peoples who had neither draught beasts nor beasts of burden, neither cows, cereals, nor vines; peoples who were not acquainted with the wheel, and had not reached the Iron Age; peoples among whom man was reduced to the *rôle* of a quadruped, whose bloody religion admitted human sacrifices, and who had markets for human flesh?

If the conquistadors destroyed much and practised needless cruelties—destruction and cruelties which are as nothing beside those of modern war—they blazed the trail for the missionaries who saved for history everything that was essential in those embryonic civilisations, and but for whom we should know absolutely nothing about pre-Columbian America.

CHAPTER XXIII

The Viceroys and the Missionaries

OVER against the conquistadors, a little army lost in an immense continent, was the enormous mass of natives, whom they could not hope to destroy and, indeed, did not want to destroy, since they had come expressly to convert them and save their souls.

Towards these pagan Indians, these new subjects of the Catholic Sovereigns, what was to be the attitude of the clergy, and of the government? There was not the least hesitation: they were to be made Spaniards and Christians. It was a strict duty, an obligation of conscience. It was for this that the Pope, master of all countries known and unknown, had given them as subjects to the King.

The men of that time would not have admitted for a moment the present-day system, which consists in respecting everything in the customs and traditions of colonial peoples that is not absolutely contrary to the essential principles of our civilisation, and in allowing them to evolve, as it is said, within the framework of their own civilisation. They would have regarded it as a monstrosity, a regular piece of impiety, to make such compromises with obvious barbarism, and above all to let these peoples wallow in their old superstitions, their old fierce and bloody idolatries.

These peoples had only to bow down before their new masters, who brought them truth, humanity, and civilisation, to be, in theory at least, regarded as brothers. For this colonial imperialism was entirely impregnated with Christian fraternity: it justified itself solely by anxiety to save souls and elevate inferior races to the level of human dignity. Such was the generous conception—generous despite its narrowness and arbitrariness—which in practice was to collide with almost insuperable obstacles.

If the Church and the King proclaimed that the natives were to be treated as brothers, the rough men who were to change the face of the New World regarded the Indian as a being of incurable inferiority, who could not be anything but a labour-machine and a beast of burden, and whom it was essential, for his own good, to keep in slavery. In practice the native was not to count. These new countries which had just been conquered could be administered only by Spaniards and their half-breeds. Spain had not come to America to maintain indigenous rudimentary civilisations, but to found new Spains there.

This transformation was accomplished with a rapidity which bordered on the miraculous, if one bears in mind the remoteness of the motherland and the difficulties of navigation. In less than half a century the South American continent, with the addition of Mexico, was staked out with Spanish towns and covered with a complete administrative network which, at least on the map, made it, as it were, a prolongation of the Iberian Peninsula.

There were in the first place simple governors, then viceroys, to represent the royal authority and exercise its functions. Side by side with the governors and the viceroys, there was also the important institution of *audiencias*, which shared many governmental prerogatives with them.

The *audiencia* was defined in the first place by its judicial attributes. It was created essentially to render justice, as much to the natives as to the Spanish colonists. But it had also other attributes. It participated in administration properly speaking, in the control of war and finance, with the governors, the captains-general, and even the viceroys.

As to the viceroys, they were theoretically the visible image of the Catholic Sovereign or the Emperor. But in reality their almost absolute power was limited by all kinds of restrictions—a mere measure of prudence, given the extent of the territories which they were supposed to administer, equalling or exceeding that of the greatest European states. At the outset there were only two viceroyalties: that of Mexico and that of Peru. Later there were instituted those of Santa Fé de Bogotá and Buenos Aires.

In the first place the metropolitan authority, fearing lest the viceroys should come to regard themselves as regular sovereigns of these distant lands, did not leave them long in their offices—six or seven years at the most. The case of Antonio de Mendoza, who was viceroy of Mexico for fifteen years, before proceeding to Peru, where he held the same position, was an exception. In the next place, the viceroys were sent "visitors" to check their proceedings: sometimes a general visitation, sometimes an extraordinary visitation in particular cases.

Finally, when they were recalled, they had to render account of their administration before a Judge of Impeachment (*Juez de Residencia*). The visitors and the judge of impeachment summoned to the sound of trumpets all those who had any complaints to make against the retiring viceroy. An inquiry was immediately instituted, which often went on for years and years, with the result that accusers or accused might die before judgment was delivered.

These minute precautions show how much the Spanish sovereigns distrusted their administrators, even the most honest and the best intentioned. We are told that the remedy was often worse than the disease; but, in any case, these regulations attest how seriously the sovereigns designed to fulfil their *rôle* as protectors and civilisers of the Indians.

Other institutions organised in the motherland, such as the Council of the Indies, and the *Casa de Contratación*, whose seat was at Seville, proposed to leave nothing to chance in so far as concerned alike the administration and the exploitation of the New World. The *Casa de Contratación*, created in January, 1503, "inaugurated a whole system of administration and jurisdiction, a new method of commerce and of geographical exploration. As emigration office, trade clearing-house, mercantile tribunal, nautical college, it was the centre of activity which had the most influence upon American enterprises. . . . As to the Council of the Indies, it was, like all the other Councils of the Crown, a consultative and law-making assembly, as well as a tribunal, an administrative office, and an academy of studies. The geography and the history of America owed much to the services of the Council of the Indies."[1]

There were here two administrative organisations which found no equivalents until modern times. Out of them, in the course of the sixteenth century, emerged a formidable body of legislation, comprising no less than six thousand articles dealing with economy, justice, administration, worship, health, education, letters, and the arts, in short, everything that concerned the regime in the New World.

This solicitude of the Spanish sovereigns towards the Indies and the Indians was affirmed from the very beginning of the conquest. One of the most eloquent testimonies which can be adduced—among a swarm of others—is this too little known passage in the Testament of Isabel the Catholic: "When the Apostolic Holy See granted us the Islands and the *Tierra Firme* of the oceanic sea, our principal intention, in soliciting from Pope Alexander VI the concession of the lands discovered and to be discovered, was to convert their peoples to our holy Catholic faith. . . . I beg the King my lord very affectionately, I order and command the Princess my daughter and the Prince my son, to execute and accomplish this intention.

"Let this be their principal end, and let them apply all their diligence to it. Let them not permit, or be the cause, that the Indians inhabiting the said islands and mainland suffer any damage in their persons or their property. *They shall be vigilant, on the contrary, to see that these peoples be treated with justice and kindness.* And if they receive any prejudice, let this prejudice be repaired, and let it be seen to that the mandate which was confided to us by the Apostolic letters is faithfully executed."

Isabel's successors respected the wishes of the pious Queen. In 1526, Charles V issued ordinances at Granada which once more recalled the religious object of the conquest. Finally, after the complaints of Las Casas against the tyranny and the cruelties of the colonists, other ordinances, which were called "the new Laws," were issued in 1542 by the same sovereign. In them it was prescribed notably: "that no Indian may be reduced to slavery, either for reason of war or rebellion, or for any other reason, seeing that all are vassals of the royal Crown of Castile"; "that none shall employ an Indian as servant or in any other capacity against his will"; "that no

[1] Carlos Pereyra: *Breve historia de America*, p. 229.

viceroy, or any officer, may grant commanderies of Indians, and that those which belong to a deceased *encomendero* be restored to the royal Crown."

Unfortunately these generous measures were not applied. The royal ordinances, received with submission, remained a dead letter. (*Lo que el Rey manda se obedece, no se cumple*: what the King commands is obeyed, but not executed.) It was the eternal conflict between colonists and the administrators and legislators of the motherland.

A motherland, we must recognise, too often legislates to the detriment of its interests and in complete ignorance of the unfortunate or cruel conditions with which the colonists have to deal— and this on grounds of humanity for which the native is not in the least grateful to it. On the other hand the colonist, living in a barbarous and hostile environment, is only too strongly tempted to employ reprisals and exploit a disarmed enemy.

Accordingly the viceroys, caught between the royal injunction and the ill-will of the colonists, found their efforts almost useless. Their *rôle* was only too often confined to deriving the utmost possible advantage from an always dangerous office. Nevertheless some among them, who left a reputation as great administrators, exerted themselves to reconcile the interests of the colonies and the crown with the principles of humanity recommended or imposed by the sovereigns. Such, for example, was Antonio de Mendoza, who was the first viceroy of Mexico, from 1535 to 1550, at which date he went to Peru to exercise the same functions there.

Such, again, was Francisco de Toledo, who was nicknamed the Peruvian Solon, and began by devoting five whole years to visiting the territories entrusted to him. He never applied a measure until he had satisfied himself that it was applicable, remembering what his great predecessor Mendoza had repeated: "that before changing anything whatsoever in the kingdom, one should see things with his own eyes, to which purpose he needs good health and, even more, youth."

But the actions of the viceroys, given their false position and also the short duration of their exercise of their functions, could not yield either very solid or very lasting results.

The influence of the clergy—an influence not merely religious, but also civilising in the widest sense of the word—was considerable in a different way.

Inasmuch as the object of the conquest was the propagation of the faith, it is obvious that the clergy were bound to play a preponderant *rôle* in it. It is difficult for us to realise to-day with what enthusiasm, what ardour of faith, the Spanish monks threw themselves into this spiritual conquest. We must endeavour to imagine the intoxication of joy and pride, the great outburst of daring, self-confidence, temerity and heroism, which possessed the victorious nation on the morrow of the taking of Granada. It must have been something analogous with the outburst of faith and conquering impetuousness which launched the companions of the Prophet to the attack on the old Greco-Roman world.

The field of the Crusades was enlarged indefinitely, so to speak. In the same way as the fever of gold took to America a swarm of poor men and adventurers hallucinated by chimerical paradises, so the fever of evangelisation brought out of their cells armies of monks thirsting for martyrdom, or thirsting for movement and liberty, consumed with desire to win souls, build churches, found monasteries, educate and control obedient masses, and be themselves discoverers and founders.

Accordingly we find enrolled among these conquistadors of Christ and the Church great lords and personages of royal blood, such as the Franciscan Peter of Ghent, a relative of the Emperor Charles V. Elderly men, weak and infirm, men incurably ill, like the Dominican Louis Bertrand, insisted upon setting out with the young and strong. Despite his weakness, his ulcerated leg and the fever that wasted him, Louis Bertrand devoted himself for years to converting the Caraibs of New Granada. At the age of eighty Juan de Zumarraga, the first Archbishop of Mexico, conceived the idea, together with the Dominican Betanzos and Las Casas, who was as old as himself, of crossing the Pacific, recently opened to European navigation, and going and preaching to the Chinese.

Unlike the seekers of gold and the Spanish administrators, these apostles regarded the Indians as brothers who must be enlightened and led. The *encomenderos*, to whom territories and whole populations of Indians were granted on the condition of feeding them and instructing them in the Christian faith—these colonists declared that there was nothing to be done with the Indians. As lacking in intelligence as animals, they could be nothing but beasts of burden and labour.

The religious and the bishops protested indignantly against such ideas and tendencies. Fray Julián Garcés, Bishop of Tlascala, stood out particularly through a letter of protest addressed to Pope Paul III, which made a great impression in Europe as well as America.

"Where," asked this prelate, "is the man presumptuous and impudent enough to dare to affirm that the Indians are incapable of receiving the faith, when we find them practising the mechanical arts and when, within the limits of our ministry alone, we can attest their natural goodness, their fidelity and their diligence? . . . It is but just to recognise them as rational beings, fully conscious and endowed with understanding. Their children surpass ours in their mental capacity and quickness of intelligence. . . . To-day they are happily so well educated (I speak of the children) that they write in Latin and in Castilian better than our Spaniards."

The good bishop was, no doubt, generalising from exceptional cases, or neglecting to investigate these infant prodigies very closely. In the same way as Las Casas regarded his Indians as "gentle sheep," Fray Julián Garcés attributed to his, for the purposes of his argument, aptitudes and talents probably much exaggerated. Be that as it may, the Sovereign Pontiff re-echoed his protest in a famous Bull, the Bull *Ipsa veritas*, of which the essential passage was as follows:

"He Who is Truth itself and can neither deceive nor be deceived said to the preachers of His faith, when He sent them to exercise their ministry: *Go and preach to all nations*. He said "all nations" indifferently, because all are capable of receiving this teaching. . . . But the Enemy of the human race has persuaded some of his ministers to affirm, the better to satisfy their cupidity, that the Indians and other peoples recently come to our knowledge ought to be treated as brute beasts and reduced to servitude, as being incapable of receiving the Catholic Faith. . . .

"Desiring to bring remedy to such a state of things, in the name of our Apostolic authority we declare by the present letters that the Indians and other peoples recently known to us, even if they are outside the Christian faith, be not and cannot be deprived of their liberty, or of the possession of their property, and that they must by no means be reduced to slavery."

Unhappily it was the same with the Pontifical Bulls as with the royal ordinances. They changed nothing, or almost nothing, in an inveterate evil. Slavery, ill-treatment, and cruelty continued. All that the religious could obtain was the moderation or the partial amelioration of the regime.

But let us not be in a hurry to condemn the colonists, for whom there was a swarm of extenuating circumstances, which anybody who has lived in colonial countries will understand. The life of these men was something of a torment as well as a heroism—and that deserves the recognition of their descendants. Let me repeat, moreover: to judge what they were driven to do, we should need to have lived that life of theirs and known the dangers of all kinds by which, and the merciless enemies by whom, they were surrounded.

In any event, the principal object of the propagators of the faith was achieved: they won a whole continent for Christianity. In less than fifty years they obtained what four centuries of crusades had never accomplished, a conquest which surpassed the wildest dreams of the most conquering Popes.

In the history of Western humanity, this was a result of extreme importance. Converted to Christianity, the conquered peoples were to accept the essential principles of our culture, and not merely the external or material part of our civilisation, as in the case of Asiatic or African peoples who remain faithful to their ancestral religions.

The American Indian or half-breed is closer to us than the most cultured Musulman, Buddhist, or Shintoist.

Apart from any religious consideration, these missionaries of the New World must be regarded as great civilisers. Not only did they abolish human sacrifice and cannibalism, together with fetishism and idolatry; they also ceaselessly combated slavery in all its forms. They did not confine themselves to evangelising; they also exerted themselves to elevate and educate their catechumens. The Franciscans, the Dominicans, and, after them, the Augustinians and the Jesuits, were the great educators of the Americans.

It was the Franciscans who founded the first colleges. Peter of Ghent, who founded that of Mexico City, succeeded, we are told, in assembling as many as a thousand pupils, to whom he taught not only Latin, sacred music, and Castilian, but also all kinds of arts and crafts. Similar foundations multiplied in Mexico, thanks to the initiative of the clergy or the viceroys. One of the most remarkable was that established by Archbishop Juan de Zumarraga, who, in his college of Santiago de Tlaltelolco, grouped a select band of young natives, in order that, once they were in possession of the Castilian language, they might teach their own language to future Spanish preachers.

After that, universities were created in the principal centres: first in Mexico, then in Lima, where, in the middle of the sixteenth century, there was opened the University of San Marcos, a daughter, like that of Mexico, of the University of Salamanaca, and enjoying the same privilege. Thanks to its enormous revenues, it was able to maintain as many as thirty-two Chairs. "There was also to be found at Lima the *Protomedicato*, a centre independent of the University."[1]

There were other centres, for example, Sante Fé de Bogotá, which possessed two universities. One was that of Santo Tomas, founded in 1627 by the Dominicans, as a development of a grammar school created in 1572. For their part the Jesuits had founded the Universidad Javeriana, placed, as its name indicates, under the protection of Saint Francis Xavier.

In addition, New Granada numbered twenty-three colleges and a very large number of primary schools, for every monastery had one of its own. In Argentina the great university centre was Cordova del Tucumán, where the Jesuits established their Colegio Maximo in 1613. There was another at Charcas, whose teaching was preferred to that of Lima.

All this assumed a learned equipment: printing-presses and libraries. The first printing-house in the New World was installed in Mexico, about the year 1535, by Archbishop Zumarraga. There were early in Mexico, as at Lima and Santa Fé, important libraries founded by the religious, which, together with works of philosophy

[1] Cf. Carlos Pereyra: *La obra de España en America*, p. 130 *et seq.*

and theology, comprised collections of the Greek and Latin classics and treatises on physics and mathematics.

But perhaps the greatest service which these monks rendered America was that of studying its languages and its history—in fact, all its past anterior to Columbus's discovery. In order to preach directly to the natives, they wanted to know even their humblest dialects. They composed grammars, lexicons, and dictionaries. They made themselves not only grammarians and lexicographers, but also ethnographers and historians. From geography and mineralogy to the study of religious and political systems they embraced everything, and poured the treasure-trove of their researches into books which are regular scientific compendia.

Among other capital works of this class, the *History of the Incas of Peru*, by Garcilaso de la Vega—who, if not one of these monks, was at least one of their pupils—and the *General History of the Things of the New World*, by Father Sahagun, are still regarded to-day as regular monuments of erudition, repertories as abundant as they are indispensable to anybody concerned with studies of this kind.

I have already referred to the charge so often formulated against the Spaniards and against the missionaries in general: that of having destroyed the treasures of the old American civilisations through fanaticism and ignorance, and we have seen how, in order to increase the guilt of these iconoclasts and vandals, these civilisations have been ridiculously overestimated.

Neither the conquistadors nor the missionaries were so much to blame. It is already some little time since the eminent Mexican scholar, Joaquín García Icazbalceta,[1] dealt adequately with these monstrously exaggerated accusations.

That destructions of idols, temples, and hieroglyphic paintings took place was certainly the case. But these destructions in no way diminished the sum of the ideas that we can form about the history and religion of the primitive peoples of America—those peoples who did not know the art of writing, and whose history was limited to rude chronological notations. Everything there was to be known was obtained by the monks and missionaries, who had the patience to interrogate the Indians of their time, to collect still living traditions, and to describe what they saw in the way of monuments still standing.

I may add that in teaching the Indians to read and write, and teaching them languages as perfected as Latin or Castilian, they provided them with mediums of expression of which they had no previous conception. They enabled them to become conscious of a past which was on the point of foundering in their memories.

Naturally, in the intentions of the missionaries, all this intellectual culture was subordinated to religious propaganda. What dominated

[1] See, in particular, p. 373 *et seq.*, in his *Biografía de D. Fr. Juan de Zumarraga, primer obispo y arzobispo de Méjico.*

all their efforts was the propagation of the faith and anxiety to maintain that faith in all its purity. Hence it was that the Inquisition was not slow to be introduced into the New World, as it had been into Spain. The first Inquisitor was precisely that Juan de Zumarraga who founded the first colleges and the first printing-houses in Mexico.

It would be preposterous and, indeed, absurd, to defend the Inquisition. But it may be said that the number of its victims in South America was much less than certain historians have imagined; that burnings of warlocks and men possessed were also frequent in Protestant countries; and, finally, that this persecution of dissidents was rendered obligatory, for the royal officials as for the religious, by the very terms of the mandate which the Crown of Spain had assumed in accepting the conquest and domination of the New World. Their *rôle* was to extend and defend the Faith. In consequence, anybody who opposed this programme must be treated as an enemy.

This was why the American Inquisition, during the first century of its existence, persecuted especially Lutheran English and Dutch, and Jews or Judaisants escaped from Spain and Portugal. From the political and commercial point of view, these heretics might also be dangerous rivals and enemies. The other persons condemned were bigamists and sodomists or common law criminals, found guilty of cannibalism and ritual murders. The Inquisition tended more and more to assume the functions of an ordinary tribunal or a secret police organisation.

It is not a question of condemning or whitewashing proceedings which we regard to-day as absolutely iniquitous and odious. It is a question of determining what the New World owed to its Spanish conquerors and its missionaries. It is impossible to dispute that it owed them everything that we understand by the word "civilisation."

But for the uncompromising and indomitable faith by which these last Crusaders were carried away, it is certain that America would not have been thrown so widely open to the influence, and to the immigration, of the Christian peoples, and that the whole of America would not have become what it is to-day—namely, an extension of our old European world.

CHAPTER XXIV

The Work of Spain in America

THE winning of gold, the other motive force of the American enterprise, was at first only a mirage, which inflicted cruel disappointments on the early colonists. The discovery and exploitation of the mines demanded considerable time. Before anything else, it was necessary to win the soil, and render it habitable and supporting for the European immigrant. But for the planters and the graziers of Cuba and San Domingo, it would have been impossible to equip the expeditions and extend the conquest on the mainland.

This conquest and this peopling of American soil were a regular piece of creation: a Spanish creation. To us, habituated as we are to our countries of long-standing cultivation, to flora and fauna domesticated for centuries, it is hard to realise what such an undertaking meant. We who find the table laid, and have only to stretch out our hand to pluck a fruit, cannot imagine what life must be like in countries where human cultivation does not exist.

The conquistadors had to import into America, together with their food, the animals and the working implements which would enable them to master the soil. One may say that it was the horse, steel, and powder which founded Spanish domination in America. We may add the dogs, which were regular combatants side by side with the conquistadors. Without them, and without their cavalry and artillery, the converters sent by His Holiness and His Cæsarian Majesty would have been promptly annihilated by the natives.

The horses brought from Spain multiplied so rapidly throughout the South American continent that in some regions they rapidly reverted to the wild state. Asses and mules, also imported from Castile, took the place of the llamas and the vicuñas of Peru for work in connection with the mines and all kinds of transport.

At the same time as draught beasts, beasts for consumption were also introduced, especially pigs, whose rearing became the principal resource of the first colonists, and then cows and sheep. Goats were also imported, as those of the country were regarded as inferior to the strains which the Spanish ships brought from Guinea or the Canaries. Finally the native species were improved by all kinds of crossings. Castilian hens, ducks, and turkeys filled the farmyards of Mexico and Peru.

The most precious gift which Spain made to America was wheat. It was unknown there before the conquest. All that was known was maize and manioc. I have already recalled the story, or the legend, of Inés Múñoz planting three grains of wheat, which had come from Spain, in a flower-pot, and how the ears that came out of this pot sowed Peru. This story is repeated in other forms in all the American countries. Up and down the continent, in the monasteries of Santa Fé or Mexico, reverend Fathers tell the legend of the first grain of wheat that came from Castile, and show you the flower-pot which produced that wheat, the father of the harvests of the New World.

The vine was not slow to follow corn. It prospered especially in Peru. At the outset, however, the smallest vine-branch was worth its weight in gold. Those who had planted a few slips in their *huertas* had to have them guarded by armed men, so rare were the plants. The same applied to the olive tree, which was brought to Lima by Inés Múñoz's second husband, Antonio de Ribera, who arrived from Spain with a case of young olive trees which came from the Ajarafe of Seville.

Only one of these olive trees survived, and it became enormous. It was called the Castilian olive tree, and soon had a whole history. When it had grown, its owner, on the occasion of a procession, cut a branch of it and placed it in the path of the Holy Sacrament: a proceeding which aroused the greed of everybody present. To save the precious branch, a monk took possession of it and made a present of it to the owner of a *huerta*, one Gonzalo Guillén, but on the condition that, if the branch took root and grew, they should share the crop.

The branch grew so well that the colonist thought it more advantageous to buy out the monk's interest with a bar of silver. Having become sole owner of the tree, he sold shoots of it, which brought him in from four to five thousand pesos. Finally there was a regular grove of olive trees in the *huerta* where the monk's branch had been planted.

Naturally the first olives were very dear. To offer five or six to one's guests was regarded as a refinement of generosity. Other fruits and vegetables imported from Spain and acclimatised in America produced similar miracles and similar greeds—oranges, lemons, asparagus, and even mere carrots. Garcilaso de la Vega, who was a half-breed of Inca and Spaniard, tells us with charming simplicity what an event was the appearance on his father's table of the first three sticks of Castilian asparagus.

"I remember," he says, "that in the year 1555-1556 Garcia de Tuelo, a native of Trujillo, then treasurer of savings in the imperial city of Cuzco, decided to send Garcilaso de la Vega, my dear father and lord, three asparagus, produce of Spain, of which he made him a present as something exquisite. . . . These asparagus were very fine, but unequal, because there were two as thick as one of the fingers of the hand, and much longer than a quarter of an ell. But, as to the third, it was much thicker and also much shorter, and all three were so tender that they broke of themselves.

"To do greater honour to these new plants, my father had them cooked in his room, in the presence of the seven or eight gentlemen who were supping at his table. When they were cooked, he had vinegar and oil brought, and then my father divided the two longest among the guests, to every one of whom he gave a little, and he reserved the third for himself, saying that they would pardon him, *because it was a question of a novelty of Spain.*"

I have reported this anecdote at length, because it is highly typical and significant. This ceremonial taking of three sticks of Spanish asparagus in a special room was something like a solemn communion with the motherland. There was more affection than epicurism in the episode of Garcilaso's father reserving the third stick to himself alone, because, as he said, it was "a novelty of Spain." What these colonists sought was to give themselves the illusion of the home-land that they missed, to create new Spains in America.

Everything proves this superabundantly, from the names of the cities which they founded and the viceroyalties which they con-quered and organised, to the fruits and vegetables which they exerted themselves to acclimatise in the soil of exile. There are thousands of other examples to show us that these conquerors, seekers of gold or hunters of souls, religious or colonists, were before all else cultivators and graziers, eager to develop the land as well as its inhabitants, and create there a new fertility and a flora and fauna which the untilled soil had never known.

The native products, in their turn, were improved and cultivated intensively. The cultivation of the sugar-cane was not slow in becoming the main source of wealth of the Antilles. Some colonists even tried to introduce the silk industry into New Spain. The first experiments gave excellent results—so brilliant, so unexpected, that Father Motolinia, in his *Historia de los Indios de la Nueva España,* went so far as to say that the silks of Mexico would supplant all others in the markets of Christendom. Unfortunately the dis-covery of the Philippines and the diffusion of Chinese silks dealt a fatal blow to the young Mexican industry.

This transformation of the soil by the Spanish colonist no longer strikes the eye to-day. His contribution is merged in the native wealth. But what it is impossible not to see is the profound imprint which he stamped upon his conquest.

In a few years he changed the face of it. With a kind of joyous haste, analogous with the transport and delirium of procreation, he sowed towns and centres of population wherever he went. These towns have an individual, unforgettable physiognomy, like that of the proud individuals—who were, indeed, heroes—that founded them.

This must obviously be true if even to-day, after a century of unrestrained Anglo-Saxonism and Germanism, North American writers find themselves compelled to recognise it. "New Spain," writes Sylvester Baxter in his *History of Spanish Architecture in Mexico,* "never experienced the long period of colonial simplicity of the English possessions. The land was transformed as though it had been illuminated by Aladdin's lamp. Thanks to the startling energy of the conquerors, greedy for wealth and power, animated at the same time by a profound faith, the new Spain became flourishing within a few years, and was metamorphosed into a marvellous kingdom, whose immensity was dotted with splendid cities which arose suddenly in the midst of the desert, or occupied the site of an old native town."

The contemporaries of this heroic period, who were able to compare the two conditions of the country, before and after the conquest, express an admiration for the Spanish achievement in which national pride doubtless plays a large part, but which nevertheless seems to correspond to the facts of the case.

"Let curious readers," says Bernal Díaz, "consider how many cities, towns, and villages peopled by Spaniards there are in this country. There are so many that, not knowing all their names, I shall not speak of them. Let them pay attention to the ten bishoprics, without counting the archbishopric of the most worthy city of Mexico, and to the three royal seats. Let them look at the holy cathedral churches, the monasteries peopled by Dominicans, Franciscans, Fathers of Charity and Augustinians, the number of hospitals and their great blessings, and the devout house of Our Lady of Guadalupe.

"Let them take account also of the University of Mexico, where are studied and taught grammar, theology, rhetoric, philosophy and other arts and sciences; its master-printers and its presses for printing all kind of books, both in Latin and in the vulgar tongue; and that here are conferred degrees of licenciates and doctors."

After these foundations of an intellectual or spiritual kind, he deals with the natural wealth of the country: the mines of gold and silver brought into exploitation, the industries created by the conquerors, the transformation effected in the customs of the natives, who practise all the professions of the Europeans, and have their own police, their local administration, their officers of justice. "Every year they elect their ordinary *alcades*, *regidores*, registrars, constables, stewards of taxes and savings. They have their town-halls with their sheriffs. They assemble there twice a week, rendering justice, securing payment of debts, and, for some criminal offences, whipping and chastising."

The Indians, too, "have their churches very richly provided with altars and all the accessories of Divine worship, such as crosses, chandeliers, candle-sticks, chalices, patines, salvers small and large, censers, the whole in wrought silver. In rich communities, the copes, chasubles and frontals are commonly of velvet, damask, satin and taffetas of varied colours and embroideries, and the ornaments of the cross subtly worked with gold, silk and sometimes pearls."

The obliging chronicler does not stop at these splendours. He vaunts the luxury of the chiefs, who have carriages and horses of price. He enumerates the festivals devoutly celebrated by these new Spaniards, who have the same amusements as in Spain: ring-tilting, single-stick contests, bull-fights. The Castilian colonists might cherish the illusion that they had never left their native *pueblo*.

What is certain is that they gave their new cities a profoundly Spanish character. There is a Spanish colonial architecture. These men, who were often dying of hunger and short of clothes, possessed in a high degree the Latin sense of beauty and magnificence. Proud of their race as of their deeds, proud of their country as of their sovereigns, they wanted to do honour to Imperial Spain by building edifices worthy of her greatness in the conquered territory. Nothing was fine enough or great enough for the glorious subjects of his Cæsarian Majesty.

Other countries may think of economy in their colonies, and be basely practical and utilitarian. Their buildings may reek of administrative parsimony and lack of imagination. The architecture of the Spaniards in America is truly monumental in character and it includes some conceptions of genius, such, for example, as the cathedral and the great square in Mexico City.

In general the churches and the palaces, everything that had to do with worship or the royal majesty, had an air of grandeur, austerity, and strength, and, at the same time, a very Spanish appearance. All South America is full of such churches, palaces, monasteries, hospitals or schools, and you are immediately reminded of the university cities or the religious metropoles of Old Spain—or, again, of such-and-such a street-corner, cross-roads, or little square in a small town of Andalusia or Estremadura.

All the Spanish styles have left examples in Spain, from the declining Gothic to the severe style of the end of the eighteenth century, by way of plateresque, baroque, and the most disordered churrigueresque. Earthquakes and revolutions have destroyed many of these old colonial edifices; but descriptions of some of them have been preserved for us. We know that on the morrow of the conquest of Mexico, a few years after the entrance of Cortés into the Aztec capital, there was a Royal Palace in Mexico City, which served as the residence of the viceroy.

A contemporary writer vaunts its façade, "with its high galleries adorned with slender columns and its stone balustrades . . . the great hall, with its platform hung with rich tapestries and its dais of damask spangled with gold, where are placed the seats of the councillors. That of the viceroy is of velvet, provided with a cushion, also of velvet, for his feet."

A century later another writer, describing the same royal palace, gives us an idea of the development which it had undergone since the days of Cortés and Bernal Díaz. It was a whole world to itself, a labyrinth of courtyards, galleries, and corridors, with monumental staircases. At the entrance was an octagonal fountain, in white marble, surmounted by a bronze horse. Everywhere throughout the halls there was a profusion of hangings, velvets, crimson damasks bearing the royal arms embroidered in relief; portraits of the sovereigns, seats of the councillors, the dais and throne of the viceroy.

But, more than all this external magnificence, what we must bear in mind is the moral imprint given to a whole continent by the Spanish genius. Not only in those American cities where you breathe the air of Castile and Andalusia, where you rediscover their colour and their atmosphere, but everywhere else as well, from one end of the continent to the other, among the natives and the half-breeds no less than among the colonists of pure Iberian race, you find a spiritual unity which relates to one another all these peoples separated by thousands of leagues and subject to the most widely differing climates: which, in short, relates them with their ancestors or their Spanish or Portuguese masters of the early period.

With all their defects, which are many, they represent a new form of Latinity, in other words, of Western civilisation in its highest form. In face of Anglo-Saxon pressure, of the machinism and collectivism of the North, they represent the resistance of the individual and the free activity of man.

These people of Buenos Aires, Rio, or Lima are closer to us Latins than those of New York or Chicago. They perpetuate, in a world younger than our own, a conception of life, traditions of culture and of intellectual elegance, a sense of pleasure and of beauty, a need of leisure, even of idleness, which are the condition of great works of art and thought and do honour to humanity.

CHAPTER XXV

The World Balance-Sheet of the Discovery

LET us imagine the effect that would be created in our modern world by the discovery in the South Polar seas of an unknown land; a land inhabited by peoples possessing a civilisation of their own, with a climate and products which upset all our historical and scientific theories, our geology as well as our philology; a land reached by a new route which was regarded as impracticable—and we shall have only a faint idea of the emotion which seized hold of our Old World at the news of the prodigious voyage of Columbus and his return from it.

We find an echo of this emotion in the enthusiastic letters which Pedro Martir addressed to his learned and aristocratic correspondents. On September 13, 1493, he wrote to the Count of Tendilla and the Archbishop of Granada: "Lift up your hearts, veterans of learning! Columbus announces that he has discovered marvels!" Again, in a letter to the philosopher Pomponio Leti, he wrote: "You exulted with joy and you could not restrain your tears when I confirmed to you the news of the discovery of the world, hitherto hidden, of the Antipodes. Your reply enables me to judge your emotion."

This enthusiasm, this marvelling, have been disputed, as everything in the least extraordinary or heroic in the story of the Discoverer has been disputed. We are asked to believe that it was he who provided all the expenses of his publicity and that he organised it cleverly himself. Nevertheless, the mere extracts from letters which I have just quoted testify to the impression that was produced in literate and erudite circles.

It is unquestionable that Columbus's exploit enjoyed a popular success as well. Otherwise it is not to be explained that he should have found so many volunteers for his second voyage. We know, moreover, that within the same year the fame of his exploit spread throughout all Europe. In Italy and in Germany, poems celebrated the isles of gold discovered by the intrepid admiral of the oceanic seas.

The fact was that the old Mediterranean world had collapsed. Millenary barriers were broken. That world was no longer blockaded by Islam at the two outlets from the Mediterranean. The horizon expanded, and new ways were opened to human activity, and to human thought. The world escaped at last from that little inland sea where there had been so much scuffling and struggling among European peoples for centuries. Men felt themselves liberated and, at the same time, increased in strength. The power of man had grown, coincidently with the extension of his dominion over new seas and lands. It was, in short, a New Man who was born.

This New Man, who became the model more or less avowed, more or less envied, of all Christendom, was the Spaniard of the sixteenth century. The man of the Renaissance modelled himself, consciously or unconsciously, upon the Spaniard of his time. That model was in the first place a cosmopolitan, inasmuch as he was, in the first place, a great traveller. He had fought in Italy, Germany, and Flanders. He had conquered islands and continents in the New World. He had seen strange countries, many strange countries. He had lived there, he had struck roots there, he had founded cities and kingdoms there.

This cosmopolitan knew the world better than our tourists or even our colonial officials of to-day, who merely rush through exotic countries or see them pass by, at full speed, from the window of a sleeping-car or the cabin of an aeroplane. Colonist, soldier, or official, captain-general or viceroy, he was as much at home in Lima as in Mexico, in Rome or Milan as in Brussels. Hence arose an assurance and an audacity, a spirit of initiative and enterprise, a need of adventure, which the Christian world had forgotten.

This Spanish Man was confident in himself and his future. Was it not he who had vanquished Islam—that Islam whose menace had weighed for centuries upon Christendom and which, even beaten, was still to be feared? Had he not, with a few ships and a handful of bold comrades, conquered and subjected a whole new world?

He was very full of the sense of his strength and his valour. He was bursting with pride and presumption, with a swaggering and a swashbuckling which bordered upon rhodomontade. Spaniard and Catholic, he represented the highest aristocracy in the world. So let nobody dare to dispute his precedence in the ante-chambers of the Pope or his victory on the battle-field!

It was because he was high-minded as well as strong that everything was due to him: wealth and domination. He wanted luxury, grandeur, beauty, voluptuousness around him. His manners grew polished. He became, for the rest of Europe, the type of perfect gentleman, as much through the elegance and sober distinction of his costume as through his courtesy and his art of enjoying life.

His cities, like his palaces, beautified themselves. Flanders sent him her tapestries and her linen; Italy her pictures, her statues, her jewellers' ware, her perfumes; America her timber and her precious metals. By the end of the sixteenth century, Madrid became a great cosmopolitan centre—a centre not only of politics, but also of business and the arts. From all parts of the vast Spanish Empire, men on the make and intriguers flowed thither, together with merchants, bankers, painters, artists, and craftsmen of all kinds, men of learning and travellers.

The lower orders themselves acquired polish in their turn, and felt their pretensions growing through contact with such magnificent and gallant lords. In the seventeenth century, it was not unusual to see mere craftsmen bearing swords. Menial occupations were left to foreigners or to peasants come from the most backward provinces of

Spain. It was French Auvergnats who cleaned the boots of the hidalgos and acted as knife-grinders, porters, and water-carriers in the Spanish capital.

To this enlargement of material life corresponded another enlargement—and of greater importance—in the intellectual sphere. Carried by the navigators and discoverers, propagated by a whole literature of explorations and voyages, new notions made their way into men's minds and changed the face of reality, together with the fundamental axioms of learning. Throughout the sixteenth century and into the seventeenth, the Spanish writers of the New World—among whom were a certain number of natives—diffused an enormous mass of facts and ideas all through Europe and the whole world: whether they were historians or linguists, botanists, naturalists, metallurgists, soldiers or explorers, or even simple travellers who told of their ship-wrecks and their sufferings in the unknown islands. Spanish-American literature fills square kilometres of archives and libraries.

The first consequence of this afflux of new ideas was a diminution of the respect paid to antiquity, sacred as well as profane. Columbus, through his discoveries, had proved that antiquity was wrong, not only in its pagan philosophers, but also in its Fathers of the Church and its theologians. Modern rationalism, so far as it stands opposed to the slavishness and the superstition of antiquity, derives from this —from the confidence which the man of the sixteenth century discovered in himself; from the liberation and the enlarging of his intelligence, on the threshold of a new world and of unsuspected realities.

Here, in itself, is something that the Renaissance owed to Spain, apart from her own art and literature, whose richness and originality are unrivalled. The share of Italy, and that of Greco-Latin antiquity, in the work of the Renaissance have been immoderately exaggerated. The most modern share, the part that was most alive, most full of promise for the future, obviously belongs to Spain.

What a strange thing it is!—the American enterprise, the last Crusade against Islam, thus presents itself to us as the final flowering of the thought of the Middle Ages, as the liquidation of a whole, long past. It was out of this religious idea that was born the modern world, sceptical and rationalist.

§ VII

THE SPANISH HEGEMONY AND THE ESTABLISHMENT OF THE ABSOLUTE MONARCHY

CHAPTER XXVI

The Policy of the Catholic Sovereigns. The Wars of Italy. The Royal Marriages. Settlements in Africa

" NOTHING can make a prince more esteemed," writes Machiavelli, "than his great enterprises and the fine examples which he gives. We have in our days Ferdinand of Aragón, at present King of Spain. One may almost consider him as a new prince, inasmuch as, from his being the weak monarch he was, his glory and his renown have made of him the first monarch of Christendom. It you consider his actions, you will find them all great and some of them extraordinary. At the commencement of his reign he assaulted Granada, and that was the beginning of his greatness."

This eulogy smacks a little of the courtier. There was nothing great about Ferdinand, who was rather a man of petty means and tortuous ruses, but of a practical and singularly realist turn of mind. His chief merit, in the eyes of his compatriots, was that, more or less unconsciously, he paved the way for Spanish hegemony, which really was a great thing and was to last more than a century and a half. As Machiavelli truly remarks, the beginning of his fortune coincided with the taking of Granada, which occurred on January 2, 1492.

Already, several years earlier, his marriage with Isabel of Castile, by completing the *de facto* unification of Spain, had put in his power one of the most important States of Christendom. His victory over the Moors, his possession of the kingdom of Granada, the political marriages of his children, the successes of his arms in Italy, the fortunate manœuvres of his diplomacy; and finally the discovery of America, the sudden enrichment of the Spanish nation, and the intoxication of conquest which seized upon it, after all these unexpected triumphs, gave Spain a prestige such as had not been known in Europe since the collapse of the Roman Empire.

Such good fortune could not fail to provoke jealousies and rivalries. At that moment the designated rival of Spain was France, her nearest neighbour: a kingdom more united than Spain, which the excellent administration of Louis XI had just made stronger than she had ever been before.

A struggle between the two nations was inevitable. They had urgent frontier questions to settle, in the direction of Navarre as well as in the direction of the Cerdagne and Roussillon. Competition over heritages was to divide them still more.

Ferdinand of Aragón and the young King Charles VIII of France had more or less debatable rights over the Kingdom of Naples. Ferdinand I, bastard son of Alfonso V of Aragón, held this kingdom in defiance of his cousin Ferdinand, the husband of Isabel of Castile. His exactions had dissatisfied the Neapolitan nobility, who, in order to get rid of him, invoked the rights of the Crown of France to the kingdom of Naples, which had belonged to Charles of Anjou, brother of Louis XI.

Since an Aragonese dynasty had supplanted the Angevin dynasty, the rights of France seemed to have lapsed. But René of Anjou, who had just died, had revived them by bequeathing his territories and titles to Louis XI and his descendants. Accordingly Charles VIII could regard his pretensions to Naples as legitimate, and entertain the offers which were made to him by the Neapolitan barons.

By way of further justification of an expedition to Italy, the King of France declared that he would only call at Naples, and that the real object of the campaign was to go and attack the Turks in Constantinople. He was setting out, he said, on a new Crusade. It was this religious pretext which covered all the wars undertaken at that time, just in the same way as in our time wars require social or humanitarian ends. It is no longer religion, but civilisation or humanity, which one is said to be defending.

This war of Italy is usually regarded as a juvenile folly on the part of the young Charles VIII: the itching of ambition in a feeble mind. To argue in this way is to ignore the political necessities which made the possession of Italy a question of the first importance for France and Spain. According to the manner in which it was decided, one or the other of the two rivals would be put in a position of inferiority.

Spain could not allow France to gain a footing in Italy, especially in the kingdom of Naples. Ferdinand of Aragón was in possession of Sicily, whence he kept watch over the Barbaresques, the eternal enemies of Spain and her trade, who, recently expelled from Andalusia, continued to harry and raid the Andalusian coasts through their pirates. Could she tolerate a neighbour as dangerous as the French installed in Campania, whence they would certainly attempt to gain Sicily at the first opportunity? Was it prudent, above all, to let them occupy southern Italy, the advanced bastion of defence against the Turks?

Spain, even after the taking of Granada, lived in terror of a descent by the united Ottoman and Barbaresque fleets. In 1480 the Turks had seized Otranto and threatened the whole Italian peninsula. But an even worse danger, in Ferdinand's eyes, was that of seeing the King of France acquire his rich heritage of Naples and augment his maritime power by occupying new ports in the Mediterranean, which would compete with the eastern Spanish ports.

On the French side fears were no less intense. If Ferdinand supplanted his cousin in Naples, as he looked like doing, being already the possessor of the whole of the southern coast of Spain, together with Sicily, he would turn the western Mediterranean into a Spanish lake. All trade would pass into the hands of the ship-owners of Barcelona, Valencia, and Málaga. The King of Spain would become master of the straits which commanded navigation of the eastern Mediterranean.

Moreover, if Spain gained a footing in Italy, whence she could lend a hand to various enemies of France, she would become a very serious danger. Such a further aggrandisement, after her throwing-back of the Moors to Africa, would in itself be a great source of anxiety to France. This anxiety was only increased some years later, when the Catholic Sovereigns married their children to princes and princesses whose standing added still more to the prestige of the Spanish hegemony.

In 1497, the Infante Don Juan married Margaret of Austria, daughter of the Emperor Maximilian. Shortly afterwards the Infanta Juana married the Archduke Philip the Fair, brother of Margaret and son of the Emperor. Through his mother, Marguerite of Burgundy, the Archduke was sovereign prince of Namur and heir to Brabant, Hainault, Holland, Zeeland, Luxembourg, in short the whole of Flanders. Moreover, as the government of Charles VIII had made the mistake of restoring Artois, the Franche-Comté and the Charolais to him, this son-in-law of the Catholic Sovereigns, master of the French northern and eastern frontiers, could penetrate into the heart of France when he chose.

Ferdinand set the seal upon his work by giving his daughter Catherine to Henry, Prince of Wales, the future Henry VIII, who, if need be, could threaten the King of France in his own kingdom, should he presume to proceed to Italy with conquering intentions.

France thus ran the risk of being encircled by land and sea. The astuteness of Ferdinand was in process of creating around her a barrier which was to last for two centuries. If Spain became, in addition, master of Naples and in the Milanese, it meant that France would be reduced to an inferior *rôle* in the Mediterranean and, above all, threatened on all sides by her worst enemies.

This grip upon Italy was of capital importance for Spain. Through the Milanese she would effect a junction with the Emperor, the relative and ally of her sovereigns. When the Emperor was at the same time King of Spain, as was the case under Charles V, and when this Emperor married his son to the sovereign of England, as happened in the case of Philip II and Mary Tudor, the encirclement of France would be complete. The Spaniards would block all the French frontiers from the Bidassoa to the Somme, by way of the Alps, the Jura, the Franche-Comté, Flanders, and Artois. The two seas would be in the hands of themselves and their allies.

The wars of Italy were, therefore, a vital necessity for France, and not, as has been blindly repeated, a mere sport of princes. For Imperial Spain, the upper hand in Italy was the very condition of the exercise of power. Without free passage through Italy, she could not communicate with Germany, the seat of the Empire, or even with her Flemish possessions; for the French privateers made the sea passage dangerous.

The councillors of the Emperor Charles V—Charles I of Spain—perfectly understood all these necessities. The remonstrances which they submitted to him at the beginning of his reign very clearly defined the reciprocal interest which the Kings of France and the Kings of Spain had in making themselves masters of Italy. "The first consideration," says one of these monitory letters,[1] "is that the duchies of Milan and Genoa are the keys and the door to the possibility of holding and dominating all Italy, and *Italy occupied and duly reduced to your subjection is the true seat and sceptre for dominating the whole world. And, inasmuch as the French your enemies know it very well, and hold this point in more estimation than the defence of their own kingdom, it must be contemplated that at all and any times when they find an opportunity of being able to return there, they will do so.*"

The councillors of Charles VIII of France, on their side, must have realised, or at least sensed, all the gravity of the situation which was created for France by the successive aggrandisements of Spain from the marriage of the Catholic Sovereigns down to the taking of Granada, and by Ferdinand's pretensions to the kingdom of Naples.

Accordingly, in the month of August, 1494, a French army crossed the Alps under the command of the young King, and, after traversing Italy, entered Naples almost without striking a blow. Charles VIII had thought to buy Ferdinand's neutrality by returning to him Roussillon and the Cerdagne, which had been occupied by France since the time of Louis XI. But, with his usual perfidy, the King of Aragón, after recovering these two provinces, was able to find a pretext for contesting the legitimacy of Charles's possession of the kingdom of Naples.

This meant war between the two rivals: the beginning of those long wars of Italy which were to last nearly a century. After alternating successes and reverses the French, beaten by Gonzalo de Cordova, Ferdinand's best general, who was known as "the Great Captain," had to evacuate their too easy conquest, and the King of Aragón became in fact King of Naples.

Under Louis XII, Charles VIII's successor, the struggle was resumed, this time for possession of the Duchy of Milan, over which the new King of France had rights through his grandmother, Valentina Visconti, Duchess of Milan. It was a question for him not so much of asserting his rights to a heritage difficult to keep, which would always cost more than it paid, as, once more, of preventing the Spaniards and the Imperialists from gaining a footing there and joining hands to invade the French marches.

Hence it arose that Louis XII and Ferdinand both exerted them-

---

[1] Cf. Ernest Gossart: *Charles Quint, roi d'Espagne* (advice given to the Emperor Charles V by the first lords, councillors and ministers of State for the good government of his kingdoms and estates), p. 236.

selves to the utmost to dislodge the other from the Milanese. The King of France devoted himself to the task until the very eve of his death, which occurred on January 1, 1515. Beaten at Novarra and definitely expelled from Milan, he was attempting to regain the advantage, and it was in the midst of warlike preparations that death surprised him.

He handed on to his successor the heavy heritage of the Italian wars—and this in unfavourable conditions, after territorial losses which had further weakened the kingdom. On the other. hand, Ferdinand of Aragón, thanks to the agility of his diplomacy and the success of his arms, had scored nothing but gains all along the line.

His wife Isabel had died in 1506, and he governed both Castile and Aragón. He was, therefore, the effective master of all the Spains, including the kingdom of Granada. He held, along with Sicily, the kingdom of Naples. On the French side, he had recovered Roussillon and the Cerdagne, and, profiting by the excommunication pronounced by the Pope against Jean d'Albret, sovereign of Navarre, he had seized that country, despite the armed intervention of Louis XII.

Nevertheless, he did not lose sight of the Musulman danger; for attack by the Turks or the Barbaresques was still possible. For the maritime security of Spain, in fact, it did not suffice that the kingdom of Granada and its ports should be occupied by the troops of the Catholic King. So long as Africa was in the hands of the Barbaresques, more or less aided by the Turks, the Andalusian coast was always menaced, and, in any case, Spanish trade in the Mediterranean was exposed to the risks of piracy.

For southern Spain to feel safe, it was necessary that the Barbaresque ports should be held or watched by the Spaniards. The Arabs themselves, when they were masters in Spain, and the Visigoth kings before them had realised the fact. The Visigoths, like the Caliphs, had always sought to seize the African coast, or at least to occupy the embarkation points.

To see in such African expeditions evidence of megalomania, unbridled ambition or even fanaticism, is to close one's eyes to the necessities which were imposed upon the Spaniards. Historians who overlook these necessities proceed to be surprised that the Spaniards should never have tried to press their conquests into the interior of Africa, but stopped at the ports and the coast. This wise course of action is precisely the proof of the absence of any ambition for conquest in this case. It sufficed to the Spaniards, in the interests of their security, to occupy a few strategic positions on the coast and the principal embarkation points. To advance beyond these into the interior would have been sheer madness and led them nowhere.

The Catholic Sovereigns, doubtless on the advice of Cardinal Cisneros, felt the force of all this reasoning. This former Franciscan

seems to have known the Musulmans very well, particularly the
Berbers of Africa. He guessed that at the first favourable opportunity the Moors, expelled from Spain, would attempt to return.
They must be deprived of the means of doing so. Moreover, the
footholds which the Portuguese had made on the Moroccan coast
might prejudice Spanish influence there. In the course of the
fifteenth century, taking advantage of the difficulties of Castile, they
had seized Ceuta and attempted to establish themselves at Algiers.

For all these reasons several expeditions were organised against
the Barbaresques. In 1497, Melilla was taken by the fleet of the
Duke of Medina Sidonia. In 1509 Cisneros, with the help of Captain
Pedro Navarro, captured the Peñon of Vélez, Oran, the Peñon of
Algiers, Bougie, and Tripoli: conquests which were precarious, but
for some time at least diminished piracy and reduced the Moors to
impotence.

So Ferdinand of Aragón, helped by a number of favourable circumstances, and fortunate in his collaborators, left when he died, in
1516, a Spain which, if not completely unified, was at least enormously aggrandised and powerful: a Spain, mistress over all her
frontiers, whose hegemony over Western Europe was to go on
developing throughout the course of the new century.

CHAPTER XXVII

*The Emperor Charles V. Renewal of the Wars of Italy. The Protestants.
The Barbaresques*

FERDINAND OF ARAGÓN left as his successor his grandson Charles,
the future Emperor Charles V, son of his daughter Juana—
known as Joan the Mad, owing to her mental weakness—and
the Archduke Philip the Fair, son of the Emperor Maximilian.

He would have preferred, however, to hand on his Spanish kingdoms to Charles's younger brother, his second grandson Ferdinand,
for whom he had a predilection, and who, having been brought up
in Spain—unlike Charles, who was a regular Fleming—seemed to
him, quite rightly, more likely to be popular than his elder brother.
Charles's position, moreover, was delicate in his capacity as heir to the
throne of Castile. While he was the lawful heir to the throne of
Aragón through his grandfather Ferdinand, it was to his mother
Juana, who was still alive, that Castile belonged. Joan the Mad, shut
up in the castle of Tordesillas, had many partisans, hostile to Charles
and his Flemish councillors.

For these reasons, because he had in effect to conquer his Spanish
kingdoms and fight against the ill-will of his future subjects; and also
because he was preparing to assume the succession to his grandfather
Maximilian, and was actively engaged in his election as Emperor, the
young Archduke felt obliged to walk warily with his powerful
neighbour, the King of France, who might still further complicate
the difficulties in which he was involved. Accordingly he began by
negotiating with François I and compromising with him. The King
of France hastened to take advantage of these favourable circumstances.

Leaving Spaniards and Flemings entangled in their affairs of suc-
cessions, he lost no time in asserting his rights over the Milanese once
more. The wars of Italy were to begin again. I cannot too strongly
insist that this was not for François I a question of vainglory, or of
personal ambition, or even, as some imagine, the lure of the pleasures
and the arts of Italy. It was a matter of the first importance to the
French Government.

The French could not admit that Spain should be mistress of the
Italian peninsula. The Spaniards, who were in possession of Naples
and Sicily, already held the Milanese as well through Duke Maximilian Sforza, their ally. If Charles of Austria, after becoming King
of Spain, succeeded his grandfather Maximilian as Emperor of
Germany, it was not only Italy, but also the whole of Central
Europe, which would pass under Spanish hegemony. France must
hasten to bar the way to the troops of the future Emperor who, at
the same time, was going to be King of all the Spains—and the best

means of barring his way towards Germany was to seize Genoa and the Milanese.

So it was that, in the month of August, 1515, a considerable army, commanded by François I in person, started to cross the Alps. It was "a great and powerful army," as he put it in the letters patent which appointed his mother Regent of the kingdom. He was determined to make a supreme effort, in view of the importance of the matter for the destiny of France.

François, victor at Marignano, went so far as to play with the idea of advancing South and, with the support of the Holy See, on which he thought that he could count, driving the Spaniards out of Naples. But Pope Leo X dissuaded him. He returned to France, hugging the illusion that he had re-established French supremacy in the North of Italy. The treaty of Cambrai, signed in 1517 between Charles and himself, seemed to stabilise the *status quo*.

But matters could not rest there. Neither of the two Powers could admit the interference of the other in Italy. That the French should be back in Milan and Genoa was contrary to the most elementary principles of Spanish policy. As soon as Charles had suppressed the revolt of his Castilian subjects—the *comuneros*, as they were called—and secured his election as Emperor under the name of Charles V (July, 1519), he concerned himself with renewing the struggle for hegemony.

François I provided him with a pretext and an occasion by supporting the pretensions of the Prince of Béarn to the crown of Navarre. The Emperor concluded a defensive league with Pope Leo X and the Republic of Florence, and hostilities between France and Spain began again. The French armies were defeated on the Bicoque (1522), and then in the battle of Pavia (1525), which was a regular disaster. François I was captured and imprisoned in the Alcázar of Madrid.

There he remained for a year, as his adversary laid down unacceptable conditions for his ransom. Finally a treaty of peace was signed at Madrid at the beginning of the year 1526. The King of France ceded the duchy of Burgundy to the Emperor, and renounced his rights over Flanders, Artois, and the duchy of Milan.

He considered himself entitled not to respect this treaty, which he regarded as extracted from him by force. But he was, in fact, definitely expelled from Italy. He refused to accept the fact. He returned to the attack several times, but was never able to maintain himself there.

These Italian wars were not popular in France. Public opinion was hostile to them on account of the enormous expense which they entailed. The government itself did not understand the importance of them. Accordingly they were never carried on with the energy and the sense of continuity which were required. This contributed to the inferiority of France during more than a century, and, at the same time, confirmed the Spanish hegemony.

Because France had been defeated at Pavia and had not recovered from that defeat, she was to experience Spanish encirclement on all her land frontiers and be exposed to the menace of the House of Austria, in alliance with Spain, until the end of the seventeenth century. Italy, definitely withdrawn from French influence and divided up into Spanish viceroyalties, was to become the corridor of communication between the two Austrian royal families, that of Vienna and that of Madrid. It was to demand all the efforts of Henri IV, Richelieu, and Louis XIV to annul the political consequences of an Italy surrendered to the Spaniards and the Imperialists.

In short, Charles V had triumphed over his rival. He had expelled him from the Empire and driven him out of Italy. Spain, unified not without resistance, ended by accepting Charles's domination and even, dazzled by the Imperial Majesty, by becoming proud of it.

But the authority of the Germanic Cæsar was more brilliant than real. Germany, torn by religious quarrels which masked grave political and even social conflicts, was in a state of perpetual war and anarchy. The preaching of Luther had unleashed a regular revolution there. The Emperor might have him condemned by the Diet of Worms (1521); he found himself nevertheless obliged to make all kinds of compromises with the Reformer and with the princes who were his partisans.

After a long period of such compoundings, interrupted by reconciliations and ruptures with the rebels—a period which lasted from 1530 to about 1546—Charles made up his mind to strike a great blow. This effort ended in the victory of Mühlberg (1547), won by the Spanish and Italian troops. But the Emperor, betrayed by his ally Maurice of Saxony, was forced to accept the convention of Passau (1552), which was in effect a defeat for the imperial authority.

After that, he could not even assure to his son Philip his succession to the Empire, which he had wanted to make hereditary. He found himself confronted by the hostility of the German princes, whom the King of France, Henri II, hastened to support in their resistance. The results of this new conflict were frankly unfavourable to the Emperor. The Duc de Guise seized the Three Bishoprics of Lorraine (1553) and constrained Charles to withdraw.

The Emperor had to accept the *fait accompli* and leave things as they were. Once the religious sovereignty of every Germanic principality or republic had been recognised by him, the unity of the Empire became a chimera, and Germany slipped between his fingers.

He was scarcely more successful in his struggle against the Turks and the Barbaresques. The Musulman danger was no sooner conjured away than it reappeared again. This time it seemed more threatening than ever. The Sultan Selim I, after subjugating all the East, from Persia to Egypt, turned his arms against the West once more. He advanced as far as the walls of Vienna, and the Pope was afraid lest he should organise an expedition against Italy.

In Africa the renegade Barbarossa, having succeeded in seizing Algiers and Tunis, had acknowledged himself a vassal of the Sultan. The Spanish coasts were more than ever exposed to raids and descents by the Barbaresque pirates. In the hope of making an end of this centuries-long peril, Charles V organised an expedition against Tunis (1535). He succeeded in expelling the usurper Barbarossa from it and seizing the port of La Goulette.

Master of Tunis, he delivered thousands of captive Christians. This fortunate operation had a resounding effect throughout Christendom. But its results, like those of all campaigns against the Barbaresques, were very superficial and lasted a very short time. In 1541 Charles V had to equip another fleet against Algiers. This suffered a regular disaster, and it was only with great difficulty that the Emperor was able to reach Spain again.

The Islamic danger, therefore, was far from being suppressed. We shall meet it again in the reign of Philip II. Meanwhile the Moriscos of Andalusia were restless, and their attitude demanded the greatest vigilance on the part of the Spanish Government.

In short, the magnificent hopes which had been brought to birth when the Imperial throne was mounted by the grandson of the Catholic Sovereigns were frustrated. Despite his tireless efforts, seconded by collaborators of the first order, Charles V, by the time he passed his fifties, experienced this sense of disappointment himself. He felt himself no longer equal to the task of governing such vast possessions. The most humiliating thing for him was that he could not secure the Empire for his son.

For all these reasons—and perhaps for religious reasons also, to prepare himself for death—he decided to abdicate and retire to a monastery in Estremadura, at San Yuste. The act of abdication took place solemnly in Brussels in 1555. Charles laid aside the Imperial crown in favour of his brother Ferdinand, and passed on to his son Philip, together with Flanders and his rights over Burgundy, his kingdoms of Aragón, Castile, the Two Sicilies, and all his Italian possessions.

This abdication of Charles V marked the separation of Spain and the Germanic Holy Roman Empire. But the alliance subsisted between the two royal families and the two states. The sovereigns of Vienna and those of Madrid continued to constitute, and to represent, that House of Austria against which France was to fight until the dawn of the eighteenth century, and which was to weigh so heavily upon the destinies of Europe.

CHAPTER XXVIII

Philip II. The Apogee of the Spanish Monarchy and the Counter-Reformation

THE succession to Charles V was a very heavy burden; but, when one thinks of the difficulties of all kinds, financial as well as religious, which weighed at that time upon all the European states, one may regard it as still privileged and singularly brilliant. Even after the death of the Emperor, the King of Spain still remained the first sovereign of Europe.

Since his father had abdicated the Empire, Philip II might naturally fear a diminution of his prestige. As a matter of fact, he was relieved of a very onerous title, which would have conferred upon him only the most precarious authority. The Empire, having passed into the hands of Charles V's younger brother, assumed the appearance of a mere delegation of power granted by the head of the family, and became in a sense an extension of the Spanish monarchy.

This monarchy in itself presented a most imposing *façade*. The mere enumeration of its kingdoms, viceroyalties, fiefs, and possessions filled whole pages in diplomatic documents. Henceforth the Iberian Peninsula was completely unified under the same sceptre. Philip, heir through his mother to the crown of Portugal, annexed this kingdom to his states (1581). Apart from Castile and Aragón, he had inherited the kingdoms of Valencia, Naples, and the Two Sicilies, Tuscany, the Milanese and Liguria. From his father, heir of the House of Burgundy, he held Flanders.

To put the corner-stone upon this colossal political edifice, Charles had married him to Mary Tudor, daughter of Henry VIII, and, until the death of this princess, he was regarded as the rightful King of England. Finally, he was the master of the Americas, of their mines of gold and silver, and of any number of unknown lands which remained to be discovered and conquered.

So Spain continued to cut a great figure in the world. She continued also to encircle France, her rival. More than ever France was blockaded by land and sea. The treaty of Cateau-Cambrésis, concluded in 1559 between Philip II and the King of France, in addition to leaving the French northern and eastern frontier open, and in addition to securing the restitution to Philip of a number of small fortresses, accorded Philip the right to intervene in French affairs, in his capacity as heir through his wife to the throne of France, if the sons of Henri II died without children. Under the terms of this treaty the Catholic King was to marry Elizabeth de Valois, daughter of Henri II and Catherine de Medici.

What was to be the policy of the new monarch at the head of this great empire, whose principal disadvantage was that it was disjointed and severed by arms of the sea or foreign states, but which presented such an imposing *façade*? He might well have been intoxicated by the excess of his power and conceive a thousand plans of aggrandisement and conquest.

Philip II, however—he repeated it over and over again, and with all the sincerity in the world—contemplated nothing but preserving the heritage which had been handed down to him by his father, and maintaining it in its territorial integrity and in the purity of its faith.

He regarded himself as the great protector of Catholicism. In the same way as he would not yield an inch of his territories, so he would not permit heresy to contaminate his states. The whole of Philip II is summed up in this twofold *rôle* of defender of the faith and maintainer of the Spanish monarchy.

He was not an ambitious or a violent man. Fundamentally he did not like men of war. He always distrusted them and their appetites. It must be recognised that most of the time he was right. He resorted to war only in the last extremity, being convinced that diplomacy and compromise achieved much more than force. Nobody could have been more impregnated with the idea that time works in favour of policy. Hence arose his slowness in action and in administration.

He prided himself upon his kindliness and clemency, and it is quite certain that in doing so he believed himself to be sincere. He did not like fuss, disturbance, disorder, bloodshed, and execution. When the crime was secret, the punishment, in his opinion, ought to be so, too; he had a horror of scandal. He resorted to the scaffold or the stake only when he thought that he ought to make an example.

He was a man of the study, extraordinarily painstaking, obstinate, and self-willed, who believed in the efficacy of calculation and craft, in their superiority over brute force, and who therefore exhausted himself in abstruse and tortuous schemings. A dissembler, surrounded by spies, he certainly added to the hypocrisy of manners as well as to the sinuosity of the diplomacy of his time. But, to judge him in this respect, we must first of all bear in mind what the diplomacy of that time was, the perfidy of heads of states, and the unscrupulousness and brutality of his contemporaries. In such a world, dissimulation was prescribed as a royal virtue.

Passionate in his youth and very fond of pleasure, he forced himself to kill all passion in himself. In proportion as he grew older, he sought to make himself more unmoved, more detached than ever. He sacrificed himself completely to affairs of State and religious duty. In perfect good faith, he tried to imitate Saint Louis of France by exerting himself to become the perfect type of Christian monarch.

In any case, nobody could rival him in being a master. With Louis XIV, his great-grandson, he was the model of absolute sovereign, who not only knew how to make up his mind, govern, and foresee, but also proposed to direct everything himself, see everything that was going on to the smallest detail, decide everything and sign everything with his own hand. As he was at the same time a man of uneasy mind, tortured by scruples, and as he wanted to leave nothing to chance—persuaded as he was that everything ought to be subordinated to mental processes—he was slow in arriving at his smallest decisions. In consequence, this grimly determined man has been regarded as weak and irresolute.

As a matter of fact, he never strayed from his programme: to maintain the Spanish monarchy and defend the faith. Whatever disappointments, whatever reverses he experienced, one may say that he realised his twofold design and that, on the whole, this man of strong will made events yield to it.

We can recognise the perseverance, finally victorious, of this design in all Philip's external policy. In the first place, so far as concerned Italy, the perpetual object of French desires, he succeeded in keeping her, despite all the efforts of France and of Pope Paul IV. This Pope, who was a Neapolitan, and as such detested the Spaniards, the oppressors of his country, exerted himself from the beginning of Philip II's reign to organise a league against him.

Paul IV told the ambassador of Venice, which he tried to bring into this league: "Be sure of this, the Spaniards intend to make Italy their colony. They are beginning at the weakest point. After the Papal States, they will attack you. Do you not see all that they possess already—the kingdoms of Naples and Sicily, Tuscany, the greater part of Lombardy and Liguria? They lack nothing but your State."

Some days later Henri II, in concert with the Pope, declared war on the King of Spain. Philip, who could not abandon Italy without weakening his close alliance with the House of Austria, sent the Duke of Alba to oppose the French armies commanded by the Duc de Guise, who was defeated in Italy. The struggle continued in France, and, after a series of reverses, which included the taking of Saint-Quentin and the battle of Gravelines, Henri II, with his kingdom invaded, found himself obliged to treat with his adversary. The result was the famous treaty of Cateau-Cambrésis, by which France renounced Italy, apart from a few fortresses in Piedmont. It amounted to recognising a situation which in fact had lasted for nearly a century.

The presence of Spain in the Milanese was to render the struggle of France against the House of Austria much more difficult under Henri IV and Louis XIII. Not only did Philip II yield nothing in Italy; he also consolidated himself there from one end of the peninsula to the other, and maintained a threat to the French Alpine frontier. In fact, he reduced France to a minor *rôle* throughout his reign, and ceaselessly intervened in her affairs in the course of the wars of religion.

At the time of the League, a Spanish garrison occupied Paris.

Alexander Farnese defeated Henri IV under the walls of the French capital. After the assassination of Henri III, Philip even conceived the idea of having his daughter Isabel Clara Eugenia elected Queen of France, as the legitimate and most direct heiress through her mother Elizabeth de Valois. The Infanta, married to the Archduke Albert of Austria, would have founded a new dynasty, and thus France, under the hegemony of Philip, would have become a Spanish viceroyalty.

This project, which was incapable of realisation because it wounded French national feeling too deeply, may have failed, despite the complicity of the League. Philip nevertheless maintained his position completely. The treaty of Vervins, concluded in 1598 between him and Henri IV, made no change, in effect, from the situation created by the treaty of Cateau-Cambrésis, which had been regarded as so disastrous for France. While it confirmed the French acquisition of the Three Bishoprics, it left the French frontier still open to the North and East. France still began at the Somme. The Duke of Savoy, Philip's ally, was at Annecy and Chambéry, and Spain had viceroys in Naples and Milan.

In short, if Philip had gained nothing from France, neither had he lost anything—which was in conformity with his programme—and he had obtained from her the renunciation of Italy; a renunciation purely formal, no doubt, but whose moral effect might be considerable.

In Germany, despite the fact that he was not loved there, Philip was also able to maintain the position which he had acquired. There were some disagreements between him and his relatives in Vienna on the subject of the Lutherans. But the alliance between the two branches of the House of Austria became, if possible, closer than ever. Ferdinand, Philip's uncle, had received the Empire at the hands of Charles V. The King of Spain finally married his cousin, the Archduchess Anne, daughter of the Emperor Ferdinand. He gave his own daughter, the Infanta Isabel Clara Eugenia, to the Archduke Albert, his nephew, son of the Emperor Maximilian II. Thus the family pact which linked the Habsburgs of Vienna with those of Madrid, and was to last two centuries, became consolidated.

This matrimonial policy, which served them so well, nearly gave England to Philip II as well. This ascetic man—this man, at least, who early became one, and married four wives for reasons of State—had married Mary Tudor, daughter of Henry VIII, in 1554. But incompatibility between husband and wife immediately manifested itself, and Philip, for reasons which are only too easy to understand, made himself unpopular with his wife's subjects. He wanted to win them over to Catholicism and his indiscreet zeal had only the effect of exasperating the majority of the English.

In this case it was defeat for him all along the line. Completely unsuccessful in re-establishing the Catholic religion in England, he was no more successful in giving the throne to Mary Stuart.[1] The great expedition which he organised in 1588 to punish Elizabeth for the execution of Mary Queen of Scots was a lamentable disaster. "The invincible Armada," as it was called in derision by the Protestant enemies of Spain, left on record in history the memory of the most resounding defeat that the world has ever seen. The crowning humiliation was that the English fleet pursued the Spaniards even into their own waters, and Cádiz was taken and sacked.

Meanwhile the English privateers had been giving chase to the galleons coming from America, and inflicting serious losses upon Spanish trade, as well as compromising the security of Spanish communications. The expedition of the Armada, therefore, had not merely a religious object; it was designed also to defend the shipowners of Seville, and the revenues of the Crown. Despite the most intense and persistent efforts, Philip never succeeded in suppressing this danger.

Those who refuse to see in him anything but a fanatic ignore the practical and national character of most of his actions and his warlike undertakings. He attacked England for reasons of security and to protect the trade of his subjects. Religious reasons were undoubtedly uppermost in his mind; but we should not ignore the other reasons. It was the same thing in America. He did not concern himself with it only as a converter; he exerted himself also to improve its administration.

During his reign the conquest was consolidated and extended, despite the obstacles which were put in the way of the Spanish advance by the rivalries of all the European nations and the continual attacks of the privateers. Colonisation proceeded from Peru and Chili in the direction of Paraguay and the North of Argentina. *Audiencias*, bishoprics, new cities, and seats of government were established.

Though the production of the Peruvian and Mexican mines has been exaggerated, it is nevertheless true that Spain under Philip II was the richest nation in gold in Europe. She preserved this superiority throughout the seventeenth century—a superiority which was recognised, not without acrimonious jealousy, by Colbert himself. Even apart from this, the mere possession of immense dominions in the New World conferred a very great prestige upon the Spain of Philip II, of which we must take account in drawing up the balance-sheet of his reign. This prestige was so real that—no

---

[1] It must also be remembered that in the early years of Philip's reign the accession of Mary to the English throne would have strengthened the international position not of Spain, but of France, owing to the dynastic ties which united the Houses of Stuart, Valois, and Guise. This possibility explains much of Spanish policy towards England, and not least the postponement, at Philip's request, of the excommunication of Elizabeth until 1570. Of these divisions among her enemies the English Queen took full advantage both at home and abroad, so that when Philip could afford to strike it was too late.

C.P.

doubt with the object of maintaining the Imperial dignity which his father had abdicated—Philip contemplated asking the Pope for the title of Emperor of the Indies.

Islam still remained the great European danger. Spain, in contact with the Barbaresques through her southern coasts and her African possessions, and at the same time exposed to attack by the Turks in her Italian viceroyalties, was especially menaced.

Philip had to resist these secular enemies to the best of his ability; but his activity against them was hampered by a thousand and one difficulties—in the first place the necessity which was imposed upon him of fighting on several fronts at the same time, and, above all, the incoherence of European policy.

France, in pursuance of François I's example, intrigued with Stamboul. She did something more serious, and scarcely credible: at the beginning of Philip II's reign, she came to an understanding with the Holy See to launch the Ottoman squadrons against the Spanish dominions in Italy. The coasts of Campania were devastated, and thousands of captives were carried away to the galleys and the harems of the Levant.

In order to bar the passage of the Turks into the Western Mediterranean, Philip endeavoured in the first place to occupy the island of Djerba and Tripoli. He recovered the Peñon of Vélez, and delivered the Island of Malta, which was an excellent observation-post for pursuit of Ottoman or Barbaresque corsairs. In 1572, in concert with the Pope and the Republic of Venice, he organised against the Turkish fleet an enormous maritime expedition, under the command of Don John of Austria, an illegitimate son of Charles V, which ended in the victory of Lepanto: a regular disaster for the Turks, which made a great impression throughout Christendom. The Turks had to set numbers of captives at liberty.

But, as usual, the effect of the victory of Lepanto was moral rather than definite in the practical sphere. The Turks and the Barbaresques soon resumed the offensive. The Spaniards were driven from Djerba and La Goulette, as they had already been from Bougie and Algiers. They retained only Oran, Mers el Kebir, and Melilla. In 1577 Philip, who was heavily committed elsewhere, made a truce with the Sultan.

Clearly the results of his long and hard struggle against Islam were not brilliant. But, here again, he had more or less maintained his position, and—what was more important—he had demonstrated to the Turks, through the victory of Lepanto, that any attempt to invade the Western basin of the Mediterranean was doomed to disappointment. All that they could do on one side or the other was to pillage one another by sea, and carry on a stealthy little war of piracy. The Catholic King, distracted from this field of battle by the grave revolt in Flanders, had nevertheless shown that he could hold his own against Islam. That was all he wanted for the moment.

In Flanders the struggle was a much more serious matter. Here Spain had not merely great political interests to be defended, but other matters of principle of the highest importance. Over and above local quarrels, the very existence of Catholicism was at stake.

What was at issue between Philip II and his Flemish subjects was, in fact, the defence of the Catholic faith. The Reformation had invaded all the North of the Low Countries, it found adherents and sympathisers in the Belgian provinces, and it was supported by the French Huguenots. The situation became more and more disquieting for the King of Spain. Liberty of conscience played only a very minor part in this affair: it was a pretext which was invoked for the moment, to be cast aside as soon as the upper hand was gained. Liberty of conscience involved political liberty, and, in Philip's eyes, therefore, every Huguenot was a rebel—and so, as a matter of fact, he was.

At the same time, this revolt constituted a menace for all the neighbouring countries. Under the cloak of heresy, it was agitating and dividing France after doing the same thing in Germany. If it triumphed in France after contaminating all Flanders, Spain herself would be exposed to the contagion: Spain still precariously unified, where whole populations of Moriscos asked nothing better than to make common cause with the enemies of the Spanish monarchy, whoever they might be. It is understandable that Philip should have bestirred himself to arrest the conflagration, or at least to localise it.

He endeavoured to do so to the utmost of his power, and by any means, even the most cruel. The Flemings, as I have said, were in his eyes not merely heretics, but also the most dangerous rebels. What they wanted was their more or less complete independence under the nominal suzerainty of Spain. At the back of the religious question, there was the matter of privileges, immunities, and political rights.

The Flemings wanted to preserve their communal liberties, the sovereignty of their states in the matter of taxes. They protested against the introduction of the Spanish Inquisition and against the creation of new bishoprics and new universities—all measures intended to strengthen the royal authority. In other words, they would not admit that Flanders should be subject to the Spanish regime. Below the middle-classes and the nobles fermented a lower order eager to sack the monasteries and churches under the cloak of religion.

If this revolutionary movement carried the day, it was necessary to contemplate the complete independence of the Low Countries. But it was a dogma of Castilian policy that, without Flanders, Spain would cease to be a European Power. This territory was the guarantee of her hegemony over Europe.

As early as the time of Charles V, his ministers had assured him that Flanders was "a citadel of steel" for his House, "a shield which enabled him to receive the blows of England, France, and Germany far away from the head of the monarchy." It was by way of the Flemish frontier that France was most vulnerable; it was in that direction that Spain could keep her "under perpetual restraint." Finally, if Spain lost this advanced post, whence she could watch the whole of Central Europe, she would lose also her right to intervene in European affairs. The possession of Italy itself had no value for her unless she simultaneously possessed the Low Countries, which enabled her to bear upon France, England, and Germany at one and the same time.

For all these reasons Philip II found himself obliged to keep Flanders at any price. He tried all means: kindness, conciliation, craft and duplicity, and finally force. Force proved to be the most efficacious. The Duke of Alba, appointed governor, drowned the revolt in blood, as it was said. He struck in the first place at its chiefs. The Counts of Egmont and Hornes were beheaded, the Baron de Montigny was strangled in his prison, the Prince of Orange was compelled to take refuge in Germany.

But, though these drastic measures might indeed terrorise the country, they did not pacify it. The revolt dragged on. One may say that it lasted throughout the reign of Philip II, who used up his governors and his generals in the thankless task of mastering the Flemings. By dint of temporising, he ended by tiring them out.

Though the provinces of the North, the Low Countries properly speaking, succeeded in detaching themselves from Spain under the leadership of William of Orange and proclaiming themselves independent by the abjuration of The Hague (1581), the Belgian provinces remained faithful both to the Catholic King and to Catholicism. To give them a semblance of satisfaction, by conceding them a semblance of autonomy, Philip II decided to hand over Flanders to his son-in-law, the Archduke Albert—on the condition that he should forbid Protestantism in his States. Moreover, if the Archduke died childless, Flanders would revert to the crown of Spain.

In reality, Philip had given away nothing. Spanish domination continued, almost as rigorously as before. The authority of the Archduke was nullified by that of the military governors, and Spanish garrisons maintained obedience in the country. Philip II had localised the conflagration by resigning himself to the loss of Holland. Apart from these Protestant provinces of the Low Countries, he had lost nothing of his paternal heritage. By way of compensation, he had added Portugal to the Spanish Monarchy. Finally, he had maintained both Catholicism and his own authority in the southern provinces.

At the same time as he was combating the Reformation in Flanders, he was trying also to conquer it in France. He proposed to profit by his intervention in the religious quarrels of France to such good purpose as to establish Spanish suzerainty there, as in the Low Countries.

He began by forming a defensive league with Henri II, who, like François I, realised that Protestantism was becoming more and more a danger to French unity. Then, when Henri II died prematurely, he attempted to persuade Catherine de Medici and Charles IX to take drastic measures against the Huguenots. He supported the Guises and the Catholic party, and later the Duc de Mayenne and the League.

He protested against the policy of Henri III, who ended by recognising the Protestant Henry of Bourbon, the future Henri IV, as heir to the throne. He caused the latter to be defeated under the walls of Paris by Alexander Farnese. He intrigued against Pope Sixtus V to prevent him from recognising Henri IV and accepting his abjuration, and even threatened the Pontiff with deposition by a national council if he insisted upon recognising a Huguenot as King of France.

When Henri III died without children, Philip put forward his daughter, the Infanta Isabel Clara Eugenia, as claimant to the succession to the last Valois. In this connection he multiplied offers of military support and subsidies, always finding very active partisans in the League. But for this persistence, this tenacity of Philip, the aid which he never ceased to give the Catholic party, it is probable that Henri IV would have still further deferred his conversion, and so prolonged the division and weakness of France.

The French Catholics, as a matter of fact, did not want either a Spanish king or a Protestant king like William of Orange or his brother, Louis of Nassau. But it is nevertheless true that at a certain moment, at the instance of Coligny, Charles IX was on the point of making an alliance with the Protestants of England and the Low Countries against the King of Spain, and that at this moment there was a possibility of France's becoming Protestant.

No doubt, if Philip II intervened in French religious quarrels, it was with the idea of definitely reducing France to the *rôle* of a satellite of Spain at the back of his mind. But to refuse to admit anything but these political intentions is to misconstrue the man of ardent faith that he was. Above all it was for the sake of his religion, for the triumph of his religion, that he interested himself in the affairs of France. It is quite certain that, if France remained Catholic, it was partly to his energetic influence that she owed the fact.

To the utmost of his ability, therefore, he fulfilled his *rôle* as Defender of the Faith. In acting as he did in Flanders, he raised a barrier against the Reformation, he prevented it from invading the Latin countries, and, by doing so, he saved the spirit of Latinity and Latin civilisation. It may perhaps be said that he had no intention of doing so, that he never thought of doing so. That makes no difference, if the result was obtained indirectly through his efforts.

This man of faith, moreover, was a connoisseur and a collector, a lover of fine things, a lover of books and a lover of learning. The new art which was to develop in the Catholic countries, under the inspiration of the Council of Trent, had no more fervent patron than Philip II.

CHAPTER XXIX

*The Government of Philip II. The Absolute Monarchy. The
Inquisition*

WITHIN Spain, despite some resistance, despite some rebellions
which were crushed with merciless rigour, one may say that
the authority of Philip II was uncontested and absolute. The
modern monarchical regime, in its autocratic and centralised form,
had been established, at least in fact, by Ferdinand and Isabel.
Under Charles V it was further perfected. Under Philip II, it assumed
that definitive shape which it preserved in Spain until the extinction
of the Habsburg dynasty. This Castilian autocracy served as model
to all the reigning houses of Europe.

Henceforth the King was the master of peace and war, and of
alliances and negotiations with foreign countries. Diplomacy and
external affairs were in his hands. He alone had the right to issue
money. He deprived the nobility of all the prerogatives which had
made any fief of importance a State within the State. Having episcopal sees at his disposal, he held the bishops at his discretion, and
tended more and more to make them mere officials of the crown. He
restricted the *fueros* of the provincial communities as much as he
could, and also the influence of the *Cortes* by assembling these
parliaments as seldom as possible.

At the same time, it would be a mistake to suppose that the monarchy thus constituted knew no limitations in the exercise of its
power. As a matter of fact, this so-called absolute authority encountered a swarm of hindrances and restrictions, a swarm of little
local authorities which refused to abdicate and only sought an
opportunity to make themselves completely independent. Neither
the aristocracy nor the provincial communities resigned themselves
to State discipline.

To understand Philip's severity we must bear all this in mind. It
may be said that, to obtain the smallest war subsidy from his Catalan
or Aragonese subjects, he was compelled to go and beg for it in
person before their *Cortes*. Hence arose his persistent efforts to
suppress or diminish these troublesome bodies little by little. He
proposed to govern by himself. He would have no more ministers,
who ended by usurping the royal authority. The Spanish autocrat
confined himself to consulting councils or *juntas*, with which he
shared the various departments of administration.

Under the Catholic Sovereigns, apart from the Council of State,
the Council of Justice, and the Council of Finance, which were
already in existence, those of the Holy Brotherhood, of the Inquisition, of the Military Orders, and of the Indies were created. The
most important was the Council of Justice, which was reorganised
by the sovereigns. They introduced into it jurists belonging to the

middle classes and trained in the principles of the old Roman law, who, inasmuch as they owed their elevation to the sovereigns, became docile instruments in their hands.

Philip, perfecting the governmental mechanism, added to these councils those of Castile, Aragón, Flanders, and Italy. Each of these organisations, together with the Council of the Indies, corresponded to the divers regions of his vast Empire. It must, however, be emphasised that these *juntas* had only a consultative voice, and that it was the sovereign who decided in the last resort. Philip, very jealous of his authority, never shared his right of deciding and ordering with anybody.

I have already indicated some of the inconveniences of this regime, the chief of which were arbitrariness and, above all, slowness in the conduct of affairs. Contemporaries were keenly alive to all these defects and criticised them. But, in substance, they accepted this terrible power. One might almost say that they were flattered at obeying a prince who, on equality with God, had become a Majesty. The title of Majesty, then in all its novelty for the Kings of Spain, was repeated by his subjects at every opportunity, and with a strange accent of devotion. This majesty was as sacred as the person of the sovereign. The throne was approached only with trembling.

Philip inspired a regular terror in the unfortunate people who obtained audience of him. His icy coldness, his fixed stare, his silence or the fewness of the words he spoke, unintelligible as those of an oracle—all this made him a fearful person to approach. Besides, beyond the majesty of the royal person was to be sensed the majesty of an Empire which embraced two continents. Only Napoleon, conqueror of Europe, ever enjoyed such a prestige.

On the whole this autocracy, with its centralisation, its police, its tribunals, its armies, which guaranteed security at home and abroad, struck contemporaries as a considerable advance upon the Middle Ages. If the regime was not exactly loved, it was surrounded by much respect and obeyed with pride. The royal power was regarded as the source of all legitimate authority. The conquistadors, who made themselves masters of kingdoms greater than all the Spains, did not consider themselves entitled to control them unless they had obtained the royal note of hand conferring the title of viceroys or governors upon them. They did not hesitate to cross the ocean to solicit this title.

They might fight among themselves, but each claimed to cover himself with the royal authority. The name of the king was over and above all quarrels. In his tragedy *The Cid*, Corneille well translated this profoundly Spanish sentiment, when he put into the mouth of Don Diego these humble and proud words:

> "It is the respect which absolute power demands
> That none should question when a king commands."

One of Philip II's shrewdest achievements was to add the prestige of religion to the royal prestige. Like the Musulman caliphs, his predecessors, he proclaimed himself Defender of the Faith. He ended —for that matter with the best intentions in the world—by making out of religious authority an instrument of royal authority.

This instrument was the Inquisition. It had, indeed, existed long before him; but nobody ever used it so cleverly, or in a more effective and terrifying way. Doubtless Philip would always have defended himself against the charge of subordinating spiritual interests to temporal interests. He never proposed to act except to the greater glory of God. But the result was the same as though he had acted solely in order to strengthen his power and in the interests of the State, as he understood them.

Nowadays nothing is more repugnant to us than religion put at the service of politics and used as a cover for atrocities. That secret police of minds and souls, as it was organised in Spain in the sixteenth century, that vast organisation of spying and informing, that bloody tyranny over thought, inspired a veritable horror even in contemporaries. Neither France nor the Low Countries were prepared to tolerate it.

The issue is decided. There is no question of rehabilitating the Inquisition. The *rôle* of the historian is to try and understand, and make understandable, how it was that such a regime was able to secure toleration and even acceptance by the Spaniards, and to what necessities of the moment its institution answered.

In a sense it had always existed, among the Christians as well as among the Musulmans and in the pagan world of antiquity. At all times the Church reserved the right to seek out and judge heretics and inflict punishments upon them in proportion to their offences. Throughout Christendom bishops were invested with this right. It was only in the thirteenth century, at the time of the rising of the Albigenses, that there appeared a special organisation charged with persecuting heresy: an organisation superior to all local jurisdictions and directly answerable to the Pope. This was the Roman Inquisition.

The Spanish Inquisition was only a delegation of the Roman Inquisition. For the reason that it was responsible to no kind of constituted authority, it might have been a great source of disturbance in Spain unless the royal power succeeded in laying hands upon it. That was what Philip II succeeded in doing; and it is unquestionable that in doing it he aimed at employing this terrible tribunal for the greater good of religion and the Spanish nation.

Under the Catholic Sovereigns, the Inquisition was already functioning in Aragón. It seems probable that it was Ferdinand who decided Isabel to introduce it into Castile. The Dominicans of Seville, supported by the Papal nuncio, took the initiative in demanding from the sovereigns exceptional measures against the *conversos* who swarmed in Andalusia: in other words, the Jews who claimed to be converts and the Musulmans who had followed their example. Ferdinand counted especially in this matter upon lucrative confiscations, which would fill the treasury opportunely on the morrow and on the eve of costly wars.

Isabel, influenced by her confessors, but foreseeing possible injustices with which she did not want to charge her conscience, hesitated for some time. She ended by yielding. In the month of November, 1478, Pope Sixtus IV promulgated a Bull which authorised the introduction of the Roman Inquisition into Castile, with the object of bringing heretics and Judaisants back to the Christian faith.

Startled by the excesses which followed as soon as the Bull was promulgated, the Pope manifested an intention to withdraw it. What influences intervened? In any case, two years later, in 1480, a new Pontifical Bull organised this exceptional tribunal which, for the next century, was to play the *rôle* of the French revolutionary tribunals of public safety: in other words, paralyse any reaction by terror, hunt down the guilty and even the suspect, and exterminate them with merciless rigour.

How is it to be explained that such a monstrosity could be established and could last? What was happening in Spain—what grave events were there which made these odious means of repression seem the only ones possible? It is quite obvious that the regime of the stake, like that of the guillotine, could only be imposed with the assent of a whole section of the nation.

When one studies this question, two facts are particularly striking. In the first place, it was the Dominicans of Seville who obtained these drastic measures against the *conversos*. In the next place, these measures had already been demanded on several occasions by the local populations themselves. Numerous petitions were addressed to Isabel by the Old Christians, denouncing the proceedings of the *Marranos* to her and demanding their punishment and expulsion.

It is to be noted, moreover, that Isabel, in her struggle against the partisans of La Beltraneja, her rival for the throne of Castile, was supported by the Old Christians and consequently opposed more or less openly by the *conversos*. She therefore had some reason for resentment against them.

But the most significant fact is the intervention of the Dominicans of Seville. It was the eve of a decisive war against the Moors—the final attack, with the object of wresting the kingdom of Granada from them and throwing them back to Africa. The monks, vigilant guardians of orthodoxy, realised with alarm that Seville and Andalusia—that is to say, the region nearest to Granada—were full of false converts, Jews and Moors, who, under cover of Catholicism, continued to practise their religions more or less openly, setting a bad example to the Christian people and scandalising them by the display of their wealth.

In short, they divided the people and favoured a state of rebellion: a state the more dangerous on the eve of an enterprise which demanded unanimity on the part of the Spanish people. Moreover, by reason of their affinities of race, they were regarded as the secret allies of those Moors whom it was proposed to expel from Granada.

On its side, the government reckoned upon the proceeds of fines and confiscations. The money of the *Marranos* would be excellent to pay for the war. Besides, the government wanted to withdraw from the Moors the possibility of support by the *conversos*. Accordingly, the regime of terror began to function in Seville and throughout Andalusia.

At the outset, therefore, the Inquisition was not directed against the orthodox Jews who remained faithful to their beliefs and were left free, one might say, to practise their religion. The grievance was only against false Christians, Judaisants and Moorish renegades, who were suspected, not without reason, of seeking to ally themselves with the Moors and the Jews of Granada.

It was only after the taking of this last citadel of Islam in Spain that the general expulsion of the Jews was decreed, for the reasons, both religious and political, which I have already indicated. What was specially feared was the alliance of the Jews with the Granadine Moors who remained in Spain. Such an alliance was, so to speak, traditional whenever the Jews were persecuted.

Resentments of very long standing were gratified against them. They were accused of having summoned the Arabs to Andalusia at the time of the Visigoths. The Jews of Narbonne were especially accused of having delivered Septimania over to them. Montesquieu notes, in his *Esprit des Lois*, that the Spanish Inquisitors only renewed against the Jews the measures already framed against them by the Visigoths.

Once the Jews were gone, there remained to occupy the Inquisition only the Judaisants, the Moriscos, the Lutherans, and those mysterious dissidents who were called the "illuminati"—"*los alumbrados.*"

Astonishment and indignation have been expressed that there should have been such determination in persecuting the Moriscos and the Lutherans. To find an explanation of this cruel repression, we must try and imagine what that still inadequately unified Spain of the sixteenth century was like: a Spain in which the very numerous Moriscos constituted a people apart, especially in certain regions such as Andalusia and the kingdom of Valencia; in which the coast populations lived in perpetual dread of raids by Barbaresque or Ottoman pirates; and for which a Musulman invasion, a disembarkation of Turks or Africans, was a constant obsession and often a very real danger.

The monks continued to see in these dissidents more or less secret corrupters of the public faith. Merely by their way of life they set a contagious example. Together with their vices or their loose morals, the Christians acquired from them a tendency to jeer at their own clergy and their own religion, without imitating the dissidents' ardent faith.

The men responsible for the government of Spain were afraid of these people who gnawed their ropes in silence, while they awaited the hour propitious for deliverance foretold by their prophecies. It was obvious that the Moriscos would turn traitors; there was daily proof of the fact. It is true that they had good reasons for doing so; but, even if they had been well treated, they would nevertheless have turned traitors at the first favourable opportunity.

It was this fear of the internal enemy—the fear of adding to the Musulman peril that of Spaniards or foreigners who were accomplices of the Protestants of France, England, Germany, and Flanders —which, in a more or less subconscious way, made the Inquisition so suspicious and so stern towards Protestants during the reign of Philip II. Bishops such as the Archbishop of Toledo, Bartolomé Carranza, and monks such as Fray Luis de León, were arrested and imprisoned because the Inquisition, like the King himself, suspected them of favouring the new doctrines. The worse matters went in Flanders and the more formidable the Huguenots became there, the more Philip II felt himself bound by conscience to put Spain beyond the risk of contagion.

Despite the strictest vigilance, Protestant propaganda nevertheless penetrated into the Peninsula. The number of Protestant books[1] which were printed outside the kingdom in the Spanish language was larger than, or at least equal to, those printed in other languages. From the printing-houses of Germany these books were sent to Flanders and thence to Spain—at the outset by sea, and then, when the governmental surveillance became stricter, in the first place to Lyons, whence they were introduced into Spain by way of Navarre and Aragón. The centre of this smuggling traffic was to be found at Frankfort, where twice a year, during the fairs, Spanish and Flemish merchants came to renew their stocks, which they then dispatched to their correspondents in Spain.

Propaganda books arrived by the bale. A certain Wilmann, a bookseller of Antwerp, had branches at Medina del Campo and at Seville, where Latin and Spanish translations of Protestant writings could be procured. These books, printed at Frankfort, were sold at a very low price in order to promote their circulation. From Spain money was sent to these clandestine printing-houses, and was passed on to Spanish refugees who had fled to Germany.

These *émigrés* were the most active agents of propaganda. They made continual journeys between Frankfort and the Low Countries, despite the risk of falling into the hands of the Brussels police. The

[1] Cf. *Documentos inéditos para la historia de España*, Vol. V, pp. 399–400.

provinces of Spain where this proselytism made the most progress were Andalusia and Aragón. Matters came to such a point that Calvin's famous work, *The Christian Institution*, was actually printed at Saragossa.

It is easy to understand why Aragon and Andalusia were chosen by the Protestants as centres of propaganda .It was because these provinces were full of Moriscos and Judaisants, upon whose complicity they counted; and also because they were the two provinces where rebels could most easily come to an understanding with foreigners and receive help from them—the Aragonese from France, and the Andalusians from Morocco and the Barbary States.

In any event, heresy was pitilessly strangled. The atrocity of the means employed is only too evident. What is most repugnant to us in these measures of repression, I repeat, is religion put at the service of a bloodthirsty policy. But the result, dearly bought though it was, is also incontestable.

These executions and these expulsions *en masse* saved the still weak plant of Spanish unity. They spared Spain the horrors of interminable civil wars, anarchy and division—and perhaps another attempt at invasion, as at the time when the Berbers crossed the Strait of Gibraltar to put everything to fire and sword in the Peninsula.

CHAPTER XXX

The Golden Century

UNDER Charles V and under Philip II, Spain's internal prosperity did not by any means correspond with the brilliant *rôle* which she played in the world. This was for many reasons. The first was her conquering and colonising expansion.

During all that period which followed the taking of Granada, one might say that Spain was deserted by the Spaniards. Immense horizons opened before them, which lured them out of their motherland. It became nothing more than the old ancestral home where one went to rest and die, after spending his life fighting on all the battle-fields of Europe, or to enjoy the small fortune gained by exploiting the sugar-canes of Cuba and San Domingo, or the gold and silver mines of Mexico and Peru.

Exodus of soldiers, exodus of colonists—this explains first the progressive decrease of the population, and next the impoverishment of the soil and the decay of the few industries which had previously prospered in some cities of the Peninsula. For that matter, except in Catalonia and in the southern provinces, Spain had never been a country of intensive cultivation and highly industrialised. I may add that the expulsion *en masse* of the farming and industrial Moriscos and the trading Jews completed the decline.

Nevertheless, the gold of the New World flowed into Spain. The greatest wealth rubbed shoulders there with extreme poverty, and magnificence displayed itself in the midst of sordid wretchedness. The government was embarrassed in its finances, like governments of all periods and particularly those of that period. It was embarrassed in its finances because its fiscal regime was extremely lenient—positively paternal by contrast with our present-day regimes—and because taxes were imposed only upon the least rich part of the nation, with the result that their yield was very small.

Driven to address itself to financiers who robbed it, the Spanish Government found the greater part of the ingots which were brought to it by the galleons of America disappearing into the coffers of the bankers of Antwerp, Augsburg, and Genoa. The dealers in gold, expelled from Spain, revenged themselves by emptying her purse and starving her people.

But, by way of compensation, this period of Spanish expansion and hegemony coincided with an extraordinary intellectual, literary, and artistic development. This great movement maintained its impetus for nearly two hundred years, and its influence extended all over Europe and even to the New World. It was what the Spaniards called their "Golden Century."

At this period a number of universities were founded, side by side with the old university centres of Alcalā and Salamanca. There were more than thirty of them in the Peninsula. Inasmuch as these universities, like the Musulman universities, and for that matter like all those of the Middle Ages, were above all theological colleges, whose degrees led to ecclesiastical benefices, the multiplication of them ended by creating a regular intellectual proletariat, since the Church could not support all its bachelors and all its licentiates. The starveling student then became a literary type.

It was the Jesuits who modernised teaching, by giving a larger place in it to the study of the humanities and by reviving the study of classical antiquity. Colleges of theirs were established in the principal cities of the kingdom. In Spain, as elsewhere, they educated generations of humanists.

For reasons of a practical kind, schools of law—political law, international law, above all canon law—were more flourishing than ever in the universities. Philosophy, as among the Spanish Musulmans of the time of the Caliphate, was a timid enough follower of theology, which dominated the intellectual field for two centuries. The necessity of replying to the learned men of the Reformation gave a new impulse to studies of this kind.

The unique contribution of Spanish theology was its mysticism, which is really incomparable. Saint Theresa of Avila, Saint John of the Cross, to mention only the greatest among the Spanish mystics and to consider them only on the purely intellectual side of their work, veritably opened unknown worlds to psychological introspection. They corresponded, in the spiritual sphere, with the discoverers of America and the conquistadors.

Science properly so-called did not flourish in the Spain of the sixteenth century. But it was the same thing in all the other countries of Europe. Science was barely at its birth. Only cosmography and astronomy were seriously studied. Spain at that time had excellent cosmographers, but none of the first rank. At the same time it must not be overlooked that Philip II devoted much attention to the discoveries of his time and their scientific application.

Not only did he have bridges, aqueducts, and fortifications constructed in all directions, but he also encouraged the projects of the boldest inventors and engineers of that period. He tried to bring the water of the Tagus right up to Toledo by means of a system of hydraulics. He even thought of canalising this river and making it navigable from Lisbon and the Ocean. Toledo as a port was one of his dreams.[1]

If the positive sciences had little place in the "Golden Century," the intellectual sciences, on the other hand, were exceedingly flourishing. Historians and monograph-writers were legion, and they have left us a very considerable array of work, admirable for the

[1] See my *Philippe II à l'Escorial*, pp. 195 *et seq.*

most part, especially their contributions on American and pre-Columbus antiquities.

But all this pales beside the purely literary production of this Spanish Renaissance. All literary forms are represented in it in extraordinary profusion. After the romances of chivalry, the pastoral *genre* enjoyed a prodigious success. The seven books of Montemayor's *Diana enamorada* were imitated by all European literatures, and in particular by the French. The play and the novel, not to speak of lyric poetry and epic poetry, had a vogue still greater and more lasting than the pastoral. For two centuries they provided subjects for French dramatists and novelists, among them Corneille and Lesage.

This Spanish drama, especially that of Lope de Vega, was astonishing in its wealth of imaginativeness. While Cervantes created an immortal figure in his *Don Quixote*, and was a moralist and a depicter of customs of the first order in his *Novelas Ejemplares*, he did not exhaust, or nearly exhaust, the whole range of conception of the Spanish school of fiction. Side by side with him and after him, there was a very large number of novelists and short-story writers, especially the "picaresques," who, despite certain conventional characterisations imposed upon them by public taste, have left us the most authentic paintings of Spanish society at all its levels.

This tradition persists even to-day. The novel, the short story, are among the most alive, the most fertile *genres* in present-day Spanish literature. It was a *genre* that developed, even under Philip II, with a liberty, a freedom of thought and expression, which surprise those who see nothing in the Spain of that period but the country of the Inquisition.

Finally there were architecture, the plastic arts, jewellers' work, painting—the last of them absolutely unequalled. It is a current prejudice among tourists, and even art critics, that there is nothing interesting in Spain in the way of architecture except Moorish architecture. Apart from the Alcázar of Seville, the Alhambra of Granada, and the Mosque of Cordova, there is nothing worth even a glance, so we are told.

Nevertheless—not to speak of Roman and Visigoth architecture, which has left monuments worthy of admiration from one end of the country to the other, such as the cathedrals of Burgos and Seville and the monasteries of Ripoll and Poblet—if we confine ourselves only to the period of the Golden Century, there was during that period an architectural flowering which can challenge comparison with that of the most privileged Latin countries.

All styles are represented in it, from the expiring Gothic to the "grotesque," by way of the plateresque, the churrigueresque, and the neo-classic of Herrera. The cathedrals of Salamanca, Santiago de Compostela, Jaen, Murcia, and Granada are magnificent edifices which have nothing to yield to the most prodigious creations of Gothic art. Among any number of civil and religious edifices, contemporary with it, the Escorial of Philip II stands out as the most complete expression of Imperial Spain and Castilian character, soldierly and Catholic at one and the same time.

It is the same in the case of sculpture, which is absolutely unique of its kind. This also is one of the most imposing and revealing manifestations of the national genius. From the second half of the fifteenth century to the first half of the sixteenth, it maintained itself at about the same level. This long sustained achievement sufficiently demonstrates its strength and the fact that it drew its inspiration from the inmost springs of Spanish consciousness.

Doubtless it is not to be compared with the idealist art of the French sculptors of Chartres, Amiens, and Rheims. But it is closer to reality. It is realist as Spain herself, as her literature, her painting, her mysticism. Like all true and great realists, beginning with Saint Theresa, it carries its realism through to the end. It takes the humblest thing as its starting-point, by no means despising it and often lingering over it lovingly; and it culminates in the most transcendental thing, in which it expires seemingly with the same satisfaction. From hell to Heaven, by way of the terrestrial globe—such is its progress, such is its domain.

With evident predilection, this sculpture employs wood—polychrome wood—because this material, which can be carved more readily than stone or marble, lends itself to the expression of everything that is violent and passionate in the human body, all of the paroxysms of pleasure and pain, and indeed of everything that is most subtle and most sublime in the human soul. It starts from commonplace reality to end in ecstasy. One may even say that it is concerned with form only for the purpose of stirring the soul. It is Catholic art at its most ascetic and its most orthodox, and as such it was practised by all those wonderful workers in wood, Becerra, Montáñez, Alonso Cano.

This integral realism, this specifically Spanish realism, which embraces all aspects of reality, from the humblest realities that fall within the sphere of the senses to the supra-sensuous realities that are accessible only to mystics—this realism also inspires the painting of Morales, Zurbarán, El Greco, and Murillo, as well as that of Ribera and Velázquez.

Spanish painting is perhaps the most original that the world has ever seen. Trained in the school of the Flemings and the Italians, it has all the sumptuousness of the one, all the virtuosity of the other, but together with something unique: the sense of life. It is living reality, life in action, life surrounded with splendour and zest.

In writing this I am thinking especially of Velázquez, that great realist who in any fragment of reality, isolated as it were at random, succeeded in discovering and expressing this sense of splendour in life—to such a point that, under his brush, a blacksmith, a spinner at work assume an epic grandeur, and his picture *The Ladies in Waiting* is as intensely, as profoundly poetical as a great historical and military canvas such as his famous *Surrender of Breda*.

This taking possession of life has such a sovereign, such a triumphal air in Velázquez that other painters, by comparison with him, descend to the level of mere picture-makers. At one time his principal works were exhibited in the great central gallery of the Prado, side by side with the canvases of Raphael, Titian, and Van Dyck. All of them were eclipsed by his own, all of them seemed trifling beside his. Only his work appeared to express the seriousness and the magnificence of life.

His portraits have the same epic air about them. Those of his emulators, if they do not possess the same grandeur of style, have at least realism, psychological penetration and sometimes exact lyricism. These Spanish portraitists were painters of the very first rank. All of them, the mystics as well as the realists, handed on to their modern descendants, together with the sense of life, a vehemence in execution and a colourist's gift which have perpetuated, right down to our own time, the mastery of El Greco and Velázquez.

PART II
THE HISTORY OF SPAIN SINCE THE
DEATH OF PHILIP II

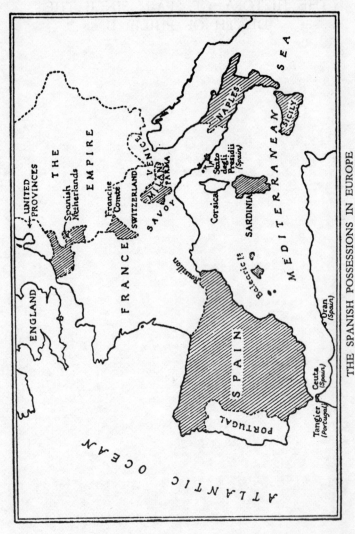

THE SPANISH POSSESSIONS IN EUROPE

After the Peace of Westphalia, 1648. The Franche Comté was ceded to France in 1678.

CHAPTER XXXI

The Reigns of Philip III and Philip IV (1598–1665)

THE death of Philip II ushered in a new period in Spanish history. The old monarch had been his own minister, and there was no department of the State which was not under his personal supervision. This policy was completely reversed by his son and grandson. The accession of Philip III initiated the reign of the favourites, who exercised the royal authority in the name of the monarch.

This change was partly due to a lack of application on the part of the later Habsburg Kings of Spain, but the early age at which they succeeded to the throne was also not without its influence. Philip III became King when he was twenty, and Philip IV when he was sixteen, while Charles II, when his father died, was only a boy of four. It is not without interest to note that Philip II had foreseen this development, for just before his death he said, "God, who has given me so many kingdoms, has denied me a son capable of ruling them. I fear that they will govern him."

In spite, however, of the indolence of her sovereigns, the mediocrity of her ministers, and the reverses which had marked the last years of Philip II, Spain still held the hegemony of Europe, and her prestige was very high indeed. Apart from the United Provinces, which had detached themselves from the Spanish monarchy, but to which the latter had not yet by any means abandoned its rights, Philip II passed on to his son the same wide dominions that he had inherited from his father. The King of Spain was still master of Naples and Sicily, the Milanese, the Franche Comté, Artois, and Flanders, while all of the New World that was yet inhabited by white men was subject to his rule. Philip II had even added to this vast heritage by the annexation of Portugal, which also meant the incorporation in the Spanish Empire of Brazil, as well as of the various Portuguese colonies in the East.

The problem which faced the successors of Philip II was the preservation of these dominions, and particularly of that portion of them which lay in Europe. Spain had played no part in the world until she had acquired possessions outside the Iberian Peninsula, and if she was to retain her supremacy she must continue to hold her Italian dominions, as well as the inheritance of the Dukes of Burgundy. For centuries she had been too absorbed in her battle against the Moslem invader to take a hand in European politics as such, and although her final victory over the Crescent had vitally affected the destiny of Europe, she had not reaped any immediate benefit. In short, Spain had fought for Christendom, but she had no voice in its counsels.

The acquisition of Naples, Sicily, and the Milanese, combined with the marriages which brought the Burgundian heritage, had changed all this. She was the mistress of Italy; she was installed upon the Rhine; and, above all, by her possession of the Low Countries she was able to dominate the most vulnerable frontier of her great rival, France. Her situation was indeed an advantageous one, and on the sole condition that she had the adequate military and naval strength at her disposal, she was mistress of Europe.

The preoccupation of Spanish policy throughout the seventeenth century was to perpetuate this state of affairs at all costs. To maintain the closest connection with Austria, and to let nothing be decided in Europe without the consent of Madrid and Vienna; to preserve free communication with Germany and Flanders through the Tuscan ports and the Milanese (this was especially important in view of the growth of English and Dutch naval power); and to hold France in check by the menace of the Flemish garrisons: these were the objects of Spain during the reigns of her last three Habsburg monarchs.

Above all, France was the enemy whose growing power must be curbed, and to do this the Spanish watch upon her frontiers must never be relaxed. In consequence, the whole century was one long struggle between France and the two branches of the House of Austria, until, finally, the former broke the bonds which held her, and Louis XIV set a French prince upon the throne of Ferdinand and Isabel.

Philip III was a well-meaning man, and was certainly not a fool, but, while amiable, he was both weak and idle, with the natural result that he was a tool in the hands of others throughout his life. During his reign the real ruler of Spain was not the King, but Don Francisco de Sandoval y Rojas, Duke of Lerma. From the accession to the death of Philip III the favourite controlled every department of State, and he secured his hold over the monarch by pandering to the latter's weaknesses.

In marked contrast with the austerity of Philip II, ostentation now became the order of the day, and full vent was given to that love of display which ere long provoked the biting satire of Quevedo. Madrid made no secret of its dislike of Lerma, who accordingly persuaded his master to transfer the capital for a time to Valladolid, where there was less criticism of his methods of government. Some idea of the extravagance which prevailed can be gleaned from the fact that while Philip II spent upon his household 400,000 ducats a year, the cost of his son's establishment was more than three times that amount. Even allowing for the steady fall in the value of money during this period, it is clear that the Cortes had considerable reason for its repeated complaints of the royal expenditure.

Throughout the reign of Philip II the problem of the Low Countries had transcended in importance every other international question, and shortly before his death that King had attempted to settle it by handing over the provinces concerned to his daughter, Isabel, and her husband, the Archduke Albert, as a semi-autonomous principality under Spanish protection. Unfortunately this proved to be no solution at all, firstly, because the Archdukes, as they were called, could not maintain themselves without Spanish money and troops, and secondly, because, as they were childless, it was only a question of time when the Low Countries would revert in full sovereignty to the King of Spain. In actual fact, Philip III found himself as fully committed to war against the Dutch as ever his father had been.

When the Archdukes arrived at Brussels they found the situation critical in the extreme. In their absence the Archduke Andrew and Juan de Mendoza had occupied the hitherto neutral territories of Cleves and Westphalia, with the consequence that the Protestant princes of Germany had made common cause with the Dutch, who were also receiving a certain amount of support from England and France. In desperation, the Archdukes opened negotiations with their enemies, and a conference was held at Boulogne in 1600. This proved abortive, and when war was renewed Maurice of Nassau, though he failed in an attack on Nieuport, swept the Spaniards out of Cleves. These events clearly established the fact that the Archdukes would never be able to maintain themselves with their own resources, and accordingly every effort was made to retrieve the situation by the despatch of money and reinforcements from Spain and from the Spanish possessions in Italy.

Fortune, which had so long favoured the Dutch, now began to incline towards the Spaniards. In 1603 Elizabeth of England died, and as much of her animosity towards Spain was personal, there was little difficulty in obtaining from her successor, James I, a promise that he would "not succour the Hollanders or allow English ships to trade in the Indies." Furthermore, in the Marquis of Spinola the Spaniards found a general capable of making head against Maurice of Nassau.

In these circumstances the war began to pursue a different course. Ostend surrendered to Spinola after a siege of three years, and the Spaniards pushed the campaign across the Rhine, and along the Dutch eastern frontier, from where, in the autumn of 1605, Spinola threatened Friesland with invasion. In spite, however, of these successes, it was clear that neither side could hope for a final victory, and a truce was made in 1607. Two years later another truce, this time for a period of twelve years, was concluded, and Spain at last admitted the United Provinces to be a government *de facto*.

At the expiration of this time hostilities were renewed, and Spinola gained several more triumphs, notably the surrender of Breda in 1625. He was, however, required for the campaign in Italy, and his successors were not so fortunate. The war against the

Dutch had now also become merged in the Thirty Years' War, and the varying fortunes of the one affected the other. Finally, by the Treaty of Westphalia in 1648, Philip IV recognised the United Provinces as an independent state, and this brought to a close a conflict which had been in existence for eighty years.

Spain was forced to give up the struggle against the Dutch, partly because she was unable to supply the men and money required, but also because communications with the Low Countries became increasingly more difficult with the passage of time. The defeat of the Armada, and a series of Dutch naval victories, rendered the sea route highly insecure, while the growth of French power threatened the line of communication from the Milanese through the Franche Comté. At the same time, the recognition of the independence of the United Provinces, if inevitable, was a heavy blow to the prosperity of those which remained in Spanish hands, for the Dutch held the mouth of the Scheldt, and they closed it to international navigation. Antwerp was ruined, and the Spanish Netherlands were deprived of their natural outlet to the sea.

In addition to these commitments in the Low Countries, Philip III had also inherited from his father the burden of a war with England, and he and Lerma determined to make one more effort to detach at any rate Ireland from Elizabeth's dominions. Messages from that country came in to the effect that now was the time to strike, but that unless the Earl of Tyrone and The O'Donnell were supported by Spain the chance of expelling the English from Ireland would be lost for ever. Lerma agreed with the Irish representations, and he induced the Cortes to vote an extraordinary tax of 24,000,000 ducats spread over six years.

The expedition sailed from Lisbon early in September, 1601, under the command of Diego Brachero, and consisted of thirty-three ships, carrying 4,500 men, commanded by Don Juan del Aguila, and a large quantity of war material. As so often in the history of Spanish attempts upon England, a storm drove many of the vessels back to port, and although del Aguila effected a landing, it was not long before he found himself invested in Kinsale by an English army under Lord Mountjoy.

In reality his position was hopeless in view of the failure of Tyrone to give any effective help. Reinforcements were sent from Spain, but these were unable to join del Aguila, and they accordingly disembarked at Castlehaven, Baltimore, and Dunboy, only, however, to be invested in these places in their turn. In 1602, therefore, the Spanish commander came to terms with Mountjoy, and evacuated Ireland.

For all practical purposes this terminated the hostilities between Spain and England in Europe, for although there was a project to dethrone Elizabeth by means of an army commanded by Spinola, it was never put into execution. The proposal to substitute Arabella

Stuart for James VI of Scotland as the Tudor Queen's successor was also favoured by Spain, but Elizabeth died before the necessary arrangements could be made. The new King of England realised that no useful purpose was being served by the continuance of the war, for all danger of England becoming a Spanish province had been averted, while the existing situation seriously hampered English trade with the Low Countries. Lerma, too, was weary of the struggle, and in 1604 peace was signed.

The Treaty of Vervins in 1598 had already brought the war with France to an end, though had Henry IV not been murdered twelve years later, it would probably have been renewed, for Spain could hardly have remained unaffected by the contest which then appeared to be inevitable between that monarch and the Emperor. His murder, however, completely changed the situation, and under the regency of Marie de Medici French policy was definitely favourable to Spain. This state of affairs continued until the outbreak of the Thirty Years' War, and the rise of Richelieu to power.

There can be no question but that Lerma was right in putting an end to these foreign wars which were draining the resources of Spain, but he did not know how to utilize peace once he had secured it. His main difficulty was that it was an age when the value of money was falling, while prices were consequently rising, as a result of the stream of gold from the New World, and the unsatisfactory nature of Spanish financial administration rendered the crisis more acute. An infinite number of petty taxes upon industry, commerce, and food hampered trade without producing the necessary revenue, and Lerma's extravagance, and the corruption of those by whom he was surrounded, only made matters worse. By 1605 every source of revenue had been pledged for years ahead at ruinous rates of interest, while the Milanese and Naples could no longer pay their way, but had to be subsidized by Spain.

Fundamentally, the problem was the same as in every other European country, but it was aggravated in Spain by the incompetence of the government, and by the particularly futile financial system. In these circumstances peace did not result in the national revival that might have been expected.

The most important event in the Peninsula itself during the reign of Philip III was the expulsion of the Moriscos, that is to say of the Moors who still lived on Spanish soil and were converts to the Christian religion. The Moriscos were for the main part engaged in agriculture, partly because other occupations were closed to them, and partly because the Old Christians regarded farm-work as menial and beneath their dignity. At the same time, it should be remembered that the Moors had not brought their processes of agriculture and irrigation with them from Africa, but had merely employed those which had been in use in Spain for centuries before their arrival.

The charges against them were that they still practised Islam clandestinely, and that during the recent wars they had entered into treasonable relations with the national enemies. That the latter accusation was justified can hardly be doubted, and in view of their number the Moriscos thus constituted a very real danger. Moreover, they were chiefly to be found in the kingdom of Valencia, whence they could easily communicate with the Turks and the Barbary corsairs. In the reign of Philip II it had been found necessary, for these reasons, to expel the Moriscos from Andalusia, and their resistance had resulted in the war of the Alpujarras. In 1609 they once more seemed so dangerous that it was decided to take drastic measures against them, and in that year Philip III signed an edict for their total expulsion from the Peninsula.

This decree is usually treated as having been issued by a weak administration, which, without due consideration, had yielded to the pressure of a fanatical clergy. In actual fact the whole question had been pondered and discussed for years, and the final decision had only been taken after considerable hesitation. Furthermore, the problem of the Moors had been calling for settlement for over a century, so that whatever charges may be preferred against the Spanish government the latter cannot be accused of acting precipitately. The Church certainly called attention to the importance of the problem, for in its eyes the secret practice of Mohammedan rites by those who were receiving Christian sacraments was sacrilege, and the lead was taken by the Archbishop of Valencia, in whose diocese the Moriscos were most numerous.

Accordingly, a *junta* was convoked at Valencia to consider the question solely from a theological standpoint, and to decide whether it was possible to continue administering the sacraments to those who manifestly treated them as a mockery. The answer was in the negative, and as this was equivalent to putting the Moriscos outside the pale of the Church, the problem of expulsion became critical.

Even then, the measure seemed so grave that the government was reluctant to adopt it. The Pope, as well as a certain number of the Spanish bishops, declared against it. Needless to say the great landed proprietors, who had Moriscos working on their estates, adopted the same course, and some of them went so far as to declare that if the religious education of the Moriscos was at fault, the blame must rest with the clergy themselves.

What finally decided the government was the danger of invasion from abroad coinciding with an insurrection in the Peninsula, as may be seen from a letter which Philip III sent to the deputies at Valencia: "Desiring to reduce the New Christians by means of conciliation and kindness, I ordered the *junta* about which you are informed to assemble at Valencia, in order to proceed a second time to their instruction and conversion, for the greater ease of my conscience, and to see whether it was possible to avoid expelling them from the kingdom. But I have learned through divers channels, all of them sure, that those of Valencia and Castile pursued their evil courses, since, at the moment when we were concerned with their conversion, they sent emissaries to Constantinople and Morocco to treat with the Turk and King Mouley-Sidan, asking them to send their forces in aid and support next year; and assuring them that they would find a hundred and fifty thousand men in arms, ready to adventure life and property in this enterprise; and that the difficulties were not great in view of the fact that our kingdoms were lacking in men, arms, and trained soldiers. In addition to this, I have learned also that they are in communication, and are plotting, with the heretics and with other princes, enemies of our monarchy, and that both have offered to aid them with all their strength."[1]

The expulsion of the Moriscos *en masse* was clearly disastrous, but from the national point of view it seems to have been inevitable. While the Spanish armies were fighting in Flanders, Italy, and Germany, the government could not allow an important section of the population to intrigue with the enemy, and plot to throw open to them the best ports of the kingdom. Even if the Moriscos had been left free to practise their own religion, which would have been contrary to all the ideas of the period, they would never have ceased to regard themselves as a separate people, and to conspire against the Spanish government with their co-religionists abroad.

Philip III died in 1621, and his death meant the downfall of Lerma. For some years the opposition to the minister had been growing, since his extravagance annoyed the Cortes, while the expulsion of the Moriscos ranged the landed proprietors against him. The Prince of Asturias was completely under the influence of Don Gaspar de Guzman, the Count-Duke of Olivares, who was the enemy of Lerma. The moment that Philip III was dead, Olivares obtained from his successor full powers to deal with the minister. Lerma and his partisans were put to death or exiled, and Spain was henceforth ruled by Olivares in the name of Philip IV.

Olivares was an abler man than Lerma, but he did not possess the talents necessary to rescue Spain from the slough into which she was sinking. Edicts against luxury were issued, and Philip IV set an example by a reduction in the expense of his court. All this, however, was to no purpose, for prices were steadily rising, while the whole financial and economic system was antiquated. The cost of collecting the taxes was frequently in excess of the amount obtained, and every monopoly, of which there were many, had its own

---

[1] Evidence in support of this charge is to be found in a letter addressed by the Moriscos to Henry IV of France. It was discovered in the archives of the Duc de La Force, and was published by the Marquis de Lagrange, in his edition of the *Mémoires authentiques de Jacques Nompar de Caumont, duc de La Force*, Paris, Charpentier, 1843, Vol. I, p. 341.

officials. Owing to the *alcabalas* or taxes on sales, tolls, inland customs-dues, and *octrois* to which goods in transit were subject, it was quite out of the question for them to compete with those of foreign origin, except at first-hand in the place where they were produced.

In these circumstances, it is not surprising that there was continual friction between the government and the Cortes in Castile, Aragón, Valencia, and Catalonia over the granting of subsidies, and these differences had much to do with the separatist movements that marked the middle years of the reign.

Three years before Philip IV came to the throne the Thirty Years' War had begun, and into that struggle Spain was inevitably drawn, both on account of the close family relationship between the Emperor and the Spanish King, and of the necessity of maintaining the encirclement of France. In the latter country the rise of Cardinal Richelieu to power in 1624 meant a return to the policy of Henry IV, and consequently a renewal of war.

On the other hand, both the contemporary Kings of England, James I and Charles I, realised the importance of friendship with the master of the Spanish Netherlands too well to sacrifice it. Accordingly, although the visit of Charles, when still Prince of Wales, to Madrid did not result in a marriage with a Spanish princess, there were, save for an English attack on Cádiz in 1625, no serious hostilities between the two countries until Cromwell revived the old policy of Elizabeth. A formal peace was made in 1629, and was ratified by Rubens as a special envoy to England in the following year.

The war with France began in Italy. During the last years of the reign of Philip III the Spanish forces had occupied the Valtellina, the valley which connected Lombardy with the Tyrol, for the purpose of keeping open the communications with Vienna. The victories of Spinola in the Low Countries, and the success of the Imperial arms in Germany and Bohemia, determined Richelieu to strike before it was too late, and the French accordingly invaded the Valtellina.

In spite of the exhausted condition of Spain the energy she displayed was remarkable, and notwithstanding early French successes Richelieu was compelled by the Treaty of Monzon, in 1626, to relax his hold upon the disputed valley, whose inhabitants recovered their independence on payment of a tribute to the Swiss canton of the Grisons. The interests of France and Spain were, however, too strongly opposed for this settlement to be anything more than a truce, and the succession to the duchy of Mantua led to another outbreak of hostilities. In this struggle the Spaniards were not so fortunate, and by the Treaty of Casale, in 1630, the claimant supported by France obtained the duchy, though subject to the suzerainty of the Emperor, while the French received the fortress of Pinerolo.

In spite of a heavy expenditure both of men and money Spain gained nothing.

Meanwhile, in Germany the fortune of war had changed with the intervention of Gustavus Adolphus and the Swedes, and even after the death of the former in the hour of victory at Lutzen the Imperialists were unable to make any effective head against their opponents. In these circumstances Philip IV and his minister determined to strike a blow at France by checking the progress of her allies, the Swedes and the German Protestants, for the re-establishment of the Imperial power in Germany would perpetuate her encirclement, the basis of Spanish policy, and also prove a standing menace to the Dutch. Accordingly, Philip's brother, the Infante Don Fernando, the governor of the Spanish Netherlands since the death of the Archdukes, was sent to the aid of the Emperor with 18,000 of the incomparable Spanish infantry. The stroke was brilliantly successful, for at Nordlingen, in 1634, the Swedes and the German Protestants were routed, leaving 8000 dead on the field and 4000 prisoners in the hands of the enemy.

The defeat was a serious blow to the policy of Richelieu, but the Spanish victory rendered it more important than ever that France should break the bonds which imprisoned her. Hitherto, she had not taken a direct part in the Thirty Years' War, but had acted through the Swedes and the German Protestants. Nordlingen made it imperative that she should intervene directly, or see the Habsburg hegemony in Europe more firmly established than ever.

Accordingly, Richelieu declared war against both Spain and the Emperor, and encouraged the Dutch to attack Don Fernando in the rear. Flanders, Germany, and Northern Italy were the scenes of the fighting, and in these three theatres the war dragged on with varying fortunes. In 1636 the Spanish armies advanced so far as to threaten Paris itself, and two years later Lombardy was completely cleared of the French, who had occupied it: successive efforts on the part of Richelieu to invade Spain were also unsuccessful. On the other hand, the Dutch finally wrested from the Spaniards the command of the sea, for in October, 1639, a Spanish fleet of 70 ships, carrying 10,000 men, was destroyed by Van Tromp in the Downs.

At this point the energy of Spain was still further distracted by the outbreak of revolts in Portugal, Andalusia, Biscay, and Catalonia.

The old jealousy between the Spaniards and the Portuguese had in no way diminished as the result of their allegiance to a common crown. On his conquest of the country in 1580 Philip II had done his best to conciliate his new subjects, and had kept his word to preserve all their national privileges, to respect their autonomy, and not to burden them with Spanish taxation: official posts were filled entirely by Portuguese, and the nobles of Portugal were always made welcome at the Spanish court. Philip III followed his father's policy, and almost his last act was to attend a meeting of the Portuguese Cortes. Indeed, had these conciliatory methods continued to be employed, it is possible that the union of the two countries might have endured, but with the accession of Olivares to power all discretion was thrown to the winds.

In the first place his followers were installed in the more lucrative Portuguese posts, for there were not enough Spanish sinecures to satisfy their greed. Then, again, the continual wars in which Spain was engaged were definitely harmful to the interests of Portugal, which saw her old possessions in America, Africa, and the East harried by enemies with whom she had no sort of quarrel, while at home Cádiz was taking away from Lisbon much of its commerce. This was the moment chosen by Olivares to introduce, in 1636, the Spanish tax of 5 per cent upon all property, movable and immovable, and a rising was the result. This was suppressed, but instead of taking the warning to heart, Olivares imposed a fresh special tax upon the Portuguese as a punishment, and announced a plan for abolishing the Portuguese Cortes, and bringing the representatives to sit in the Cortes at Castile, of which kingdom Portugal was in future to be a province.

The strongest claimant to the Portuguese throne was the Duke of Braganza, and his popularity among his fellow-countrymen was great. As the rule of Spain became more unpopular, all eyes were turned towards him, and at the instigation of the Archbishop of Lisbon an organization was formed for the purpose of placing the crown upon his head. The Regent for the King of Spain was Margaret, the widowed Duchess of Mantua, but although she knew that the storm was brewing, she had not the necessary resources at her disposal to do anything.

When the revolution did take place, on December 1st, 1640, it was carried through with consummate ease. The conspirators, not above four hundred in number, rushed the palace in Lisbon, compelled the Regent to surrender the citadel, and the Duke of Braganza, after a three hours' revolt in which he had himself done nothing, found that he was King of Portugal under the title of John IV. Subsequent Spanish attempts to regain the country were unsuccessful, but the war dragged on for years. Finally, in 1665, the Portuguese won a decisive victory at Villaviciosa, and three years afterwards, by the mediation of Charles II of England, a treaty was made in which Spain recognised the independence of Portugal and her colonies, Ceuta alone remaining in Spanish hands.

In the state of the Peninsula at this time separatism was highly contagious, and hardly had Portugal established her freedom than Andalusia attempted to follow suit. The Duke of Medina Sidonia was not only the greatest landed proprietor in that province, but he was the brother of the new Queen of Portugal. His project was to make himself King of Andalusia with Portuguese help, but like his ancestor who commanded the Armada, he was a poor creature, and had not the resolution necessary to carry out his project. The details of the plot leaked out, and Olivares, determined to prevent a repetition of the Portuguese revolution, heavily reinforced the garrison of Cádiz. Medina Sidonia thereupon made his submission, and although his life was spared, he was not allowed to return to Andalusia.

A few years earlier, in 1631, Biscay had also broken out in revolt against what it held to be a violation of its privileges by the proposed creation of a salt monopoly, and order was not restored until the project had been abandoned.

Most serious of all was the rebellion of Catalonia. For years there had been difficulty with Madrid over financial matters, as well as over the billeting of Spanish soldiers in the province, and it was this latter grievance that precipitated the outbreak. The Spanish troops were in arrears with their pay, and they proceeded to live on the country in the same manner as they did in Italy and the Low Countries. The Catalan peasants retaliated, and the trouble spread to Barcelona, where, in June, 1640, a rising took place in which the Viceroy was killed.

The insurgents at once realised that they could not stand alone, and invoked the aid of Richelieu, who sent envoys to treat with them on the basis of the creation of a Catalan republic under French protection, or of the recognition of Louis XIII as Count of Barcelona. It was the latter alternative that was finally adopted.

The Catalan rebellion, and the proclamation of Louis XIII as Count of Barcelona, meant that the war against France had been transferred to the soil of the Peninsula, and Olivares quickly grasped the danger which this implied. An army was hastily assembled at Tortosa, and it advanced in triumph to Barcelona, only, however, to be routed at the battle of Montjuich (1641). French troops poured into Catalonia, and by the end of 1642 the outlying provinces of Cerdagne and Roussillon had been lost, in spite of the gallant defence of Perpignan by its Spanish garrison.

Philip IV took the field in person, and this did much to restore his subjects' spirits, while the failure of Condé to reduce Lerida after attempts which lasted for three years served to discourage his opponents. Furthermore, the Catalans discovered that they did not really like the French any better than the Spaniards, and it was not long before there was a party among them in favour of returning to their old allegiance. Nor was this all, for the death of Richelieu in 1642 ushered in a period of instability in France which proved highly advantageous to her enemies.

Finally, Philip IV entrusted the command of the Spanish forces to his illegitimate son, Don John of Austria, and the latter captured Barcelona in October, 1652, after a siege which lasted for fifteen months. The pacification of Catalonia, however, cannot be considered as complete until the signature of the Treaty of the Pyrenees with France in 1659.

The immediate consequence of these separatist movements in the Peninsula was the fall of Olivares. His enemies were numerous, and Philip could no longer refuse to listen to them. Accordingly, one morning in January, 1643, the King went out hunting, having left a note behind him dismissing the minister in the most friendly manner, and that was the end of the long ministry of Olivares.

There can be little doubt that the favourite had been influenced by the example of Richelieu to pursue in Spain that same centralising policy which the Cardinal was putting into effect in France, but he lacked the ability of his French contemporary, and in place of unification he merely achieved revolution. His manner was too arrogant to allow of his becoming popular, while his ignorance in economic matters made his task the more difficult in an age of economic crisis. After the dismissal of Olivares the King for a time took a more active personal share in the administration, but gradually the power passed into the hands of Don Luis de Haro, a nephew of the fallen minister, and it was not long before he was as powerful as his uncle had been.

The death of Richelieu, shortly afterwards followed by that of Louis XIII (May, 1643), encouraged Spain to strike another blow at France. The Infante Don Fernando had died in Brussels in 1641, and he had been succeeded in command of the Spanish forces in the Low Countries by Don Francisco de Mello, a Portuguese noble faithful to Spain. This general was at first highly successful, for he captured Lens, and in 1642 inflicted a crushing defeat upon the French at Honnecourt.

In the following year, after a feint on Picardy, he entered Champagne through the Ardennes, and laid siege to Rocroi. Condé determined to attack the besiegers, in spite of the fact that the bulk of them consisted of the veteran Spanish infantry which was acknowledged to be without a rival in the world. The French won the day by the adoption of new tactics. The solid mass of pikemen, which constituted the military strength of Spain, wedged together in close formation, could resist all cavalry attack by their stubborn endurance, and by sheer weight could bear down all opposition. If, however, the mass became once disorganised, it could never reform. Gustavus Adolphus had shown at Breitenfeld how it could be broken by artillery, and Condé applied the lesson at Rocroi. He alternated his squadrons of cavalry with musketeers, and used the one or the other against the Spanish phalanx as the situation demanded.

Time after time the Spaniards drove the French back, but at last their formation broke, and they were slaughtered where they stood. They lost 7000 killed and wounded, 5000 prisoners, and all their stores. The battle of Rocroi is notable in that it sounded the death-knell of Spanish military prestige, though it was far from bringing the war to an early conclusion.

The immediate effect of Rocroi was the French penetration of the Low Countries. Condé lost no time in entering Hainault, and he pushed his scouts almost as far as Brussels. He then turned to the East and captured Thionville, but his further progress was stopped for the moment by a victory of the Spaniards and the Imperialists over the French at Tuttlinghen, which threatened to open the Alsace frontier to invasion. Nevertheless, the succeeding years saw the loss to Spain of a great part of Western Flanders, and of Dunkirk, while in 1648 Condé won another resounding victory at Lens. In Italy, too, the Spaniards lost ground, and were driven out of Mantua, Tuscany, and the islands of Porto Lonzone and Piombino.

By this time the Thirty Years' War had exhausted not only Germany, in which it had for the most part been fought, but also the other countries that had participated in it. Negotiations for its termination had been begun as early as 1641, and they were now brought to a conclusion by the Peace of Westphalia in 1648. Of the three treaties which were made at this time only one concerned Spain directly, namely that with the Dutch, which was signed at Munster. By this document Spain formally recognised the United Provinces as an independent state, together with the colonies in the East which the Dutch had conquered.

The Peace of Westphalia did not terminate the struggle with France. Mazarin, who now controlled the policy of that country in place of the dead Richelieu, was desirous of exchanging Roussillon and Catalonia, which were in French hands, for the Spanish Low Countries and the Franche Comté. This proposal was unacceptable to Spain, and it was also the reason why the Dutch made a separate peace with Philip IV, for it revealed French ambitions so clearly that henceforth the United Provinces are to be found on the side of their ancient enemy in opposition to their old friends, the French.

In consequence, the war between France and Spain lasted another eleven years, and owing to the outbreak of the Fronde, which paralysed the French arms, the Spaniards were able to recover much of the ground which they had lost in previous campaigns. For a time, too, Condé was in the Spanish service, and in 1656, he and Don John of Austria severely defeated a French army under Turenne which was besieging Valenciennes. This reverse drove Mazarin to make an effort to come to terms, but the intervention of England on the side of France so encouraged the latter that the French government refused to consider any terms which Spain could accept.

The causes of this sudden hostility on the part of England were many. The English republican ambassador in Madrid had been murdered by supporters of the Stuarts; there were complaints of the maltreatment of English subjects by the Inquisition; and there was the desire to compel Spain to open her American possessions to

English trade. Above all, Cromwell looked at Europe through the eyes of Elizabeth, and to him Spain constituted the same threat as in the previous century.

The appearance of England on the side of France involved the loss of Jamaica, the victory of an Anglo-French army at the battle of the Dunes in 1658, and the recapture by the French of all that the Spaniards had recovered during the preceding years. In Italy, too, the armies of Philip were worsted by the combined forces of France, Savoy, and Modena. At the same time, Spanish privateers inflicted enormous damage upon English trade, and Cromwell's mistaken policy in regard to Spain precipitated an economic crisis that had much to do with bringing about the restoration of the monarchy.

In spite of these successes, however, France was weary of the war, and in 1659 the Treaty of the Pyrenees brought it to an end. Louis XIV married the daughter of Philip IV, but she renounced her right to succeed to the Spanish throne on condition of receiving a dowry of 500,000 crowns. Spain surrendered Roussillon and Cerdagne to France, and also all Artois except St. Omer and Aire. Gravelines, Bourbourg, St. Venant, the Sluys, Landrecy, Quesnoy, Thionville, Montmédy, Damvilliers, Irovy, Marienberg, Philippeville, Rocroi, Chatelet, and Limchamp remained in the hands of the French, while to the English was ceded Dunkirk. The fortresses in Burgundy were returned to Spain, with Oudenarde and Dixmude in Flanders, and France renounced all claim to Catalonia.

The Treaty of the Pyrenees undoubtedly strengthened France, but it did not enable her to break the circle of Spanish possessions by which she had been surrounded ever since the days of Charles V. The peace was only an expression of the lassitude of the two countries which had been at war for so long. Spain came to terms because she had no more men or money, and because Philip IV, although not old, was an invalid; France was glad of the opportunity to profit by an advantageous military situation that might change, and also because, in the event of the King of Spain dying without male heirs, she wished to make in peace the necessary preparations to grasp the Spanish heritage.

The Treaty of the Pyrenees did not mark finality. The governors of the Catholic King continued to command in Lille and Besançon, while his viceroys held the Two Sicilies and the Milanese, and could, in case of need, effect a junction with the Emperor. In short, France still possessed no guarantee of security except the financial impoverishment and the military weakness of the government at Madrid.

Philip IV only survived the Treaty of the Pyrenees for six years, for he died in September, 1665. His letters to the nun Maria de Agreda have enabled posterity to form a better estimate of his character than was possible for his contemporaries. They reveal a passionate man whose outward impassivity was but a mask. Indolent and self-indulgent, Philip was very far from being a fool, and his great failing was not a lack of ability, but a want of application. Unfortunately for Spain, Philip II had devised a system of government which imposed a life of unremitting toil upon the monarch, and neither his son nor his grandson had the will to shoulder this burden.

In spite of the decline of Spanish power during the reigns of Philip III and Philip IV, both Kings were the patrons of literature and art, in which Spain continued to lead the world. The Spanish theatre was the pattern upon which the European stage still modelled itself, and the great Lope de Vega did not die until 1635, or Tirso de Molina until 1648, while Calderón was at the zenith of his fame in the last years of Philip IV. Cervantes himself died a subject of Philip III, and it was in that monarch's reign that both *Don Quixote* and the *Novelas Ejemplares* were published. Spanish literature at this time could also boast the great satirist, Quevedo. In art the period was distinguished by El Greco, Ribera, Zurbarán, Murillo, and above all, Velázquez.

In fine, the reverses suffered by the Spanish arms, and the growing poverty of the country, were entirely without influence upon its literature and art, which continued to enjoy their old supremacy, and the seventeenth century may justly be described as the golden age of Spanish civilisation.

CHAPTER XXXII

Charles the Bewitched, and the Succession Question
(1665–1700)

IF Spain was in a state of decadence on the accession of Charles II
the fact left her inhabitants profoundly indifferent. If the national
finances were in disorder; if poverty was increasing with the rise
in the cost of living; and if the population was declining, as always
happens after a period of great prosperity, it does not appear that the
Spanish people were particularly unhappy during the reigns of
Philip IV and his son.

In Madrid, at any rate, leisure was general. With sword and dagger
at their sides, the members of the lower orders jostled those of the
upper classes in the streets, and, by their swagger, maintained their
pretension to be treated on the same footing as the aristocracy. It is
true that there was no longer any industry worth the name, but one
went very elegantly dressed in cloth and linen that came from Holland
and Flanders. Most professions were in the hands of foreigners, and
the few ships that plied between the Spanish ports were Dutch.
Under Philip IV there were already 40,000 French in the capital; a
fact which shows that there was still money to be made there, or
they would not have come. Moralists might groan about the public
depravity, the frivolity of all classes, and the increasing number of
prostitutes, but it made little difference, for the theatres and pleasure-
resorts were always full.

Nevertheless, beneath this external light-heartedness there remained the conviction that Spain was the greatest country in the
world; so great, in fact, that the loss of an outlying province might
pass as an accident of no importance.

Charles II was a boy of four when his father died, and he was a
very delicate boy at that. He was the son of Philip IV by his niece,
Mariana of Austria, and he was the only one of that monarch's
legitimate children to survive, with the exception of Maria Theresa,
the wife of Louis XIV, and Margaret, who married the Emperor
Leopold I.

He possessed the physical peculiarities of his family to an extent
that made him a monstrosity. His chin was so enormous, and stood
out to such an extent, that he could masticate nothing; while his
speech was almost unintelligible owing to the abnormal size of his
tongue. Up to the age of ten he was treated as an infant, and in
order not to endanger his feeble health his education was neglected,
with the result that he was incapable of transacting the ordinary
business of the State.

This weakness of body and mind, combined with the fact of his
extreme youth when he came to the throne, condemned Charles

from the beginning to constant tutelage. Philip IV had nominated his widow as Regent, and he had appointed a council to assist her, but from the outset there was jealousy and intrigue. That Charles would be the last of his branch of the House of Habsburg was generally believed both in Spain and abroad, and the shadow of the succession began to darken the politics of Europe. Such being the case, it was not long before French and Austrian parties were formed at Madrid.

Although the Regent declared that the era of favourites was at an end, but a short time passed before her confessor, the Jesuit, Father Nithard, became all-powerful, and was appointed both Inquisitor-General and a member of the Council of Regency. Father Nithard was a Tyrolese of good family; he was a man of ability; and as a foreigner he was disinterested, but it was this very fact of being a foreigner that made him unpopular. Furthermore, he attempted to curb the extravagant display in the capital, which roused its pleasure-loving inhabitants against him, and by making proposals for a reform of taxation he alienated the innumerable and powerful individuals who had a vested interest in the existing system.

From the beginning the Queen and Father Nithard were faced with the opposition of Don John of Austria, the son of Philip IV and an actress named Maria Calderón. For the time being Don John was under a cloud owing to the failure of his attempts to reconquer Portugal, but it was clear that he would avail himself of the first opportunity of attacking the Regent and her minister.

The death of Philip IV, and the unconcealed partiality of his widow for her relatives of the Austrian branch of the Habsburg dynasty, was an occasion for the renewal of the war with France. The dowry of the French Queen had not been paid as stipulated in the Treaty of the Pyrenees, and Louis therefore set up a claim, based upon a custom in Brabant called devolution, on her behalf to the Spanish Netherlands. He also cited in his favour the precedent of the elder daughter of Philip II, the wife of the Archduke Albert, who had succeeded to Flanders upon her father's death.

The claim was rejected by the Regent, and in May, 1667, the French invaded the Low Countries, where the Spaniards were unable to offer any effective opposition to the advance. Charleroi, Courtrai, Oudenarde, Tournai, Lille, Alost, and a number of smaller towns fell into the hands of France, while in the East the Franche Comté was likewise wrested from Spain.

At this point, however, the Regent was saved by the intervention of England, Holland, and Sweden, who had no desire to see Louis XIV become too strong. Under pressure from these Powers, therefore, peace was made at Aix-la-Chapelle in 1668. France restored the Franche Comté, though with its fortresses dismantled, to Spain, but retained Charleroi, Binche, Ath, Douai, Scarpe, Tournai, Oudenarde, Lille, Armentières, Courtrai, Bergues and Furnes.

The termination of hostilities was the signal for an attempt on the part of Don John of Austria to obtain control of the government. By order of the Regent one of his friends was arrested, and subsequently murdered in prison, without any charge having been preferred against him. This gave Don John his opportunity, and after a fruitless effort on the part of Nithard to arrest him, he advanced on Madrid at the head of a considerable force, and amid the undisguised sympathy of a large part of the population. The Regent was obliged to yield, and the Jesuit withdrew to Rome, where he spent the remainder of his days.

Protracted negotiations then took place between the Queen and Don John, during the course of which several reforms were promised by the Regent, and at last a reconciliation was effected: Don John was made Viceroy of Aragón, and after making his submission to the Regent he departed to Saragossa. For the moment there was no minister who was pre-eminent, but the tradition of a royal favourite at the head of affairs had become so firmly rooted that it was clear no long time would elapse before another made his appearance.

The Treaty of Aix-la-Chapelle had hardly been signed before French diplomacy set to work to undo it. The alliance of the three Powers that had forced its signature was broken by the secret Treaty of Dover between England and France in 1670, while a subsidy to the Swedes brought them once more, as in the days of Gustavus Adolphus, within the French orbit.

At the same time Louis XIV endeavoured to obtain possession of the Spanish Low Countries by direct negotiation with Madrid. First of all he made an offer to buy them for cash, and when this suggestion was rejected he proposed to exchange them for Roussillon, Cerdagne, and part of French Navarre. The Regent refused to entertain this proposal either, and Spain concluded, in 1671, the treaty with the Dutch, by which the two countries promised to come to one another's aid if attacked by France.

Unfortunately for Spain, the result of this was to precipitate war. Charles II of England, who wished to destroy the maritime power of the United Provinces, for commercial reasons, promised armed support to his French ally, and early in 1672 Louis XIV declared war on the Dutch.

Spain was unprepared, and all she could do during the first year of hostilities was to send 4000 men to the Low Countries, and reinforce the garrisons in Catalonia. At sea the Dutch managed to hold their own, chiefly owing to the lack of co-operation between the French and the English, but on land they were clearly powerless to make head against the magnificent armies of Louis XIV. The danger of the total subjugation of the United Provinces by France was obviously so great that in 1673 the Treaty of The Hague ranged Spain, the Emperor, and the Duke of Lorraine on the side of the Dutch.

The reply of Louis was a declaration of war against Spain and the Emperor, and the concentration of his efforts upon the conquest of the Franche Comté. The 15,000 Spanish troops there were quite unable to resist French forces of more than thrice this number, and before the summer of 1674 was far advanced the province was once more, and this time finally, in the possession of France. At last Louis had put an end to the encirclement that had lasted since the days of Charles V, and it was no longer possible for the Spanish armies in the Low Countries to be directly reinforced from the Milanese.

The succeeding years were equally disastrous for Spain. An offensive in Roussillon, which promised to be successful, had to be abandoned owing to the outbreak of an insurrection in Sicily, aided by the French, and this absorbed all the energies of Spain in the Mediterranean, more particularly after the defeat of the combined Spanish and Dutch fleets by the French off Palermo in 1676. Negotiations for peace began in the following year, but the Spanish terms were too high, and it was not until a further series of reverses had placed Ghent and Ypres in the Low Countries, and Puigcerda in Catalonia, in French hands, that Spain gave way. Peace was signed at Nimwegen in 1678, and by it the Franche Comté was added to France. On the other hand, Spain actually recovered Charleroi and some of the smaller towns she had surrendered by the Treaty of Aix-la-Chapelle.

In view of her defenceless condition, Spain came out of the struggle better than might have been anticipated, but this was largely due to the conditions in which warfare was carried on at this time. It was extremely difficult to crush an enemy owing to the fact that it was only on the rarest occasions that a general had enough troops to follow up a victory, and so wars went on for years. In this way, Spain was enabled to hold out decade after decade, risking only a very small number of men, and reducing her territorial losses to the minimum.

The progress of the war had not put an end to the intrigues at Madrid, and before long a successor to Nithard had appeared in the person of Fernando de Valenzuela. It was the story of Lerma and Olivares over again, though on this occasion the enemies of the favourite were in a stronger position in that they had Don John of Austria to help them.

Charles II came of age in 1675, and a decree appointing Don John as chief minister was all ready for his signature on the morning that he attained his majority. Don John's partisans had persuaded the king to sign it, but under the influence of his mother he changed his mind, with the result that Valenzuela became more powerful than ever. Two years later an attempt on similar lines was made again, and this time it was successful. The Queen was ordered to leave

Madrid, Valenzuela was sent to the Philippines, and Don John became dictator of Spain.

Once in power he proved no more competent than the fallen minister, but before his opponents had gathered sufficient strength to overturn him, Don John died, in 1679. The immediate consequence of this was a reconciliation between the King and his mother, and the return of the latter to the capital, where she resumed her old sway over the feeble monarch.

The question of the succession was now beginning to loom ever larger in the eyes, not only of Spain, but of all Europe, and Don John had, shortly before his death, taken the necessary steps to ensure that the King's marriage should weaken, rather than strengthen, the party of his mother. The bride selected for Charles was Princess Marie Louise of Orléans, the child of the brother of Louis XIV and Henrietta of England, the daughter of Charles I.

The marriage took place in November, 1679, but it was a failure from the start. Marie Louise had been brought up in the gay court of the early days of her uncle's reign, and the rigid etiquette that surrounded the Spanish throne was antipathetic to her. She made no effort to reconcile herself to her surroundings, and she did not take the trouble to acquire the mastery over her husband, which she could easily have done. Worst of all, the royal couple remained childless. In short, Marie Louise was a complete failure from every point of view, and her want of tact played completely into the hands of her mother-in-law, so that the triumph of the Austrian faction was complete. Ten years after her marriage Marie Louise died, in 1689, and the problem of succession was no nearer settlement than it had been when she first entered Spain.

While this struggle between Austria and France had been taking place in the palace, the administration of the country had, since the death of Don John, been carried on, first of all by the Duke of Medina-Celi, and then by the Count of Oropesa. Both did what they could in the matter of reforming the most obvious abuses, and the latter, realising the danger to Europe of the Turkish siege of Vienna, sent an army of 12,000 men to the aid of the Emperor; but the designs of Louis XIV were their preoccupation.

War with France broke out again in 1681, and lasted till 1697, save for the Truce of Ratisbon (1684–1686). The diplomacy of Oropesa was successful in bringing to the aid of Spain, by the formation of the League of Augsburg, Sweden, Austria, the Pope, and eventually, England and the Dutch. The war was fought on many fronts, and Spain had to defend herself in Flanders, Catalonia, and the Balearic Islands. At first she was successful, but by the time that the Treaty of Ryswick was signed in 1697 the French had conquered most of Catalonia, including Barcelona. In Flanders, though it was Spanish territory, the contest was mainly one between the English, Dutch, and the allies on the one side, and the French on the other, for Spain was unable to make any serious effort in that theatre.

What finally brought the war to an end was not the victory of one side or the other, or even the exhaustion of both, but rather the fact that the King of Spain could obviously not live much longer. He had been married again, this time to Princess Mary Anne of Neuburg, a sister of the Empress, but there was no heir, nor the likelihood of any, and it was clear that Charles II would be the last male of his line.

In these circumstances the Powers preferred to divide his heritage, if possible, peacefully, and so the Treaty of Ryswick was concluded. By this the French restored Catalonia, Luxembourg, Mons, Ath, and Courtrai to Spain, but it was also agreed that the Dutch should garrison the chief frontier fortresses in the Spanish Low Countries, since their nominal master had proved so incapable of defending them against French attack.

The claimants to the Spanish throne were three in number, viz., the Dauphin, the Electress of Bavaria, and the Emperor Leopold I. The Dauphin was the nearest heir to Charles II by blood, for he was the son of the eldest daughter of Philip IV, but his mother had renounced all claim to the Spanish crown when she married Louis XIV. The Electress of Bavaria, the daughter of Charles's younger sister, and of the Emperor Leopold I, was next in succession, but her mother had likewise renounced her rights when she married the Emperor. Lastly, there was Leopold himself, for his mother, the aunt of Charles II, had made, unlike her nieces, no renunciation. If, therefore, the renunciations held good, the Emperor's claim was the best, but if not, then the Dauphin was the lawful heir.

It was, however, clear from the beginning, that in the regulation of the succession to the Spanish throne, legal interpretations would have to give place to practical considerations. The Spanish monarchy was still by far the greatest of all Christian realms. In Europe it included Spain, the Milanese, Naples and Sicily, Sardinia, and the Spanish Low Countries, and in the New World all South America (except Brazil and Guiana), Central America, Mexico, Cuba, and other West Indian islands, while in the East Indies the Philippines also belonged to Spain. If the Emperor succeeded to this inheritance the empire of Charles V would be revived, whereas if France obtained these vast dominions the rest of Europe would feel its very independence threatened.

Accordingly, Louis XIV entered into direct negotiations with William III of England, and in 1698 the First Partition Treaty was signed. This stipulated that the Electoral Prince of Bavaria, the weakest of the three claimants, should have Spain, the Indies, and the Low Countries; Naples, Sicily, the Tuscan ports, and Guipúzcoa were to fall to the Dauphin; and the Milanese was to go to Leopold's son by his second wife, the Archduke Charles. In February, 1699, however, the Electoral Prince died, and the negotiations had to be begun afresh.

In the following year the Second Partition Treaty was made between England, France, and the Dutch, and by this the Archduke Charles was given Spain, the Low Countries, and the Indies, while the Dauphin was to have the Two Sicilies, the Milanese, the Tuscan ports, and Guipúzcoa. The Emperor protested against this arrangement when the news of it leaked out, while the Spanish ambassador in England used such strong language that he was requested to leave the country.

Meanwhile, in Madrid all was confusion. The Queen Mother had died in 1696, and Oropesa had been dismissed, recalled, and dismissed again. The Queen inclined to the party which favoured Austria, but the partisans of France, headed by Cardinal Portocarrero, steadily gained ground. All Spaniards were opposed to a partition of the empire, and it was obvious that, if any one could prevent its dismemberment, it was Louis XIV.

So far as Charles II could appreciate any argument, this carried great weight with him, although his natural inclinations were in favour of his relatives at Vienna. Finally, he signed a will leaving the whole of his dominions to Philip, Duke of Anjou, the younger son of the Dauphin, and appointed a council to carry on the government until the new King arrived in Spain. If Philip refused to accept the inheritance, the right to it was to pass wholly to the Archduke Charles.

On November 1st, 1700, Charles died at the age of thirty-nine. Louis XIV, anxious above all things to prevent that fresh encirclement of France which the accession of an Austrian to the Spanish throne would imply, accepted the will, and the Duke of Anjou was presented to the assembled courtiers at Versailles as Philip V of Spain.

CHAPTER XXXIII

The Spanish Domination in Italy and America

THE Spanish dominions in Italy consisted of the Duchy of Milan, the Kingdom of the Two Sicilies, and the "Presidi." The last-named were five coast places which Cosimo I of Tuscany had been obliged to leave in Spanish hands as pledges for his loyalty, and they provided Spain with a ready means of access to the Italian peninsula should Genoa ever be closed to her. The "Presidi," therefore, possessed great strategic, but no other, importance.

The supreme authority was the Council of Italy, a mixed body of Spaniards and Italians, which sat at Madrid, but in actual fact the Viceroys in Naples and in Milan had things very much their own way. It is usually stated that the administration of the Spanish dominions in Italy is one of the scandals of history, and it certainly left a good deal to be desired. At the same time, the same financial and economic problems, owing to the steady rise in prices, were present there as in Spain itself, and their consequences were equally serious.

It is true that sinecures were found in Italy for the relatives of a Lerma and an Olivares, but Spain, at any rate in the seventeenth century, made no profit out of her Italian possessions. Far from contributing to the Spanish exchequer, the Milanese was run at a loss, and the deficit there usually had to be made up out of the surplus, if any, in Naples. What the Kings of Spain did get out of Italy was generals, such as Parma and Spinola, and soldiers, and at the death of Philip III, for example, no less than thirteen of the *tercios* into which the Spanish army was then divided were composed of Italians.

The Milanese was regarded primarily as a *place d'armes*. Its strategical importance was very great indeed, for it not only linked Spain with Austria, and, through the Franche Comté, with the Low Countries, but it served as a barrier against a French advance into Central or Southern Italy. In consequence, the Lombard towns were all strongly fortified, as were also the frontiers of the Duchy. There was a permanent garrison of about 5000 of the famous Spanish infantry, besides Italian troops, which included a native militia, for which each Lombard commune had to provide and equip its quota of recruits. The military power was always predominant over the civil, and although the Senate of Milan continued to exist, it was invariably beaten in any trial of strength against the Spanish Viceroys. There was, however, a considerable measure of municipal self-government, and in the rural districts there was a great deal of local patriotism in the communes.

The chief event, unfortunately, in the history of Lombardy in the seventeenth century was the plague in 1630, which depopulated several districts. The inability, too, of the King of Spain to pay his troops regularly resulted in the latter pillaging the inhabitants upon whom they were billeted, though eventually barracks were built, and this relieved the situation somewhat. Nevertheless, in spite of a good deal of grumbling, the Lombards made no determined effort to overthrow the rule of Spain, for they realised that independence was out of the question, and that they would merely be exchanging government from Madrid for government from Paris.

In Naples the position was somewhat different. The Viceroy, at least in theory, was supposed to consult the Collateral Council, and the old Neapolitan Parliament, with its three estates, was still summoned to vote supplies. In the city, the municipal administration was conducted by district councils, called *Piazze*, five for the nobles and one for the people, each of which chose an *eletto* to transact business with the Viceroy. Actually, the country was so divided against itself that this machinery never functioned properly.

The memories of the old feuds between Ghibelline and Guelf, and between Aragón and Anjou, prevented any common action on the part of the aristocracy, while the people were too fickle to remain united long enough to achieve any one object. A good deal of money was, it must be admitted, spent by the Viceroys upon public works, and the military element was not supreme in Naples as it was in Milan. The real trouble, as elsewhere, was finance (taxation was trebled between 1558 and 1620), and the cumbrous and wasteful Spanish fiscal system.

Sicily was in a happier position, in spite of the fact that it suffered from many of the same disadvantages to which Naples was subject. It had belonged to Aragón for centuries before Spain herself had become united, and it retained its medieval constitution, and consequent independence of political life, which enabled it to resist the bureaucratic tendencies of Spanish rule. Moreover, the memory of the Sicilian Vespers was sufficiently fresh to make the Spaniards cautious, so Parliament continued to make laws and vote taxes, and the nobles to retain their feudal authority.

The towns were specially active and independent, and the export of corn made them wealthy. The rivalry between them, particularly between Palermo and Messina, was bitter, and for their own ends this was encouraged by the Spaniards, who, however, eventually allowed it to go so far that it ultimately led to the most dangerous Italian revolt which they had to face in the seventeenth century. For the rest, Sicily was specially useful to Spain as an outpost against the Turks.

The reign of Philip III witnessed a struggle between Spain and the Duke of Savoy, Charles Emmanuel I, who claimed Montferrat on the death of Francis I of Mantua in 1613. At first the Governor of Milan was prepared to assist Charles Emmanuel, but orders arrived from Lerma that the Savoyard claim was to be opposed, and this so annoyed the Duke that hostilities broke out in 1614. Charles

Emmanuel hoped to annex the Milanese, and he called upon the Italian States to aid him in driving the foreigner from the country, but his appeal fell upon deaf ears. The fighting went on with alternating success, partly in Piedmont and partly in the Milanese, until it was terminated by the Treaty of Pavia in 1617.

The unexpected strength displayed by Charles Emmanuel undoubtedly shook, for a moment, the hold of Spain over Italy, but the Italian States were too divided to make the concerted effort which alone could have rendered success possible, and the peninsula had to wait more than two centuries for its unification.

About this time took place the plot which is known in Venetian history as the "Bedmar Conspiracy," and which well illustrates the practical independence enjoyed by the representatives of the King of Spain in Italy. To this day it is by no means clear exactly what was intended, but it is certain that the Duke of Osuna and Don Pedro of Toledo, respectively Viceroys of Naples and Milan, in conjunction with the Marquis of Bedmar, the Spanish ambassador in Venice, were meditating some desperate act against the Republic of St. Mark.

The Council of Ten was informed of what was afoot, and it announced that the real object of Osuna was to make himself King of Naples. Philip III and Lerma may not have believed this charge, but it seems to have aroused their suspicions, for Osuna was shortly afterwards recalled to Spain. In any event, the Thirty Years' War was just beginning, and Lerma had no desire to see protracted hostilities with Venice added to his other difficulties. The departure of Osuna was welcomed in all quarters, and not least by the Neapolitans, who preferred, as the ultimate resident authority, a Viceroy who could be removed to a monarch who would of necessity be permanent.

Yet it was in Naples that Spain encountered most opposition, and it was there that took place one of the most famous insurrections in history, namely that led by Masaniello. This revolt had, however, been preceded by several earlier disturbances.

Philip III was hardly seated upon his father's throne when, in 1600, the peasants of Calabria rose at the bidding of a mystic called Campanella, but the movement was suppressed. In 1621 there were riots in Naples itself owing to the rise in the cost of living, but these, too, were put down. By 1646 the cost of Spanish participation in the Thirty Years' War made it necessary to impose fresh taxation upon Naples, and the Viceroy put a gabelle upon fruit, the staple article of Neapolitan diet.

This provoked an explosion, and Masaniello, a fishmonger, became the symbol, rather than the leader, of the agitation which followed. The Viceroy had but few troops at his disposal, and being himself of a timid nature, he conceded all the demands of the insurgents. The consequence of this was mob-law both in town and country, and in the anarchy Masaniello, whose arrogance had become insufferable, was murdered. At this point, Don John of Austria arrived with a fleet, but his bombardment of Naples, far from inducing the insurgents to surrender, drove them to abandon the last pretence of loyalty to the Spanish throne, and to proclaim a republic.

With Condé winning victories in the Low Countries, and with Portugal and Catalonia in revolt, Spain was in no position to coerce Naples, and she must have lost that kingdom had the Neapolitans not been so fickle, or had they received adequate support from France. Henry, Duke of Guise, did come to Naples, where he passed as the heir of the Angevins, and at first he met with an enthusiastic reception. He could, however, get no serious assistance from Mazarin, who distrusted him, and he soon quarrelled with the Neapolitans, who wanted him to be a kind of Stadtholder on the Dutch pattern, while he was determined to be King.

In these circumstances all who had anything to lose saw that the only hope of restoring order lay in the re-establishment of Spanish rule, and the revolt soon afterwards collapsed. The Spaniards returned without conditions, and when the new Viceroy reduced the gabelles, the Neapolitans allowed him to hang the leading rebels without protest. The Duke of Guise made another attempt in 1654, but received no support. For the remainder of the reign of Philip IV, save for a severe outbreak of plague in 1656, and during the whole of that of his son, the history of Naples was uneventful: indeed, there was a definite revival of prosperity owing to the energy of the Viceroys at this time in reforming taxation and suppressing brigandage.

In Sicily the most serious rising against Spanish rule took place in 1674, and it was to no small extent due to the rivalry between Palermo and Messina. The latter had been allowed a monopoly of silk, and when this was cancelled there were riots. The Viceroy declared that these constituted a revolt, which he was determined to crush, but the people of Messina fortified their town, and invoked the aid of France. In 1675 Louis XIV sent troops to Sicily, but although they might have conquered the whole island, they in fact did very little. France regarded the expedition merely as a method of distracting Spanish attention from the other theatres of war, and as soon as the Messinese discovered this they refused to obey the French generals.

The struggle dragged on until 1678, when the French evacuated Sicily. The victorious Spaniards were unexpectedly moderate in their hour of victory, though all the privileges of Messina were taken away. So long as Charles II lived the Sicilians gave no further trouble to Spain, and when, early in the eighteenth century, they were separated from the Spanish monarchy they were dissatisfied.

Whether there was war or peace in Europe, hostilities never ceased in the New World and in the East Indies.

The reign of Philip III witnessed the Dutch expansion in the East, and this naturally led to conflicts with Spain, who owned the Philippines. The object of the Dutch was to cut the communications between Manila and Mexico, and to embroil the Spaniards with the Javanese, in the hope of eventually securing the Philippines for themselves. However, the power of the United Provinces began to decline before this purpose could be accomplished, but to Spain this brought no real relief, for the threat from the Dutch was succeeded by the far greater danger from the Buccaneers in the West Indies.

Their origin may be dated from 1625, when a band of English and French adventurers founded a settlement on St. Christopher, from which they made raids into San Domingo. In 1630 they moved to Tortuga del Mar, which lay in the main route of trading vessels. Here they were joined by kindred spirits from all parts of Europe, and for many years were a terror to Spanish ships and to the Spanish settlements on the mainland. The Buccaneers were greatly aided by the British capture of Jamaica in the days of the Commonwealth, for they obtained considerable, if unofficial, assistance from that island, and it was in the reign of Charles II that they did the greatest damage.

Hitherto the Buccaneers had generally operated separately, but about this time they found in Henry Morgan a leader who possessed the necessary ability to induce them to act together. One of his earlier exploits was the sack of Puerto Bello, but in 1671 he accomplished the feat which has made him famous. He crossed to the mainland with a fleet of thirty-nine vessels, and after marching across the isthmus, he fought a pitched battle, and then sacked Panama in circumstances of the greatest barbarity. Morgan's later career was equally notable, for he was knighted by Charles II of England, and appointed deputy-governor of Jamaica. The success of Morgan caused him to have many imitators, and for some years no town in America was safe from attack. In 1680 John Coxon captured Santa Maria, and took several vessels in the Bay of Panama, while three years later Van Horn sacked Vera Cruz, and Davis and Swann harried the Pacific coast at will.

This, however, was the high-water mark of the Buccaneers' power, for the breach between England and France in Europe soon prevented any co-operation between their respective nationals even in the pursuit of piracy. The other Powers, too, gradually realised that the Buccaneers were a public menace, and assisted to curtail their activities. Pirates, of course, there were on the Spanish Main until well into the nineteenth century, but they never again became as formidable as they had been in the days of Charles the Bewitched.

In spite of wars in Europe, and of the raids of the Buccaneers, the work of exploration and colonisation in America was steadily pursued. In the reign of Philip III, Sánchez Vizcaíno explored the coast of California in the hope of finding a suitable harbour for ships coming from the Philippines, and one result of his expedition was the foundation of the city of Monterey. Fernández de Quiros about the same time discovered the New Hebrides, and the coast of New Guinea and Australia, while in 1605–1609 the Northern part of Florida was opened up and in 1617–1618 Cape Horn was explored.

The remainder of the century witnessed the progress of these explorations. The Spaniards gradually worked their way North in California, and up the great rivers of South America, adding vast tracts of territory to the known world. Other nations, too, endeavoured to obtain a permanent footing in this part of America, but without success, save in Guiana, and at the mouth of the Mississippi, where the French established the colony of Louisiana.

It was during the seventeenth century that the administration of Spanish America attained the form which, with some modifications, was to characterise it until it was finally overthrown in the reign of Ferdinand VII. For this reason it is convenient to give an account of it here, indicating at the same time the changes which were made when the House of Bourbon succeeded that of Habsburg on the Spanish throne.

The basic principle of the administration was that it should approximate as closely as possible to that in Spain itself, and this had been clearly laid down by Philip II. The kingdoms of Castile and Aragón on the one hand, and the Indies on the other, belonged to the same monarch, and their laws and government were to be alike in so far as their natural differences would permit.

These instructions were obeyed, but, unfortunately, by the time that America had been settled on any considerable scale the machinery of government in the Peninsula itself was breaking down under the strain of supplying the needs of a world-empire, and the natural consequence was a state of confusion that was transplanted to America, where, since everything was on an infinitely bigger scale than in Europe, the results were even more disastrous.

Spain was not, as has been shown, a unitary State after the fashion of England and France: it was rather a collection of kingdoms and duchies whose only link was the fact that they belonged to the same monarch. These different units had their own laws and customs, and the memory of past strife was still fresh. Furthermore, the system of administration which had, on the whole, worked well enough in the Middle Ages was collapsing, and it was not until the accession of the House of Bourbon to the throne in the person of Philip V that administrative reforms were undertaken; even then the more important ones had to wait for another half-century, and the succession of Charles III.

The fact is that at the time when she was exercising the greatest influence over her American possessions, Spain herself was beginning to decline, and it was the seeds of her own decay that were in too many instances transplanted across the Atlantic. At the same time, there is no justification for the charge that the Spanish government paid no attention to the Americas. The *Recopilación de las leyes de las Indias* in nine books, published in 1680, is in itself a refutation of this accusation, and the earlier ordinances display an equal care for the affairs of the New World. In fact, the intentions of the home government were excellent, but the machinery for carrying them out was defective, and was quite unable to overcome the opposition of local vested interests. It is an arguable proposition that Spain lost America because she interfered too much, and in the wrong way, but on the evidence it is quite impossible to maintain that her chief sin was indifference.

During the rule of the House of Austria the Spanish possessions on the mainland were practically divided between the Viceroyalties of New Spain (Mexico) and Peru, but with the advent of the eighteenth century several important changes took place.

First of all, two new Viceroyalties were created, New Granada and Buenos Aires. The former, which was finally established in 1739, consisted of part of Tierra Firme and the kingdoms of Santa Fé de Bogotá and Quito, while the latter, which came into existence in 1776, was composed of the provinces del Plata, Paraguay, Tucumán, and four Peruvian districts. In 1731 Venezuela was separated from San Domingo, and created a Captaincy-General by the name of Caracas. Chile and Puerto Rico were granted the same status, which was also that of Louisiana with Florida. There were thus at one time four Viceroyalties (New Spain, Peru, New Granada, and Buenos Aires), and eight Captaincies-General (Guatemala, San Domingo, Cuba, Chile, Puerto Rico, Venezuela, Louisiana, and the Philippines).

This creation of smaller governmental units ultimately provided a great impetus towards independence, for it became possible for those who lived in them to think and act together in a way that was quite out of the question in the enormous Viceroyalties of earlier times.

The Viceroy was at the head of the whole administration, and he was usually a nobleman whose possessions in the Peninsula were such as to constitute a guarantee that he would not attempt to establish an independent kingdom in the Americas. There were few men of outstanding ability among the Viceroys sent out by the Habsburgs, but with the accession of the Bourbons there was a decided change for the better, and the viceregal office was held by administrators of the standing of Vertiz, Ceballos, Amat, Manso, Buccarelli, Gálvez, Azanza, O'Higgins, and the Marquis of Croix.

Beside, rather than beneath, the Viceroy was the *audiencia*, which was composed of lawyers, and whose members were known as *oidores*. This body had two separate functions, for it was at once the Viceroy's privy council and a court of law, from which the appeal lay to the Supreme Council of the Indies at Seville: when it met in the former capacity the Viceroy presided, and when in the latter its own president took the chair.

The *audiencia* had certain rights with regard to the Viceroy, which severely circumscribed his authority. When his term of office expired, it could inspect and pass his accounts, and at any time it could make a report upon his conduct to the authorities in Spain, while if he died it carried on the administration until the arrival of his successor. Furthermore, a decree of Charles I authorised the return to the Peninsula of any Spaniard who wished to inform the King personally of abuses in the colonial administration, though, as may be supposed, those who desired to take advantage of this permission were likely to find every possible obstacle placed in their path by the Viceroy and the *audiencia*.

In effect, then, the administration of the Americas was based upon a system of checks and balances calculated, not so much to produce good government in the colonies, as to prevent any tendency to break away from Spain. On the other hand, it must be admitted that the Spanish government was by no means unmindful of the interests of the native population, though the measures which it enacted on their behalf were liable to be honoured rather in the breach than in the observance on the other side of the Atlantic.

Beneath the Viceroys, the Captains-General (for all practical purposes the powers of the latter were the same as those of the former), and the *audiencia* was an elaborate municipal system, for the Spaniard, like the Roman, colonised from and through the towns. The *cabildos*, or town councils, soon became self-electing, and at the end of their year of office the outgoing *regidores*, or councillors, nominated their successors. The *alcalde*, or *corregidor*, i.e., the mayor, could not hold office again for two years, while twelve months had to elapse before the re-election of a *regidor*. In actual fact, long before the end of the seventeenth century these offices were bought and sold, and the same corruption characterised the municipalities of the Americas as marked those of every country at this period.[1]

The *cabildos* enjoyed considerable judicial and administrative power. The *alcalde* presided over a court of first instance for both civil and criminal cases, and the *cabildo* could act as a court of appeal in civil cases where the amount in dispute did not exceed a certain sum, but the jurisdiction of both *alcalde* and *cabildo* was liable to be severely circumscribed by that of the judges appointed by the *audiencia*. In administrative matters the municipalities were, theoretically, autonomous, but, in fact, they generally took into account the wishes of the higher authorities. When any unusually important decision affecting the municipality had to be taken a kind of town's

[1] In this connection it is not without interest to note that the Corporation of Oxford, which was heavily in debt, offered to secure the election of 1766 f the sitting members in return for a loan of £4000 free of interest.

meeting, known as a *cabildo abierto*, was summoned, and it was attended by the more influential citizens.

At one time it even appeared possible that this municipal system might afford a basis for self-government in some form, for as early as 1530 Charles I had laid down regulations for convening a congress of representatives from the various *cabildos*, and during the course of the sixteenth and seventeenth centuries there were about forty such meetings. The difficulties of transport and of communication, combined with the jealousy which always existed between the Viceroy, or Captain-General, and the *audiencia* on the one hand, and the *cabildos* on the other, effectively prevented any development of this tendency, which may be said to have been checked by that feeling of suspicion which pervaded every part of Spanish colonial administration.

The closing decades of the eighteenth century witnessed, in addition to the fresh grouping of the Americas for administrative purposes, the introduction of *intendentes* and *subdelegados*. Even before this there had existed *visitadores*, whose duty it was to inspect the public administration, and to call attention to abuses. The power of the *intendente*, however, was greater, for he possessed a jurisdiction in matters of police, justice, finance, and war, so that he could intervene in all those departments of government that had formerly been the preserve of the Viceroys, Captains-General, and *audiencias*, and what he was to them the *subdelegados* were to the *corregidores*. The first legislation on this matter was enacted in 1782, and it attained its final form in 1803.

In effect, the centralised administrative system of France, which Philip V had introduced into Spain, was being transplanted by his son and grandson to the colonies at the very time when the Spanish Crown, upon which in the last resort everything was to depend to an even greater extent than in the past, was itself on the eve of eclipse. To this may be attributed much of what was to follow.

The preoccupations of the Spanish government in Flanders, Italy, and the Americas in no way caused it to abandon the age-long campaign against the Turks and the Barbary corsairs, and throughout the whole of the seventeenth century the fight went on in the Adriatic, the Aegean, and the Eastern Mediterranean, as well as on the African coast in Tunis and Algeria. Lerma attempted to distract the forces of the Sultan by an agreement with the Shah of Persia, and at one time he seriously considered the conquest of Algeria, but nothing came of the project in the end. Raids were made on the Moroccan coast, where Larache was captured, and also on Tunis, Egypt, and Albania, while Turkish attacks on Messina and Malta were repelled.

All this, however, did little to curb the activity of the Barbary corsairs, who were continually raiding the Spanish coast, and pushed their forays as far as Galicia and Asturias. The reign of Philip IV was too troubled for Spain to spare any great effort against the Moslems, though the latter were growing increasingly more bold, and the plate-fleets from America were often attacked. In spite of the weakness of Spain under Charles II the struggle was continued, and in 1673 the Island of Alhucemas was captured by the Spaniards. This success was offset by the fact that in 1689 Larache fell into the hands of the Moors, though an attack on Ceuta four years later was driven off.

The century closed with the issue still undecided, and with the threat from Africa still formidable: indeed, in 1688 the French ambassador in Madrid wrote to Louis XIV that if the Moors again invaded the Peninsula they would meet with little resistance. These circumstances explain, if they do not justify, the expulsion of the Moriscos by Philip III.

CHAPTER XXXIV

The Early Bourbons (1700–1759)

WHEN Louis XIV presented the new King of Spain to his court, he said to him, among other recommendations, "Be a good Spaniard, but remember that you are French by birth, so that you may maintain union between the two nations."

Philip V certainly became a good Spaniard, but he was inclined to be a little too mindful of his French birth. He remembered it, that is to say, in the sense that, despite all written renunciations of the French throne, he long cherished the hope of becoming King of France. He was the most direct heir after Louis XV, and so long as that monarch had no children Philip nourished this ambition, and did not hesitate to further it by intrigue. The consequence of this was that for many years he regarded his residence in Madrid as temporary, and this, in its turn, made the pursuit of a consistent policy on the part of Spain very difficult, and placed serious obstacles in the path of reform. Before, however, Philip could cast eyes on the throne of France he had to settle himself firmly on that of Spain, and this was only accomplished after a long European war, usually known as the War of the Spanish Succession.

The new King arrived in Spain in January, 1701, and his first act was to remove the members of the old Austrian party from all positions of responsibility. The widow of Charles II was required to leave the capital, and the nephew of Cardinal Portocarrero was appointed Viceroy of Catalonia in the place of the Prince of Hesse-Darmstadt. To strengthen still further the French connection the Duke of Harcourt, the French ambassador, was made a member of the Council, while the national finances were entrusted to another Frenchman, Orry. Above all, there was the Princesse des Ursins, whom Louis XIV had sent for the express purpose of guiding the steps of his grandson and his wife, Maria Luisa of Savoy.

The King himself was only seventeen when he ascended the Spanish throne, and in his youth his vigour and activity gained him the affection of his subjects; in later life he became the victim of acute melancholia, and thus belied, to some extent, the promise of his earlier years.

At first it even appeared as if the acceptance of the will of Charles would not be seriously opposed by the other Powers, with the exception of the Emperor. William III of England was, as usual, ready to fight, but his ministers, and still more his subjects, were not; and so, in April, 1701, Great Britain recognised Philip V, and the Dutch and the smaller states were compelled to do likewise.

Unfortunately for the new King of Spain his grandfather soon afterwards committed a technical violation of the Treaty of Ryswick by recognising James III as King of England on his father's death, and this provided William with an excuse for plunging his country into war with France once more. The Whig oligarchy which controlled England became alarmed for its possessions, and the representations of the Emperor met with a cordial reception in London.

The reply made to the French King was the formation, at The Hague in September, 1701, of the Grand Alliance between the Emperor, England, and the United Provinces, who accordingly declared war on France and Spain, an action in which they were soon joined by Savoy and Portugal, in spite of the fact that the Duke of Savoy was Philip's father-in-law. At the same time the Emperor ceded his rights to the Spanish throne to his younger son, the Archduke Charles, who was thereupon acknowledged as King of Spain by the members of the Grand Alliance.

The first hostilities took place in Italy, where the Emperor fomented a rising in Naples, and sent an army under Prince Eugene into the Milanese. Philip, leaving the Queen as Regent, went to the rescue of his threatened Italian possessions, and success attended his efforts. Prince Eugene was defeated at Santa Victoria and Luzzara by the French and Spaniards under the Duke of Vendôme and the Count of Aguilar, while an outward appearance of calm was re-established in Naples. Further progress was rendered impossible by the course of events in Spain itself, which necessitated the King's return to that country.

In August, 1702, an Anglo-Dutch fleet, under the command of Sir George Rooke, appeared off Cádiz, and demanded the submission of the town to the Archduke Charles. The plan, which owed its inception largely to the Prince of Hesse-Darmstadt, was to use Cádiz as a lever to provoke a general insurrection in Andalusia. Before this threat the Queen fell back upon the support of Castile, which had already perceived that this was no mere dynastic struggle, but the real issue was the unity or the dismemberment of Spain.

Faced with the certainty of determined opposition, Rooke made off to Vigo, where he attacked the plate-fleet, which was lying in the harbour protected by French men-of-war: he captured one or two galleons, but the majority were sunk by those in charge of them. Two years later the Archduke himself landed at Lisbon, and it was this news that brought Philip back from Italy. Once more he was successful, for the Franco-Spanish troops invaded Portugal, and compelled the Archduke to abandon his intention of an advance upon Madrid from that quarter.

The year 1704, however, was not wholly fortunate for Philip, for although Rooke failed both to organise a rising in Catalonia and to capture Ceuta, he did succeed in taking Gibraltar, not, it is to be noted, in the name of the Archduke, but on behalf of his own country. The subsequent attempt of the Spaniards to recover the fortress resulted in failure.

The following year, 1705, was a disastrous one for Philip. In the spring the Earl of Peterborough succeeded in bringing about a Catalan rising, which was nominally in favour of the Archduke, but was actually more a revolt against Castile. In October the Habsburg entered Barcelona as Charles III of Spain, and before the end of the year he had been acknowledged by the greater part of Aragón and Valencia. Philip made an effort to retake Barcelona at the beginning of 1706, but he was unsuccessful, and the Anglo-Portuguese forces in the West, under Lord Galway, took advantage of his preoccupation to pass from the defensive to the offensive, and to invade Spain, where they made themselves masters of Ciudad Rodrigo and Salamanca.

Meanwhile Louis XIV was in no position to send help to his grandson. Two years before his German schemes had been checkmated at Blenheim, and the summer that saw Galway on Spanish soil also witnessed the defeat of the French at Ramillies by the Duke of Marlborough, and before Turin by Prince Eugene. The Spanish aristocracy thereupon inclined to what seemed to be the winning side, and Philip was forced to leave Madrid for Burgos. The Archduke entered the capital in July.

What appeared to be the darkest moment of Philip's fortunes was to prove the commencement of their revival. The North-west of Spain, the Castiles, Estremadura, and Andalusia declared for Philip, and against his rival, who came to claim their allegiance at the head of an army chiefly composed of their old Portuguese enemies, of foreign Protestants, and of Catalan separatists. The energy of the King in the defence of his crown also touched a sympathetic chord in the hearts of his people, and he became known as *el animoso*, or "the spirited." The struggle became national, and it was one of the Gothic-Celt-Iberians against the men of Romance blood.

The first evidence of this development was the frigid reception with which the Archduke met in Madrid, and which, taken in conjunction with the threat from Philip's army under the Duke of Berwick, induced him to abandon the city not long after he had entered it. The King thereupon returned to his capital, in October, and was received with the warmest of welcomes by its inhabitants.

The army of the Archduke under Galway withdrew from Madrid to Valencia, and Berwick took up a position at Almansa, where he proposed to await the arrival of reinforcements which the Duke of Orleans was bringing from Italy before taking the offensive. Galway determined to attack his adversary before such a junction had been effected, and he did so in April, 1707. The result was an overwhelming victory for Berwick, who immediately followed up his success by the reconquest of Valencia and Aragón, whose privileges were immediately abolished by Philip as a punishment for their rebellion. The same year witnessed the recapture of Ciudad Rodrigo, but in 1708 Sardinia and Minorca were lost, and the Algerines took Oran.

The war had now reached a point at which all the combatants were desirous of its termination, but when negotiations to this end were commenced it was found that the Powers of the Grand Alliance were still insistent upon the renunciation by Philip of the Spanish throne. Peace was clearly impossible on these terms, and both sides made preparations to fight to a finish.

The Archduke and his English allies determined to strike what it was hoped would prove the final blow in the Peninsula, and in the summer of 1710 Philip's forces were beaten at Almenara and Saragossa. Once more the Archduke entered Madrid, but he was so badly received there, and in Castile generally, that it was clear his cause was hopeless. Louis XIV, too, was not inactive, and he sent Vendôme to put an end to the Spanish war. The Archduke was forced to leave the capital, but even retreat could not save his troops and those of his allies.

Stanhope and the English were overthrown at Brihuega on December 9th, and on the following day the Imperialists who were marching to their aid met a like fate at Villa Viciosa. The Archduke managed to reach Barcelona in safety, but his last hope of becoming King of Spain had vanished. Nor was this all, for in 1711 his elder brother, the Emperor Joseph I, died, and the Archduke succeeded him as Charles VI. This completely changed the whole international situation, for neither the English nor the Dutch had any desire to see the re-creation of the empire of Charles V, even in favour of their ally.

Accordingly, negotiations were opened in London, and subsequently carried on at Utrecht, where the Treaty of that name was signed in April, 1713. The Emperor refused to be a party to this settlement, but French victories at Freiburg and Landau convinced him of his inability to continue the struggle alone, and in March, 1714, he concluded the separate Treaty of Rastadt.

By these treaties Philip was recognised as King of Spain and the Indies, but he had to waive his rights of succession to the French throne. To Great Britain he had to cede Gibraltar and Minorca, as well as certain commercial privileges in the Americas. The Duke of Savoy obtained Sicily, but the island was to revert to Spain if ever the Savoyard male line should become extinct. The Emperor obtained the Spanish Netherlands, with the exception of the frontier towns, which were to be occupied by the Dutch, and of Gueldres, which went to Prussia. The Milanese, Naples, and Sardinia were also ceded to the Emperor.

Neither Charles nor the English did anything for the Catalans, who, however, continued their resistance. Barcelona was stormed in September, 1714, and with the capture of Palma, in Majorca, in the following year Philip was at last master of his own kingdom. The privileges of Catalonia then met the same fate as those of Aragón and Valencia.

During the years of the war the predominant influence in the government had been the Princesse des Ursins, while Orry had done his best to restore the finances. At the beginning of 1714 the Queen died, and before the year was out the King had married again, this time Elizabeth Farnese, the daughter of the Duke of Parma. This marriage marked the commencement of a new period in the reign of Philip V, for it brought the French influence to an end, at any rate in its old form.

Even while Louis XIV was alive his grandson had not infrequently refused to take his advice, but as soon as he was dead relations between Paris and Madrid became very strained. Philip regarded himself as the heir presumptive to the French throne, in spite of the provisions of the Treaty of Utrecht, and he was on the worst of terms with the Regent, the Duke of Orleans. The new Queen influenced her husband to attempt the reconquest of the lost Spanish possessions in Italy, and as time went on this became the ruling passion of her life.

Philip's sons by his first wife, Louis and Ferdinand, would succeed to the Spanish crown, and as Elizabeth Farnese began to bear children of her own, she grew more determined that they should eventually occupy Italian thrones. Accordingly, the Princesse des Ursins was sent away, and Cardinal Alberoni was brought from Italy to enable Spain to tear up the Treaty of Utrecht.

Alberoni is one of the greatest names in Spanish history, and he would have been able to effect more had time been allowed him. He revived the army and navy, and the abolition of the internal customs barriers went a long way towards restoring the economic situation, but it was in foreign affairs that he displayed the greatest skill. His object was to isolate the Emperor, and then to over-run his Italian provinces.

With this end in view James III was invited to Spain, and an expedition prepared to place him on his throne, while all the enemies of the French Regent were goaded into activity. By this means it was hoped to prevent England and France from coming to the assistance of the Emperor. At first all went well, and in August, 1717, Sardinia was occupied without difficulty. Soon afterwards the Duke of Savoy was driven out of Sicily, but this was the high-water mark of Spanish success.

The rest of Europe grew alarmed at the obvious revival of the power of Spain, and there came into existence the Quadruple Alliance of France, England, the Emperor, and Savoy. In August, 1718, the Spanish fleet was defeated by the English off Syracuse, and Austrian troops were poured into Sicily.

Nothing daunted, Alberoni conceived the grandiose scheme of persuading Charles XII of Sweden and Peter the Great of Russia to lay aside their differences, and invade Scotland for the purpose of restoring the Stuarts. The death of Charles XII in December nipped this project in the bud, and there was nothing for it but a direct Spanish attack upon Great Britain, while every effort was made to provoke a rising in Brittany against the Duke of Orleans.

James III arrived in Spain in March, 1719, and was received with all the honours due to a reigning monarch. At Cádiz a fleet of five warships and twenty-two transports was ready to convey 5000 men, and arms for 30,000 more, to England, under the command of the Duke of Ormonde, and James was to join the expedition at some northern Spanish port. While this was taking place, a smaller force, with the Earl Marischal, was to go to Scotland, and rouse the clans. However, hardly had the expedition put to sea than it was dispersed by a storm, and all idea of a direct invasion of England had to be abandoned. The attempt in Scotland, known in British history as the Nineteen, also failed, and the few Spanish troops which had landed were compelled to lay down their arms. Meanwhile, the same lack of success attended the efforts to rouse the Bretons, and French troops began to occupy strategic points in Guipúzcoa and Catalonia.

Philip and Elizabeth Farnese had to give way, and peace was made at The Hague in 1720. By this treaty Spain had to yield both Sardinia and Sicily, the former to the Duke of Savoy and the latter to the Emperor, but the son of Philip and Elizabeth, the Infante Don Carlos, was recognised as heir to the duchies of Parma, Piacenza, and Tuscany. Cardinal Alberoni was dismissed before the treaty was signed.

The immediate effects of the treaty were a revival of friendship with France, for the Queen had come to the conclusion that her Italian ambitions would be easier of achievement with the aid of that Power, rather than in the teeth of its opposition. In order to cement this alliance it was arranged that the Prince of Asturias should marry the daughter of the French Regent, and that the infant daughter of Philip and Elizabeth should in due course marry Louis XV. The two princesses were duly exchanged at the frontier, and the Prince of Asturias was married to his bride in January, 1722.

Two years later Europe was startled by the news that Philip had abdicated in favour of his son, Louis, but the event proved of no ultimate importance, for the new King only lived for seven months afterwards, and his father then reascended the throne. This brief reign nevertheless had a definite constitutional importance, for the Cortes that was summoned to recognise Ferdinand as the new heir to the crown for the first time contained representatives from all the Spanish kingdoms.

The second reign of Philip V lasted twenty-two years, and Spanish policy was as tortuous as it had been in the earlier period, and for the same reason. The ambition of the King to play a part in French politics, and the determination of the Queen to seat her sons on Italian thrones, were the determining motives of the government of Spain in its relations with other powers.

There was sitting at this time at Cambrai a European conference which was endeavouring, amongst other things, without much success, to settle the outstanding differences between the Emperor and Spain. The former was demanding that the European Powers should guarantee the Pragmatic Sanction, which declared his daughter, the Archduchess Maria Theresa, to be his heir, and should recognise the duchies of Parma, Piacenza, and Tuscany as Imperial fiefs. This last request was a direct blow at the rights of Don Carlos, and could not be admitted by Spain for a moment. However, Elizabeth Farnese determined to see what could be done by a definite reversal of all Spanish policy since the death of Charles II, namely direct negotiation with Vienna.

The minister who was entrusted with this task was the Baron Ripperdá, who had originally come to Spain as the representative of the United Provinces, and was the very type of an adventurer. This individual was accordingly sent on a secret mission to the Austrian capital in November, 1724.

Ripperdá's visit to Vienna coincided with the rupture of the marriage contract between France and Spain, and the Duke of Bourbon, whom the death of the Duke of Orleans had placed at the head of the French government, sent the prospective bride of Louis XV back to her own country. This affront angered Philip to such an extent that he ordered Ripperdá to accede to almost any terms to bring about an alliance with Austria, and the first Treaty of Vienna was signed in November, 1725. The Infante Don Carlos was acknowledged as heir to the duchies, but in return all the Spanish ports in Europe and America were to be thrown open to Austrian trade, and the companies established at Trieste and Ostend were to conduct it.

Unfortunately, the news of this agreement leaked out prematurely, and at once the Alliance of Hanover was formed to frustrate it by Great Britain, France, the United Provinces, and Prussia, all of whom felt their interests to be adversely affected in some way. Ripperdá's garrulity was the cause of this disclosure, and when the fact came to the ears of the King and Queen his fall was clearly but a question of time. Finally, it was discovered that the Emperor had no intention of marrying Maria Theresa to Don Carlos, as Ripperdá asserted to be the case, and the minister was arrested. Eventually he managed to escape, and after embracing Islam, became Grand Vizier to the Sultan of Morocco.

Ripperdá had gone, but the fruits of his policy remained. The Spaniards once again besieged Gibraltar, and the English attempted to blockade Puerto Bello, but in neither case did success attend the attackers. The Emperor made no effort to assist his Spanish allies, and Walpole, on the other hand, had no desire to see hostilities become general, for he knew that war on a large scale would mean the overthrow of the Hanoverian dynasty, and of the Whig oligarchy that governed England in its name.

In these circumstances an arrangement was not difficult, and at the Congress of Soissons Cardinal Fleury took the lead in promoting a settlement. What the French government desired was to bring Spain over to its side, and at the same time to drive in a wedge between England and her old ally, Austria, and all this was accomplished by Fleury in the Treaty of Seville in November, 1729. This treaty, which left the Emperor isolated, was signed by England, France, Spain, and the United Provinces, and it provided for the sending of Spanish garrisons to the Italian duchies to support the claims of Don Carlos, when he should succeed. At the same time all the commercial privileges which England had obtained at Utrecht were restored.

The death of the Duke of Parma, the last male Farnese, in 1731, precipitated another crisis, and enabled Walpole to have his "tit for tat" with Fleury. Austrian troops had marched into the duchy, and once more there appeared to be every prospect of war, but Patiño, the new Spanish minister, had no mind for adventures. In any event, the Infante could not get his troops easily to Parma without the aid of the British fleet, so active negotiations ensued between London and Madrid. The outcome was the second Treaty of Vienna in 1731 between Spain, England, the United Provinces, and the Emperor.

The Pragmatic Sanction was guaranteed on condition that Maria Theresa did not marry a Bourbon; the Ostend East India Company was abandoned; and Don Carlos was recognised as Duke of Parma, and heir to Tuscany. France was, for the moment, isolated, as the Emperor had been two years before. In October, 1731, the 6000 Spanish troops to occupy the duchies sailed from Barcelona with an escort of English men-of-war, and the new Duke of Parma met with an enthusiastic reception from his subjects upon his arrival among them.

The restoration of Spain to her old place in the councils of Europe, which these events amply proved, was very largely due to the work of José Patiño. A Galician, he had originally been a Jesuit novice, but had forsaken the ecclesiastical profession, and had played an important part in the organisation of the army during the War of the Spanish Succession. Alberoni transferred Patiño from Seville to Madrid, and on the fall of Ripperdá, he was appointed Minister of Marine and the Indies, and later, Minister of Finance.

His first care was to reorganise the navy, and so successful was he that in 1732 a fleet of no less than 600 sail, with an army of 30,000 men, went from Alicante, and recovered Oran from the Moors. By means of a system of bounties Patiño encouraged Spanish trade with the Americas and the Philippines, while his financial reforms carried on the work that had been initiated by Alberoni. When he died in 1736 he had enabled Spain to conquer two kingdoms in Italy, and he had restored her prestige almost to what it had been in the days of Philip II.

The later years of Philip V were marked by more cordial relations between France and Spain. It was clear now that Louis XV would not die without offspring, and his uncle was forced to reconcile himself to the fact that the French throne would never be his. In 1733 the King of Poland died, and in the complications which ensued it became clear that the interests of France and Spain were much alike. At first the Queen was in favour of an attempt to secure the Polish crown for Don Carlos, but as France wanted it for the father-in-law of Louis XV, this would have caused dissension between the two Bourbon Powers. Patiño therefore suggested that while the Emperor was busy about Poland, Don Carlos should seize Naples and Sicily, where the inhabitants were weary of Austrian rule.

This project was particularly agreeable to France, for it meant the diversion of some of the Emperor's energies from Central Europe. In November, 1733, a treaty on these terms, usually known as the First Family Compact, was made between France and Spain, and in May of the following year Don Carlos entered Naples, after having encountered resistance only at Gaeta and Capua. Sicily proved to be an equally easy conquest, and in 1736 the Third Treaty of Vienna recognised him as King of the Two Sicilies, though at the price of relinquishing the duchies.

Spain was not, however, destined to remain at peace for long. Quite apart from the Queen's determination to place her children upon Italian thrones, there were the complications attendant upon the British trade with the Americas, which was a perpetual cause of friction.

By the Treaty of Utrecht the monopoly of the slave trade had been given to Great Britain, as well as many commercial privileges in America. British factories in one form or another existed at Panama, Vera Cruz, Buenos Aires, and Cartagena, and ships trading with slaves were exempt from examination or duty. This enabled the colonists in Jamaica, who had already enriched themselves by the plunder accumulated by the Buccaneers, to carry on an active contraband trade to the great loss of the Spanish government.

Recriminations and reprisals followed, and in the course of them an English merchant captain named Jenkins was said to have had his ear cut off by a Spanish officer. At any rate, he produced a severed ear in a box on his return to London, and in the public mind Jenkins's ear became the symbol of the ill-treatment to which British citizens were subject in the Spanish dominions.

Spain did not want war, and made every effort to avoid it. By the Convention of the Pardo in January, 1739, she agreed to pay an indemnity of £95,000 pending a peaceful settlement of the questions outstanding between the two countries, namely the right of search and the delimitation of Georgia. In return, Spain pressed for the payment of certain claims made by her against the South Sea Company. England, however, was intent upon hostilities, and the Walpole administration, which was tottering to its fall, was forced to declare war on the most flimsy pretexts.

The campaign that followed showed how well Patiño had done his work. The war began with a Spanish reverse, for Admiral Vernon sacked Puerto Bello, but the news of this disaster roused all Spain. Within a few months Spanish privateers had captured English shipping to the value of £234,000, and Gibraltar and Minorca were being threatened. The British government determined to strike its principal blow in America, and Vernon was sent to attack Cartagena with the assistance of 10,000 troops.

The Viceroy, Sebastian de Eslava, himself conducted the defence, and after an initial British success the invaders failed to capture the citadel in spite of their vastly superior numbers. Soon afterwards, the climate compelled the abandonment of the attempt, and when Vernon subsequently tried to capture Santiago de Cuba a similar failure attended his efforts. In October, 1740, the death of the Emperor Charles VI, and the seizure of Silesia by Frederick the Great, caused the struggle between Spain and Great Britain to be merged in the War of the Austrian Succession.

For Elizabeth Farnese, except during the period immediately after the first Treaty of Vienna, the Empire's extremity had been her opportunity, so she persuaded her husband to claim the whole inheritance of Charles VI on the ground that he was the senior descendant of Charles V. In actual fact the Spanish claim was only intended as a lever for obtaining the Austrian dominions in Italy, that is to say, the Milanese, Parma, and Tuscany (the last now possessed by Maria Theresa's husband, who had exchanged Lorraine for it on the extinction of the male line of the Medici in 1737), which would make a kingdom of respectable size for Philip, the second son of the King and Queen of Spain.

Italy was invaded by the Spaniards, and the plan of campaign was that they should be joined by the Neapolitans, but it miscarried from the start. The King of Sardinia, as the Duke of Savoy had now become, sided with Austria, while the British fleet appeared in the Bay of Naples and gave Charles III an hour to agree to withdraw the Neapolitan contingent from the Spanish army under the threat of an immediate bombardment of the capital. The King agreed, much to the detriment of the Spanish cause, which was still further jeopardised by the Treaty of Breslau in July, 1742, when Prussia withdrew from the war, and Austria was proportionately strengthened.

Fortune was not long in favouring Spain again, for in the following year the death of Cardinal Fleury, the French Prime Minister, proved the signal for the adoption of a more vigorous policy on the part of France. In October, 1743, the Treaty of Fontainebleau was made between the two Powers, which were henceforth to stand shoulder to shoulder: Gibraltar and Minorca were to be taken from the English; and Parma, Piacenza, and Milan were to be won for young Philip. As a result of this treaty the war was carried on in Italy with great energy, but with varying success. In 1744 the Franco-Spanish forces invaded Piedmont, but were driven out again, and the same experience befell them in the Milanese in 1745-1746.

At this point Philip V died, and his successor, Ferdinand VI, had no particular interest in waging war in Italy for the benefit of his stepmother's children. In 1746, too, a popular rising in Genoa against the Austrians permanently checked the latter's victorious career, and all the belligerents were ready for peace, which was made at Aix-la-Chapelle in 1748. Philip did not get the Milanese, but he was recognised as sovereign Duke of Parma, Piacenza, and Guastalla, while, by the Treaty of Aquisgran in the next year, the outstanding differences between England and Spain were duly settled. Elizabeth Farnese now retired into the background, but she had succeeded in her object of placing her sons upon Italian thrones.

In spite of the many wars in which she was involved, Spain made enormous progress during the reign of Philip V. It is true that the old uneconomic system of taxation had not been fundamentally altered, and the *alcabalas* of 14 per cent on all sales were still supposed to be collected, but many modifications had been introduced. Monopolies and exemptions were granted, while bounties were paid to certain industries, which in many cases counteracted the effect of the high taxation. The abolition of the internal customs-houses also had a beneficial result in increasing production, and the Valencian textiles, for example, were once more able to supply the home market, the number of looms increasing from 300 in 1717 to 2000 in 1722.

The revenue was naturally the gainer by this revival of prosperity, and it rose from 142,000,000 reals in the year of Philip's accession to 211,000,000 reals in 1737. Spain was not a country in which it was possible to proceed with reforms except by very easy stages, but the succession of the Bourbons to her throne undoubtedly initiated a revival, as Great Britain had learned to her cost when war came.

By his first wife Philip had had four children, of whom only his successor, Ferdinand VI, survived him. By Elizabeth Farnese he had six children, of whom four were living at the time of his death, including the King of Naples, the Duke of Parma, and the Cardinal Don Luis. The new King was thirty-four years old, and both he and his wife, Barbara of Braganza, were determined that once the War of the Austrian Succession was at an end Spain should pursue a policy of neutrality in international politics.

Ferdinand was above all else a patriotic Spaniard, and unless the interests of his country demanded that he should fight he was resolved to keep the peace. The King's task was not an easy one, for the two leading ministers, José de Carvajal and the Marqués de la Ensenada, were desirous of taking sides, the one for England and the other for France, and they were naturally encouraged by the British and French ambassadors, Sir Benjamin Keene and Duras. In spite even of the outbreak of the Seven Years' War in 1756, Spanish neutrality was preserved until Ferdinand's death, and it is at home rather than abroad that the real importance of his reign is to be found.

Ensenada had held various important offices during the latter years of Philip V, but it was not until the accession of the new King that his power became supreme. He told Ferdinand quite frankly that it would be madness to suggest an army equal to that of France, and a navy of the same size as the British; what he aimed at was to raise the military, naval, and financial strength of Spain to a position which would enable her to make her neutrality effective, and to maintain her independence in the councils of the world. The King thoroughly agreed with this policy, which was energetically carried out. New regiments were called into existence, and Barcelona, Majorca, Cádiz, Ferrol, Corunna, and the Portuguese frontier were carefully fortified. Six ships were laid down every year in Cádiz, Ferrol, Cartagena, and Havana, and before long both the Atlantic and the Mediterranean fleets of Spain were of formidable proportions.

This activity aroused the hostility of Great Britain towards Ensenada, and in consequence he became more and more closely identified with the French party at Madrid. Finally, his zeal outran his discretion, for Keene discovered that he had given secret instructions to the Viceroy of Mexico to molest English traders, and upon this being represented to the King, the minister was dismissed.

Both Ensenada and Wall, an Irishman who succeeded him, continued the financial and economic policy of Patiño. Agriculture was revived, roads improved, canals made, and manufactures assisted in every possible way. The Spanish mines were re-opened, and the ban on the export of metal was removed, while a royalty of $3\frac{1}{2}$ per cent in Spain and 6 per cent in America was imposed. The farming of taxes was abolished, and the revenue rose by 5,000,000 ducats a year.

In addition, the intellectual progress of the country at this time can hardly be exaggerated. The foundation of academies and learned bodies went on apace; subsidies and scholarships were granted liberally to scientists, artists, and men of letters to enable them to pursue their researches both in Spain and abroad, and foreign scholars were welcomed. When Ferdinand VI died in 1759, Spain was once more a prosperous nation, with a powerful fleet, and three millions sterling in the treasury.

CHAPTER XXXV

The Reign of Charles III (1759-1788)

FERDINAND VI was succeeded by his half-brother Charles III, the King of the Two Sicilies, who was already exceedingly popular with his Italian subjects. By the Treaty of Aquisgran it had been provided that the throne of Naples should pass to the Duke of Parma if Charles came to that of Spain, and that Parma, Piacenza, and Guastalla should be divided between Austria and Sardinia. By a combination of skilful diplomacy and a cash payment, Charles persuaded the Powers concerned to waive this stipulation, and in its place an arrangement was made by which Naples was to pass to his third son, Ferdinand. The eldest, Philip, was excluded from the succession in consequence of his insanity, and the second son, Charles, became Prince of Asturias on the accession of his father to the Spanish throne.

Charles III was an excellent example of those "enlightened despots" who were so prominent a feature of the latter half of the eighteenth century. He was easily the best and the most intelligent of the Bourbon Kings of Spain. With something of the yokel about his appearance, and with a long, pointed nose and piercing blue eyes, he had a strange mask of a face which recalled Louis XI. There was much of the *dilettante* about him; he was a lover and patron of the arts; and he was a man of taste upon whom his long residence in Italy, amid the monuments of an ancient civilisation, had made a profound impression.

Charles was greatly under the influence of French ideas, and this fact also goes far to explain his Francophil policy. His motto, and that of several contemporary monarchs, might well have been "Everything for the people, but nothing by the people," which is by no means an unsatisfactory doctrine. Nevertheless, as will be seen, the people revolted more than once against the improvements which the King and his ministers sought to impose upon them.

The Seven Years' War was at its height when Charles came to the throne, and in 1761 he made another Family Compact with France. This necessitated hostilities with Great Britain, but instead of the support given by Spain to the French cause doing anything to restore the balance, it merely involved the former country in the series of misfortunes which France was experiencing.

In the West Indies, the British captured Grenada, St. Vincent, St. Lucia, and Tobago, and in August, 1762, Havana itself fell into their hands with 15,000,000 dollars of treasure, an enormous quantity of arms and stores, and twelve men-of-war. In the Pacific the Spaniards were also unfortunate, for another English expedition captured Manila. In Europe there had been a Spanish invasion of

Portugal, but although it met with some success at first, the arrival of English troops to reinforce the Portuguese soon compelled the Spaniards to withdraw to their own side of the frontier. The only compensating advantage gained by Spain was the conquest of some Portuguese territory on the River Plate.

Charles realised that in coming to the aid of France at such a time he had made a mistake, and he accordingly opened negotiations for peace, which a change of government in England now made possible. The Treaty of Paris in 1763 brought the war to a termination. Spain had to cede St. Vincent, Tobago, and Grenada, though St. Lucia was restored to her. The British also obtained Florida, the right to cut logwood in Honduras Bay, and the Spanish renunciation of all fishing claims in relation to Newfoundland. In return Great Britain surrendered her conquests in Cuba and the Philippines, while France, unable to secure the restitution of Minorca, handed over to her ally New Orleans and all Louisiana West of the Mississippi.

Charles III had made no change in Ferdinand's ministers, beyond the addition of the Marquis of Squillaci (Esquilache as the Spaniards called him) to their number, but after the conclusion of the Treaty of Paris, Wall resigned on account of bad sight. He was replaced by Grimaldi, and the two Italians proceeded to accelerate the pace of reform. They made no secret of their determination to limit very drastically indeed the power both of the Church and of the Inquisition, and they united against them elements capable of precipitating a revolt which came within an ace of being a revolution.

The immediate cause of the outbreak was a trifle. For many years the Spaniards had worn wide-brimmed hats, side-locks, and long cloaks (in which daggers were too often and too easily concealed), and they disliked the cocked hats, bag-wigs, and coats in which Charles wished them to appear. In March, 1766, an order was issued forbidding the wearing of cloaks beyond a certain length and of wide-brimmed hats, and officials were posted in the streets to cut offending garments to the required dimensions. The attempt to enforce this pragmatic led to rioting, and to a demand for the head of Squillaci, who was forced to fly. During the disturbances the Walloon guards fired on the crowd, and this roused the latter to a frenzy. The Walloon guardsmen were killed at sight, and the capital was in the hands of the mob: the King was forced to give way, but immediately he had done so he left Madrid for Aranjuez.

Charles took care that Squillaci got safely out of the country, and then he reformed the administration, placing at its head the Count of Aranda. The latter was a man of great ability, but also of considerable vanity, and, like his predecessor, he was anti-clerical. During the summer of 1766 the agitation continued, and a plot to murder the King was alleged to have been discovered. Finally, however, Charles got his way, and in December he re-entered Madrid to find his subjects, if still discontented, attired after the new fashion.

Both King and minister were convinced that the clergy in general, and the Jesuits in particular, had been at the bottom of the trouble, and they were determined to put an end to clerical opposition to their reforms. In this resolution they were greatly influenced by contemporary events in Portugal, where an attempt to murder King Joseph had been laid at the door of the Jesuits, and where the Marquis of Pombal had already adopted strong measures against them.

In April, 1767, an order was suddenly issued for the expulsion of the Jesuits from Spain, and it was executed in a manner which inflicted the greatest hardship on those concerned. The priests were not allowed to take anything with them but their personal belongings, and they were conveyed in unseemly haste to the coast, whence they were shipped to such foreign countries as were willing to receive them. The same procedure was adopted in America, with the result that the work of civilisation which the Jesuits had been doing in Paraguay came to an end, and the Indians in that country relapsed into savagery.

In his attack on the Jesuits the King of Spain secured the support of his son in Naples and, for a time, of his nephew in Parma. Louis XV adopted analogous measures, for Choiseul was then in power in France, and he was responsible for the policy, which subsequently had to be reversed, of endeavouring to placate the *Parlements*. Charles was, however, the moving spirit in the attack, which he continued after Louis XV had wearied of it, and the Duke of Parma had changed his mind. In the end he gained his point, and in 1773 Clement XIV signed the decree suppressing the Society of Jesus throughout Christendom.

The campaign against the Jesuits was only part of a general offensive against the Church, for Aranda was completely under the sway of the French Encyclopædists. The Inquisition also became the object of attack, and in 1780 its last victim, an old witch, was burnt alive at Seville. Education, too, which had been taken out of the hands of the Jesuits, was nationalised and secularised.

Whether these measures were wise from the point of view of the monarchy is another matter. For centuries the Spanish throne had been invested with a religious sanction, and Church and State had been almost indistinguishable. Charles undoubtedly increased the power of the Crown, but he placed the monarch in a position of dangerous, if splendid, isolation. The Cortes was nothing but a name, the Inquisition was powerless, and the very foundations of the Church were undermined. When the storm came, the monarchy had no outside support upon which it could rely.

It is a curious coincidence, if nothing more, that less than two decades after the suppression of the Jesuits the oldest throne in Europe came crashing to the ground, and that the violence of the subsequent upheaval has been most severely felt in those countries which had adopted the attitude of Charles III of Spain.

The policy of Aranda in civil matters was much less open to criticism, and it was largely an intensification of that of Ensenada. In particular, rural depopulation was arrested by internal colonisation, and Bavarian immigrants to the number of 6000 were settled in thirteen new villages in the Sierra Morena. The import and export of grain were permitted under certain restrictions with regard to price levels in the home market. A government registry for titles and mortgages was created to render the transfer of land both easy and cheap, and the coinage was reformed and unified. Raw material was allowed to enter the country free, but a prohibitive tariff was put upon such manufactured articles as were likely to compete with Spanish products. The social services also received attention. Hospitals, asylums, and alms-houses were established all over Spain, as well as savings banks, benefit societies, and philanthropic institutions of one sort or another.

The glass factory of La Granja, the porcelains of Buen Retiro, the cotton velvets of Avila, the fine leathers of Seville and Cordova, and the fancy goods of Madrid, all became famous at this time. During the reign of Charles III the population of Spain rose to 10,250,000, which represented an increase of 1,500,000 since the death of Ferdinand VI, while the revenue during the King's last years had grown to 616,300,000 reals, or more than three times what it had been a century before, and that in spite of a definite decrease in taxation.

If all remained quiet in Europe after the Treaty of Paris, the rivalry of Spain and Great Britain in America continued unabated. Choiseul was determined to precipitate a conflict between the two countries if it were in his power to do so, and in 1770 he persuaded Charles to make effective the Spanish claim to the Falkland Islands. An expedition was accordingly sent from Buenos Aires, and the English were ejected. War appeared imminent, but Louis XV had no desire to engage in a Spanish quarrel, and he made it clear that if Spain fought she would fight alone; he also dismissed Choiseul. Charles had hoped that France would aid him by virtue of the Family Compact, but when Louis washed his hands of the matter he had to evacuate the islands in dispute.

In consequence, Aranda's many enemies succeeded in bringing that minister down, and his successor was, first Figueroa, and then the Count of Campomanes. This was not the first difficulty that Spain had experienced in America since the Treaty of Paris, for the colonists of Louisiana had objected to the transfer of sovereignty, and they finally had to be reduced to obedience by force.

In 1775 the Spanish arms met with a reverse in Africa. The Moors had for some time been besieging Ceuta and Melilla, and an expedition was sent to relieve both places, which it did very successfully. This encouraged Charles to attempt to capture Algiers, which was the headquarters of the Barbary Corsairs. A force of 20,000 men under Count O'Reilly was despatched for this purpose, and it was hoped to take the Algerines by surprise. Unfortunately the news of what was afoot had already leaked out, and O'Reilly was defeated with heavy loss. The rout of the general caused the fall of his patron, Grimaldi, who was replaced by the Count of Floridablanca.

Nevertheless, Charles did not renounce the historic Spanish mission of fighting Islam, and in 1783–1784 Algiers was severely bombarded by his fleet. By the end of his reign treaties had been extorted by force or diplomacy from the Sultan of Morocco, the Dey of Algiers, and the Bey of Tunis in which those rulers not only pledged themselves to refrain from attacking the ships and coast of Spain, but also agreed to the establishment of Spanish consulates in their territories, and to freedom of worship for Spanish subjects. A treaty of peace was also made with their suzerain, the Ottoman Sultan. In this way Charles III put an end to a menace which had threatened the Peninsula for centuries.

The year following O'Reilly's defeat was marked by an outbreak of hostilities with Portugal over the vexed question of the frontier of Brazil. Pombal, the energetic minister of that country, embarked upon a policy of expansion in America that very soon brought the Portuguese into conflict with Spain. Charles ordered a counter-offensive, and in 1776–1777 the Spaniards captured various places in Rio Grande do Sul.

What might have developed into a serious war was terminated, however, by the death of the King of Portugal, Joseph, and the subsequent fall of Pombal. A treaty was then made between the two Powers by which Sacramento, as well as the navigation of the rivers Plate, Parana, and Paraguay, became Spanish, while Spain also acquired the islands of Annobon and Fernando Po in the Gulf of Guinea. In exchange, Charles recognised the Portuguese right to some territory on the Amazon which was in dispute.

While these events were taking place in the Mediterranean and in South America the relations between Great Britain and her American colonies were getting steadily worse, and in 1776 came the Declaration of Independence. From the first the temptation to Spain to take advantage of this opportunity to reverse the verdict of the Seven Years' War was great, and when, in the spring of 1778, France recognised the United States, the pressure upon the King to adopt a similar policy was overwhelming. Charles, however, was mindful of the disasters which had attended the last appearance of Spain in the field as the ally of France, and he had not forgotten the latter's attitude at the time of his dispute with Great Britain over the ownership of the Falkland Islands. If Spain fought, it would be for her own hand, and not to suit the convenience of Louis XVI. Accordingly, Charles waited to see how the struggle was going, and in the meantime he offered to mediate, but England refused to listen to him.

Saratoga convinced him that the British without a Pitt to lead them were not a very formidable proposition, and when news arrived that attacks were pending on Nicaragua and the Philippines, Spain declared war (June, 1779). A few weeks previously, when hostilities were already certain, a secret treaty had been made with France by which that Power promised to aid in the reconquest of Gibraltar, Florida, and Minorca, and in the expulsion of the British from Honduras.

Spain had never been so well-prepared for war as she was on this occasion. In Europe alone she had sixty-eight ships of the line afloat, as well as many smaller craft, and in the Americas both her naval and military power was considerable. Moreover, the friendship of Portugal deprived England of an ally, and of a base of operations, which had proved of inestimable advantage to her in previous wars.

The Franco-Spanish plan of campaign had as its immediate objectives the invasion of Great Britain, and the capture of Gibraltar and Minorca. The British fleet was reduced in numbers through the usual neglect in time of peace, and the coast was badly defended. Accordingly, the Franco-Spanish armada swept up the Channel without encountering any serious opposition, but it made no use of its opportunities, and not a soldier was disembarked. Nevertheless, something had been attained, for the loss of the command of the sea had prevented the English from interfering with the arrival of the plate fleet from America, and it had deprived the armies that were fighting Washington of the reinforcements which they so urgently required.

In the other theatres of war the Spaniards were more fortunate. They invested Gibraltar, expelled the English from Honduras, and co-operated with the Americans in Florida and on the Mississippi, with the result that by March, 1780, Mobile was in their hands. At this point the British Government opened negotiations for peace, but its terms were still too high for Spain to accept, and the war went on. Floridablanca left no stone unturned in his efforts to bring England to her knees, and he was largely instrumental in forming the Armed Neutrality, which refused to accept the British view of blockades and the right of search. In 1782 the Spaniards, this time in co-operation with the French, achieved a further success with the capture of Minorca.

The most notable event of the war was the siege of Gibraltar, defended by Lord Elliot. The fortress had been blockaded at the very commencement of hostilities, but it was relieved for a time by Rodney in January, 1780. After the reduction of Minorca the attack was begun again, and in the attempt to reduce the place floating batteries were employed by the besiegers. They were constructions of enormous size, very heavily armed, and great results were expected from them. At first they caused considerable damage to the defence, but the British used red-hot shot against them, and with the most disastrous consequences. Finally, in October, 1782, Howe ran the Franco-Spanish blockade, and the re-victualling and re-arming of the fortress rendered its capture hopeless.

Meanwhile, the American cause was victorious on the other side of the Atlantic, and the object of the war was achieved. Peace was made by the Treaty of Versailles in September, 1783. In so far as it concerned Spain, she was confirmed in her conquest of Minorca and Florida, but she agreed once more to allow the English to cut logwood in Honduras Bay.

The Treaty of Versailles gave Spain her revenge for the humiliation of twenty years before, and her power in the New World was at its zenith, for in addition to the possession of all South and Central America, except Brazil and Guiana, she was mistress in North America of Mexico, California, Louisiana, and Florida. Nevertheless, the establishment of the United States was an encouragement to the Spanish colonies themselves to revolt, and the results of this were not long in being felt.

Five years later, on December 14th, 1788, Charles III died, and with his death an epoch of Spanish history came to an end.

From the point of view of internal policy the reigns of Philip V, Ferdinand VI, and Charles III may be regarded as a whole. The Spanish monarchy at this period approached very closely to the French type, not in the sense that the royal power became more absolute, but rather that centralisation tended to become more complete through the restriction of local privileges. As has been shown, regular ministers replaced the favourites of the previous century, and the *juntas*, or councils of government, disappeared, giving place to regular departmental ministries. The nobility and the clergy found themselves more and more subjected to the central authority, and, so far as the latter were concerned, a Concordat with the Holy See was made in 1754, by which ecclesiastical nominations depended almost entirely upon the King.

In the intellectual, literary, and artistic spheres there was, in spite of the efforts of successive monarchs, certainly a decline in comparison with the great preceding age, namely that "Golden Century" which in reality embraced a period of nearly two hundred years. Literature was less original, although in certain aspects of it, particularly in the drama, there was still a very widespread activity.

On the other hand history more than maintained its position. The study of antiquity and the examination of archives gave birth to such learned publications as *España Sagrada*, which was begun by Father Enrique Flores. Mention has already been made of the foundation of learned societies. The Royal Spanish Academy was founded in 1713, the Academy of History in 1738, and the Academy of Fine Arts of St. Ferdinand in 1744. Charles III, in particular, was distinguished by his taste for architecture and for painting, and the patronage which he accorded to the arts and to artists was very considerable indeed.

At the same time there was no longer the exuberance or genius of the great period, but architecture, in its new forms, maintained itself on a level that was still sufficiently high. There has been much criticism of the style which was popular at this period with its ornamentation, its luxuriance, and its overloading, and it has been called "the romanticism of rococo"! Yet we owe to it some charming creations, for example, the Palacio del Marqués de Dos Aguas at Valencia. The same observation applies to baroque in its classical and grandiose form. Italian, and above all, French influences are certainly recognisable in it, but the native genius is still preponderant. The Royal Palace in Madrid and the Castle of San Ildefonso at La Granja are very fine specimens of architecture, and can bear comparison with the best work that was being done at that time in other European countries.

Painting also held its own. If it had produced nothing more than an artist like Goya, it could still, thanks to him, be said to have maintained its own prestige. Spanish realism finds its expression in the work of this harsh Aragonese, with a strength and intensity and a psychological penetration hitherto unknown. The new spirit reveals itself in his creations, and in the whole range of his philosophical symbolism.

Nevertheless, it is no longer the national realism, the realism of Velázquez, with its depth, and its classical qualities of proportion and complete impersonality. It is a deviation from it, often impetuous and verging on frenzy, towards the fantastic, the grotesque, and the macabre. In short, it is no longer purely Spanish.

What may be observed in the art of Goya is the keynote of the reigns of the earlier Bourbons. The same deviation from the old realism began to affect the national spirit. Under outside influences, especially those of France, the Spanish soul lost its moral and intellectual unity, which, in the domain of art as in that of thought, had produced unique works. Foreign ideas began to have their effect upon the national genius; they were to serve as the ferment of approaching revolutions, and they have distracted the Peninsula throughout the whole of the nineteenth century, and down to the present day.

CHAPTER XXXVI

Revolution and Restoration (1788–1833)

CHARLES IV was a worthy man full of good intentions, somewhat like Louis XVI. He was, unhappily, timid, and his character was weak, while he was completely under the domination of his wife, Maria Luisa of Parma. She, in her turn, was influenced by her lover, Manuel Godoy, the guardsman whom she caused to be created successively Duke of Alcudia and Prince of the Peace.

The King's accession was almost immediately followed by the outbreak of the French Revolution, and the whole of the reign was overclouded by the shadow of this upheaval. Spain was pulled hither and thither by France and by the Powers, notably Great Britain, opposed to her, until she became a mere plaything in their strife. At last her navy was destroyed by the English and her independence by the French. The whole reign of Charles IV led up to the tragedies of Trafalgar and the Dos de Mayo.

The new King had hardly succeeded to the throne before a dispute with England proved that Spain could place no reliance upon the support of revolutionary France, and that the days of the Family Compact were over. In May, 1789, an expedition sent by the Viceroy of Mexico discovered that the British had established a trading-station at Nootka Sound, in Vancouver, and seized the ships that it found there. The British Government demanded satisfaction, but Floridablanca refused on the ground that all land on the West coast of America as far as 60 degrees North latitude belonged to Spain, and that in any event Nootka had first been discovered by a Spaniard. Pitt replied that these pretensions were inadmissible, for there had been no effective occupation, and both sides began to prepare for war.

Floridablanca thereupon called upon the French Government to fulfil its obligations under the Family Compact, but the National Assembly, after grandiloquently declaring that the French nation had renounced wars of conquest, proceeded to offer assistance on terms which included the restitution of Louisiana. The Spanish ministry in this dilemma preferred to treat with England, and a settlement was effected on the basis of a declaration that Nootka was a free port, and of compensation for damage done. The alliance between France and Spain was clearly at an end.

These events, and the progress of the revolution, caused Florida-blanca to abandon the policy of reform which he had pursued during the reign of Charles III, and an attempt which a Frenchman made on his life in June, 1790, caused him to impose a rigorous censorship upon all books and pamphlets that came from the other side of the Pyrenees. Nor was this all, for the dangerous position of the French Royal Family soon began to alarm their relatives in Madrid, and

Floridablanca at the time of the flight to Varennes attempted to intercede with the National Assembly on behalf of Louis XVI.

His mediation was indignantly rejected by that body, and he then had a census made of all the foreigners in Spain, after which they were compelled to swear fidelity to the King, the laws, and the religion of Spain. This infuriated the French, and when the Spanish Government went on to demand that Louis XVI should be allowed to depart to a place of safety their anger at so humanitarian a proposition knew no bounds. Immediate war appeared inevitable, but Charles was persuaded to dismiss Floridablanca in February, 1792, and Aranda was appointed to succeed him.

For a time this change of ministers preserved peace, but when the Convention demanded that Spain should recognise the Republic, and gave her the choice of an alliance or war, Aranda found himself in the same position as his predecessor a few months before. In November of the same year he was suddenly relieved of his office, not for political reasons, but because the Queen desired to see Godoy at the head of affairs.

Godoy was an adventurer with more ambition than brains, and his appointment signified a return to the days of Lerma, Olivares, and Valenzuela. It alienated public opinion, accustomed to the able ministers of the previous monarch, and it caused serious dissensions in the Royal Family itself, where the Prince of Asturias strongly resented the relations of Godoy with his mother. The policy of the new minister was to save the life of Louis XVI, and to avoid the alternatives put forward by the Convention, but in the end he failed to do either. In March, 1793, France declared war, and a few days later Spain signed a treaty of alliance with Great Britain, thus joining the First Coalition.

The outbreak of hostilities was popular in the Peninsula, where the revolution had alarmed all classes. Three armies were formed: one in Guipúzcoa and Navarre under Don Ventura Caro; another in Aragón commanded by the Prince of Castellfranco; and a third in Catalonia with Don Antonio Ricardos at its head. The campaign of 1793 was very favourable to the Spaniards. Ricardos conquered Roussillon, and won several victories over the French: Caro repulsed all attacks, and captured Hendaye: while the Prince of Castellfranco frustrated a determined attempt at invasion. At sea, the Spanish fleet aided the British in the occupation of Toulon, until the fire of Napoleon's cannon compelled its evacuation.

The next year witnessed a complete reversal of fortune, largely owing to the death of Ricardos. Not only did the French sweep the invading Spaniards out of Roussillon, but they assumed the offensive in their turn, and captured Figueras, which was defended by 10,000 men and 200 pieces of heavy artillery. In 1795 the Spanish arms fared even worse, for though the French advance in Catalonia was checked, at the western end of the Pyrenees, where Irun, Fuenterrabia, San Sebastian, and Tolosa had already been captured in the preceding year, Bilbao and Vitoria were lost, and by June the French had reached Miranda de Ebro.

These reverses, combined with the defection of Prussia from the Coalition, decided Godoy to make peace. By the Treaty of Basle the French gave up all their conquests, while Spain ceded to France her half of the island of San Domingo, and also allowed her neighbour certain commercial advantages in the Peninsula. For his share in this treaty Godoy was created Prince of the Peace.

Save during the reign of Ferdinand VI it had always proved impossible for Spain to remain neutral when England and France were at war, and so it was on the present occasion. Spain had to side with one or the other, and as the British had shown themselves to be very unsatisfactory allies, Godoy concluded in August, 1796, the Treaty of San Ildefonso with the Directory. The English reply was a declaration of hostilities, and the Spaniards were heavily defeated in the following February off Cape St. Vincent, while in America the island of Trinidad was captured by the British. On the other hand, attacks on Puerto Rico, Cádiz, and Santa Cruz de Tenerife were repulsed. In the following year Godoy was replaced at the head of the ministry by Saavedra and Jovellanos, though he remained at court, and continued to exercise great influence in the administration.

In 1801 three further treaties were made with France, where Napoleon was now First Consul, as a corollary to the Treaty of Luneville, which had just been concluded between France and the Emperor. By the first of these the kingdom of Etruria was created for the son of the Duke of Parma, who had married a daughter of Charles IV, and it was stated that the new realm was to be a dependency of Spain, while Louisiana was ceded to France. By the other treaties Charles promised to supply ships for the formation of four Franco-Spanish squadrons, and to declare war on Portugal if that Power would not terminate her alliance with England.

The command of the Franco-Spanish forces that were to bring the Portuguese to reason was entrusted to Godoy, and the short campaign which ensued is known as the War of the Oranges, from the bough of this fruit which Godoy sent to the Queen from Olivenza. The allies occupied almost the whole of Alemtejo without much difficulty, and Portugal sued for peace, which she obtained on payment of an indemnity to France, and on the cession of Olivenza to Spain. In the following year the Treaty of Amiens brought about a general pacification, and Spain recovered Minorca, which she had again lost, but she was compelled to relinquish Trinidad to the British.

The Treaty of Amiens was a mere truce, and when war was renewed between England and France in 1803, Napoleon compelled Spain, as the price of her neutrality, to pay a monthly subsidy, and to negotiate a commercial treaty. The British thereupon proceeded to treat her as an ally of France, and seized the plate-ships from America whenever an opportunity occurred. The result was a Spanish declaration of war, and in October, 1805, the allied fleets of France and Spain were destroyed by Nelson at Trafalgar.

Spain was always unfortunate in her alliances, and she was now inextricably entangled in the meshes of the Napoleonic web. The French Emperor, having failed to effect a direct invasion of England, was determined to bring that country to its knees by means of economic pressure, and he therefore instituted the Continental Blockade, in the winter of 1806–1807. To make this complete it was essential that all countries on the mainland of Europe should close their ports to British ships, and as Portugal refused to do so Napoleon decided to apply compulsion. Moreover, he wished to obtain possession of the Portuguese fleet to compensate him to some extent for the loss of his own ships at Trafalgar.

The Emperor resolved to act with Spain as he had done in 1801, and in October, 1807, the Treaty of Fontainebleau was signed, by which it was agreed that the combined armies of France and Spain should conquer Portugal. That kingdom was then to be divided into three parts; the northern provinces were to be given to the King of Etruria in exchange for his dominions in Italy, which were to be annexed to the French Empire; the central portion was to be held by France until the conclusion of peace; while the southern district was to be formed into an independent kingdom for Godoy. In pursuance of this treaty a French army under General Junot marched across the Peninsula, and by the beginning of 1808 Portugal was in French hands.

Meanwhile the strife of parties at the Spanish court was growing ever more bitter, and it soon provided Napoleon with an opportunity for meting out to Spain the same treatment that Portugal had received. The Prince of Asturias took part in a plot against Godoy, and was thrown into prison. He appealed for help to Napoleon, and the King also applied to the French Emperor to arbitrate upon his differences with his son. This afforded Napoleon an excuse for sending further troops into Spain, and an army under Murat approached Madrid. These events gave rise to the rumour that Charles was about to leave the country in the same way that the Prince Regent of Portugal had done, and an insurrection broke out in Madrid: Godoy was maltreated, and the King abdicated in favour of the Prince of Asturias, who took the title of Ferdinand VII.

Napoleon refused to accept this abdication, and summoned both the King and his son to Bayonne. When the Spanish Royal Family were all assembled in that town, both Charles and Ferdinand were forced to resign their rights to the Spanish throne, which was at once conferred by Napoleon upon his brother, Joseph, until then King of Naples. On May 2, 1808, Madrid rose against the French, and the War of Independence began.

The desperate nature of the struggle which began at this date is apt to obscure the fact that Spain was not unanimously in arms on behalf of the absent Ferdinand. It is true that there were few who desired the restoration of Charles IV, but among the educated classes Napoleon did not fail to make some converts to the idea of substituting for the Bourbons a Bonapartist dynasty in the person of Joseph. The French Emperor endeavoured to cover his acts with the cloak of legality by convening at Bayonne a meeting of the Spanish notables, who received at his hands a constitution on the French model, while Ferdinand sank so low as to offer his congratulations to his supplanter.

Napoleon's clemency was useless. In spite of the fact that Joseph was superior to Ferdinand both as a man and as a monarch, and that the new constitution was far in advance of anything that Spain had hitherto possessed, the country would tolerate neither the *"rey intruso"* nor his methods. It soon became obvious that a new phenomenon was being witnessed in the shape of a popular rising, and although the French armies easily overcame all organised resistance, the methods which had been so successful in other parts of Europe were quite ineffective in Spain.

The provinces fought for themselves, and if the struggle was everywhere carried on in the name of the absent Ferdinand, the leaders in the field took little notice of any central authority. Those Spaniards who were prepared to acquiesce in a change of dynasty were held up to the universal execration of their fellow-countrymen under the title of *"los afrancesados,"* while the notables who had refused Napoleon's invitation to Bayonne became at once objects of popular adoration.

The insurrection on May 2 had compelled the French to retire beyond the Ebro, but the Emperor placed such forces at his brother's disposal as to enable him to reach his capital with ease. Marshal Bessières defeated the best Spanish army under General Cuesta at Medina del Rio Seco, and Joseph entered Madrid on July 20. On that very day, however, the French sustained the worst defeat with which their arms had met since the Revolution, for General Dupont was compelled at Bailen to surrender to General Castaños with 20,000 men.

In reality this victory had been achieved by the regular Spanish infantry, always renowned for its hard-fighting qualities, but it was generally believed to have been won by armed peasants, and the news that the French veterans had been defeated by such means roused the greater enthusiasm. All over the Peninsula men sprang to arms. In Portugal, too, there was disaster, for the country had risen against the French, and the arrival of a British army compelled Junot, by the Convention of Cintra in August, 1808, to evacuate that kingdom.

It hardly need be said that Napoleon was far from expecting such disasters, for he had become so accustomed to victory that he could not understand the change in his affairs. He looked, however, on these two events as of merely temporary importance, and proceeded to the Congress of Erfurt. When this was over he determined to visit Spain himself, and put an end to the opposition to Joseph.

Accordingly, he invaded the Peninsula at the head of an army of 135,000 men, the pick of the French forces, and joined his brother, who had left Madrid after the capitulation of Bailen, and had retreated behind the Ebro. Napoleon marched straight upon the capital: Marshal Soult defeated the Spanish army of the centre at Burgos; Marshal Victor routed the Spanish army of the left at Espinosa; and Marshal Lannes overwhelmed the Spanish army of the right at Tudela. In spite of the snow, the Emperor forced the pass of the Somo Sierra, and on December 4, 1808, received the capitulation of Madrid.

These victories, combined with the rapid and successful advance on the capital, convinced Napoleon that the difficulties of the Spanish war had been exaggerated, and the result of this impression was that in after years he neglected to strengthen his armies in Spain sufficiently, and attributed all failures to the incompetence of his generals instead of to the warlike qualities of his opponents.

After occupying Madrid the French Emperor next determined to turn his strength against the English forces in the Peninsula. Almost the first thought of the Spanish patriots had been to look to Great Britain for help, and already in June the representatives of the Province of Asturias had arrived in London. Canning and his colleagues in the Cabinet at once realised the importance of what had happened, and it was decided to send to the Peninsula an army that had originally been intended for Venezuela. Peace was made with Spain, and Hookham Frere, who had been British minister at Lisbon for some years, was appointed to act as intermediary between the Foreign Office and the Spaniards.

Sir John Moore had assumed the command of the British forces in October, and his instructions were to co-operate with the Spanish armies that were then holding the line of the Ebro. Owing to such circumstances as the difficulty of securing the necessary transport, Moore's advance was extremely slow, and by the middle of November the British army had not got any farther than Salamanca. By that time, as has been shown, the whole position had changed for the worse. Moore, somewhat unaccountably, spent four whole weeks at Salamanca, where the news of the successive disasters reached him, and he determined to make an attack upon the French lines of communication. The only result of this was to postpone, rather than prevent, the French occupation of Andalusia, while Moore eventually had to retreat to Corunna. A battle was fought there in January, 1809, to protect the embarkation of the British, and in it Moore himself was killed.

While these events were taking place in the West, Saragossa had been holding out in a manner which augured ill for the final success of the French, and it was only after the most desperate resistance that the city was captured in February, 1809. In Aragón and Catalonia the campaign chiefly consisted of the reduction of small fortresses, which invariably resisted fiercely, although in the open field the Spaniards were always defeated. From Madrid Joseph acted in two different directions. Marshal Moncey took Valencia; Marshal Victor defeated Cuesta at Medellin; and General Sebastiani prepared to invade Andalusia.

In order to prevent this last stroke, Sir Arthur Wellesley, who was now British commander-in-chief, invaded Spain from Portugal, and in July defeated the French at Talavera. He was not, however, able to effect his object. In November the Spaniards were routed at Ocana, and the whole of Andalusia, with the exception of Gibraltar and Cádiz, fell into the hands of the French.

The years 1810–1811 marked the height of French power in Spain. During almost the whole of this period Wellington, as Sir Arthur Wellesley had now become, was forced to remain on the defence in Portugal. On the other hand, Joseph only exercised his sway over the districts where his brother's bayonets were present to support it. He had even less hold over the country than the Archduke Charles a century before, for there was no province upon which he could count. The French lines of communication were constantly being cut, stragglers were killed, and so active were the *guerrilleros* that before long it was unsafe to send a letter from France with an escort of anything less than two hundred men.

Even so, it might have been possible for Joseph to have established himself had Napoleon appreciated the true nature of Spanish warfare, but, as it was, the Emperor tried to direct the campaigns from Paris, and he never trusted any one of his marshals enough to give him a free hand. For the rest, all the benefits conferred by Joseph counted for nothing, and the Spaniards would accept neither the abolition of the Inquisition nor of feudalism, neither religious tolerance nor good laws, from a foreign monarch imposed by Napoleon.

In the South only Cádiz still held out, but in the East there were still a few organised Spanish forces in the field. In 1810 and 1811 Suchet campaigned in Aragón and Valencia, and defeated a Spanish army under General Blake at Albufera. In the next year Napoleon's pre-occupation with Russia gave Wellington and the Spaniards their chance.

First Ciudad Rodrigo, and then Badajoz, were taken from the French, and in July, Wellington won an important victory over Marmont at Salamanca. This caused Joseph to evacuate Madrid, and after withdrawing all his troops from Andalusia he fell back behind the Ebro. Wellington occupied the capital, and then advanced upon Burgos, which, however, defied all attempts to capture it. Once more the British had to retire to Portugal, and Joseph returned to Madrid for the last time.

While this campaign was being fought Lord William Bentinck, who commanded the British forces in Sicily, was requested to make a diversion on the East coast of Spain. The operations, however, were badly combined, for Sir John Murray was driven from before Tarragona, and subsequently Lord William himself failed to make any impression on Suchet's position at Alicante.

When the campaigning season opened in 1813 it was clear that Napoleon's sun was setting, and the progress of events in Central Europe rendered it impossible for any further assistance to be given to Joseph by his brother. Wellington accordingly broke up his quarters in the early summer, and marched North-East with the intention of cutting the communications between Madrid and France. This move had the desired effect. Joseph fled from the capital with all the troops he could collect, and attempted, as on previous occasions, to hold the line of the Ebro. Wellington, however, turned the French positions on that river, and in June he overthrew Joseph and Marshal Jourdan at Vittoria.

This victory sealed the fate of the French in the Peninsula, for not only did Joseph retreat at once into France, but Suchet had to abandon Valencia, and fell back through Aragón and Catalonia to the French frontier. In the West the advance of Wellington was rapid. San Sebastian fell into his hands on the last day of August, and by the end of the year Bayonne was invested. The War of Independence was over.

The efforts of the Spaniards themselves in this war have rarely received recognition. When it began, the military establishment of the country consisted of 80,000 troops of the line, including 16,000 cavalry, and 30,000 militia; but the ranks were far from being complete, and the total effective force, including the militia, was under 100,000 men. From this number were to be deducted 16,000 under the Marquis of Romana in Holstein, 6,000 in Tuscany, or on the march from there to the North of Germany, and the garrisons of the Canary and Balearic Islands, so that the actual number of troops that could be brought into the field did not at the utmost exceed 70,000.

When it is further remembered that the departure of the Royal Family had thrown the whole administration into chaos, the resistance made to the French in the first year of the war is the more remarkable. The Spaniards were left to bear alone the brunt of the attack by the finest troops in Europe, for Sir John Moore signally failed to co-operate with them. Thereafter, with their old army broken up, they were forced to fight as irregulars, and in this capacity the Spaniards were invaluable. What is surprising, in view of the history of the two previous decades, is not that the Spaniards did so little in the War of Independence, but that they were able to do so much.

Meanwhile, the struggle against Napoleon was not without important results from the constitutional point of view. The whole administration of the government had for so long been centred in the monarch that when he was removed no one knew who was to exercise authority in his place. The Council of Castile made a hesitating attempt to secure the reins of power, but it was too uncertain of its position, and some of its members were too strongly suspected of sympathy with the invader for the effort to be successful. Meanwhile *juntas* sprang up all over Spain as the struggle against the French proceeded, and they owed a more or less nominal allegiance to a *Junta Central*, which changed its place of meeting according to the vicissitudes of the military situation. This body, be it noted, was intensely loyal to Ferdinand, and all business was transacted in his name.

In 1810 the *Junta Central* repaired to Cádiz, which at that time was one of the few towns still in the hands of the patriots, and resigned its power to a Council of Regency; but before doing so it convoked a Cortes of all Spain in two houses, which were later reduced to a single chamber. This was a purely revolutionary measure, since no such body was known to the constitution, for the union of the crowns of Aragón and Castile had not been followed by the formation of a single Cortes as had been the case when León and Castile became united.

When the assembly met in September, 1810, it at once became evident that two parties were struggling for mastery: on the one side were those who realised how little Spain desired representative government, and how angry Ferdinand would be at such a step having been taken in his absence, while on the other were the men who were infected with the ideas to which the French Revolution had given birth, and who were determined to take advantage of the suspension of all regular government to put them into practice. The strength of this latter lay in the seaports, which have always been the home of Radicalism, and, as they were at that time almost the only part of Spain able to send representatives to the Cortes, it is not surprising that the extremists had a majority on that body.

The Council of Regency soon found itself unable to work with the new masters of the country, and resigned, only, however, to be succeeded by another more in harmony with the views of the larger part of the deputies. At length, in 1812, the Cortes completed the work upon which it had been engaged, to the almost complete neglect of the conduct of the war against Napoleon, and promulgated the memorable Constitution which has since taken its name from the year that saw its birth.

The main points of this extraordinary document were that Spain was to be governed by a moderate hereditary monarchy, with the right of making laws vested in the Crown and one chamber, and for the election of the latter all males over twenty-five were to possess the franchise, while the actual selection of the deputies was indirect, and involved four separate processes. Whether this constitution would have worked in a country that had been accustomed to representative government for several centuries is a moot point, but that it was totally unsuited to Spain at the beginning of the nineteenth century cannot for a moment be in doubt. It placed in a subordinate position both the King and the Church, and yet these were the only two institutions which the country had known since the days of Ferdinand and Isabel.

More important than the actual details of the Constitution of 1812, for it proved quite useless when put in practice, is the influence which it came to exercise over the politics of Southern Europe. For nearly a generation after the fall of Napoleon every popular rising, not only in Spain itself, but in Portugal, Piedmont, and Naples, demanded the immediate enactment of the Constitution of 1812, and it was not until the rise of Republicanism in the middle of the century that it began to pass into oblivion.

It soon became apparent that the opponents of this measure had gauged the feelings of their countrymen more accurately than those who supported it, for, as the provinces were liberated from the French, and their deputies began to attend the Cortes, the Liberal majority rapidly sank, while the members of that party became more violent in their demands when they realised that power was passing from them. Such was the case when the Cortes was dissolved and a new one was elected in October, 1813. The most desperate efforts of the Liberals had only secured them a very narrow majority in the new house, and they were at once faced by the prospect of Ferdinand's immediate return from exile.

In vain they attempted to regulate his movements, and to compel him to take an oath to observe the Constitution of 1812. Ferdinand temporised until he had ascertained for himself the state of public opinion, but his journey through Catalonia was so triumphal a progress that he realised there was no further need for procrastination, and at Valencia, in May, 1814, he condemned the Constitution, restoring the old order in its entirety. The step was accompanied by the arrest of all the leading Liberals, and thus brought to an end a by no means unimportant epoch in Spanish history.

Ferdinand returned to the Peninsula almost entirely unknown to his subjects, and himself realising little of the changes which had been brought about by six years of war. He had, of course, made a serious blunder in not withdrawing into Andalusia in 1808, and so putting himself at the head of the national resistance to the invader. The French invasion, however, had obliterated from the memory of most Spaniards the behaviour of the Royal Family in 1808, and of the even more disgraceful events which had preceded it, and few restored monarchs have returned from exile with greater advantages than Ferdinand VII.

Unfortunately, he was not the man to avail himself of the favourable circumstances in which he was placed, for, although he was not the monster his opponents have painted, he was obstinate and narrow-minded. He was also addicted to low company, and replaced the ministers by a personal council, consisting, for the most part, of men of little worth. The King's anger after his return was principally directed against the *afrancesados* and the Liberals. The former must have repented bitterly of the step they had taken, for during the reign of Joseph the burden of taxation had fallen entirely upon them, since it was from them alone that it was possible for the invader's government to collect the revenue, while after the return of Ferdinand they were treated as public enemies, and those who had not taken the precaution of following Joseph into France were left to face the prison and the scaffold.

The King's hand was no less heavy upon the Liberals, and he made no difference between the moderates and the extremists, so that the same dungeon held both the Jacobin and the supporter of constitutional monarchy. In short, Ferdinand had neither the men nor the skill to govern the country on the old lines, and although sporadic Liberal revolts were easily crushed, it soon became evident that some change must take place before long.

In international affairs Spain stood alone, and at the Congress of Vienna she was refused the position and the vote of a first-class Power. No support was given to the claim of a member of the Spanish Royal Family to the Duchy of Parma. The district and fortress of Olivenza, near Badajoz, was assigned to Portugal in spite of Spanish protests. The slave trade, on which the prosperity of a large part of her colonies depended, was abolished. The small contingent under Castaños which she sent to France during the Hundred Days was scornfully sent back to its own side of the frontier.

Meanwhile, the American colonies were in revolt, and Ferdinand was thus unable to gain any laurels abroad which might restore his prestige at home. In addition, the country was exhausted by the long struggle to regain its independence, and the moral and social anarchy was even more marked than the political and economic chaos. At the same time, Ferdinand was not personally unpopular with the large majority of his subjects, and it was not the despotism of the restored monarchy which precipitated the crisis, but its stupidity; and the first blow was struck by its own chosen implement, the army.

In 1819, Ferdinand determined to make one last attempt to reassert his authority in America, and for that purpose all the available forces were concentrated at Cádiz. Unfortunately, the Spanish marine had been so neglected that there were no transports available, and the troops were kept in idleness pending the arrival of some ships which had been sent by the Czar of Russia. The army was honeycombed with masonic lodges and secret societies, which had penetrated into Spain and spread there as a result of the French invasion, and during this period of enforced inactivity, revolutionary propaganda was particularly effective.

On New Year's Day, 1820, Ráfael Riego, an Asturian battalion commander, raised the standard of revolt, by proclaiming the Constitution of 1812. At first the attempt met with little success, and its author was compelled to take to flight, but at the very moment when the Liberal cause appeared to be most hopeless the towns began to rally to it. Ferdinand was too astute not to realise that opposition would be futile, and might prove dangerous, so he took an oath to observe the Constitution. There was little or no popular feeling behind the revolutionary movement, which was, in fact, the first of a long series of *pronunciamientos*, which have ever since marred the progress of Spain.

The Cortes met in July, and among its members were thirteen deputies who had been chosen to represent the American colonies, although most of the latter had already asserted their independence. At first men of moderate views were in the majority, but, as in the case of all revolutionary movements, the power soon passed into the hands of the extremists. Riego was the hero of the Radical mobs, and the position of Ferdinand was becoming perilous when a Liberal attack on the Church gave the Royalists an opportunity to recover much of the ground which they had lost.

To the political demands of the Liberals the majority of the nation was indifferent, and those who took any interest in such matters probably supported the reformers, but when the Church was called into the question every peasant realised that a vital principle was at stake. Ferdinand's adherents formed the *junta apostólica*, and commenced to harass their opponents at all points.

The progress of events in Spain soon attracted the attention of the other Powers, not least because the Spanish rising had been followed by revolts in Naples and Piedmont: in the former the Constitution of 1812 had been proclaimed by the revolutionaries, although there was not a single copy of it in the kingdom. It was in these circumstances that the Congress of Verona met in October, 1822, and the story of its transactions may be briefly told.

The French representative opened the proceedings by asking for a definition of the attitude which the other countries would adopt if France found herself compelled to intervene in the Peninsula. To this Austria, Prussia, and Russia replied that they would support such action by withdrawing their representatives from Madrid, but they hesitated to promise any material aid, which suited the policy of the French government very well indeed, as that was the last thing it wanted.

Wellington, who represented Great Britain, took the opposite line, and declared that his government would not be committed in advance to the approval of the attitude of any other Power. This attitude convinced both Louis XVIII and the Holy Alliance that nothing was to be expected from England, and when Wellington declared that the British Minister at Madrid would confine himself to allaying the ferment which the communications of the other Powers must inevitably excite, they excluded him from the more private deliberations. Finally, the Holy Alliance gave France a free hand in Spain, of which she was not slow to avail herself.

The moment was extremely propitious for intervention. Once they had attained power the Spanish Liberals had proved themselves just as intolerant as Ferdinand, and considerably more incompetent. While their leaders were corresponding with Bentham as to the principles upon which the new code was to be based, anarchy prevailed all over the land and in every branch of the administration. The years which followed the *pronunciamiento* of Riego were marked by a series of *coups d'état*, changes of ministry, riots, and revolts which, combined with the anti-clericalism of the country's new rulers, helped to fan the flames of civil war.

The Inquisition, which had been revived by Ferdinand, was, indeed, again abolished, but when the Madrid mob broke into its prisons to release the martyrs for civil and religious liberty, all they found there, apart from a few hams and some barrels of wine, was a French priest, whose extravagant royalism had culminated in a crazy mysticism; this individual was comfortably housed in an attic, which he was most reluctant to forsake.

Intervention in Spain was popular with almost all sections of French opinion. The more extreme Royalists wished to lend aid to a King in difficulties with his subjects; the army clamoured for a renewal of the glories it had known under Napoleon; and the *bourgeoisie* was anxious for the fate of the 200,000,000 francs which it had invested in a Spanish loan. In January, 1823, Louis XVIII announced to the Chambers that he had withdrawn his ambassador from Madrid, and that about 100,000 Frenchmen were about to march "invoking the God of St. Louis, for the sake of preserving the throne of Spain to a descendant of Henry IV, and of reconciling that fine kingdom with Europe."

In April the French army, under the command of the Duke of Angoulême, crossed the Bidassoa. It was the first time for thirty-four years that French troops had marched under the Bourbon lilies, and there was some doubt how they would behave. At the frontier they were met by a party of Bonapartist exiles carrying the tricolour, but they showed no hesitation at firing upon the flag of the Revolution, and from that instant the result of the campaign was not in doubt.

The French progress proved to be little more than a military promenade. Angoulême's plan was to press forward to Madrid as rapidly as possible, leaving corps of observation to mask the fortified cities on his road, in order to allow the government no time to mature its plan of defence, and, above all, to prevent the assembling of guerrilla bands. This strategy, which is said to have been suggested privately by Wellington during the Congress of Verona, was entirely successful.

The Cortes, taking Ferdinand with them, fled to Seville, and by the end of May, the French were in Madrid. In other parts of the Peninsula the scattered Spanish forces were dealt with in detail, and by the middle of June the Cortes had retired to Cádiz, where they kept the King in captivity. In August the French, who had been blockading Cádiz for some weeks, began the siege in earnest, and on August 31 they stormed the Trocadero, the key to the city. Fighting continued for a little longer, but by the end of September all resistance was at an end, and Ferdinand was at liberty.

Before the King was released he had taken an oath to grant a general amnesty, but as soon as he was free he ignored it on the ground that it had been obtained from him by force. The most rigorous methods were adopted towards all who had been implicated in the recent disturbances, and such severity was used as thoroughly to disgust the Duke of Angoulême, who finally showed his disapproval of the King's proceedings by refusing the decorations offered him for his services.

The principal figure in the administration during the last ten years was Calomarde, who, as Minister of Justice, was responsible for the persecution of the Liberals. That the means he employed were violent cannot be denied, but they were no worse than those of his opponents during their tenure of power, and at least the country was not troubled by civil war. Indeed, there was a very large section of Spanish opinion which held that Ferdinand was too moderate, and the "Society of the Exterminating Angel" was formed for the purpose which its title sufficiently indicates. This development left the King midway between the more extreme Absolutists and the Constitutionalists, and he endeavoured to retain this position. It was not without considerable justification that he told a French ambassador that in upholding absolutism he was in agreement with the majority of his subjects, and that it was only with the greatest difficulty that he had been able to prevent a second revival of the Inquisition.

The personal popularity of Ferdinand was never in question. The French troops were finally withdrawn in 1828, but the King had no difficulty in maintaining himself even after the triumph of Liberalism in France in July, 1830. He spent the winter of 1827–1828 in Barcelona, and then took an extended tour of the kingdom, being everywhere received with acclamation. Nor was the administration during this latter period of the reign by any means contemptible. The court was not at all extravagant, and the skilful finance of Ballesteros gradually repaired the damage caused by a generation of war and revolution. This minister drew up a code of commercial law, appointed consuls to represent the country abroad, founded an Exchange, and promoted the first exhibition of Spanish industries. Economy was the order of the day, and in its interests Ferdinand even allowed a considerable reduction in the army, although he appeared to run great risks in so doing. Prosperity was followed by contentment, and those who desired a change were a mere handful.

Although Ferdinand had been married three times he was still childless, and the heir to the throne was his brother, Don Carlos, to whom the Absolutists looked as their leader. In 1830, however, the King entered into matrimony once more, on this occasion with Maria Cristina of Naples, and in due course it was announced that the Queen was expecting a child. This event at once raised a constitutional problem of the first importance, for the principle of the succession to the crown had not been settled; indeed, it was still very much open to question.

The *Siete Partidas* of Alfonso X had recognised the right of females to succeed to the throne of Castile and León in default of male heirs of an equally near degree of consanguinity, and that this right had also been admitted in practice is proved by the succession of Isabel I: it was recognised, too, in Aragón, for the claim of Charles I was through his mother, Juana the Mad. With the advent of the Bourbons a change was made, and in 1713 Philip V introduced the Salic Law, which established the French procedure. The matter was still further complicated by the fact that, for some obscure reason, Charles IV, in 1789, convoked the Cortes in secret session, and, on his initiative, a resolution was passed asking him to revert to the old order of succession, but the necessary decree had never been promulgated.

In March, 1830, Ferdinand VII promulgated the Pragmatic Sanction of Charles IV, and in June of the same year, he made a will in which he left the crown to his unborn child. Don Carlos could not, and did not, object to the principle of leaving the crown by will, for it was owing to an act of this nature on the part of Charles II that the Bourbons were in the Peninsula, but he protested against the promulgation of the Pragmatic Sanction. He denied that it was genuine, and declared that, in any case, since he was alive at the date of its enactment it could not be retrospective. Ferdinand at one time gave way, and revoked the Pragmatic Sanction, but he eventually destroyed the revocation, and when his daughter, Isabel, was born, he recognised her as his heir.

In 1833, the King died, and thus, in his own words, the cork was removed from the fermenting and surcharged bottle of Spain. Ferdinand VII was certainly not the inhuman monster of Liberal historians, but he did his country a great disservice when he altered the order of succession, even if his act may to some extent be extenuated on the score of parental affection.

CHAPTER XXXVII

The Loss of America

THE later years of the eighteenth century were marked by more than one rising in America against Spanish rule. It is true that there had always been sporadic revolts due to local or temporary causes, but during the reign of Charles III and his son talk of independence first began to be heard. Not only had the reforms of the former monarch, as has been shown in an earlier chapter, created smaller units of government, but by abolishing many of the old restrictions upon commerce they had whetted the appetite of the colonists for unshackled trade with all the world.

The most formidable rebellion, however, was not of the creoles but of Tupac Amaru, who claimed descent from the Incas, and wished to revive their empire. The struggle lasted during the greater part of 1780–1781, and at one time more than 50,000 Indians were in arms, and the rising was only suppressed with the greatest difficulty.

The establishment of the United States was also by no means without its influence upon Spanish America, and Aranda, in 1783, advised Charles III to make such concessions as might serve to prevent this growing feeling of nationalism from becoming hostile to the Spanish connection. His project was to bring direct rule in America to an end, and to create kingdoms in Mexico, Peru, and New Granada for the Infantes. The King of Spain was to take the title of Emperor, and to make a Family Pact with these new monarchs: there was also to be a commercial treaty to which France, but not Great Britain, was to be a party.

Nothing came of this scheme, but it was revived in 1804 by Godoy in a slightly different form; there was to be no commercial treaty, and the Infantes were merely to be regents. The series of catastrophes that befell Spain shortly afterwards caused this plan, too, to be consigned to oblivion.

Great Britain had not failed to take advantage of the growing discontent in Spanish America, and Francisco Miranda, the Venezuelan patriot, had for some time been urging Pitt to assist his fellow-countrymen to break with Spain. In 1806 a British force under Sir Home Popham captured Buenos Aires, but was soon driven out again, not by regular troops, but by the colonists themselves, a fact which gave an enormous impetus to the separatist movement. At the beginning of the following year fresh troops came out from England, and Montevideo was taken. General Whitelocke then arrived to take supreme command, but he proved so incompetent that within a few short weeks not only had he failed to retake Buenos Aires, but he had lost the greater part of his army, and had been forced to surrender Montevideo.

These failures, together with the arguments of Miranda, caused the British Government to direct its attention farther North, and as soon as Canning was installed at the Foreign Office it was decided to send a large force to Venezuela under the command of Sir Arthur Wellesley. The outbreak of the War of Independence, of course, put an end to these schemes, for Great Britain could not encourage her ally's colonists to revolt, but the little aid that Spain had been able to afford the latter when danger threatened was not forgotten.

The greater part of the Spanish colonies in America were, therefore, ripe for revolt in the early years of the nineteenth century, and it only required a spark to cause a conflagration. The attitude of Spain towards Napoleon revealed only too clearly the weakness of the government in the Peninsula, while the confusion which resulted in America from orders sent simultaneously by Charles IV, Joseph Bonaparte, and Ferdinand VII served materially to loosen the ties between the colonies and the mother country. To give the *junta central* its due it realised the danger, and by a decree of January, 1809, it was announced that the American colonies were an integral part of the monarchy, and, as provinces, were entitled to direct representation on the Cortes. Three individuals from each capital were to be selected by the municipalities, and from them the representative to the Cortes was to be chosen. Ordinances were also enacted to mitigate the restrictions which existed in respect of the commerce and trade of the colonies.

Whether this change of policy would have prevented the spread of separatist feeling it is impossible to say, for a year later the Regency abolished the ordinances. This emboldened the independence party among the colonists to make a supreme effort to obtain for themselves that freedom which they now considered it hopeless to expect under Spanish rule.

Caracas, where Miranda had already secured many followers, was the scene of the origin of the movement which culminated in the independence of the Spanish colonies. In April, 1810, the municipal council of that town was constituted into a *junta*, and refused to recognise the authority of the Regency, though it still expressed its loyalty to Ferdinand VII. Further complications were caused by the arrival of emissaries from Joseph, who demanded the recognition of his right to the crown on the part of Venezuela.

The real leader of the rebellion in this part of America was Simon Bolivar, a man who came from the highest ranks of the colonial aristocracy. Although he had been born as recently as 1783, Bolivar had travelled extensively in Europe, and shortly after the outbreak of the Venezuelan revolt he visited England in the hope of obtaining aid against the Spaniards. In this he was unsuccessful, as the British Government was the ally of Spain, but when he returned to Venezuela he managed to bring a small supply of arms and ammunition with him.

For some years the war was marked for both sides by alternating triumphs and defeats. At first the Spaniards were quite unable to cope with the revolutionary movement, but two years later General Monteverde recovered control of the greater part of Venezuela, and by 1812 the cause of the rebels appeared gloomy in the extreme. What was taking place was, in fact, civil war, and this explains the vicissitudes which marked the struggle. This aspect of the revolutionary movement has become obscured owing to the latter's triumph, but almost to the end no inconsiderable number of Americans remained loyal to the Spanish connection, and, as in all civil wars, a change of sides on the part of the combatants was by no means infrequent.

More and more the cause of the rebels became personified by Bolivar. When Monteverde appeared to have Venezuela in his grip Bolivar, who had sought asylum in Curaçoa, collected all the refugees from Venezuela and New Granada, and landed with some 800 followers at Cartagena. He marched from that town into Venezuela, where he was joined by many thousand volunteers, and in a series of battles routed the Spanish forces. In August, 1813, Bolivar entered Caracas in triumph, and was proclaimed dictator until such time as Venezuela could unite with New Granada.

Once more there was a reverse of fortune, for in an energetic campaign the Spanish General Boves caused Bolivar to evacuate Venezuela and retire to Cartagena. By this time the War of Independence in the Peninsula was at an end, and Ferdinand VII, restored to his throne, made the necessary preparations to re-establish his authority in America. Venezuela and New Granada, being the parts of that continent most easy of access, were indicated as the first field for these efforts at reconquest, and Bolivar was accordingly appointed Captain-General of both provinces.

At this point those differences which so often divided the colonists during their struggle with Spain once more made their appearance, with the result that, in spite of some early successes, Bolivar was compelled to retire to Jamaica, and by the end of 1815 the Spaniards were in occupation of Cartagena itself. This catastrophe impressed upon the rebels the necessity of union, and they once more turned to Bolivar. He organised a naval expedition, which succeeded in defeating the Spaniards, and he then landed in Venezuela, where he was joined by Paez.

The latter was one of the most remarkable figures in the American revolt against Spain, and he has become something in the nature of a legend in Venezuela. On one occasion he captured a whole flotilla of Spanish gunboats on the Apure river by swimming his cavalry out and ordering them to board the ships: on another he was credited with having killed forty Spaniards himself in one fight. The combination of Bolivar and Paez was a fortunate one for the insurgents, though it was not until the end of 1818 that the fortune of war definitely inclined in their favour. In that year López Méndez recruited in Europe some 9000 men for the revolutionary cause, and their arrival definitely turned the scale.

From 1818 the success of the rebels was never in doubt. Victory after victory was gained by the revolutionary armies, and in December, 1819, New Granada and Venezuela were united under the name of the Republic of Colombia. For a time the Spaniards struggled to retrieve the situation, but in 1821 they were crushed at the battle of Carabobo and the remnants of their force retired to Puerto Cabello, where they eventually surrendered. In the same year the constitution of Colombia was formally ratified, and Bolivar was proclaimed President.

He realised, however, that if the independence of Colombia was to be maintained it was essential that the Spaniards should be entirely driven out of America, and his first act was to organise an expedition to Ecuador. The turning-point of this campaign was the battle of Pichincha in 1822, where General Sucre overthrew the Spaniards, and by the end of that year Spanish rule in Ecuador was a thing of the past.

Bolivar was determined to do in Peru what he had effected in Ecuador. Peru was the citadel of Spanish rule in America, and unless it were captured the provinces which had already achieved their independence would never feel safe. The insurgents in Chile and Argentina had already made some impression in that quarter, and in 1820 a fleet under the command of Lord Cochrane had defeated the Spaniards at sea, with the result that a force of 5000 men commanded by the Argentine General San Martín had been able, in 1821, to capture Lima. Nevertheless, the Spaniards maintained a stout resistance at Callao and elsewhere, and it could still be said that they were in effective occupation of Peru.

In 1824 the final battles were fought which put an end to the Spanish rule in this part of America. In August, Bolivar gained a decisive victory at Junin, and in December, General Sucre at Ayacucho completely overthrew the Spanish forces, capturing the Viceroy himself, and all the principal civil and military officials. Sucre then proceeded to Bolivia, or Upper Peru as it was then called, and in a very short time he had completed the subjugation of that province, which in 1825 became an independent republic with Sucre as its President.

In the South of the continent the struggle was prolonged, not so much owing to the resistance of the Spaniards and their supporters, as because of the differences in the ranks of the insurgents. In 1810 a revolt broke out in Argentina, when the French conquest of the mother-country appeared complete, and the Viceroy retired from Buenos Aires to Montevideo, which remained in Spanish hands for four years longer. Fighting continued between the partisans of Spain and those of separation until 1816, when a congress at Tucumán proclaimed Puyredón dictator, and in July of that year the Act of

Independence of the United Provinces of the Rio de la Plata was ratified.

Paraguay, on the other hand, secured her freedom from Spain without a fight. Isolated as she was in the centre of the continent, and with the respect for authority which the Jesuits had inculcated still a powerful factor, Paraguay did not take readily to the idea of revolution. When, therefore, in 1810, an Argentine army attempted to free Paraguay, that country showed no desire to be freed, and the invaders were defeated in a pitched battle some forty miles from Asunción. The course of events elsewhere, however, soon began to exercise its influence, with the result that in the summer of 1811 Paraguay too proclaimed its independence, and Rodríguez de Francia entered upon his long dictatorship.

In Chile the movement in favour of independence may be said to have begun in 1810, and at first the insurgents appeared to be carrying everything before them. Three years later General Paroja re-established the authority of Spain, and it became clear that without outside help Chile would never be able to overthrow Spanish rule. Accordingly, the aid of Argentina was invoked, and in 1817 San Martín crossed the Andes with an army 4000 strong. The Spaniards were defeated at Chacabuco, and the independence of Chile was officially proclaimed. The war, however, was not yet over, for a Spanish army from Peru inflicted a serious defeat on San Martín, which came within an ace of robbing him of the fruits of his campaign, before it was itself routed at Maypú in April, 1818. This victory finally secured the independence of Chile.

In Mexico the rule of Spain had been undermined for many years before the final collapse took place, and it is difficult to resist the conclusion that it was the policy of Charles III which made independence possible. There, even more than in the rest of the Americas, the Spanish domination rested on the Church, and the suppression of the Jesuits struck a blow at its very foundations. The treatment meted out to them shocked the leading colonists, who were mostly their old pupils. The mass of the population remained unaffected, and the Jesuits had a sufficient number of enemies even among the clergy, who were only too pleased to assist in their destruction. The King thus received plenty of support at the time, but in attacking the Jesuits he was in reality weakening the position of the Church as a whole, for the royal authority and the ecclesiastical were inseparable.

Then came the War of American Independence, which, for geographical reasons, meant far more to the Mexicans than to those who lived in distant South America. Finally, in order the better to protect the Viceroyalty against British attack, Charles permitted the formation of a creole and *mestizo* militia. Spanish regular officers might, and did, sneer at this force, but the militia provided the nucleus of the armies that established Mexican independence.

Such was the position when the news that Spain was a mere puppet in the hands of Napoleon began to filter out to Mexico, and there were unmistakable signs that Spanish rule was approaching its end. One of the later Viceroys even entered into a conspiracy with the creoles to bring about colonial self-government, but the *audiencia* deposed him, and sent him back to Spain. In 1807 Mexico remained loyal to Ferdinand VII, but there were no Spanish troops in the country, and it began to act for itself.

Independence would probably have been proclaimed, as in Argentina, two years later when Napoleon appeared finally to have made himself master of the Peninsula, but for the revolt of a half-crazy priest called Hidalgo. This individual led an Indian rising against the creoles and *mestizos*, and he committed such excesses during the course of it as to rally the menaced classes to the Viceroy and the existing order. Hidalgo was eventually defeated and put to death, and for a little time longer the fiction of Spanish rule continued.

What caused the final breach was the events of 1820. The revival of the Constitution of 1812 alarmed the clergy, for the men who were now in power in Spain were the declared enemies of the Church, whose property it was their known intention to secularise. In these circumstances the Mexican clergy hesitated no longer, but threw in their lot with the party of independence. The Spanish regime collapsed like a house of cards. A few soldiers continued to hold the fortress at San Juan de Ulloa for a time simply because the Mexicans had no naval force, and the castle stands on an island, opposite Vera Cruz. The Viceroy himself, however, signed a document which announced the end of the old order which he represented. There can also be little doubt but that the sale of Florida to the United States by Ferdinand in 1819 had been regarded by the Mexicans as further proof of the weakness of Spain, and so had the more encouraged those who desired separation.

As soon as the Spanish colonies began to rise against the mother-country it was only natural that the other Powers should begin to fish in the troubled waters. The Holy Alliance desired that the rule of Spain should be restored in some form as an assertion of the legitimist principle; France was influenced by much the same motives, though in her case the wish to obtain commercial advantages in the Americas was the predominant factor in her policy; and Great Britain and the United States were determined that if Ferdinand could not reduce his rebellious subjects to obedience by his own efforts, no other monarch should aid him in the task.

Many schemes were discussed at one time or another, and in 1820 France was in negotiation both with Madrid and Buenos Aires for the establishment of the Duke of Luccá, who had been temporarily dispossessed of Parma in favour of Napoleon's widow, upon the throne of Argentina. Castlereagh protested vigorously against this proposal, and one of his last acts before his death was to recognise the Spanish colonial flags.

The year 1823 was decisive, for the French invasion of the Peninsula determined Canning, who had succeeded Castlereagh at the Foreign Office, to prevent the Duke of Angoulême from repeating his Spanish triumph on American soil. Accordingly, he made adroit use of President Monroe's message to Congress to impress upon Europe the fact of Anglo-American solidarity, which was non-existent, and he gained his point. The British command of the sea prevented France or the Holy Alliance from coming to Ferdinand's assistance in the New World, and in 1824 the issue was decided at Ayacucho. Many years, however, elapsed before Spain officially recognised the independence of her late colonies.

In view of her own internal weakness it is remarkable that Spain should have been able to maintain the struggle in America for so long, and she would not have been able to do so had it not been for the strength of the royalist party among the colonists. In short, the contest which resulted in the independence of the Spanish colonies was a civil war, and the support which the King of Spain was able to afford to those who were fighting his battles was at all times negligible from a military standpoint.

CHAPTER XXXVIII

Isabel II (1833–1868)

BY the will of Ferdinand VII his widow, Cristina, who was herself only twenty-seven years of age, became Regent for their infant daughter, Isabel II. From the first it was clear that the Carlists, as the supporters of Don Carlos were called, would contest the succession of the new Queen, but they were handicapped by the refusal of their leader to take any steps on his own behalf while his brother was still alive.

In consequence, all the most important positions in the State were already in the hands of the supporters of the Regent, who thus enjoyed the enormous initial advantage that the whole machinery of government was at her disposal. Don Carlos was a man of uncompromising frankness and straightforward honesty, and his absolute refusal to countenance any manœuvring for position before Ferdinand's death probably lost him the throne. One of the first acts of the Regent was to outlaw her brother-in-law, and to confiscate his property; to which Don Carlos, who was himself still in Portugal, replied in November by calling upon his followers to take up arms.

This breach in the Royal Family was the cause of most of the troubles which have afflicted Spain during the past century. It weakened the monarchy by depriving it of the support of those who were its natural defenders, and the throne was forced to rely upon politicians and generals who wished to impose upon Spain a method of government which was quite alien to her genius and to her traditions. Moreover, the interference of the army in public life dates from the death of Ferdinand VII, and the *pronunciamiento* would in all probability not have been so prominent a feature of Spanish history had the throne been occupied by Don Carlos and his heirs.

The dependence of Isabel upon the Liberals also necessitated the adoption of their anti-clerical policy, and this widened the gulf between throne and altar which had existed since the days of Charles III. In 1834–1835 there took place the first of those assaults on convents and churches which have since been repeated on more than one occasion. It marked the end of that close association between Church and State which had been the keynote of the policy of Spain in the days of her greatness.

Before considering the political history of the reign, however, some account must be given of the efforts of the Carlists to place their leader on the throne.

The summons to arms issued by Don Carlos precipitated the first Carlist war. This was in the main a confused struggle, and was carried on by small bodies of *guerrilleros*. Like all civil wars it was marked by extremes of heroism and savagery, and on more than one occasion local and personal jealousies played a greater part than the principles which underlay the struggle. The war was centred in two districts, one comprising the three Basque provinces, namely Biscay, Alava, and Guipúzcoa, together with Navarre, and the other comprising parts of Catalonia, Valencia, and Aragón.

The force behind the Carlist cause was the well-grounded fear of the Basques that the establishment of a Liberal regime at Madrid would result in the abolition of their *fueros*, or special privileges. There was also the religious fervour which was excited by the anti-clerical policy of the Regency, while the cause of Don Carlos also appealed to the monarchical instincts of many Spaniards. In the districts that supported his claim Don Carlos was recognised as Charles V, and for some time regular administration existed in the Carlist provinces. The treasury was supplied by contributions from the provinces which favoured Don Carlos, fines levied on Liberal families and villages, customs-dues collected on the French frontier, and gifts from foreign legitimists.

The war may be divided into two main periods, namely before and after the first siege of Bilbao in June, 1835. In Biscay and Navarre the Carlist leader was Tomás Zumalacárregui, who had sacrificed his commission in the army for the sake of Don Carlos. He was a man of the finest character, and his support of the Carlist cause brought it many adherents. In Castile and Aragón the Carlist leaders were Merino and Cabrera. For some months the war continued in a desultory fashion. The government generals endeavoured to draw the Carlists down to the plains, where they would be at a disadvantage in conflict with regular troops, while Zumalacárregui resisted all attempts to conquer the provinces which were the stronghold of Don Carlos.

The summer of 1835 was the high-water mark of Carlist success. In May Don Carlos established his court at Estella, and in the following month General Espartero was routed by the Carlists at Descarga. This tempted the Carlists to undertake the offensive, and siege was laid to Bilbao. The reason for this step was the urgent need for a seaport through which to obtain supplies, and it was also believed that in the event of its capture, Austria, Prussia, and Russia would recognise the Carlists as belligerents.

Unfortunately on the fifth day of the siege, Zumalacárregui was wounded, and he died nine days later. His death marked the turning-point of the Carlist fortunes, for there was nobody to take his place. The cause of Don Carlos was henceforth on the defensive, and a rebellion in such circumstances is foredoomed to failure.

The war also degenerated in character, and was marked by atrocities of the most revolting type. A government general had the mother of Cabrera shot, while in Barcelona the mob was allowed to break into the prison and massacre the Carlist prisoners. For a brief space success once more attended the Carlist arms, and under General Gómez the supporters of Don Carlos actually reached the gates of Madrid. There was, however, no general rising, as had been anticipated, and Gómez fell back to the mountains of the North. A similar attempt under the command of Don Carlos himself met with a like failure, though for a few days it was anticipated by friends and foes alike that Charles V would enter his capital.

After two years of desultory fighting the Convention of Vergara in 1839 put an end to the war in the Basque provinces, but it was not until the following year that hostilities were terminated in Aragón and Valencia by the withdrawal of Cabrera into France. The first Carlist war was over, but the divisions which it had caused in Spanish national life remained.

When Ferdinand died the Prime Minister was Zea Bermúdez, and at first he and the Regent showed little inclination to change the method of government; but, as has been said, Cristina soon discovered that without the support of the Liberals she would be unable to withstand Don Carlos, and to gain the help she needed she was compelled to move to the Left. Zea Bermúdez made way for a Prime Minister of more moderate tendencies, and in 1834 the Royal Statute was promulgated; but this document was little more than a translation of the *Charte* which Louis XVIII had issued on his restoration, and it failed to satisfy the Liberals.

More serious still was the disaffection which, about this time, became noticeable among the troops, and resulted in the *pronunciamientos*. The apostles of Liberalism in the army were the sergeants, and owing to the incompetence of the officers (due to the absence in the Carlist ranks of those who would have held commissions) their influence was even greater than is usually the case. The mob of the large towns also became infected with the extreme views which were preached in their midst, and, as in the French Revolution, this fact was responsible for much of the violence that took place. The struggle, however, did not become a social one until a much later date, and on the Liberal as well as on the Conservative side there were to be found some of the noblest families of Spain throughout the whole of the nineteenth century.

In September, 1835, Mendizabal became Prime Minister, and he possessed one advantage over his predecessors in that he was a convinced Liberal, and consequently desired to make constitutional government a reality; but he proved as incompetent as most of the Spanish ministers of this period, and was replaced by a statesman, Isturiz, whose views were more in accordance with those of the Regent. The Radicals, however, had now become definitely revolutionary, and in their efforts to secure a constitution of which they approved they did not hesitate to use force.

Risings took place everywhere, and in a mutiny at La Granja the Regent and Isabel were captured, with the result that the former was compelled to assent to the re-establishment of the Constitution of

1812, and Radicals were appointed to all places of trust. A Constituent Cortes met and passed a measure suppressing nearly two thousand religious houses; but even among its most fervent supporters it was now realised that the Constitution of 1812 was unworkable, and a new one was drawn up. This proved to be much more moderate than had been expected, since it increased the power of the Crown, and also made provision for two chambers; in fact, it was a modification in the Liberal sense of the *Charte*.

The central government, however, was so shaken by mutinies and rebellions that it was quite incapable of performing its duties under any circumstances, and Spain had much to suffer before she obtained a settled administration. The elections held under the new constitution resulted in a Conservative majority, and a measure was at once introduced to limit the franchise. This act caused a military revolt, headed by Espartero, who overthrew the government, and was soon afterwards appointed Regent in place of Cristina.

The history of the reign of Isabel is largely a record of the struggle for power between the three generals, Narváez, O'Donnell, and Espartero. All three worked with various groups in the Cortes, and used their military influence to further the objects of themselves and their political friends, but there was, nevertheless, a considerable difference between them, in character, if not in methods. It has been said that "Espartero rose by making himself the servant of the mob, Narváez by obedience to an earnest but limited sense of duty, O'Donnell tortuously by intrigue and open-eyed pursuit of self-aggrandisement."

Narváez was, above all else, a man of honour, and in an age when treason was the order of the day, his personal integrity remained unquestioned. Espartero was the typical Spaniard, a creature of spasmodic energy, broken by long periods of lethargy, and it was to the fact that he possessed to the full all the virtues and all the failings of his fellow-countrymen that he owed his position among them. As a general he was lucky rather than skilful, and his victories were due not so much to his strategy, as to his popularity with the troops he commanded. O'Donnell was a courtier, and in his pursuit of power he changed sides even more often than most of his contemporaries. In matters of internal policy Narváez leaned to the Right, and Espartero to the Left, while O'Donnell flitted between the two extremes.

The regency of Espartero lasted for two troubled years, and in 1843 he was overthrown by a coalition of Conservatives and discontented Liberals. The decade which followed was marked by a Conservative policy for which first General Narváez, and then Murillo, was responsible, and in 1845 a revision of the Constitution took place which considerably narrowed the bases of the Cortes.

It soon, however, became clear that the reign of Isabel, who had

by now come of age, would resemble the regency of her mother in all
its essential details. There was the same desire on the part of the ruler
to be absolute, and only to accept Liberal measures in the hope of
being able to reverse them in the near future. Isabel's position in any
case was not an easy one, for the traditions of government which had
existed since the days of Ferdinand and Isabel had been rudely
broken by the French invasion, and the restored absolutism had
proved too inefficient when compared with that of Charles III to win
men's minds back to the old ways. On the other hand, the Radicals
and the growing republican party declared that in democracy alone
would Spain find salvation, and as their remedy had never been
tried it was hard to deny their argument.

Above all, there was the difficulty that the larger part of the population was politically apathetic, and those who took any interest in the
government of their country were either Carlists or Radicals. Isabel
had no principle upon which to base her rule, and there was no
section of the community to which she was able to turn for support
with any certainty of finding it, since the middle classes were hardly
yet in existence, and those whose creed was "Church and King" did
not rally round her throne, but marched under the standard of Don
Carlos. In these circumstances the monarchy was forced to rely
on some chance grouping of factions in the Cortes. As if this was
not enough, the army was in a perpetual state of mutiny, and the
generals thought more of seizing the reins of government than of
enforcing discipline among their men.

Isabel's position would thus in any case have been extremely
difficult, but she rendered it hopeless by her scandalous method of
living; the ancient Spanish loyalty to the royal line had been shaken
by the Carlist movement, and the Queen came very near to destroying it altogether.

Meanwhile, the question of the Queen's marriage had given rise
to serious complications both in Spain and abroad. Isabel, together
with her younger sister Luisa, was, by the year 1846, of an age to
marry. The Regent, in default of a suitable Austrian Archduke,
desired to unite both the Queen and her sister with French Princes.
It was, however, objected by the Powers, and chiefly by England,
that the Treaty of Utrecht was still in force, and that Europe could
never tolerate a union between the crowns of France and Spain,
even although both were at that time in possession of monarchs
whose thrones were not based upon the principle of legitimacy.

At first the matter was discussed between the British and French
Governments, and between Queen Victoria and King Louis Philippe.
Lord Aberdeen made it clear that Great Britain would raise no
objection to the marriage of Queen Isabel to one of the descendants
of Philip V, and would refrain from pressing any other candidate;
moreover, in the event of the Queen having children it would not see

any objection to a union between the Duke of Montpensier, a younger son of the King of France, and the Infanta Luisa. On this basis an agreement was reached.

Of the five available Bourbon Princes three were rejected for various reasons, and the choice lay between two cousins of the Queen, namely Francis, Duke of Cádiz, who was favoured by France, and his brother, Henry, who was preferred by England. Isabel herself preferred the latter, but he was hated by the Queen-Mother on account of his Liberal views, and Cristina, therefore, made overtures to Prince Leopold of Coburg. By this means she hoped to create a breach between France and England, and thus secure a French match for both her daughters.

Guizot, who was at that time Prime Minister of France, could not resist the temptation of scoring a diplomatic success, and when Palmerston, who succeeded Aberdeen at the Foreign Office in June, 1846, announced his intention of leaving the Spanish Government free to choose between any of the candidates, Guizot regarded the neutral attitude of England towards the Coburg candidature as a breach of the agreement, and persuaded Louis Philippe to agree to the policy which he desired.

In consequence, the simultaneous marriage took place of the Queen with the Duke of Cádiz and the Infanta with the Duke of Montpensier. This was the famous affair of the "Spanish Marriages," which broke the Entente between England and France, and was also a powerful factor in precipitating the fall of the July Monarchy. In spite, however, of the diplomacy of Louis Philippe and Guizot, the French Prince was not destined to wear the crown of Spain, for Isabel had children of her own.

In 1854 the Conservative regime came to an end owing to a military revolt headed by O'Donnell, and Espartero became Prime Minister for a time, only, however, shortly to be overthrown by O'Donnell, who then governed Spain for five years with greater success than had marked the efforts of any of his immediate predecessors. In many ways O'Donnell's government may be compared with that of General Primo de Rivera two generations later, and it gave the country a much-needed rest from *pronunciamientos* and the strife of parties.

A settlement was reached with the Church in regard to its property and other matters which had been in dispute since the beginning of the reign. By this agreement the Pope recognised the validity of the sale of such Church lands as had already been sold, and he consented to the disposal of the remainder on condition that the proceeds should be handed over to the Church in the form of inalienable 3 per cent bonds.

Meanwhile, the prosperity of the country had increased even during the disturbed period which followed the termination of the

Carlist War, and the rate of increase was now considerably accelerated. Between 1848 and 1864 Spanish commerce more than trebled,
many railways were built, and extensive public works were undertaken.

The weakness of the Liberal Union, as the administration of
O'Donnell was termed, was its finance. The budgets of 1859 and 1860
showed a surplus as usual, but it was entirely fictitious. The floating
debt amounted to seven million pounds, and taxation was excessive.
As for the huge sums which had been obtained by the sale of Church
lands, in accordance with the agreement with the Pope, they simply
faded away.

O'Donnell realised that his position was by no means so secure
as might appear on the surface, and he decided to strengthen it, as
well as distract his fellow-countrymen from their internal dissensions, by adopting a spirited foreign policy. Already in 1857 a small
expedition had been sent to co-operate with the French in avenging
the murder of missionaries in Cochin China, and the Spanish troops
had fought with the valour which they always display when properly
led.

As it happened, there was a force of some 100,000 men available.
A threat of intervention by the United States in Cuba had necessitated the strengthening of the Spanish army, while on the outbreak
of war in Italy in 1859, a further increase had been made. Spain,
however, although she protested against the dethronement of the
Duke of Parma, did not interfere to prevent it, and O'Donnell
decided to use the troops for a war against Morocco. Relations
between Spain and the Moors were even worse than usual, and
O'Donnell seized his chance of embarking upon a crusade. The
Sultan of Morocco was conciliatory, but O'Donnell was determined
upon war, although, even before it was declared, he had to give a
promise to Great Britain that Spain would seek no territorial
aggrandisement.

The war began in October, 1859, and the Spaniards advanced from
Ceuta under the command of O'Donnell himself. The campaign
was sadly mismanaged, but the Spanish troops, as usual, fought well,
in spite of bad generalship, and after capturing Tetuán, they arrived
within a short distance of Fez. Meanwhile a Carlist rising had taken
place in the Peninsula, and Great Britain was drawing the Spanish
Government's attention to its promise. In these circumstances peace
was made in April, 1860, and Spain obtained little more than an
indemnity and a treaty of commerce.

Nevertheless, O'Donnell's taste for adventure had been whetted
rather than satiated, and in 1861 two further opportunities came his
way. The republic of San Domingo had grown weary of the attempt
to govern itself, and, in the hope of obtaining protection against its
neighbour, Haiti, it applied for re-admission to the Spanish monarchy. Accordingly, the repentant republic was re-incorporated by

decree, and it was hoped in Spain that this marked the first step in the re-establishment of Spanish rule in America. These hopes were completely ruined by the tactlessness of those who were sent to administer the country, for a swarm of functionaries from Cuba swooped down upon the island, and treated it as if it were a conquered province. The result was a general insurrection against the Spaniards, and after having wasted the lives of 10,000 soldiers and a sum of £4,000,000, Spain was, in 1865, obliged to relinquish her hold upon San Domingo.

In the same year that saw San Domingo temporarily re-united to Spain, O'Donnell joined with Great Britain and France in sending a force to Mexico to preserve the rights of the foreign bond-holders. Spain, however, withdrew from this venture at the same time as Great Britain, and left the French to attempt the conquest of Mexico on their own.

In February, 1863, O'Donnell resigned on account of the Queen's refusal to recognise the new Italian kingdom. He left the country restless in spite of his spirited foreign policy, for not one of the questions that vexed it had been solved, and the old animosities were unappeased.

The five years that intervened between the resignation of O'Donnell and the fall of the dynasty saw several governments in office. They also witnessed the emergence of new men, such as General Prim, Antonio Cánovas del Castillo, Emilio Castelar, and Serrano; the last of these had, it is true, been closely connected with the Queen personally, but it was only now that he made his appearance in the political arena. Unfortunately, the successors of O'Donnell shared his partiality for foreign adventures, and a needless conflict with Chile and Peru was the consequence in 1865–1866.

Admiral Pareja bombarded Valparaiso and Callao, but all that Spain gained from these operations, which revived the old colonial hatred of her in full force, was an indemnity from Peru on condition that the latter's independence was formally recognised. These wars also reduced Spanish credit abroad to the lowest ebb, and when the government of the day endeavoured to float a loan in Paris and London it was met with a blank refusal.

During these years the position of the throne was growing steadily weaker. In the earlier part of Isabella's reign the Left had been content to attack the ministers, but now it began to direct its fire upon the dynasty itself. There were several reasons for this. The private life of the Queen had become more scandalous than ever, and if her children were undoubted Bourbons on their mother's side there was only too much reason for conjecture where their father was concerned. At this time, too, both Narváez and O'Donnell died. With all their faults, both were loyal subjects of Isabel, while Castelar was a republican, and Prim had been personally offended by the Queen.

More than ever did the monarchy feel the want, owing to the Carlist schism, of its natural supports. The Church, weakened by its divisions, had lost much of its old influence, as well as most of its wealth, and the most fervently monarchist part of the country, the Basque Provinces and Navarre, watched with glee the increasing difficulties of her whom they regarded as a usurper. By 1868 the monarchy had become a mere *façade*.

When the end came it came, as was also to be the case in 1931, quickly. In 1866 a mutiny of the artillery, the *corps d'élite*, in Madrid was only suppressed with the greatest difficulty, and after much blood had been shed on both sides. Narváez was called to power to stem the rising tide of disorder; but he died, and González Bravo was installed as Prime Minister, or rather dictator, in his place. A man of strong views and great courage, he declared that he would make the generals bend their gaudy backs before his plain coat, and he proceeded to banish all the leaders of the Liberal Union who were still in Spain. His next step was to alienate the navy by drastic economies, and this drove Admiral Topete and his officers to make common cause with the exiles.

By now the throne was quite isolated. The Duke of Montpensier and his wife were negotiating with the revolutionaries in the hope of securing the succession for themselves, while Sagasta, one of the leaders of the Left, went to England to see Cabrera in the hope of enlisting the support of the Carlists: the latter, however, would not conclude an alliance with the Liberals, and placed their principles before expediency.

The final blow to the regime was struck by Topete, who first of all arranged for the return of the revolutionaries, and then, on September 18, 1868, he made his *pronunciamiento* at Cádiz. Together with Serrano, Prim, Sagasta, and some others, he issued a manifesto which was sufficiently vague to unite all the opponents of Isabel, but which carefully refrained from stating whom or what it was proposed to put in her place. It naturally declared that an era of social and political regeneration had been inaugurated, and it curiously observed that the considerations which decided the most important questions should be such as could be named before mothers, wives, and daughters.

Once the movement became known it spread, and the Queen, who was at San Sebastian, realised its seriousness, if not its danger. The issue was decided by a skirmish, for at the Bridge of Alcolea, on the Guadalquivir, General Pavia was forced by the insurgents to fall back, and this opened to the latter the way to the capital. No further resistance was attempted in any quarter, and on September 30 Isabel crossed the Bidassoa into France, exclaiming, "I thought I had struck deeper roots in this land."

The revolution of 1868 marked the end of old Spain. Isabel and, before her, Cristina had endeavoured to hold the balance even between it and the forces which had been unloosed by the French Revolution, and for which the way had to no inconsiderable extent been paved by the earlier Bourbons. Circumstances, due almost entirely to the Carlist split, had been too much for them, and henceforth the destinies of the country were to be in the hands of those who, whatever the regime, based their government upon a set of ideas that were, not Spanish, but foreign, in their origin.

CHAPTER XXXIX

The Troublous Times (1868–1885)

So long as the work of those who were opposed to the Bourbons was merely destructive it was not difficult to get them to agree, but when the time came to put forward definitely constructive proposals the fundamental differences of opinion among them were at once revealed. While the streets of Madrid were adorned with posters announcing "the everlasting downfall of the spurious Bourbon race," a Provisional Government was formed with Serrano at its head, and consisting of Prim, Topete, Sagasta, Ruiz Zorrilla, and López de Ayala.

When this had been accomplished two manifestoes were issued by the Cabinet, one for the benefit of the Powers, and the other addressed to the Spanish people. The first was a long and verbose account of the causes and aims of the revolution which had dethroned Isabel, while the second was little more than a general statement of Liberal principles, with an occasional reference to the political situation in Spain. It did, however, make clear that the new constitution was to be monarchical, though the throne was to be occupied by another dynasty than the Bourbons, and whoever was chosen as King would exercise very little power.

The next step was to convene a Constituent Cortes, and in the elections for this body the Provisional Government obtained an overwhelming majority. A few republicans, such as Castelar, and Carlists were returned, but there was hardly a deputy who would confess himself an avowed supporter of the fallen dynasty. As soon as the Constituent Cortes had met, it proceeded to draw up a constitution, a task which it accomplished in the remarkably short space of a month.

The document in question contained nothing original, and it was little more than an amalgam of the various Liberal constitutions which had been adopted at one time or another since 1812. Spain was declared to be a strictly limited monarchy, with the real power vested in two Chambers. The influence of the Church was directly attacked in the clauses which established civil marriage and guaranteed freedom of worship. The jury system was also adopted, and individual liberty was declared inviolable. The new constitution was in due course voted by 214 to 55 votes, and it was promulgated in June, 1869.

As the Constituent Cortes had voted in favour of a monarchy Serrano proceeded to call himself Regent, and Prim became Prime Minister. It was not long, however, before it became obvious that the new constitution had not satisfied anybody. The vast majority of the nation was revolted by its anti-clericalism, and in their despair of the restoration of Isabel many leaders of the Right turned to the Carlists as their only hope.

At the same time those who had been most prominent in the revolution of the preceding year derided the provisions of the constitution as hopelessly inadequate, and began to drift into the ranks of the republicans. Castelar, incomparably the greatest orator in Spain, addressed enormous gatherings, and the Cabinet did not dare to take any measures against him. The prevailing unrest made itself felt in all quarters, and at Cádiz and Málaga there were risings. Spain was breaking up.

The constitution having been voted, it now became necessary to find a King, and in the autumn of 1869 Serrano and Prim began the search for one. There were several obvious candidates, namely Alfonso, the Prince of Asturias, and son of Isabel; Don Carlos, the grandson of the original claimant, and now the head of the Carlist branch; the Duke of Montpensier; and Espartero.

The first two were barred, among other reasons, by the recent law which excluded the Bourbons from the throne. This exclusion also applied to Montpensier, who was also generally unpopular, and who was shortly to set the seal upon the suspicion with which he was regarded by killing in a duel the Duke of Seville, the brother-in-law of Isabel. As for Espartero, he could have had the throne for the asking, but he was an old man, and it is to his credit that when he had to make the choice he refused to supplant her whom he had always considered to be his lawful sovereign. The Spanish candidates having been all eliminated, it remained for the king-makers to try their luck abroad, and the crown of Spain was accordingly hawked round Europe.

The Pan-Iberians persuaded Serrano and Prim to offer the throne to King Luis of Portugal, but he refused, and announced his intention of dying, as he had been born, a Portuguese. The next to be approached was the King-dowager of Portugal, Ferdinand of Saxe-Coburg, a cousin of Queen Victoria. For a time he entertained the proposition, and both Napoleon III and the Spanish Provisional Government pressed him to accept. Finally, he, too, refused, chiefly because of the violent opposition that was beginning to manifest itself in Portugal towards any possible union of the crowns. This obliged Serrano and Prim to go even farther afield, and they then offered the vacant throne to Leopold of Hohenzollern-Sigmaringen. He also declined, but his candidature was the cause of the Franco-German War and the fall of the Second Empire.

By this time two years had passed since the flight of Isabella, and Spain was becoming restless. In despair recourse was had to the Royal Family of Italy, and, after the Duke of Genoa had declined the crown, Amadeo, the second son of Victor Emmanuel II, accepted it. In spite of the strongest pressure in the Constituent Cortes only 191 votes out of 311 were cast in his favour, while of the minority 63 voted for a republic, 27 for the Duke of Montpensier, 1 for the Duchess, 8 for Espartero, 2 for Alfonso, and there were 19 blanks. Meanwhile, in June, 1870, Isabel had abdicated, and those who had remained loyal to her saluted the young Prince of Asturias as King Alfonso XII.

King Amadeo was twenty-six years of age when, in January, 1871, he arrived in his capital. He was, like all the members of the House of Savoy, supremely conscientious, and he was determined not to overstep the limits which the constitution prescribed. In spite of his admirable personal qualities his position was hopeless from the start. The first news that greeted him was that Prim, who would have been the mainstay of his throne, had been murdered in the streets of Madrid, and there was no one to take his place.

The King himself was anathema to innumerable Spaniards as the scion of a dynasty that had risen to power on the overthrow not only of two Spanish sovereigns, the King of Naples and the Duke of Parma, but also on the seizure of the Pope's dominions. The aristocracy boycotted the new court from the beginning, and although the republicans, Carlists, and Alfonsists had nothing else in common, they united to make any prolonged occupation of the throne by Amadeo an impossibility. The second *rey intruso* was no more popular than the first.

The King entrusted Serrano with the formation of a ministry which should be a coalition of all those who supported the regime. A Cabinet on these lines was constituted, but an appeal to the country resulted in the return of an increased number of Carlists and republicans, and the government was defeated in the Cortes on the reply to the address from the throne. The result of this was a split in the ranks of Amadeo's supporters, and the short-lived administrations of Ruiz Zorrilla and Malcampo followed.

The next Prime Minister was Sagasta, who was determined to retrieve the situation if that were possible, and at the elections in April, 1872, he exerted an official pressure hitherto unknown even in Spanish history. He secured a majority of sorts, but on the morrow of his victory he had to resign owing to a charge of embezzlement in respect of a sum of £20,000 which had disappeared from the Colonial Office. Sagasta was succeeded by Serrano, who almost immediately had to give place to Zorrilla. The new Prime Minister dissolved the Cortes, and obtained a majority, but it was in no way representative of the true sentiments of Spain, which was for the most part either Carlist or republican by this time. The supporters of Don Carlos were already in arms, and the republicans now proceeded to riot both in Madrid and Ferrol.

There can be little doubt but that by now Amadeo had realised that he could not remain on the throne much longer, and he had already narrowly escaped one attempt to murder him, at the instigation, it was rumoured, of the Duke of Montpensier.

What finally brought the experiment to an end was not a clash of general principles, but a departmental squabble. Zorrilla had persuaded the King to confer a high command upon General Hidalgo, who had sided with the rebels at the time of the mutiny in the artillery in 1866. He was accordingly detested by his brother officers, who refused to serve under him in his new capacity, and proceeded to resign their commissions. Zorrilla's reply was to dissolve the artillery corps, and to promote non-commissioned officers to fill the vacancies.

Amadeo signed the necessary decree, although he did not approve of it, and at the same time he announced his own abdication. On February 12, 1873, he left Spain, and among the papers which he did not sign before his departure, although presented for his signature, was one conferring the Golden Fleece upon Zorrilla.

As soon as the abdication of the King became known, the two Chambers of the Cortes quite illegally coalesced, and declared themselves to be the National Assembly. In spite of the fact that only four months before their members had, with a few exceptions, been elected as monarchists, they then voted a republic by 258 votes to 32, and on the very day on which Amadeo left Madrid four of his late ministers were already holding office under the First Republic.

The establishment of a republican regime met with no opposition, but by the time that it took place the state of Spain was chaotic. Almost the whole of the North acknowledged Don Carlos; Barcelona had become practically autonomous; and in Andalusia the wildest anarchy prevailed, and Socialist agitators were the real rulers of that province. As if this were not enough, the republicans were hopelessly divided among themselves. Pi y Margall wished a federal republic, like the United States. Castelar wanted the republic to be unitary but Radical, as France was soon to become. Salmerón and Serrano were for a conservative republic, such as France actually was. Lastly, Pavia desired a military dictatorship under republican forms.

First of all a government of concentration was formed, with Figueras at its head, but after a few weeks it broke up, and the federalists came into office. The President, Figueras, thereupon left the country without even the formality of announcing his intentions to his colleagues, and his place was taken by Pi y Margall. Meanwhile, fresh elections had been held for the Cortes, but only a third of those entitled to vote had done so. Nevertheless, the Constituent Cortes, the sixth of the century, decided by 210 votes against 2 that Spain should be a republic.

While these events were taking place in Madrid the anarchy in the provinces was growing steadily worse, and by July the cities of Málaga, Seville, Cádiz, and Granada had become almost independent under the name of cantons. Catalonia and Valencia took the necessary steps to cut themselves off from the rest of Spain, and the latter established its own fiscal frontiers. Everywhere the troops mutinied (in many cases shooting their officers), priests were attacked and murdered, and in many instances private property was abolished.

The worst scenes were enacted at Cartagena, where the army and fleet joined the revolutionaries, and the latter was only prevented by British men-of-war from embarking upon a course of piracy. Finally, in the interests of international peace, the British authorities took possession of the Spanish ships, and interned them at Gibraltar after landing their crews. In the midst of this confusion there were two more changes of ministry: Pi y Margall was replaced by Salmerón, and two months later, in September, 1873, the latter, in his turn, had to make way for Castelar.

Both Salmerón and Castelar realised, unlike their predecessors, that order must be restored, and the former sent Pavia into Andalusia with a handful of troops that could still be trusted. In a few weeks Cordova, Seville, Cádiz, and Granada were in Pavia's hands, and the general was only prevented by the timidity of Salmerón from capturing Málaga at the same time. Castelar proved bolder, so that by the end of September that sea-port was in Pavia's possession, and cantonalism in Andalusia was at an end.

These measures were by no means pleasing to the majority in the Cortes, and Pavia urged Castelar to execute a *coup d'état*, but the President refused. On January 2, 1874, Castelar was defeated in the Cortes, and a few hours afterwards Pavia's soldiers cleared the deputies out of the Chamber. For a moment the general thought of making himself dictator, but he finally handed the reins of power over to Serrano, who proceeded to try to run the republic along the conservative lines which he had always advocated.

The state of the country by this time was desperate. At Cartagena the red flag still floated over the city and the arsenal. There were 200,000 troops in arms against the Carlists, who were nevertheless masters of three provinces, and there were 80,000 more in Cuba, vainly attempting to suppress a rebellion which had broken out there. As the year went on the situation grew steadily worse, and the credit of Spain abroad reflected the chaos at home. By the end of December, 1873, the 3 per cent Exterior Debt had already sunk to $17\frac{1}{4}$ on the London Stock Exchange, and the coupons on this issue remained unpaid for eighteen months, having to be refunded later by the government of the Restoration.

Serrano suspended the constitution, dissolved the Constituent Cortes, and announced that elections would not be held until the country was completely pacified. He then took the field against the Carlists, and it was the danger from that quarter which kept the republic alive until the end of the year, for the Alfonsists had no desire to overthrow the existing regime until they were quite certain that its successor would not be Charles VII, but Alfonso XII. As for the mass of the population, it was only weary of the anarchy which had become synonymous with republicanism, and it was prepared to accept either Don Carlos or Don Alfonso in return for the blessings of peace and security.

When it became clear by the autumn that the Carlists had shot their bolt the Alfonsists began to stir, and Serrano took no effective measures to restrict their propaganda. Alfonso himself issued a manifesto, drawn up by Cánovas, in which he declared himself a good Spaniard, a good Catholic, and a Liberal, but Cánovas deprecated anything in the nature of precipitate action, and he desired, above all else, that his master should be restored by civilians. The monarchist generals refused to consult the wishes of Cánovas, and on December 29, 1874, General Martínez Campos proclaimed Alfonso XII at Sagunto. The troops in that part of Spain at once accepted the *pronunciamiento*, and the Captain-General of Valencia, though not adhering to the movement himself, placed no obstacles in its way.

When the news of what had happened reached Madrid, the acting head of the government, Sagasta, consulted with the Captain-General, Primo de Rivera. The latter declared that he was astonished at what had taken place, so Sagasta put Cánovas in prison, and issued a proclamation to reassure the country. Within a few hours, however, the garrison of the capital declared for the *pronunciamiento*, and Primo de Rivera compelled the resignation of the Cabinet. As for the President, Serrano, he refused to return to Madrid, and when he saw the course which events were taking, he despatched a large number of telegrams to Sagasta, and then left the country.

A provisional council, with Cánovas as its head, was formed to take over the administration, and the newspapers were full of protestations of loyalty to the new King from those who forty-eight hours before had telegraphed their determination to defend the republic with their lives. Alfonso himself was in Paris when the news reached him, but he arrived at Barcelona on January 9, and entered his capital five days later.

The new King had been born in 1857, and was thus little more than a boy when he came into his inheritance. He had been educated at Sandhurst, and had also travelled extensively. During his short reign he gave evidence of qualities which would have made him an extremely capable monarch had his life been prolonged.

From the beginning he showed himself to be a patriotic Spaniard, and he never hesitated to do all in his power to alleviate the sufferings of his people. He had little opportunity to show what he could do, for Cánovas dominated the Spanish scene during the ten years he was on the throne, but by the time of his death he had already proved himself to be an apt pupil of that great statesman. On all occasions he displayed a marked inclination to moderation and mercy, and in this way he rallied to the support of the monarchy many who had previously been numbered among its enemies. Above all, his example did much to revive that respect for the throne which his mother's public and private life had unhappily alienated.

The first task of the restored monarchy was to put an end to the Second Carlist War.

There had been more than one Carlist rising, notably in 1846 and 1848, since the first Don Carlos had been compelled to abandon the fight, and in 1860 two of the Carlist Princes had been captured during an abortive attempt in Catalonia. In 1872, the Basque Provinces again took up arms, and Don Carlos was soon at the head of 14,000 men, but he was defeated by Serrano at Oroquieta, and the Convention of Amoravieta brought the insurrection to an end. The proclamation of the republic rekindled it, and for some months it seemed as if Don Carlos must inevitably achieve his purpose.

The republicans were soon holding even the line of the Ebro with the greatest difficulty, and although the Carlists failed once more to take Bilbao, their position in the Basque Provinces and Navarre was quite unshaken. In Catalonia and Valencia, too, Don Carlos had many adherents, and he sent his brother, Don Alfonso, to command in this quarter. At one moment the latter actually got as far as Cuenca, only twenty-two leagues from Madrid, but the outrages of his followers prevented those who would have joined him from doing so. Don Alfonso, despairing of making his Catalan supporters obey the rules of civilised warfare, withdrew from the field, and henceforth the war was confined to the North, though for some time longer there continued to be bands of marauders, who called themselves Carlists, in the other provinces.

The restoration of the monarchy proved that Don Carlos had missed his chance. It also deprived him of the support of many who were prepared to accept him as the only method of overturning the republic, while the Papal recognition of Alfonso XII weakened his position with the clergy and with no inconsiderable section of the laity. The King appeared among his troops in person, and in March, 1875, Cabrera deserted the Carlist cause.

This defection was the beginning of the end, although there was much hard fighting before the insurrection was crushed. All through the year 1875 the Carlists were pushed steadily back, but it was not until the beginning of 1876 that Primo de Rivera succeeded in capturing Estella, their headquarters. In March, Don Carlos, who had never failed to show himself worthy of the sacrifices that were made for him, was obliged to cross the frontier, and the Second Carlist War was over. The Basques lost their *fueros* for ever, but they were accorded certain privileges in the matter of taxation. Nevertheless, if Carlism had been defeated in the field, its spirit survived, and was to prove an important factor when another republic came into being.

It was not until March, 1876, that the new Constitution was brought forward by Cánovas in the Cortes, and it was to a large extent modelled upon that of Great Britain. Legislation was vested in a Cortes of two Chambers with the King, and the Chambers were of equal authority. The Senate consisted of eighty senators in their own right, a hundred nominated by the Crown, and a hundred and eighty elected by local bodies, the universities, and taxpayers of the highest class. One half of the elected senators were renewed every fifth year. The Chamber was elected by districts of 50,000 inhabitants, but it was not until 1890 that there was adult suffrage, and even then the vote was limited to men. There was also, in the larger towns, a form of proportional representation. The King alone had the right to summon, prorogue, and dissolve the Cortes, but a dissolution had to be followed by the assembly of a new Chamber within three months. The King was irresponsible, but his decrees had to be countersigned by a responsible minister.

The Constitution remained in force until the *coup d'état* of General Primo de Rivera in 1923. Theoretically it left little to be desired, but in the last resort it depended for successful working upon the willing co-operation of the Spanish people, and this condition was never fulfilled. Cánovas himself did not believe that his fellow-countrymen were ready for such a Constitution, but he hoped that with the passage of time it would take root. In this he was disappointed. What happened was that the political life of Spain became a hollow sham. There were two main parties in the Cortes, the Conservatives and the Liberals, led respectively by Cánovas and Sagasta, and they alternated in office as parties of the same name were doing in contemporary England. The elections were shamelessly "made" in order to give a majority to one side or the other, for the two leaders were working together to ensure that there should be an outward appearance of normal constitutional life. So long as Cánovas and Sagasta lived this illusion was sustained, but when they died the parties began to break up into groups, and as the system had no secure foundations it was very soon completely undermined.

The end at which Cánovas aimed may, or may not, have justified the means which he employed to achieve it, but the means remained long after the end had been forgotten, and the means were the "making" of the elections. The vast majority of the electorate was unable to read or write, and power in the constituencies was in the hands of the *cacique*, who resembled the "boss" of American, and the "great elector" of Italian, politics. The corruption which this system produced can easily be imagined, and it extended to the local authorities as well. During the course of an enquiry held by the Directory of General Primo de Rivera, for example, it was found that in Murcia there had been no entry in the day-books or ledgers of the municipal accounts for years; in Orense the windows of the hospital were never mended; and in Palencia there was no heating in the local maternity hospital, although it was 3,000 feet above sea-level. Such examples might be multiplied indefinitely, and all over Spain only a small proportion of the money voted for any particular purpose ever reached it. There was no awakening of the national consciousness to these abuses, though it is to be noted that the personal honesty of the ordinary Spaniard remained uncontaminated by the venality of his politicians.

On the whole the country was quieter than it had been since the death of Charles III. In 1883 there was an attempted republican *pronunciamiento* at Badajoz, largely due to the machinations of Ruiz Zorrilla, who had completely boxed the political compass since the days when he was an aspirant for the Golden Fleece, but the movement met with no support elsewhere. More serious was the agitation in Andalusia of the *Mano Negra* and *Tribunal Popular*, anarchical secret societies that preached Communism, and reinforced their teaching with murder and arson. Sagasta was in power when the propaganda was most serious, but the Liberal leader showed no hesitation in adopting strong measures against it.

In 1885 there were severe earthquakes in the South, and in the province of Granada alone 5400 buildings were destroyed, and nearly 700 lives were lost. A few months later there was a serious outbreak of cholera, in which over 100,000 people perished. On both occasions the King visited the afflicted areas, at great personal risk, and in the second instance in direct opposition to the wishes of his ministers. In spite, however, of these visitations Spain continued to progress, and the funest inheritance of the republic was gradually liquidated.

In foreign affairs both Cánovas and Sagasta looked towards Germany rather than towards France, and in 1883 a commercial agreement with the former Power was considered as the prelude to a political understanding, and to the inclusion of Spain in the Triple Alliance. In the same year the King attended the German manœuvres, and accepted the colonelcy of a Uhlan regiment stationed at Strassburg. French irritation became fiercer than ever, and on his return through Paris the King met with so frankly hostile a demonstration, that diplomatic relations between France and Spain came within an ace of being suspended. Wiser counsels happily prevailed, and the incident was soon forgotten.

Two years later Spain came dangerously near to war with Germany herself. The commander of a German gun-boat hoisted his flag on the Caroline Island of Yap, and alleged in support of his action that the Spanish claim to the archipelago had never been rendered effective by occupation, while his fellow-countrymen had long had a factory there. When the news of what had happened reached Spain the Press set itself out to rouse popular indignation, with the result that the Madrid mob attacked the German Legation, tore down its flagstaff and escutcheon, and burned them in the Puerta del Sol. Bismarck, however, had no desire to throw Spain into the arms of

France, and he showed himself most conciliatory. Germany therefore accepted the Spanish apology for the insult in Madrid, and the question of the ownership of the Caroline Islands was referred to the arbitration of the Pope, while the Spanish flag was to fly at Yap pending the Papal verdict.

In the autumn of 1885 the King's health, never very robust, began to fail. His visit to the zone affected by the earthquakes, made in the midst of a very hard winter, and to the districts stricken with cholera, had been too much for him: when he caught bronchitis in November, 1885, he had not the strength to shake it off, and on the 25th of that month he died.

Alfonso was twice married. In 1878 he married Mercédes, his cousin, and the second daughter of the Duke of Montpensier. It was a popular match, for the new Queen was a Spaniard, and it had clearly been dictated, so far as Alfonso was concerned, by affection rather than by considerations of policy. The rejoicings at the wedding had hardly ended when Mercédes died of fever. The King was overwhelmed with grief, and he seemed to lose interest in life from that moment. In November, 1879, he married Maria Cristina, daughter of the Archduke Ranier of Austria, and the wedding took place at the same time that great floods were devastating Murcia and Orihuela, so, in accordance with the royal orders, the money that was to have been spent upon the marriage festivities was diverted to aid the sufferers in the disaster.

When the King died he left two daughters, while the Queen was with child. That his widow was able to overcome the domestic difficulties of her Regency, as well as the complications of the Spanish-American War, was in no small measure due to the support which her husband had won for the throne, and for the old respect which he had so successfully revived. It is true that he was fortunate in his ministers, especially Cánovas and Sagasta, but he had the good sense to appreciate their worth. In fine, Alfonso XII found Spain in a state of chaos, moral, social, and political, after her republican experience; he left her at peace, and making considerable material progress, so that he well deserved his title of *El Pacificador*.

CHAPTER XL

The Regency (1885–1902)

THE death of Alfonso XII caused a momentary drop of thirteen points in the Spanish funds, but it called forth all the innate chivalry in the national character. The leaders of the various parties agreed upon a political truce, and Sagasta took office at the head of a ministry that lasted with little change for five years.

The Carlists were restless at first, but the strong support which the Powers and the Vatican gave to the Regency obliged them to refrain from any attempt to turn the existing situation to their advantage. As for the republicans, not only was the memory of their failure still too fresh to make them a danger, but they were divided into four sections, led respectively by Castelar, Salmerón, Pi y Margall, and Ruiz Zorrilla. Castelar alone might have united them, but he flatly refused to consider even a provisional scheme for common action. Nevertheless, the only disturbance that did take place came from this quarter, for, in January, 1886, some civilians unsuccessfully tried to bring about a rising at Cartagena, and in the following September General Villacampa attempted a republican *pronunciamiento*.

For the rest, the peace of the country was undisturbed, and the birth of Alfonso XIII on May 17, 1886, was acclaimed by a nation that was more united than it had been for a century.

The fact that the political truce lasted not only for a year or two, but for the whole of the Regency, was mainly due to the Regent. Maria Cristina was one of the most remarkable women of her age. She was a foreigner, and at the time of her husband's death she was unknown, but gradually she won the respect of all classes of the Spanish people. The most selfish of politicians came to serve her loyally, and by her tolerance and her wisdom she continued the work of her husband in rallying to the monarchy many who had been its bitterest enemies. Castelar himself gave his support to Sagasta. Evidence of the Regent's popularity was seen when the King had a severe illness, in early childhood, for all Spain rejoiced with his mother at his recovery.

Her only enemies were certain members of the Royal Family. The Infanta Isabel was asked to leave the country in 1888, and the Duke of Seville was banished to the Balearic Islands for some years for libelling the Regent. In spite, however, of these intrigues the Queen succeeded in weathering the storms which she encountered, and it was largely due to her nobility of character that, when Alfonso XIII came of age in 1902, he found the throne even more secure than it had been at the death of his father.

In domestic affairs the period of the Regency was uneventful.

Both Cánovas and Sagasta showed a firm front to all attempts on the part of the army to place itself above the ordinary law, and they refused to allow cases in which the army and newspapers were concerned to be tried by court-martial, as the military chiefs were demanding. In 1890 universal suffrage was established, but it made little difference in the general political situation except in Madrid, where in 1893 the republicans captured six out of the eight seats. The fact was that the Conservative and Liberal parties had been indulging in mock-fighting for so long that there was now little difference between them, and a change of government meant but little change of policy.

Moreover, with the grant of universal suffrage political questions ceased to agitate the country, and the real danger to the existing order was the rise of Socialism of a particularly violent type in the nineties. Barcelona became the headquarters of this movement, and in 1892 there took place the first case of bomb-throwing in that city. In the following year Martínez Campos was wounded there by the explosion of a bomb, while another thrown into a theatre killed twenty people. At the elections in 1893 there were twenty-one Socialist deputies returned to the Cortes.

Foreign affairs were dominated by the problem of Cuba and the embittered relations with the United States which resulted from it, but there were also complications in Morocco during the period of the Regency. In 1887 the probable death of the Sultan caused Spain to increase her African garrisons, and when this event did not take place the Moors themselves appealed to the Spanish government to reassemble the conference which had met in Madrid in 1880 and had fixed the relations of Morocco and the Powers. This was done, and as a reward for the initiative displayed by Spain her legations in London, Vienna, Berlin, and Rome were raised to the status of embassies.

Unfortunately the relations between Spain and the Sultan of Morocco did not remain for long on a friendly basis, and some acts of aggression by the Riffs in the neighbourhood of Melilla in 1893 very nearly caused a breach. An army of 25,000 men under twenty-nine generals was hastily assembled, and Martínez Campos was appointed to the supreme command. This display of force induced the Sultan to disown the action of the Riffs, and he sent envoys to Madrid to ratify an agreement by which he had promised an indemnity. Unhappily an inebriated Spanish general struck one of the Moors in the face on his way to an audience of the Regent, and as compensation for this affront Spain had to be content with a reduced indemnity. In other matters, in view of the dangers at home, the Regency abandoned the active foreign policy by which Alfonso XII had sought to raise the prestige of the country.

The Cuban problem had perplexed more than one government

before the Regency, and in 1868 an insurrection broke out in the island which was not suppressed for ten years. In the middle of the struggle the United States complained in a note to the Powers of the continued anarchy in Cuba, and although it took no further action, this step was sufficiently significant. In due course slavery was abolished, but there were too many sinecures in the island to allow any government seriously to tackle the question of administrative reform.

Almost the first political event of the Regency had been the rejection by the Cortes, by 227 votes to 17, of a proposal in this sense brought forward by the Cuban deputies. This vote proved to the Cubans that it was quite hopeless for them to expect redress by legal means, for the vested interests were too strong. Furthermore, Cuba was a closed market for the Catalan manufacturers, and no Spanish government would dare to defy Catalonia.

In 1895 another rebellion broke out, and Martínez Campos was sent from Spain with an army to repress it. He completely failed in this task, and was succeeded by General Weyler, who established a system of concentration camps. These events seriously affected public opinion in the United States, for American investments in Cuba were considerable, and it was plain that it would require but very little to precipitate war. It was not long before the clash came.

On the night of February 15, 1898, the United States battleship *Maine*, which had been in Cuban waters for some months for the purpose of protecting American citizens, was destroyed by an explosion in the port of Havana, and 266 of her crew perished. This event roused excitement in both Spain and the United States to the highest pitch. The American Consul reported that the explosion was due to a submarine mine, which the Spaniards denied, but offered to assist an enquiry into its causes. The United States refused to participate, and its experts reported that the explosion took place outside the ship. The Spanish experts, on the other hand, declared that it had taken place inside, through the ignition of the *Maine's* ammunition.

By this time war was inevitable, and the United States, largely under the influence of its Press, had been preparing to fight for some months past. All attempts at mediation had been made in vain. On April 1 the President reported that Spain had sent an unsatisfactory reply to his message which had demanded an armistice in Cuba, the abandonment of the system of concentration camps, and the proper distribution of relief funds subscribed in the United States. On April 11 he asked Congress for permission to use the army and navy to put an end to the war in Cuba, and nine days later the desired powers were granted. Congress declared the Cubans a free people, and called upon Spain to evacuate the island, but at the same time disclaimed all intention of acquiring territorial rights. A state of war existed virtually from April 21, though it was not formally declared by Spain until three days later.

There was a large, but disorganised, Spanish army in Cuba, and there was a considerable force in the Philippine Islands, while three Spanish squadrons were at sea. Admiral Cámara commanded the reserve squadron at home, Admiral Cervera the Atlantic squadron off the Cape Verde Islands, and Admiral Montojo the Pacific squadron in the Philippines. It was upon the last named that the first blow fell. Admiral Dewey, who had been stationed at Hongkong with the American squadron, received orders to take the offensive, and on May 1, Montojo's ships, hopelessly outmatched, were destroyed in Manila Bay. The victors, who had only lost seven men wounded in the battle, landed, captured the arsenal at Cavite, and blockaded Manila, while Aguinaldo, the leader of the native insurgents (a rebellion had broken out two years before), attacked on the land side.

When this news reached Spain it was at first decided to send Admiral Cámara to the rescue, but he had only reached the Suez Canal when he was recalled. The government realised that the situation in the Far East was hopeless, and that the squadron might well be wanted nearer home, while in any event Spain had no coaling station between her coast and the Philippines. The first week of the war had thus been disastrous for Spain, but there was worse to follow.

Cervera proceeded to Cuba on the outbreak of war, and after coaling at Curaçoa he reached Santiago on May 19. For a week he continued to hide his presence from the enemy, but on June 1 he was blockaded by a vastly superior American fleet. The Americans then attempted to bottle up the port by sinking a collier in the narrow channel, but this stratagem was unsuccessful.

Meanwhile an American army was landed at Guantamo, forty miles to the east of Santiago, and contact was established with the Cuban insurgents. At El Caney and San Juan Hill the Spaniards were driven back after a desperate resistance, and in spite of an outbreak of fever in their ranks the Americans began to shell Santiago. This made the position of Cervera untenable, and he accordingly put to sea with great gallantry, although he had no illusions about the fate which awaited him. On July 3 he steamed out of Santiago, and in the combat which followed all his ships were either sunk, burnt, or captured. A fortnight later General Toral surrendered Santiago to an inferior American force, having stipulated for the repatriation of himself and the garrison under his command.

The war was now, in fact, over, and Spain had lost the last remains of her colonial empire, for the Americans had also gained possession of the greater part of Puerto Rico. Sagasta, who was then Prime Minister, accordingly opened negotiations for peace on the basis of an agreement as to the political status of Cuba. The American President refused to consider any such limitation, and he declared his government's terms to be the immediate evacuation of Cuba, the surrender of Puerto Rico to the United States in lieu of an indemnity, and the possession of Manila pending a settlement of the ownership of the Philippines. The Spaniards demurred at the last clause, but were finally forced to accept it, and a preliminary agreement was signed on August 12.

The commissioners to arrange the terms of peace met in Paris at the beginning of October, and the two disputed points were the Cuban debt and the sovereignty of the Philippines. With regard to the former the Spanish contention was that the debt was attached to the island, and that its change of ownership did not affect the matter. As for Manila, it had been captured by the Americans after the signature of the preliminaries of peace, and Spain demanded possession of the city and the archipelago. The Americans refused to consider these arguments, and the Spanish government was given the alternative of a surrender or a renewal of the war. As Spain was in no position to fight again she had to give way, and the treaty was signed on November 28. The United States paid a sum of £4,000,000 for the Philippine archipelago.

The immediate result of the war was a great increase in the Spanish debt, for the country was obliged to take over more than a hundred millions sterling of colonial and war loans. Nevertheless bankruptcy was avoided, and in due course her credit improved. Ultimately, the moral effect of the war was more important than the political, for from the defeat came that "generation of 1898" which has since exercised so great an influence upon every aspect of the national life. The complete failure of the regime to defend the colonies produced a reaction of which pessimism and criticism were the keynote, and the intellectuals raised the cry that there must be a fresh start.

All this, however, was for the future, for the immediate effect of the disaster was small, and the storm which it was feared might overturn the dynasty did not even produce a change of ministry. There was a feeling of relief that the drain of men and money to Cuba was at an end, though the soldiers who had proved so signally incapable of defending the country were soon to show that they had no intention of abandoning their claim to control its destinies.

Yet when the Regency came to an end in 1902 the Parliamentary System upon which the restored monarchy was based had already begun to disintegrate. Cánovas had been murdered by an anarchist in 1897, and Sagasta had but one year more to live. Neither left a successor equal to himself, and the parties they had led began to split up into groups. The lapse of a generation had not sufficed to enable the principle of Representative Government to take root in Spain, and the disappearance of Cánovas and Sagasta deprived the country of the men who could give it at any rate an appearance of reality.

CHAPTER XLI

The Earlier Years of Alfonso XIII (1902–1923)

THE King had not long attained his majority before the weakness of the Parliamentary System without a Cánovas or a Sagasta to make it work became apparent. During the first four years after the termination of the Regency there were no less than fourteen political crises and eight Prime Ministers.

The Catalan question became even more embittered, and there was a violent feud between the Catalan Nationalists and the Radical Centralists led by Lerroux. The generals, too, in spite of the poor show which they had made in the war against the United States, began to interfere in politics once again, and they obtained a law by which military tribunals were allowed to try offences against military institutions. Above all, Socialist doctrines of the most advanced type were making considerable progress in the larger centres of population, and on the day of the King's marriage in May, 1906, with Princess Victoria Eugenia of Battenberg, a particularly daring attempt was made to murder the royal couple.

In due course the Liberals gave place to the Conservatives, and Don Antonio Maura became Prime Minister. His ministry coincided with a period of widespread disorder, and for a time it appeared as if revolution was inevitable. In 1909 there was an anticlerical and anarchist rising in Barcelona, which was only suppressed with the greatest difficulty and after considerable bloodshed. An intellectual of the name of Ferrer was accused of complicity in this outbreak, and Maura had him shot. This act made the Spanish government very unpopular with Liberals and Socialists all over Europe, and Maura finally resigned. For some years afterwards he was anathema to the parties of the Left, and the mere suggestion that Maura was going to take office again was sufficient to produce a storm.

Maura was succeeded by the Liberal Moret, who was soon replaced by Canalejas, one of the very few men of the first rank in this period. He was at once an ardent Catholic and a convinced reformer, and he agreed with the King probably better than any other Prime Minister during his reign.

In 1910 Alfonso, in a speech from the throne, declared that his government would insist on the reduction and control of the Religious Orders, though there would be no interference with their spiritual independence. In consequence of this attitude relations with the Vatican became strained, and the Spanish ambassador to the Holy See was withdrawn. The anti-dynastic Left hoped that the King would yield to the clamour which these events had raised against the minister, for in that case they could reckon upon the support of Canalejas in their attack upon the throne. Alfonso refused to play into his enemies' hands, and when the Prime Minister offered his resignation, the monarch declined to accept it, pointing out that Canalejas still had a majority in the Cortes.

In November, 1912, the co-operation of King and minister was brought to an end by the latter's murder in the street in Madrid. Of the many successors of Canalejas as Prime Minister none was of more than mediocre ability with the exception of the Conservative Dato, who did much in the way of social reform, but in March, 1921, he, too, perished by the bullet of an anarchist.

By this time the disintegration of the parties was complete. On the assassination of Cánovas an attempt had been made by Silvela to succeed him as the undisputed Conservative leader, but he failed to impose his authority on the Duke of Tetuán or Romero Robledo, and the groups led by them formed alliances to the Right or to the Left as the needs of the moment appeared to dictate. Villaverde was no more successful, but for a time he was head of a section of Liberal-Conservatives which by no means always voted with the supporters of Antonio Maura, known as the *Mauristas*. In 1915 the Liberal-Conservatives elected Dato as their leader, and under his influence their policy became more progressive, for it was then that measures dealing with Workmen's Insurance, Compensation for Accidents, and Regulation of Women's and Children's Work were passed by the Cortes. Dato also received a certain amount of support from the *Mauristas*, but on his death all unity was again lost.

The nominal Conservative leader was Sánchez Guerra, but the Left wing of the party followed the political heirs of Dato, the Right wing adhered to Maura, and in the Centre was Juan de la Cierva. There were other groups, of which the principal were those led by Burgos Mazo, Ossorio Gallardo, and Bugallal. The difference between these groups was purely one of personalities and of shades of opinion.

The Liberals were in no better plight. Even before the death of Sagasta his leadership was not always accepted by Gomazo and Canalejas, and before twelve months had elapsed since that event there were three Liberal groups, led by Montero Rios, Moret, and Canalejas respectively. As in the case of the Conservatives there were no fundamental distinctions between these groups, but in spite of that the Liberal party was never united again, though from time to time there were unions, blocs, and cartels. Canalejas, with his Liberal-Democrats, commanded the allegiance of most Liberals until his death, and his successor was García Prieto, Marquis of Alhucemas, who co-operated when he could with the Reformists and the republicans. The more moderate Liberals chose the Count of Romanones as their leader, but there continued to be other groups which looked to Alcalá Zamora, Ráfael Gasset, and Santiago Alba.

Farther to the Left were the Reformists. They were a fragment which had, under the leadership of Melquiades Alvarez, broken away from the republican party in 1913, when their leader had declared in a speech at Murcia that he would no longer raise the question of the regime. Melquiades Alvarez was President of the Chamber of Deputies at the time of the establishment of the Directory.

Fortunately for the monarchy, the anti-dynastic parties were, if anything, still more divided than those which nominally supported the throne. The republicans, until the last years of the reign, were easily the weakest of all the political organisations, for the defection of Melquiades Alvarez left Lerroux with a mere handful of followers. They also lost many supporters to the Socialists, who made rapid progress during the early years of the century, more particularly in the larger towns. In 1888 there were 16 Socialist groups, in 1906 there were 115, and in 1912 there were 216. The Socialists were also fortunate in possessing an extremely able leader in Pablo Iglesias.

At the other extreme stood the Carlists or Jaimists, as they became in 1909 when Don Jaime succeeded his father, Don Carlos, as legitimist claimant to the throne. They were still strong in the Basque Provinces and Navarre, and, like the Socialists, they had a leader of outstanding ability in Vázquez de Mella, but they were never the danger to Alfonso XIII that they had been to his father and grandmother. Nevertheless, they prevented many strong monarchists from rallying to the support of the throne.

Of the other groups in the Cortes the only one of importance was that of the Catalan autonomists. In 1913 their demands were to some extent granted by the ministry of Sánchez Guerra, which gave the Catalans a limited form of local government, but this policy was subsequently reversed by the Directory.

In these circumstances it is hardly surprising that on an increasing number of occasions the King had not only to reign but also to govern. More than once a considerable period elapsed between the fall of one administration and the formation of another, and unless the whole machinery of government was to come to a standstill someone had to take the initiative. When a ministry resigned consultations had to be held with the leaders of the various groups in the Cortes, and even when a new Prime Minister had been appointed there was a further delay while he carried on his negotiations with this faction or that with a view to obtaining a majority.

One result of this was to render any bold programme impossible, and another was to increase the personal power of the monarch, who alone represented continuity amid the welter of changing groups. Unfortunately this state of affairs encouraged the King, though from the most patriotic of motives, to play one politician off against another, and this policy became in course of time so much second nature to him that in the end no one really trusted him. There had been too many constitutions during the past hundred years for any particular respect to be paid to the existing one, and in any event half the electorate was illiterate.

When the European War broke out Spain remained neutral, and while it lasted she became very rich. Money poured into the country as the demands of the Allies were met, and Spain experienced to the full all the advantages of neutrality in a world that was at war, in spite of the fact that she lost 140,000 tons of shipping.

No account of the position of Spain during these years would be complete without some reference to the work of the King on behalf of the prisoners. For this purpose he maintained, at his own expense, a secretariat of forty clerks, and the cost of postage alone was over a million pesetas. His initiative led to the cessation of reprisals in Germany against French prisoners, he took up strongly the case of the civil population of Lille, and he never ceased to protest against the horrors of submarine warfare. Eight sentences of death on women, and twenty on men, were commuted in consequence of his intervention, while had the Spanish minister at Brussels had time to communicate with Madrid, Edith Cavell would not have been shot. King Alfonso XIII may have committed mistakes which cost him and his subjects dear, but his work for suffering humanity during the Four Years' War is a big item on the credit side of his account.

Increased wealth, however, caused a spread of discontent, and the period 1914–1918 was extremely disturbed. The unrest came to a head in 1917, when there took place a general strike with the object of establishing a republic on the new Russian model.

The movement was suppressed mainly owing to the army, which, in consequence, began to exercise a dominating influence in politics with the connivance of the King, and military *juntas* were formed. By 1920 their power was such that they compelled the resignation of the Conservative ministry of Sánchez Toca, and it had already become a mere question of time when a military regime, for which there were many precedents, would come into being. In many ways the army was more representative of public opinion than the Cortes, and it enjoyed the favour of the King. This development was accelerated by the course of events in Morocco.

The opening years of the nineteenth century had witnessed a considerable degree of rivalry between Great Britain, France, and Spain in Morocco, but on the conclusion of the *Entente Cordiale* Great Britain renounced her interest there, and at the Algeciras Conference in 1906 France and Spain were entrusted with the general supervision of the country. By a further Franco-Spanish agreement in 1912, the dominions of the Sultan of Morocco had, with the exception of Tangier, been divided into two zones, and it was the efforts of the Protecting Powers to establish order in their respective zones that precipitated the conflict. France was the first to succeed in the task, partly owing to the geographical configuration of the territory assigned to her, and partly owing to the fact that in Marshal Lyautey she possessed one of the greatest colonial administrators that any nation has yet produced, though it is to be noted that she made no effort to pacify that portion of the Riff area which was included in her zone.

The Spaniards, on the other hand, were hampered not only by the mountainous nature of their Protectorate, but also by the paralysis which affected every branch of their administration during the last decade of the Parliamentary regime. Such being the case, it is not surprising that the Spanish forces should have made comparatively little headway, or that when, in the summer of 1921, a general offensive was at last begun it should have ended in the disaster of Anual, a *débâcle* unparalleled in colonial history since the rout of the Italians at Adowa twenty-five years before.

The Spanish forces had first marched out of the old stronghold of Melilla in the spring of 1909. After three years of hard fighting they had established themselves permanently on the line of the Kert River, and in all the territory comprised between its right bank and the French zone. By the first months of 1921 they had, however, advanced far beyond the Kert, but only after difficulties with the Beni Said and Beni Ulchek tribes. Both of these had submitted, but incompletely, and not in a way to inspire confidence.

During the years between 1909 and 1921 some 300 miles of roads had been built behind the line of the Kert, and also two railways towards the interior. The rich iron-ore mines of Beni Ifrur on Mount Uixan had been opened, a large agricultural colony established at Monte Arruit, and a model farm at El Zaio, overlooking the Muluya River on the East. Dispensaries and Mohammedan schools had been established at every important military base, springs covered in, while Spanish doctors were frequently sent for by the tribes, or visited by the natives at the weekly markets.

No rising or threatened rebellion had taken place during these twelve years, and it was generally thought that the natives understood the benefits of civilisation sufficiently to accept the Protectorate, which, moreover, meant for them light and regular taxation, fair administration of justice, and the preservation of order. On their part the Spanish troops were beginning to become accustomed to the country and its ways, and under the influence of this false sentiment of security were leading the life of soldiers in time of peace between the Kert and the Muluya. Frequent leave was granted to the officers and men, who naturally took advantage of their proximity to their own country.

The Spanish zone in Morocco is North of a line drawn from a point a little South of Larache on the Atlantic coast, running North of Fez, and then to Cabo de Agua on the frontier of Algeria; it does not include Tangier with its immediate hinterland, which is international. Two armies were operating in this area in the summer of

1921: one under General Berenguer, based on Tetuán, was engaged in the encircling of Raisuli; and the other, under General Silvestre, was advancing from Melilla in the direction of the Bay of Alhucemas, with the intention of uniting with General Berenguer's forces as soon as the pacification of the western sector was complete. It was this latter army under General Silvestre that met with disaster at Anual.

General Silvestre had under his command 25,790 men of all arms. These troops were, however, scattered in detachments among some seventy different posts, of which a number were held by only thirty or fifty men. Of artillery there was a mountain and a field battery at Anual, and the same in the neighbourhood of Dar-Drius, with small detachments at some other posts; there were also three companies of machine gunners at Anual and two at Dar-Drius. Such were the main Spanish dispositions in the eastern sector when the fighting began.

By the end of May, 1921, General Silvestre had advanced along the coast as far as Sidi Dris, and on the 1st of June he sent a detachment to occupy Abarran at the express request of the Temsaman tribe to whom it belonged. This detachment was treacherously attacked by the natives, assisted by their fellow-countrymen in the Spanish ranks, after the occupation of the village, and the Spaniards were compelled to withdraw. On receiving news of this disaster, General Silvestre reinforced Sidi Dris by land, and revictualled it by sea, while, on the 3rd, he occupied Talilit without opposition, although a considerable concentration of Moors could be seen in the hills in the immediate vicinity.

The reverse at Abarran had caused considerable uneasiness at Madrid, and General Berenguer, the High Commissioner, accordingly proceeded to the eastern sector of the Protectorate where, on the 5th, he had an interview with General Silvestre on board the *Princesa de Asturias*, off Sidi Dris. As a result of this meeting the High Commissioner reported to the Minister of War that in view of the hostility of some tribes and the doubtful attitude of others the situation required care, but was not disquieting. General Berenguer then returned to Tetuán.

During the following week matters changed for the worse. On the 7th, the Spaniards occupied Igueriben for the better defence of Anual, and, on the 14th, General Silvestre reported great enemy activity together with the presence of Abd-el-Krim, the Riff leader. Two days later the Moors made an unsuccessful attack on the Anual position, where they suffered heavily, and for a month the whole sector was quiet.

Abd-el-Krim's brother entered into negotiations with the Spanish authorities, and General Silvestre, who had abandoned, on the instructions of General Berenguer, all idea of a further advance until after the surrender of Raisuli, was so far deceived by the apparent calm that he allowed a number of officers and men to proceed on leave to the Peninsula. On July 15 the High Commissioner received his usual monthly report from General Silvestre, but that officer had nothing to relate. Two days later the Moors attacked the Igueriben–Anual line, but were repulsed. There was still no indication of what was coming, and even General Silvestre treated the fighting as nothing more serious than a mere demonstration like that against Anual a month before. On July 19 the storm burst.

The High Commissioner up to this date had not received any communication from General Silvestre which could lead him to suppose that the latter took a serious view of the situation, but, on the evening of the 19th, there arrived a message which was distinctly alarming. In it General Silvestre announced that Igueriben was surrounded, and that after fighting all day a relief column had been driven back with casualties amounting to six officers and seventy-one other ranks; an urgent appeal for reinforcements was also made. It cannot be too strongly emphasised in view of the disaster which was to follow that this was the first warning which General Berenguer had received that the situation was in any way critical, and that even General Silvestre did not grasp the true position is proved by the fact that he did not go to Anual himself until two days later.

The High Commissioner at once sent General Silvestre's telegram to Madrid, and within forty-eight hours such reinforcements as he could spare from the western sector were on the march to their point of embarkation. Meanwhile, the most contradictory messages were arriving from General Silvestre. On the 20th he suggested that a naval demonstration should be made off Alhucemas in order to relieve the pressure on his front and to reassure friendly natives, and he also asked for more aeroplanes. General Berenguer transmitted both these requests to Madrid.

On the 21st, the culminating day of the tragedy, three messages were received from General Silvestre. The first merely announced that Igueriben was still surrounded, and that, so far as the situation was concerned, there was nothing to report. The second pressed for the naval diversion, stated that the strength of the required reinforcements should be two mountain batteries, one regiment of infantry, as well as auxiliary troops, and contained an account of the Spanish dispositions which showed that there were eighteen companies of infantry in close reserve, an arrangement which General Berenguer considered satisfactory. The third telegram contained the disturbing information that the Spanish morale was bad, but gave no reasons for this statement.

On the 21st General Silvestre proceeded to Anual with all the forces he could muster, but it was already too late. The Moors on that day stormed Igueriben, and a convoy which had been sent to relieve it was surprised in a drift by tactics closely resembling those employed by Hannibal in his defeat of Flaminius at Lake Trasimene. These disasters determined General Silvestre to fall back upon Izzumar, and he accordingly telegraphed his decision to General Berenguer, who received the report at 10.50 a.m. the following day, the 22nd, and he replied, "I hope that in these critical moments all will think of the prestige and honour of the country before everything else." No further news reached the High Commissioner until the evening, when he heard that General Silvestre was dead and that his troops were in flight.

It is clear that General Silvestre's first intention was to hold Anual until reinforcements reached him, and had he carried out this plan it is more than likely that the subsequent disaster would never have taken place. As it was, however, he changed his mind for reasons that have never been properly elucidated, and gave the order for an immediate evacuation of Anual. The morale of his men left, according to his own report of the day before, much to be desired, and it is consequently not surprising that the order to retreat was almost immediately followed by one of those sudden panics from which no army is invariably exempt. The *Cazadores de Alcántara* formed an honourable exception and endeavoured to cover their comrades' retreat, but for the rest of the troops it was a veritable *sauve qui peut*. As soon as he realised what had happened, General Silvestre put an end to his life.

General Navarro met the fugitives at Dar-Drius and tried to rally them, but so complete was their demoralisation that out of four mountain batteries which had left Anual only one could be formed at Dar-Drius. It was found impossible to make a stand, and the retreat was continued in a little better order to Monte Arruit, where the main body arrived on July 29.

The rest of the story is soon told. The Spanish forces in the eastern zone were practically annihilated, for General Silvestre had taken every available man to Anual, Monte Arruit fell on August 9, seventy posts were captured, and by the second week of August the Moors were six miles from Melilla. The total Spanish losses were estimated at 14,772 men, 19,504 rifles, 392 machine guns, and 129 guns. Much of the territory abandoned was, however, recovered by General Berenguer before the end of the year in a campaign which proved that the panic at Anual was a very rare event in Spanish military history.

Such was the disaster at Anual which was destined to affect the history of Spain most profoundly. Had it not occurred there might have been no Directory, had there been no Directory there might have been no Second Republic, and in consequence no Civil War.

A careful study of the available evidence can only lead to the conclusion that the immediate culprit was General Silvestre. He was impetuous by nature, and, like so many people of this type, was apt to lose his head in an emergency. In the present instance he committed three blunders of the first magnitude, for he failed to realize that the Moors were concentrating against him, he placed undue reliance upon his native levies, and he evacuated Anual when he should have remained there at all costs. These mistakes in themselves are enough to explain the disaster, but the circumstances of his rash advance appeared, to those unacquainted with Silvestre's impetuous character, so inexplicable that the revolutionary parties found no difficulty in spreading the rumour that he must have acted under secret instructions from the King.

The effect of Anual upon Spain itself was to drive the last nail into the coffin of the Parliamentary System. It is true that Vizconde de Eza, in his *Mi Responsabilidad en el Desastre de Melilla como Ministro de Guerra*, made a very able defence of himself and his colleagues, but contemporary opinion put the blame upon the politicians in Madrid. The Army, in particular, deeply resented the affront that had been placed upon it, and it was not long before circumstances enabled the military to have their revenge. Anual brought to a head the discontent that had long been growing in the Peninsula, and as the murdered Dato had not left any successor of his own ability it was inevitable that a change of regime must take place, and to this the King was reputed to be by no means opposed. In addition to the strain of the Moroccan campaign, the country was suffering severely from the disorders attendant upon feeble administration. Maura, Sánchez Guerra, and Alhucemas were successively Prime Ministers, but none of them proved capable of suppressing the growing disorders that were afflicting Spain.

All the native anarchy of the race came to the surface, and there were repeated revolutionary strikes, generally accompanied by bloodshed. Communist emissaries would appear at a factory, and compel those employed there to cease work without giving any reason for their action: such was the terror they inspired that they were rarely disobeyed. Murders were perpetrated with impunity, and even on the rare occasions when the culprits were caught no jury could be found to convict. In June, 1923, these disorders reached their climax in the brutal assassination of the Cardinal Archbishop of Saragossa.

Retribution was not slow to follow. In the first days of September two of the generals in Madrid went to the King, told him that the existing state of affairs could not be allowed to continue, and that the whole system must be changed. It was not surprising that they should have acted in this manner, for the Army had by no means remained unaffected by the prevalent anarchy. Quite recently the colonel of a regiment stationed in Barcelona had come to Madrid and reported to the commander-in-chief that he had seized six men in the barracks distributing anarchist leaflets to their comrades in which they were told to kill the King, shoot their officers, and pull down the flag. The colonel in question was duly referred by the commander-in-chief to the relevant article of the Military Code which prescribed a court-martial and the death penalty, but when this was reported to the Minister for War he declared that action of this nature was inconsistent with his principles. Accordingly, the men were tried by a civil tribunal, and sentenced to imprisonment for life; but in six months this was reduced to twenty years, in another six months to fifteen years, and by the end of eighteen months the men were released altogether.

King Alfonso listened to what the generals had to say, and he informed the Prime Minister, Garcia Prieto, of what had happened. The King then went to Santander, where he was rung up a few days later by Garcia Prieto, who told him that the garrison at Barcelona under the command of General Primo de Rivera had revolted. In reply to a question the Prime Minister admitted that he had taken no action whatever in the light of the information given to him before the King's departure from the capital. Thereafter events moved rapidly. All over the country the troops followed the example of the Barcelona garrison, and in face of a movement which they were powerless to control the ministers resigned, whereupon the King called upon Primo de Rivera to form a government. Such was the *pronunciamiento* of September 13, 1923.

There can be little doubt but that one of the main reasons for the collapse of the Parliamentary System was the neglect of education. Parliamentarianism was not, in any case, a plant of native growth as Cánovas had sown it, and if it was to take root an educated electorate was essential. A few pioneers, such as Giner and Castillejo, realised this, but the mass of the politicians found that the illiteracy of their constituents was very definitely to their advantage. Without statesmen to work it, or an enlightened public opinion to support it, the Constitution, excellent as it was in many respects, was doomed.

CHAPTER XLII

The Directory and the Revolution (1923–1931)

THE head of the Directory, Miguel Primo de Rivera y Orbaneja, Marquis of Estella, was a man of fifty-three, for he had been born at Jerez de la Frontera on January 8, 1870. He was a nephew of that General Primo de Rivera, also Marquis of Estella, who played so prominent a part at the restoration of Alfonso XII, and was twice Governor-General of the Philippines. It was at this uncle's hands that Miguel received his early training.

He adopted a military career almost as a matter of course, and at the age of twenty-three was awarded the Cross of San Fernando (First Class) for conspicuous bravery in the field in Morocco, while he subsequently saw service both in the Philippines and in Cuba. The close of the war with the United States brought a period of peace to the Spanish army, but, as soon as hostilities commenced in Morocco in 1909, Primo de Rivera asked to be sent to the front, and he remained in Africa until he was severely wounded two years later. This early experience of Moorish warfare was to stand him in good stead in later years, and the skilful use which he made of his personal knowledge was proved in 1925 by his handling of the operations at Alhucemas.

The talents of Primo de Rivera now began to attract the attention of successive governments, and in 1915 he was appointed Governor of Cádiz, while four years later he became Captain-General of Madrid. His tenure of both these posts, however, terminated abruptly because his outspokenness was distasteful to those in authority. For example, he severely censured the Moroccan policy of successive administrations, and he demanded the opening of negotiations with Great Britain for the restitution of Gibraltar: with regard to this latter point it is not without interest to note that he changed his mind in later years, having come to the conclusion that Ceuta had a greater strategic value in modern warfare than Gibraltar, for which it was proposed to exchange the Moorish port. In spite of these checks his upward career was only temporarily delayed, and in 1922 he became Captain-General of Catalonia, where, as has been shown, he organised his bloodless *coup d'état* of September 13 in the following year.

Primo de Rivera was a soldier above all else; that was both his strength and his weakness. He possessed all those Andalusian characteristics which have enabled the men of the South to play so large a part in the history of Spain. An unfailing courtesy, a power of leadership, and a very sincere devotion to his Church were his most notable qualities. The impression which he made upon those who came into contact with him was that of a man absolutely sincere, and prepared to make any personal sacrifice for what he believed to be right. He was also completely fearless, and he walked about the streets of Madrid in the same careless way after he had seized power as he did before that event. A true aristocrat, he deliberately avoided all ostentation, and when he returned to the capital after his victorious campaign in Africa, he entered it as a private citizen. When he went to his club or to a theatre, in nine cases out of ten his presence was unknown.

Unfortunately there was another side to the picture, and his defects in the end proved to be the undoing both of himself and of Spain. Like so many soldiers, Primo de Rivera recognised only two colours, black and white, while in politics the distinction is rarely as clear as that. With the passage of time and the emergence of fresh problems, social and economic, with which his early training had not equipped him to deal, he got out of his depth, and therein lies the explanation of the blunders which marked the later years of his tenure of office. He estranged all the old politicians, the best of whom would otherwise have helped him, and his relations with the King were never good. In these circumstances Primo de Rivera became increasingly more isolated, and only a genius, which he neither was nor claimed to be, can afford to stand alone.

At the same time there can be no shadow of doubt but that the *pronunciamiento*, and the closing of the Cortes which followed it, were exceedingly popular. Had a plebiscite been taken the Directory would have obtained an overwhelming majority. The fact that the change had been effected by the Army in no way disturbed public opinion, for Spain had become accustomed to military intervention in politics, and the army was at this moment more representative of the country than was the Cortes. Primo de Rivera himself never lost his popularity with the masses, however much the middle classes and the intellectuals might sneer at him, and the King's apparently callous treatment of him after his fall undoubtedly contributed not a little to undermine the monarch's own position.

As has been shown, when the *pronunciamiento* was made at Barcelona the King was at Santander, whence he at once returned to Madrid. He had no choice but to accept a military Directory, and it is impossible to censure him for the action which he took at this exceedingly difficult moment, more particularly in view of the fact that he had previously warned the Government what to expect. Where he did make a mistake was in not insisting upon the convocation of the Cortes, within the three months prescribed by the Constitution, to sanction what had been done. Had this course been adopted the General could easily have obtained from the Cortes not only the ratification of what had happened, but a completely free hand in the future: in that event the charge of being unconstitutional, later to be used against the monarch with such damning effect, could never have been made. King Alfonso considered that the Constitution was suspended, and such was indeed the case, but, as it contained no provision for its temporary suspension, he was, in law, acting in an unconstitutional manner. Of course, the Constitution had so often been disregarded in the past that one more breach of it did not seem to matter, but the King had sworn to uphold its provisions, and this violation of his oath placed a very effective weapon in the hands of the enemies of the throne.

This mistake was primarily due to the lack of sympathy between the King and Primo de Rivera. The General, as we have seen, had serious limitations, and one of them, not uncommon in dictators, was his failure to appreciate the force of tradition. He thus tended to ignore the Crown, and had actually arranged to replace King Alfonso by the Infante Don Juan if the former showed any signs of opposing his wishes. In time the relations between the two men improved somewhat, though they were never cordial, and the result of the treatment which the monarch received from his minister was to weaken the prestige of the throne; on the other hand, the King became identified with the minister's policy in the eyes of every enemy of the Directory.

The first task of the new regime was to re-establish respect for the law, and this was speedily accomplished by a few exemplary sentences on wrongdoers. It was proved in this way how much could be effected by firm government. Within a few weeks, too, of his arrival in office, Primo de Rivera accompanied the King and Queen to Italy, and, as a result, many analogies were drawn both in the Peninsula and elsewhere between the regimes in the two countries. In actual fact there was nothing in common between them, for Fascism had grown up from below, while the Spanish Directory was imposed from above. On his return Primo de Rivera tried to create a body in his support called the *Unión Patriótica*, but it never obtained any strong hold. It was joined by place-seekers, anxious to stand well with the authorities, but it was the palest reflection of Fascism.

The preoccupation of the Directory, however, in its earlier years was Morocco, and Primo de Rivera spent two long periods in that country, leaving the Marquis of Magaz, the Vice-President of the Directory, in charge of affairs in Spain. The situation in North Africa certainly demanded his attention. As soon as the news of General Silvestre's overthrow had reached Spain, troops were hurried to Morocco in large numbers, and much of the lost ground was recovered, but all attempt to occupy the whole zone was abandoned. The Spaniards still very largely relied upon a series of more or less isolated posts, planned on much the same principle as the British block-houses in the South African War. As a rule, however, these were not sufficiently strong to hold out for any length of time, while the difficulty with regard to an adequate water supply was almost insuperable. In these circumstances Primo de Rivera decided to cut his losses, and withdraw behind the so-called Estella Line until such time as an offensive should be practicable. It can hardly be denied that the adoption of this policy was a proof of the General's courage, for it involved the temporary abandonment of a good deal of territory, and in view of the general political situation in Spain it was a daring move to make.

During these operations the French zone, it may be observed, had enjoyed a period of complete calm, and the authorities at Rabat had not realised that the conflagration might spread. By the end of 1924, therefore, the situation was that the Spaniards were on the defensive behind the Estella Line, which did little more than cover Tetuán in the West, while the vast area of the French zone, more than twice the size of Great Britain, was held by very weak forces, often of inferior quality, and split up into innumerable small detachments.

As soon as the weather permitted, Abd-el-Krim began his advance. He contained the Spaniards, who were still in the throes of re-organisation, with the minimum number of men that would suffice for the purpose, and with the rest of his levies he invaded the French zone. The Moorish objectives were Fez and Taza, the former because it is the old capital of Morocco, and the latter in order to cut the railway which connects the town with Algeria, and in a short time the Moors were within gunshot of both places. The numerous fortified posts, upon which the French had relied for the defence of the country, proved useless, and their garrisons merely served to swell the number of prisoners in Moorish hands, while the morale of the native troops proved to be extremely bad in the hour of danger.

The first effect of this onslaught upon the French military authorities was an urgent appeal to Paris for reinforcements, and by the end of June, 1925, the forces in Morocco had been increased by some fifty per cent, a step, however, which was only rendered possible by the evacuation of the Ruhr. In this connection it is only fair to state that the French Government almost from the beginning appreciated the seriousness of the situation, and the Prime Minister himself, M. Painlevé, visited the scene of operations. Largely as a result of his investigations two very important decisions were taken, namely to entrust the command of the French forces in Morocco to Marshal Pétain, and to enter into negotiations with Spain for the final pacification of the whole country. Accordingly, Marshal Pétain arrived at Rabat in July, though Marshal Lyautey remained in Morocco in a purely administrative capacity. It was a measure of Abd-el-Krim's importance that two Marshals of France should be arrayed against him. In July, also, a Franco-Spanish conference was held at Madrid, when the plan of campaign was drawn up.

On the eve of the Franco-Spanish offensive in August, 1925, the whole of the Moroccan coast from the mouth of the River Lau to that of the River Kert was in the hands of the rebels, whose hold upon the interior was also effective from within a few miles of

Ouezzan in the West to a similar distance North of Taza in the East. On the Spanish front operations were at a standstill, but the offensive against the French was still held up rather than definitely halted when Marshal Pétain and General Primo de Rivera delivered their counter-stroke.

It had been decided at the conference in Madrid that the two Powers should strike a simultaneous blow at two separate points, the French at Biban and the Spaniards at the enemy's capital Ajdir by means of a landing at Alhucemas. For this latter operation Primo de Rivera formed two columns under Generals Fernández Pérez and Saro, consisting of some six thousand men each, while the remainder of the Spanish forces were held in reserve at Ceuta and Melilla.

By far the harder task fell to the Spaniards. Not only had they to land upon a hostile and difficult coast, but they had so to co-ordinate their movements that columns starting from bases so far apart as Ceuta and Melilla should arrive before their objective simultaneously. Nor was this all, for the covering fleets were composed of both Spanish and French squadrons, so that Primo de Rivera, who was in supreme command, had the added anxiety which is the invariable lot of a commander whose forces are drawn from different nationalities. In these circumstances the fact that the whole operation was carried out without a hitch, except for that caused by exceptionally bad weather, is the highest tribute to the Spanish forces, who showed on this, as on many another subsequent occasion, that when well led they have lost none of their ancient valour, and are equal to any troops in Europe. The landing at Alhucemas took place on September 8, and after a month's hard fighting in which, to quote *The Times*, "the Riffs were fairly and squarely beaten," the standard of Spain floated over Ajdir. Anual was avenged.

If the task allotted to the Spaniards gave them the chance to show their fine fighting qualities, that which fell to the French was equally well performed. Marshal Pétain thrust now at one sector of the enemy's line and now at another, compelling him to give ground on each occasion. The Moors fought as well when fortune was against them as when it was in their favour, but they had neither the men nor the equipment to enable them to hold their own, and when the rain suspended operations in November they had been hustled out of most of what they had occupied in the spring. Realising that he was nearing the end of his resources, for the harvest had failed and typhus was ravaging his ranks, Abd-el-Krim attempted to secure favourable terms by negotiation, and there was an armistice for this purpose in April, 1926. The discussions, however, broke down over the question of the autonomy of the Riff, which the Protecting Powers refused to recognise, and fighting was resumed early in May.

The Franco-Spanish plan of campaign was a repetition of that of the previous year, with Targuist, the Moorish headquarters since the fall of Ajdir, as the objective. Abd-el-Krim concentrated his chief efforts on stopping the Spanish advance, but General Sanjurjo, who had by this time succeeded Primo de Rivera as commander-in-chief, broke the Moorish lines by a frontal attack after some very hard fighting indeed. This proved to be the last act of the campaign, for on May 20 the French and Spanish forces joined hands on the River Nekor a few miles east of Targuist, and a week later Abd-el-Krim surrendered to the French. The war was over, though the final pacification of the Spanish zone was not effected until a few months later.

The victorious termination of the Moroccan campaign enormously enhanced the prestige of the Directory, of which it may be said to have marked the apogee. Originally the Government had been composed exclusively of generals and admirals, but in December, 1925, it was remodelled with the addition of such distinguished civilians as Calvo Sotelo, at the Ministry of Finance, and the Count of Guadalhorce, at the Ministry of Public Works. Unhappily it did not proceed to the abolition of conscription and the creation of an efficient professional army, which would have been to the advantage both of itself and of Spain. On the other hand, there can be no gainsaying the fact that the Directory did more for the country in the six years of its existence than had been effected in the previous sixty, and for a brief space it did seem as though there were a new spirit in the land. Trains ran to time, means of communication and of transport were improved out of all recognition, and Spain seemed well on the road to a veritable renaissance. Unhappily this revival proved to be a mere flash in the pan, and it is difficult to resist the conclusion that such was the case almost entirely because, as in the days of Charles III, the impulse came from above rather than from below.

A serious blunder was also made by the Directory in its handling of the Catalan problem. As in more than one similar case elsewhere, a little autonomy at the beginning would have prevented virtual independence in the end. The King of Spain was also Count of Barcelona, and much use might have been made of this fact, but Primo de Rivera set his face against any policy that savoured of concession. Yet the more moderate section of Catalan opinion, which was alarmed at the friendly relations existing between such extreme separatists as Colonel Macia and the Communists, would have welcomed co-operation with Madrid on any terms that recognised their point of view. The result of the Government's obduracy was to throw the Catalans into the arms of the Republicans and Socialists in opposition, first to the Directory, and eventually to the monarchy itself. It was a suicidal policy, and totally unnecessary.

The year 1926, which witnessed the triumph of the Directory, also marked the commencement of its decline. The failure of Spain to obtain a permanent seat on the Council of the League of Nations was a bad start, and the lack of success which attended her claim to Tangier did nothing to enhance the prestige of the administration. Curiously enough, the first sign of decay within was a revolt of those very military elements upon which it depended in the last resort for support. The artillery objected to the Government's interference with their system of promotion, and it was only the personal intervention of the King that made them give way without resorting to violence. Even so, martial law had to be proclaimed all over Spain. In the same month, September, the *Unión Patriótica* organised a national plebiscite, and although the conditions precluded the recording of any adverse votes, the fact that six million people pronounced in favour of the Directory was significant.

The most striking successes were those of the young and energetic Ministers of Finance and Public Works. Great progress was made in the matter of hydro-electric development by the establishment of autonomous corporations, each of which controlled one of the great river-basins of the country; particularly successful was the *Confederación del Ebro*, which dealt with an area covering a seventh of Spain, and with half the latter's rainfall. Contracts were given out for the construction of nearly 400 miles of railway and over 4,000 miles of road, while the telephone service was entirely reorganised by the *Compañía Telefónica Nacional*. The problem of financial reform was also attacked at its root by drastic changes in the system of taxation. Nevertheless, Calvo Sotelo was gravely hampered by the expensive schemes of Primo de Rivera, which eventually increased the National Debt by over forty per cent, with a consequent rise in the annual expenditure to meet interest charges.

The military and naval authorities, too, distinguished themselves this year by the organisation of Commandante Franco's flight to South America, and by a no less successful one from Madrid to the Philippines. Both these events created enormous enthusiasm in Spain, and were made the occasion for a reaffirmation of Hispano-American friendship, which the Directory did everything in its power to foster.

In spite of the benefits which the regime was conferring upon the country its fundamental weakness became every day more apparent. It had not created a new system; indeed, it was not possible for it to do so, for although it still enjoyed the passive support of the majority of Spaniards, there was no dynamic popular force behind Primo de Rivera. In effect, the passage of time showed ever more clearly the difficulty of reforming a nation from above. The Government itself began to feel this, and in 1927 a National Assembly was convoked to replace the Cortes. The deputies were to some extent representative of various corporations, but they had no legislative power. All that was effected by calling this body into existence was to prove that the Directory did not feel sure of its position, for the National Assembly was never regarded as anything more than a rather poor joke. Primo de Rivera was also decidedly unfortunate in his dealing with the intellectual classes, and the harsh treatment which was too often meted out to men of international reputation created the worst possible impression abroad. A further blunder was the favour which was shown to the regular clergy, particularly in the matter of teaching, for this irritated their old rivals, the seculars, while it enraged lay educationalists.

In 1929 there took place the magnificent exhibitions at Barcelona and Seville, but they proved to be the swan-song of the Directory. The health of Primo de Rivera was obviously giving way beneath the strain to which it was subjected, an extravagant economic nationalism had sent up the cost of living, and repeated conspiracies were being discovered by the police. At the beginning of 1930 Primo de Rivera, ill and worried, instituted a referendum of the commanders of the various military districts as to the advisability of his retention of office. It is to be noted that General Carmona, the Portuguese dictator, had adopted this expedient a few months before, and it may well be that Primo de Rivera was influenced by this example. The difference between the two cases lay in the fact that Spain was a monarchy and Portugal a republic, and Primo de Rivera's action was a definite violation of the royal prerogative. This left the monarch no choice but to dismiss his minister, and it is greatly to the General's credit that he was the first to admit the mistake he had made.

A few weeks afterwards Primo de Rivera died in a Paris hotel, and the fact that King Alfonso was not present at his subsequent funeral in Madrid told heavily against the Crown. With all his faults, the General was one of the greatest statesmen Spain has produced since the sixteenth century, and the tragedy was that circumstances did not allow of his government remaining in power for twenty years. Had his relations with the King been better, or had he managed to raise the nation actively to support the Directory, his achievements might well have been permanent. Probably his greatest handicap was his own character.

The fall of the Directory left King Alfonso face to face with the enemies of his late minister. There were many who censured the monarch more than the General, for they held that whereas the King had sworn to observe the Constitution the dictator had assumed no such liability. Such being the case, King Alfonso had two alternatives before him: he could either, like King Alexander in contemporary Jugo-Slavia, himself become dictator, or he could endeavour to return to the Constitution of 1876. The first course was rejected on the ground that it would mean staking the monarchy upon the result of what was a gamble: events, indeed, were soon to show that the regime was in question anyhow, but this was not yet realised either in Spain or abroad. Furthermore, the whole tradition of the reigning branch of the Bourbon dynasty was against absolutism, and to have gone back on it in this way would have been to accept the Carlist programme. The King, therefore, decided to return to normal conditions at the earliest possible moment, and he charged General Berenguer with the formation of a government for this purpose.

The situation was one of peculiar difficulty, for during the period of the Directory the old Conservative and Liberal groups had been reduced to mere shadows, and all that remained of them was their erstwhile leaders. On the other hand, the Socialists and Communists had gained considerable ground, and their organisation was intact, if subterranean. Berenguer was not slow to appreciate these facts, and he realised that as he had been appointed to bring the country back to normal the sooner he did so the better. He therefore wished to hold the elections at once, before the revolutionaries had gathered sufficient strength to become a real menace, and before they had been provided with the cry that the new administration was but the old under another name. Not the least of the many weaknesses of the Government was its essentially palatine composition, and this meant that the old monarchist politicians, who too often had the King's ear, enjoyed power without any sort of responsibility. They opposed General Berenguer, because they wished to have time to jerrymander the constituencies in the traditional manner in such a way as to secure the return of a majority of their own adherents. With this end in view they exerted such pressure as to obtain the removal all over the country of those who owed their appointment to the Directory (very often the best men in the district), and so still further undermined the regime which they pretended to support.

The ostensible reason for this attitude was that the only constitutional course was to hold the local elections first, and it was this plea that convinced King Alfonso. It is, however, impossible not to attribute some measure of blame to General Berenguer. His probity was above question, but he had never been able to control others successfully, and in the present instance he proved as helpless at checking such politicians as the Count of Romanones as he had been incapable of making General Silvestre obey his orders in the Riff nearly ten years before. Furthermore, both monarch and minister made a serious mistake in taking the old party hacks at their own valuation, for events were soon to prove that they had no followers worth the name. Nor did General Berenguer gain any gratitude for the policy he was adopting, for in due course the politicians, with the object of compelling his resignation, announced that what they really wanted was a *Cortes Constituyentes*. In this way the General Election was repeatedly postponed throughout the year 1930, while the Left gained in strength every day by asserting that the Government never intended to hold the elections at all.

In addition, Berenguer's administration had all the vices, with few of the virtues, of the Directory. It moderated the censorship, but did not abolish it altogether; it cut down expenditure on public works, thus throwing many people out of employment; and it tinkered with, but failed to control, the national finances. Nor was this all, for Berenguer was himself associated in the public mind with Anual, and his critics claimed that he had been a failure in his own profession as a soldier. The Government, too, was completely out of touch with public opinion, and if ever a ministry played into the hands of those who had sworn to destroy it, that ministry was the one of which Berenguer was the head.

The Opposition parties, that is to say the Republicans, Socialists, and Catalans, came to an understanding, known as the Pact of San Sebastian, in August, 1930. The anti-dynastic Left was still under the shadow of the failure of the First Republic, while no inconsiderable success had attended the efforts of Cánovas to rally its more moderate members to the support of the monarchy. In 1913, as has been shown, Melquiades Álvarez, one of the most prominent Republicans, publicly withdrew his opposition to the regime. This defection had proved a severe blow to his old associates, and the Republicans continued the weakest of all the parties for many years. The driving force of the Left was Socialism, and the Republican ranks did not begin to attract recruits again until the later days of the Directory. As the Crown became increasingly associated with the policy of Primo de Rivera, so those who disapproved of the latter began to declare themselves Republicans. The failure of Berenguer to hold the elections gave an added fillip to this tendency, and so the Republican party reappeared as a force in the country with the veteran Lerroux as its leader. In reality, however, a large proportion of its members were Republicans rather by necessity than by choice, and when the Second Republic did finally come into existence this was a cause of serious weakness.

The rise of Socialism in Spain has already been traced, and its able leader, Iglesias, died in 1925. Under his direction the Socialists had paid more attention to industrial than to political action, and they returned only six deputies to the last Cortes of the monarchy. The party's main support was derived from the *Unión General de Trabajadores*, of which Francisco Largo Caballero was secretary and which had a membership of a quarter of a million. The rule of the Directory had not been unpropitious to the Socialists, for Primo de Rivera dealt more kindly with them than with the other parties, and Largo Caballero was made a member of the Council of State; at the same time their ranks were swelled by the adhesion of many who were, for one reason or another, dissatisfied with the government of the day. On the other hand, Communism, as in every country, was making its appearance to the Left of Socialism, and the *Confederación Nacional del Trabajo* was formed in opposition to the *Unión General de Trabajadores*. There was also the Bolshevist *Sindicato*

Unico which had as its aim the incorporation of all workers in one big union.

The third party to the Pact of San Sebastian, namely the Catalans, were on a rather different footing, for they regarded Spain's extremity as Catalonia's opportunity. The Catalan autonomists were divided into two groups, the moderates under Cambo and the extremists under Macia. It was the latter who pledged themselves to co-operate with the Republicans and Socialists, and the failure of Cambo to induce either Primo de Rivera or Berenguer to make any concession to Catalan aspirations strengthened the hands of Macia and his group. Nevertheless, even the extremists could not demand too much, for the Spanish market is essential to Catalonia. In short, the alliance between the three revolutionary parties was an uneasy one, but it was to achieve its immediate purpose, namely the overthrow of the monarchy. That it took place at all is the measure of Berenguer's incompetence.

Such was the position in December, 1930, when the garrison at Jaca revolted. The rebels were led by Captain Fermín Galan Rodriguez and Angel Garcia Hernández, and several people were killed before the rising was suppressed. The ringleaders were shot after trial by court-martial, and at once became martyrs in the eyes of the Left. Four days later the Republicans seized some aeroplanes at the Cuatro Vientos aerodrome outside Madrid, and flew over the capital, dropping leaflets which called upon the troops stationed there to mutiny. The hero of this exploit was Commandante Franco, but it met with no more success than the attempt at Jaca. The ease with which these risings were crushed should have strengthened the Berenguer administration, but it had just the opposite effect, for the mere fact that they had happened was regarded as a sign of its weakness. The Government also made a serious blunder in its handling of them, for it gained all the odium for stamping the revolts out in blood without the advantage which would have accrued from such a policy, that is to say, fear on the part of the disaffected. Moreover, these troubles meant a further postponement of the elections.

The opening of the year 1931 witnessed another false step on the part of the Government, for early in January the entire Flying Corps was disbanded, and forbidden to wear its distinctive uniform. This merely added to the number of Berenguer's enemies, and to those of the King, who had given his consent to such a measure. By now the Government was so thoroughly unpopular that the old politicians realised their chance had come to get rid of Berenguer. Accordingly, the Count of Romanones, the Marquis of Alhucemas, and Señor Cambo informed the Prime Minister that while they would, as promised, take part in the General Election, as soon as the Cortes met they would demand a *Cortes Constituyentes*. Berenguer had now reached the limits of his patience, and on February 15 he resigned. The King realised the gravity of the situation thus created, and endeavoured to get a ministry formed on the widest possible basis. He declared himself ready to summon a *Cortes Constituyentes*, and Sánchez Guerra and Melquiades Alvárez even tried to enlist the support of Alcalá Zamora, who was in prison for his complicity in the December rebellion. It was all in vain, for personal and party feeling was too strong to allow of co-operation, and what proved to be the last ministry of the monarchy was constituted with the inclusion of such old party leaders as the Count of Romanones, the Marquis of Alhucemas, Don Juan de la Cierva, and the Count of Bugallal, as well as General Berenguer.

The constitution of the new Government made revolution inevitable, for it marked the return to power of those very politicians whom the vast majority of Spaniards, whatever their political opinions, hoped the Directory had driven out of public life for ever. Now they had returned at the King's request, and from the moment they took office the fate of the throne was sealed. Even the most convinced monarchists had no desire to fight for those whom they profoundly distrusted, while the ministers themselves had no sort of following in the country. The issue had become narrowed to a vote for or against the Crown, and all the advantages were with the opponents of the latter. They had managed, partly by their own skill but chiefly owing to the blunders of Berenguer, to unite against the monarchy all those who had disapproved of the Directory, all who had lost their jobs under the administration of its successor, and all who were determined to prevent the Government falling once more into the hands of the old politicians. It was a masterpiece of political strategy, though this cannot disguise the fact that had King Alfonso possessed reasonably competent advisers the scheme would have failed.

The new Prime Minister, Admiral Aznar, and his colleagues decided to hold the local elections on April 12, but before that date two events took place which well illustrate the incurable levity of the Spaniard in matters political, and the consequent difficulty which confronts those who have to govern Spain. The Queen returned from a visit to England, and both at the station in Madrid and during the progress through the streets she and the King were greeted with the most tumultuous reception. A week before the elections was Easter Sunday, and the elaborate ceremonial associated with that event at the Spanish Court was carried out without a hitch, in the midst of popular approval. The Spaniard was apparently quite ready to acclaim the King one day and to vote Republican the next, so that in the circumstances it is hardly surprising that no Power abroad, with the exception of the Holy See, should have foreseen what was about to happen.

The local elections were duly held on the day fixed, and they resulted in the return of 22,150 Royalists and 5,875 Republicans, but the opponents of the regime swept the larger towns. Never was the old saying that revolutions are made in the towns and restorations in the country better exemplified than in this instance. It is probable that many of those who voted Republican did so because there was no other way open to them of expressing their disapproval of the Ministry, but, however that may be, the Government completely lost its head. Aznar announced to the Press that the country had gone Republican overnight, while Berenguer, without consulting his colleagues, sent the following instructions to the Captains-General throughout the country:—

> The Municipal elections have given the result your Excellency may suppose from what has happened in the district of your command. The poll indicates the rout of monarchist candidates in Madrid, Barcelona, Valencia, and the principal capital towns. The elections have been lost. This creates a most delicate situation, which the Cabinet will have to consider when full data are to hand. At this supreme juncture your Excellency will appreciate the absolute necessity of maximum serenity, with hearts raised in the service of the highest interests of the nation, which the Army is called upon to defend at all times. Your Excellency should maintain close contact with the garrisons under your orders, calling upon all to have complete confidence in the higher command, maintaining discipline at all costs, ready to give what help may be needed to maintain law and order. This will be the guarantee that the destiny of Spain shall continue without grave disturbances along the lines imposed by the supreme national will.

Perhaps the best comment upon this document was that of the Madrid correspondent of *The Times*: "If the Republican Committee itself had been called upon to circularize the military commanders, it would hardly have drawn up instructions better calculated to serve the purpose of paving the way for a peaceful monarchist surrender."

In effect, the monarchy was not overthrown, it collapsed, as in 1868. When the result of the elections became known the Republicans in Madrid began to demonstrate, and as the authorities did nothing to stop them they became bolder every hour. The King realised that the monarchy could at this stage be saved only by bloodshed, and to his credit he refused to order the troops to fire upon his subjects. The Republican leaders, for their part, were only anxious to take advantage of the existing situation to get the Royal Family out of Spain before there was a revulsion of feeling in its favour. In consequence, King Alfonso departed by way of Cartagena, and the Queen and her children by that of Irun. The victorious Republicans were in such a hurry to see the monarch on foreign soil that he was able to leave Spain without signing any deed of abdication.

CHAPTER XLIII

The Second Republic (1931–1936)

THE most notable fact about the advent to power of the Second Republic was the ease with which it took place, and this had no little connection with its ultimate undoing. In no quarter was there the slightest opposition; on the contrary there was a general desire among all classes to give evidence of long-standing Republican sentiments. The Royalists might have utilised their strength in the countryside to embarrass the new rulers of Spain, but they did nothing of the sort. They were too dazed to act, while their complete lack of a leader, once the King had gone, was a further handicap. It must also be confessed that at this moment there was, owing to the events of the previous decade, little enthusiasm for Don Alfonso XIII, in whom the cause of monarchism was personified. It was, too, believed, with that facile optimism which always attends the morrow of a revolution, that the change which had occurred must necessarily be for the better: even on the Right it was taken for granted that the Republic would be a very moderate affair, which all save the extreme die-hards would be able to support.

This state of affairs certainly enabled the victorious Republicans to assume control with the minimum of inconvenience to themselves, but it was soon to be a serious embarrassment. The revolutionaries were, as has been shown, composed of different elements, and the one thing that might have welded them together would have been a hard fight against a common enemy. This they never had, and the resulting weakness soon became apparent. The last years of the monarchy witnessed the general formation of a coalition of Radicals, Socialists, and Catalan autonomists, while the history of the Second Republic was to be that of the disintegration of this coalition with civil war as the ultimate consequence.

The Spanish Revolution of 1931 suffered from the further disadvantage of being an anachronism. Its leaders proved themselves in only too many cases to be men with the outlook of the nineteenth century, and they were thus in conflict with the spirit of their age, which was variously interpreted as Fascist or Communist, but which was certainly not in sympathy with *bourgeois* Liberalism, or even with conventional Socialism; yet these were the forms of government which the victorious revolutionaries were, for the most part, pledged to establish. Without casting any reflection upon the motives of the leading Spanish Republicans it is impossible to resist the conclusion that they were living in the world of 1848, and the course of events which led up to the fall of the monarchy is certainly reminiscent of an earlier age. The Republic did not introduce any fresh ideas of government, and no revolution is worthy of the name which has not a spiritual as well as a material aspect. This was not, however, apparent in the spring of 1931, save to a few foreign observers, and the change of regime was generally interpreted as a step forward along the paths of progress.

The Provisional Government which was constituted on the fall of the monarchy contained representatives of the various groups which had been parties to the Pact of San Sebastian. The Prime Minister was Alcalá Zamora, who had previously been a monarchist, and had held office in more than one administration during the reign of King Alfonso XIII. At the Interior was Miguel Maura, son of Antonio Maura, the Conservative leader, and he had previously professed his father's opinions: his conversion to the Republican cause had influenced a great many waverers in the same direction. Manuel Azaña, at the Ministry of War, was almost unknown at this time, but in revolutionary circles he had already acquired a reputation for bitterness. Lerroux was Minister of Foreign Affairs, and he was probably the ablest man in the Cabinet, but he was old, and suffered from a constitutional lack of energy. There were three Socialists in the Government, namely Prieto, de las Rios, and Largo Caballero, the last of whom, as we have seen, had served under Primo de Rivera as a member of the Council of State.

One of the first tasks of the new Government was to solve the problem of Catalonia. In that province the revolution had taken the form of the proclamation of Catalan independence, but even autonomists of the school of Macia realised this was an impossibility. Accordingly, after some wrangling between Barcelona and Madrid, the province was declared to be a *Generalitat*, and in due course an Act was passed constituting her what a British lawyer would have described as a more or less autonomous body with a status somewhere between that of a colony, with an unofficial majority in the legislature, and a dominion. The immediate effect was to whet the appetite for self-government of other regions of Spain where centrifugal influences were still powerful.

After satisfying the demands of their Catalan allies in this way, the ministers decided not to embark upon any far-reaching changes until the *Cortes Constituyentes* had been elected. That this was the correct course to pursue cannot be denied, but it at once roused the hostility of the extremists. These had not gone into the streets merely to put Alcalá Zamora in the place of King Alfonso, and they determined to force the hands of the Government. As the monarchy was gone, the most prominent representative of the old order was the Church, and in May the storm against her broke all over Spain. Convents and churches were sacked and burnt, while the police made no attempt to interfere. In many districts the inhabitants, once they realised that those who were nominally responsible for the preservation of law and order intended to do nothing, banded themselves together in defence of the clergy and of their property, and thus put a stop to the perpetration of fresh excesses; while elsewhere the outrages ceased only when there were no more religious buildings to be gutted. Some idea of the damage can be gained from the fact that in Málaga alone nearly fifty churches were sacked, in Madrid libraries containing upwards of 135,000 books were destroyed, while many valuable pictures, including at least one Titian, perished in the flames in different parts of the country.

At this point it must be stressed that the Church in Spain before the advent of the Second Republic was not an institution of almost boundless wealth, upon which the clergy lived in idleness, if not in actual vice. It had been disendowed early in the reign of Isabel II, after scenes of violence to which such majestic ruins as those of Poblet bear testimony, and the small sum which was earmarked in the budgets of the monarchy for ecclesiastical purposes represented compensation of a sort for the vast revenue which the State had taken from the Church.

The case of the Order of Jesus, whose members were expelled by the new regime, is not without interest in this connection. The Jesuits had six centres of higher or university studies; twenty secondary schools or colleges, of which fifteen were boarding-schools; two observatories, at Tortosa and Granada respectively; and a leper colony at Fontilles; there were also ten seminaries. These establishments were all closed by the republican authorities, although the State had not the means of providing the necessary educational facilities itself, as may be seen by a contemporary statement of the Minister of Public Education to the effect that the State schools in Madrid catered for only 37,000 children as against 44,000 who were taught in private schools, of which the vast majority were controlled by the religious orders.

This outbreak showed that the anarchic forces in Spain were as strong as at any time in the past, and that the mere advent of the Second Republic had not solved the problem which has always been one of even greater difficulty in the Peninsula than elsewhere, namely that of reconciling liberty with order. It also had the effect of inaugurating a reaction, not necessarily against the Republican regime, but against the type of Republic that seemed to be the object of the Government. Those who had been content to see the monarchy go down without raising a finger became seriously alarmed when an attack was made on the Church, and this in spite of the fact that the Pope, through the *nuncio* in Madrid, had given proof of his desire to cultivate friendly relations with the Spanish Government. The manifest unwillingness of the authorities to interfere had the double disadvantage of encouraging the extremists on the one hand, while on the other it frightened moderate opinion into a belief that the Government was far farther to the Left than had been supposed. It cannot be denied that there was a good deal of truth in this latter view, for the driving force behind the Cabinet was exercised to no inconsiderable extent by the Socialists, who were determined that the establishment of the Republic should mark the beginning, not the end, of the revolution.

The elections for the *Cortes Constituyentes* were held at the end of June, 1931, and they resulted in the return of an overwhelming majority of deputies pledged to support the Republic. Indeed, the majority was far too large, for it soon began to break up, while it was a genuine misfortune for Spain that the Right, which was beginning to gather force in the country under the leadership of Señor Gil Robles, should hardly have been represented at all. The first sign of this reaction was at a by-election in Madrid in the autumn, when José Antonio Primo de Rivera, son of the late Marquis of Estella, stood as a candidate of the Right, and halved the previous Socialist majority. In October, too, there was a disagreement in the Cabinet between Maura, who represented the moderate wing of the Republicans, and his more advanced colleagues on the question of the separation of Church and State, and a partial reconstruction of the ministry took place in consequence.

The preoccupation of the Cortes was naturally the elaboration of a new Constitution, and this task was completed by December, 1931. It was essentially a Liberal document, though the influence of the Socialists was obvious in many of its provisions. Freedom of conscience was established, no person was to be imprisoned for more than twenty-four hours without being tried, the right of meeting was guaranteed, confiscation of property was forbidden, the irremovability of magistrates was stated, and the deportation or exile of Spanish citizens was declared to be illegal. Government was vested in the President and one Chamber. In accordance with the provisions of the Constitution, Alcalá Zamora was elected to the Presidency of the Republic, and Azaña became Prime Minister at the head of a Cabinet which was predominantly Radical-Socialist and Socialist in its composition.

Before the Constitution had been voted there had been passed a Law for the Defence of the Republic, which became part of the Constitution by virtue of an additional clause. This was one of those exceptional measures which are generally adopted on the morrow of a revolution, and it empowered the Minister of the Interior and the Civil Governors of the provinces:

1. Suspend newspapers indefinitely.
2. Close meeting-houses and clubs, whether political or not.
3. Imprison citizens indefinitely.
4. Compel them to change their domicile.
5. Force them to reside indefinitely at a given spot within national territory, or deport them to places outside the Peninsula.
6. Seize any works or industrial concerns.
7. Forbid any kind of public meeting.

8. Impose fines up to a maximum amount of 10,000 pesetas.
9. Dismiss civil servants, or suspend them from the execution of their duties.

An appeal lay to the Cabinet against any action taken under this law, but the decision of the Government was final. It will be seen that in many material points the Law for the Defence of the Republic was in conflict with the Constitution of which it formed part.

The enactment of the Constitution and the formation of the Azaña administration brought to a close what may be termed the preliminary stage in the life of the Second Republic. Between December, 1931, and the outbreak of the Civil War in July, 1936, the regime was to experience three very distinct phases. The first of these lasted during the years 1932 and 1933, and was marked by the adoption on the part of the Government of a policy even farther to the Left, which, in its turn, began to result in a growing Catholic, Conservative, and Royalist reaction. This period was also characterised by the progressive disintegration of the forces that had brought the Republic into existence; a disintegration that was only temporarily arrested by the alarm created in Republican circles by the attempted *pronunciamiento* of General Sanjurjo in August, 1932. The swing to the Right first became noticeable at the local elections in the spring of 1933, and was most pronounced in the General Election at the end of the same year. This state of affairs rendered Azaña's position impossible, and the second phase began. It lasted until February, 1936, and its chief characteristic was a series of ephemeral Centre administrations which, under pressure from the Right, retraced some of the steps of their more revolutionary predecessors. Finally, in February, 1936, the third phase was ushered in by a General Election which revealed the real weakness of the Centre: this period was marked by a growing anarchy which finally degenerated into civil war in the summer of the same year.

The most important measures of the Azaña administration were those dealing with agrarian reform and with the Church. It cannot be denied that under the monarchy the land, at any rate in some provinces, was not developed in the way it should have been, and there were a number of absentee landlords; indeed, there were tens of thousands of tenants who had never seen the man to whom they paid their rent. King Alfonso had done what he could to make landlords take an interest in their property, but his efforts had proved unavailing in face of the opposition of what was, with a few outstanding exceptions, the most selfish and short-sighted aristocracy in Europe. What was required, if the true interest of agriculture alone was to be considered, was the enactment of some law whereby owners of land must develop their property up to a certain standard under penalty of confiscation.

The scheme put forward by Marcelino Domingo, the Minister for

Agriculture, was a complicated one, and appears to have been modelled on the Russian code of 1923. By this measure the land became the property of the State, and was to be let out at an agreed rental to committees, which were to be chosen from the rural population all over the country. They determined whether the land was to be divided into allotments to be worked by different members of the local population, or whether it was to be developed communally. The committees also had the sole right of buying all necessary tools and agricultural implements, and they disposed of the produce. This project made the worst of both worlds, for it neither gave the land to the peasant nor did it establish a workable system of large-scale farming. Moreover, the confiscation of the estates of the Grandees was an act of injustice which cast grave suspicion upon the motives of the Government in respect of its agrarian policy. The definite failure of the scheme was proved by the fact that within two years the land under cultivation in Spain had diminished to the extent of 750,000 acres.

More disastrous even from its own point of view was the anti-clerical attitude of the Government. The feeble defence put up by the mass of the population on behalf of the monarchy appears to have decided the Prime Minister and his colleagues into the belief that no more serious opposition would be made to an attack on the Church, though the reaction initiated by the riots in May, 1931, should have warned them to the contrary. Here, again, there was a case for reform along moderate lines. There were too many priests, monks, and nuns in Spain, and their intellectual standard was none too high. Education, too, was largely in the hands of the Church, yet the percentage of illiterates was one of the highest in Europe, while the number of schools was hopelessly inadequate. In these circumstances the Government had an excellent opportunity of undertaking the needful reforms by raising the level of the State schools, and then insisting upon those controlled by the Church attaining the same standard. In effect, it was clearly a case for a programme spread over a period of years, and as far as possible put into practice with the co-operation of the religious authorities. Unhappily, procedure along these lines was too slow for the extremists of the Left, upon whom the administration depended for support, and an immediate attack was made upon the Jesuits, who were expelled from the country in spite of the fact that they were the one Order against the quality of whose teaching no objection could be made. In addition, Azaña also suppressed the sum earmarked in the budgets of the monarchy for ecclesiastical purposes, and confiscated all property bequeathed to the Church since the earlier disendowment.

Equally damaging to the Government was its readiness to interfere with the course of justice as a result of pressure by the extremists. Two examples of this will suffice. One of those implicated in the murder of Dato in 1921 was a certain Casanellas, who had escaped to Russia after the perpetration of that crime, and was there converted to Communism. On the fall of the monarchy he returned to Spain, and proceeded to work for the establishment of a Soviet regime. When nearly a year had elapsed he was arrested, not, as might be supposed, to be put upon his trial for his share in Dato's murder, but to be deported for his Communist activities; indeed, he actually received a free pardon for the former offence. Equally flagrant was the case of the three Miralles brothers, sons of a well-known Madrid lawyer. These youths were arrested in May, 1931, after some local disorders, and were kept in prison for two years without being brought before a magistrate. When they were tried not a shred of evidence was produced against them, and the court ordered their immediate release.

In view of the growing opposition which the measures of the Government were encountering, it is not surprising that the numerous enemies of the Prime Minister should have arrived at the conclusion that the time had come for his overthrow. Accordingly, in August, 1932, General Sanjurjo made a *pronunciamiento* at Seville, where the garrison supported him. It is not clear what he intended to do, or upon what promise of support from other parts of the country he was relying. In any event, the attempt was a complete fiasco, for his collaborators in Madrid proved quite incompetent, and such leaders of the Right as Gil Robles held themselves entirely aloof. Sanjurjo surrendered, and was condemned to death, but the sentence was commuted to one of imprisonment, and he was actually released in the general amnesty in the spring of 1934.

The immediate effect of this ill-advised attempt was greatly to strengthen the Government by rallying to its side all who feared the overthrow of the regime. For the moment all the forces which had brought the Republic into existence were again united. Azaña took advantage of this revulsion of feeling in his favour to secure the enactment of two measures which further safeguarded his position. The first of these gave the Government power to dismiss, finally and summarily, civil and military officials who might commit acts hostile to the Republic, or calculated to bring it into contempt. The second enabled the Government to confiscate the estates of those who, in the opinion of the Minister of the Interior, had taken part in Sanjurjo's revolt, or had expressed themselves in sympathy with its object. It was, indeed, only natural that on the morrow of a revolt the Government should arm itself with the powers necessary to prevent another outbreak of a similar nature, but where Azaña made his mistake was in his extensive use of those powers. Like James II after the failure of Monmouth, he threw away all the advantages which victory had conferred on him, and within a short space his administration was even more unpopular than it had been before the Sanjurjo conspiracy.

It was not only that a large number of suspected persons were kept in prison for long periods without trial, and that the Opposition Press was suspended for weeks at a time, which aroused indignation, but also the deportation by the Government of its political opponents to Africa in defiance of the provisions of the Constitution. Nearly 140 men were, in the autumn of 1932, deported with every refinement of brutality to Villa Cisneros on the order of the Minister of the Interior, and of this number hardly any had even appeared before a court, or had a definite charge preferred against them. Villa Cisneros is a barren and unhealthy spot on the edge of the Sahara, to which water is brought twice a month from the Canaries; it is likewise devoid of all sanitation. When the deportees arrived there they found no mattresses, blankets, furniture, or even habitable dwellings; they slept on planks covered with straw, and they were obliged to buy tables and chairs at their own expense. In the end, twenty-nine of the prisoners escaped in an open boat to Portugal, while the rest, after six months in Africa, were brought back to Spain, where most of them were released as the authorities had nothing against them. No reason was given for their deportation, nor were they indemnified in any way. Another political opponent of the Government, Dr. Albiñana, was relegated to Las Hurdes, the most desolate region in the Peninsula, where he was compelled to live in a stable, while the ex-Rector of Saragossa University was interned in a remote hamlet in the province of Granada.

Early in January, 1933, the Communists and Anarchists rose in revolt in many parts of the country, and were suppressed only after some hard fighting, in which about a hundred people were killed. The Government showed as much vigour, let it be frankly stated, on this occasion against the Left as it had displayed in the previous August against the Right, but, as then, it alienated public sympathy in the hour of victory by excessive severity. The incidents at Casas Viejas, a small village in the province of Cádiz, for example, roused a storm of indignation among all parties. There had been a clash in which two of the Civil Guard were killed, and the Shock Police were sent into the village to make an example of it. This they did with characteristic thoroughness, and at least twenty peasants met their death as a result. The methods employed to restore order can best be gauged from the fact that a woman was beaten to death; a cottage was set on fire, and the occupants, including a young girl, were mowed down by machine-guns as they endeavoured to escape; and an old man was shot dead in his bed. When the news of these events reached Madrid and questions were asked in the Cortes, the Government made the great mistake of resisting inquiry. The result was that Azaña and his colleagues were at once held responsible for the atrocities committed by their subordinates, and thus became as unpopular on the Left as they already were on the Right.

In April, 1933, the local elections, at which women voted for the first time, were held, and they served to show how unpopular the Government had become. Of the councillors elected, 4,586 were classed as supporters of Azaña, and 11,742 as opponents, while the percentage of votes polled by the Government candidates was only 28. This defeat was the more remarkable in that the Law for the Defence of the Republic made all Royalist propaganda impossible, while it was a notorious fact that, as always in Spain under any regime, the authorities had exerted the greatest pressure upon the electors. The result was that although the Government was not, of course, directly affected by these local elections, it lost what moral influence it still possessed, for it was clear that they were prophetic of what would happen when the Cortes itself was dissolved. In these circumstances it was only natural that Azaña's agricultural and anti-clerical policy should meet with increasing opposition.

Further evidence of the Government's unpopularity was forth-coming in September, when the elections were held for the Court of Constitutional Guarantees, appointed to supervise the proper work-ing of the Constitution. Out of fifteen members elected to the tribunal by specified regions of Spain only five of Azana's supporters (two of them very doubtful ones at that) were returned, as against four of Lerroux's Radicals and six Conservatives of the extreme Right. When the College of Advocates, composed of the lawyers of Spain, chose its two representatives to the tribunal, it elected Calvo Sotelo, the Finance Minister of the Directory, and Cesar Silio, both avowed Royalists. Faced with this rising tide of opposition, Azaña resigned.

After making every allowance for the difficulties of the position, it is not easy to reach any other conclusion than that Azaña in power was a disaster both for the Republic and Spain. He settled nothing and he unsettled everything. He practised violence, forgetting that in politics violence begets violence. He was dependent upon the Socialists for support, and he did not hesitate to use all the machinery of the State against their enemies, both to Right and Left. The Casas Viejas incident filled the Communist and Anarchist ranks, and drove them to fury. When he took office the Right was crushed; when he resigned it was a growing force. As for the Church, he acted in such a way that every practising Catholic was forced into opposition to the Government, if not to the regime. He had the chance of con-solidating opinion in support of the Republic, but he behaved in such a manner as to prepare the way for civil war. As for the interests of the country as a whole, Azaña's stewardship is best illustrated by the fact that during the course of it the value of shares in first-class Spanish enterprises fell by 50 per cent, and that the export trade of Spain decreased by two-thirds.

The fall of Azaña, who was succeeded as Prime Minister by Lerroux, ushered in the second phase of the Republic, and the elections, which were held in November, 1933, were marked by a sharp swing to the Right, who obtained 217 seats, as compared with 162 gained by the Centre and 93 by the Left. Unfortunately what this meant so far as the government of the country was concerned was that the pendulum did not swing far enough to the Right for a stable administration to be formed. The result was a series of ministries of the Centre dependent upon the Right. The latter, it should not be forgotten, consisted of several groups, of which by far the strongest was *Acción Popular*, headed by Gil Robles, who for some time was regarded by his fellow-countrymen as a second Cánovas. The son of a Carlist professor at Salamanca, he had stood as a monarchist in 1931, and since then he had worked at perfecting the organisation of his party. Closely allied with *Acción Popular* were the *Tradicionalistas* and *Acción Española*. The *Tradicionalistas* represented the old Carlist element, and were particularly strong in the North and North-east: their leader was the Count of Rodezno. *Acción Española* was composed of the supporters of Don Alfonso XIII, and was led by Antonio Goicoechea: its strength in the new Cortes was thirty-seven. Aloof from these groups stood the Spanish Phalanx, headed by José Antonio Primo de Rivera: they already had branches all over Spain, and claimed 80,000 adherents in Madrid alone.

The failure of the Left at the elections shook its faith in the parliamentary system, and some sections of it soon passed from propaganda to direct action. A Communist revolt broke out in October, 1934, but it was at once suppressed in Madrid and many other places. In Asturias, however, it soon assumed the character of civil war, for the extremists succeeded in persuading the miners to take up arms, and there was heavy fighting in and around Oviedo. The insurgents were not overcome until there had been considerable loss of life and many outrages had been committed, for the Azaña administration had so starved the Army that it was incapable of doing its work in an emergency. During the course of these disturbances, it may be added, the rebels stole £400,000 from the banks to finance their operations.

When the revolt had been put down, the Government gave abundant proof that it had learnt nothing from the mistakes of its predecessor in similar circumstances. Instead of shooting the ringleaders, and letting the rank and file go free, it put a couple of obscure individuals to death, released any rebels of prominence, and kept hundreds of others in prison without bringing them to trial. The consequence was that the Government, not its opponents, received the chief odium, owing to the tendency of the public to place the blame, not upon those whose sins are the worst, but upon those who have sinned the most recently. At the same time the fact cannot be ignored that the insurrection had been directed against the lawfully constituted Government of Spain, which had a majority in the Cortes. If it was justified, then so was that of Franco two years later; if the latter is indefensible, so was the Communist revolt in Asturias in the autumn of 1934.

Thereafter matters were allowed to drift. For some months Lerroux was Premier with Gil Robles as Minister of War, and if the general situation was better than it had been in the days of Azaña, the lull but preceded another storm. The Right was by now no means satisfied with the influence it was able to exert. It is true that Gil Robles secured the repeal of two measures which were particularly obnoxious to his supporters, namely the expulsion of the Religious Orders and the confiscation of private property, but in his position, and with his following, he could scarcely have done less. The Left was taking full advantage of the blunders of the Government on the morrow of the rising in Asturias, and began to close its ranks under the name of the Popular Front in a way that its opponents would have done well to regard as significant. Finally, several members of the Lerroux administration became involved in financial scandals, and Lerroux had to resign. The President refused to call the Right to power, and conferred the premiership on one Portela Valladares, who was not only without followers, but had not himself a seat in the Cortes. In February, 1936, recourse was had to new elections with a view to finding a way out of what had become a deadlock. The result was to make the situation a great deal worse, for the practical elimination of the Centre left the two extremes of opinion face to face. The result of the voting was as follows:

Popular Front . 4,356,000 votes and 270 seats.
Centre . . 449,000 votes and 60 seats.
Right . . 4,128,000 votes and 140 seats.

The proportion of seats won to votes obtained requires no comment. In addition, there is considerable evidence of interference with the voting by the supporters of the Popular Front, particularly in Valencia, Cuenca, and Málaga. It was already clear that only a miracle could avert civil war.

The immediate result of the election was the return of Azaña to the Premiership, but he was unable to secure the support of the extreme Left owing to the opposition of Largo Caballero, who was demanding the dictatorship of the proletariat: he was thus compelled to form his administration upon a basis so narrow as seriously to curtail its influence even with the groups composing the Popular Front. Similarly, on the Right the prestige of Gil Robles was on the wane owing to the growing lack of confidence in his powers of leadership, and there were already whispers that the only solution was a *pronunciamiento*.

One of the first acts of the Popular Front was to dismiss the President, and in so doing it certainly had the support of all sections of public opinion. The Republic's ambassador in London, Perez de Ayala, said of him, "Our political repertory swarms with picturesque and theatrical figures. For instance, Señor Zamora who with his clownish eloquence and satisfied smile is reminiscent of the traditional clown in the Spanish theatre." He had resigned the Premiership as a protest against the anti-clerical policy of the new rulers of Spain, but the offer of the Presidency, with its annual income of £60,000, reconciled him to a programme of which he had previously disapproved. While President he alienated all parties, and no one regretted it when he followed into exile the monarch whom he had supplanted. He lived on until 1949. Alcalá Zamora was succeeded by Azaña.

Meanwhile Spain was relapsing into chaos. To quote Salvador de Madariaga: "Neither life nor property was safe anywhere. . . . It was not only the owner of thousands of acres granted his ancestors by King So-and-So whose house was invaded, and whose cattle were left bleeding with broken legs on the smoking fields of his lands. It was the modest Madrid doctor or lawyer, who had a villa of four rooms and bath, and a garden as big as three handkerchiefs, who saw his house occupied by land-workers, by no means homeless and by no means hungry, who came to harvest his crop: ten men to do the work of one, and to stay in his house till they had finished. It was the secretary of the local gardeners' union who came to threaten the young girl watering her roses that all watering had to be done by union men; it was a movement to prohibit owner-drivers from driving their own cars and to force them to accept a union driver. . . . No wonder that Fascism grew. Let no one argue that it was Fascist violence which developed Socialist violence."[1]

A judge who had given a sentence of thirty years to a Fascist for the murder of a Socialist newspaper boy was shot dead in Madrid on April 13. The following day, during a parade to celebrate the anniversary of the Republic, a lieutenant of the Civil Guard was shot dead by Socialists. His funeral was regarded by the Fascists as an excellent opportunity for displaying their strength, and a running battle developed in the very centre of Madrid, through which the procession was, incidentally, passing in defiance of the orders of the Government. Such incidents were typical, not exceptional.

On June 16, 1936, Gil Robles indicted the Government for its failure to maintain order. During the first four months of Popular Front rule 269 people had been murdered, and 1,287 injured, in political disturbances; 160 churches had been completely destroyed and 231 partly damaged; 69 Right Wing political headquarters had been wrecked and 312 were damaged; there had been 113 general and 228 partial strikes; while 10 newspaper offices had been sacked and 33 damaged. On July 8 there came another fierce attack on the Government, this time from Calvo Sotelo. As he sat down, Dolores Ibarruri, better known as La Pasionaria, a Communist deputy, shouted at him, "That is your last speech."

[1] *Spain*, pp. 346 and 349.

Four days later an officer of the Shock Police by name Castillo, noted for his Communist sympathies, was murdered by Fascist gunmen outside his house in Madrid. At three o'clock on the following morning a detachment of the Shock Police came in uniform to the home of Calvo Sotelo, took him away, murdered him, and left his body at the gates of a cemetery. Another body of police visited the residence of Gil Robles, but he was already in hiding. The Government arrested the ninety men of the company to which Castillo belonged, but did nothing more. On the 18th the army in Morocco revolted, and the Civil War had begun.

CHAPTER XLIV

The Civil War (1936–1939)

THE struggle which began with the revolt of the Melilla garrison on July 18 had in its origin nothing to do with the clash between conflicting ideologies which was so prominent a feature of the contemporary international scene. The movement against the Government was purely military in its nature, and there were many precedents for it in the history of Spain. General Franco and his colleagues were thinking in terms of a *pronunciamiento* similar to that of Primo de Rivera thirteen years before, and it was only when their plans miscarried that they were forced to prepare for a civil war which had assuredly not entered into their original calculations. Certainly the movement was not monarchist in origin, for whatever the views of Franco himself, most of his generals, especially Queipo de Llano, were strong republicans at one time, and even Franco in the earlier days of the republic had refused to commit himself on the question of regime. Nor did the rising owe anything to the Spanish Phalanx, for José Antonio Primo de Rivera had been arrested and imprisoned some months before it took place, so that he could hardly have been implicated. In fact, his fate was for long in doubt, and he was referred to by his followers as *El Ausente*—the absent one—until it was established that having been condemned to death by a popular tribunal he was shot in Alicante prison in November, 1936.

On the other hand, it is clear that Franco's blow forestalled one by the Communists. Documents which fell into the hands of the Nationalists proved that the plans of the extreme Left were complete, and from them it would appear that the signal was probably the murder of Calvo Sotelo. At any rate, very early in the programme occurs the ominous phrase, "execution of those who figure on the black lists". Further items of interest were the provision for a pretended Fascist attack on the Socialist headquarters, and the appointment of Largo Caballero as the President of the Spanish Soviet. Russian complicity, it may be added, was fully established. The Communist rising was originally to have taken place between May 3 and June 29, but it was subsequently postponed until the end of July, and this change of plan enabled the Nationalists, as they soon came to be termed, to get their blow in first. In these circumstances Franco and his associates could surely claim to be following the advice given by no less a statesman than Gladstone, who once said that "if no instructions had ever been addressed to the people of this country, except to remember to hate violence and love order and exercise patience, the liberties of this country would never have been attained".

However this may be, the original plan of campaign was to paralyse the action of the Government by the seizure of all the more important centres of population at a single blow. General Franco, who was

Captain-General of the Canaries, flew to Morocco, where he assumed command of the troops, with whom he was personally popular owing to his service there in the days of the monarchy. Even more remarkable was the exploit of Quiepo de Llano, who bluffed Seville into surrender at the head of one hundred and fifty men: he first captured the radio station, from which he constantly sent out news that he was advancing on the city with an army of forty thousand: he then put his handful into lorries, and sent them out again and again to various districts to create an impression of overwhelming strength. Elsewhere Mola obtained control of a large part of the North of Spain, while Cabanellas seized Zaragoza.

These were, indeed, considerable successes, but they were far from constituting final victory, and they were counterbalanced by serious reverses. In the capital General Fanjul hesitated too long, and thus gave the Government time to arm the Workers' Unions, who overpowered him on July 20, and stormed the barracks of La Montaña. Much the same happened in Catalonia: for General Goded, who commanded in the Balearic Islands, went to take charge of the rising there, but was captured and shot. Finally, General Sanjurjo was killed in an air accident as he flew from Lisbon to join the Nationalists. Had he lived, he would have assumed the leadership of the movement, which now passed into the hands of Franco and Mola. Thus a few days after the first blows had been struck it had become obvious that the rising had neither failed nor succeeded, and that a civil war, possibly of a protracted nature, was inevitable. Such being the case, both sides began to take stock of their position.

Geographically they were curiously placed. The Government held Madrid, the whole eastern coast, La Mancha, New Castile, and Estremadura. This cut the Nationalists in the North off from those at Seville, but Guipuzcoa, Biscay, and Santander, which still acknowledged the Government, were in their turn separated from the rest of the territory under the control of Madrid. It was significant of what lay ahead that in the main this had been the line of division in previous civil conflicts. It had been so in the seventeenth century when the Catalans accepted Louis XIII as their ruler: it was the same again sixty years later when the Archduke Charles held Catalonia and much of Aragon against Philip V; and in the War of Independence the *afrancesados* were particularly strong in the East of Spain. It was the old struggle of the Gothic–Celt–Iberians against the men of Romance blood.

In several respects the Government had an advantage over its opponents. Since it had not been overthrown in the initial attempt it was in possession of the resources available to constituted authority: and the machinery of administration was in its hands, whereas the Nationalists had to improvise everything. Then, again, its enemies did not possess command of the sea, and this meant that it was highly dangerous to bring troops over from Morocco, although the Protectorate was entirely in Franco's hands. To some extent, however, this advantage was offset by the fact that the crews of the Government men-of-war had murdered their officers, generally in circumstances of revolting barbarity, and in consequence the ships were often unable to put to sea. On the other hand, the Government had practically no regular troops and hardly any officers. From the beginning, therefore, it was compelled to rely upon the workers, whom it provided with arms from the State arsenals. The effect of this upon the political situation was not long in being felt, and power began to shift even farther to the Left. At the beginning of September, 1936, the Premiership passed to Largo Caballero, and his Cabinet included men of extreme views such as Álvarez del Vayo, Indalecio Prieto, and Juan Negrín. This development was accelerated by Communist activities with the support of Russia, which had for long been desirous of fishing in the troubled waters of Spanish politics. As early as April, 1936, for example, a party of over a hundred Spaniards and pseudo-Spaniards, who had been living in Moscow, passed through Paris, and were forwarded to Madrid with every care and attention on the part of the Spanish embassy.

As summer began to merge into autumn the military situation gradually improved from the point of view of the Nationalists, for whatever their difficulties might be they were careful never to allow the strategic initiative to pass into the hands of their opponents. Before the Powers placed an embargo on the sale of munitions to either side they managed to obtain a considerable number of aeroplanes, and by this means it proved possible to get Franco's forces from Morocco across the Straits of Gibraltar. During these months, too, the command of the sea passed from the Government to the Nationalists, who were able to complete the construction of some ships which were being built at Ferrol, and after the end of September the Government men-of-war had suffered such losses that for all practical purposes they ceased to exist as an effective force. After a few days' siege Badajoz was taken, and Estremadura was cleared of Government troops, so that communication was established with the Nationalists who were operating in the North. The next step was the capture of Irun and San Sebastian, thereby closing the western end of the Franco-Spanish frontier, and so stopping the provision of supplies to the enemy forces round Bilbao. Finally, there was the relief of the garrison of the Alcazar at Toledo. When all this had been done the way was clear for an advance on Madrid.

Meanwhile an important political event had taken place, for on November 1 the Nationalists had appointed Francisco Franco as Generalissimo of their armies and Head of the Spanish State for the duration of the war. At that time, although he was only forty-three years of age, he had a distinguished and varied career behind him. His father was a naval officer, and Francisco was a second son. He joined the infantry academy at Toledo in 1907, and five years later first saw service in Morocco. In 1920 he assisted Millán Astray in the formation of the Spanish Foreign Legion, and he served with it until the end of the war, when at the age of thirty-three he was already a Brigadier-General. Franco's next appointment was that of commandant of the new military academy at Zaragoza, and he held that post when the monarchy fell in 1931. He served the Second Republic in several capacities as loyally as he had the preceding regime, saying that "soldiers should stand aside from politics and think of the nation". All the same he gradually came under suspicion as power at Madrid shifted to the Left, and he was virtually exiled to the Canary Islands, where, as has been shown, he was Captain-General in the summer of 1936. The death of Sanjurjo, it may be added, did much to bring Franco to the fore.

What may be described as the purely Spanish phase of the Civil War ended in the first week of November, 1936. During this period it is true that France, then under a Popular Front administration, supplied the Government, and Italy the Nationalists, with a number of aircraft, but no political colour was thereby given to the struggle, nor was there any serious foreign attempt to interfere with its conduct. After November the nature of the contest changed, and for a space there was a real danger that, as at the beginning of the eighteenth century, a Spanish quarrel might develop into a European war. That this did not take place was largely due to the efforts of British diplomacy, but, in spite of all the exertions of London, intervention there was, and Spain experienced, though happily only to a modified extent, the fate of Germany in the Thirty Years' War: that is to say she became the place where were tested the latest theories in strategy and politics.

It had been generally believed abroad that the *pronunciamiento* would either succeed or fail in a relatively short period: what had not been anticipated, either in Spain or out of it, was a prolonged civil war. When this proved inevitable it was only natural that, given the existing division of Europe into two armed camps, the various Powers should take active steps to see that the conflict terminated in a manner favourable to their interests. France was the first in this field, and it was estimated that by June, 1938, more than a hundred of the aeroplanes brought down by the Nationalists were French. Nor was this all, for during the course of a debate in the French Chamber of Deputies in December, 1938, it was stated that from twenty to thirty thousand Frenchmen had gone to fight against the Nationalists in Spain. In effect, French intervention was probably more powerful than that of any other country on either side, and it was just as much official intervention as that of Italy and Germany: the only difference was that no secret was made of the activity of the Axis Powers, while France posed all the time as the protagonist of non-intervention. What finally caused the Popular Front administration in Paris to change its policy was a realisation of the fact that arms could not be spared for Spain in face of the rapid rearmament of Germany, as the events of the late spring of 1940 were abundantly to prove.

Russia contented herself, largely in view of her remote geographical situation, with the provision of a few senior military officers, a number of experts, and airmen in considerable quantity. By the end of June, 1938, the Nationalists claimed to have brought down eight hundred Russian aeroplanes, and at the beginning of that same year there were said to have been over three thousand Russian prisoners in captivity. In every country in the world the efforts of the Soviet in aid of the Spanish Left were unceasing, and this fact was fully recognised, for when the first units of the International Brigade marched through Madrid in October, 1936, they were greeted with shouts of "*Viva Rusia*". Everybody knew who had sent them, although there were very few actual Russians in their ranks. The greatest contribution to the Government cause was, indeed, this same International Brigade, though its exact strength is not easy to determine in the absence of reliable statistics. The official Nationalist figure put them at 100,000, but other observers estimated them at anything between 50,000 and 150,000. In any event they seem to have been at least as numerous as the foreigners who fought for Franco.

Germany and Italy recognised the Nationalist Government on November 18, 1936, and thereafter reinforcements from those two countries arrived in not inconsiderable numbers, though there were never more than 46,000 Italians and 7,000 Germans, the latter being entirely airmen and technicians; these forces, it may be added, were openly kept up to strength by their respective countries until April, 1938.

In effect, the war began to take on a different complexion, and in its new form it did not at once go well for the Nationalists, who suffered several reverses during the ensuing winter. Franco at first endeavoured to end the contest by combining his forces for an attack on Madrid at the beginning of November, but the first units of the International Brigade arrived in the capital just in time to forestall him. In March, 1937, Franco's Italian allies, who were not of high quality, were routed at Guadalajara, and this convinced the Nationalist leader that before anything more was attempted on this part of the front his troops required further training. In this connection he had the great advantage over his opponents that it was never necessary for him to guard his lines of communication, which was proof where the sentiments of the people lay, and so he was able to make the most effective use of his man-power. In February, 1937, the Nationalists captured Malaga, but during the rest of that year they concentrated their energies on Mola's campaign in the North, and this was highly successful; by the end of October the towns of Bilbao, Santander, and Gijon, with the surrounding country, had been lost to the

Government. It is to be noted that while these events were taking place a Russian General Staff, headed by General Goriev, had installed itself in the War Office in Madrid.

By this time the danger of the conflict becoming an international one was very great indeed, and it could only be avoided with considerable difficulty. The initiative in this matter was taken by Great Britain, for it was by no means to her interests that Europe should be divided into two armed camps. What was required was clearly a lightning-conductor of some sort. The League of Nations would have been the natural instrument for this purpose, but Germany was no longer a member, and Italy viewed Geneva and all its works with the gravest suspicion and disfavour. Therefore the Non-Intervention Committee was called into existence in London under the chairmanship of Lord Plymouth: it first met on September 9, 1936, and in the following December the Council of the League of Nations expressed is approval of the policy pursued by the British Government. What all this really amounted to was that intervention was only to be on a scale which was unlikely to result in an extension of the struggle beyond the frontiers of Spain.

As time went on even this modest aim became extremely difficult of attainment. On May 24, 1937, an Italian patrol-ship was bombed off the Balearic Islands by Spanish Government aeroplanes, while five days later the German cruiser *Deutschland*, on patrol service in the same area on behalf of the Non-Intervention Committee, was also attacked, and several of her crew were killed. As a reprisal Hitler ordered the bombardment of Almeria, while both Italy and Germany withdrew from the patrol service and the Non-Intervention Committee. This step was followed by a number of mysterious sinkings in the Mediterranean, and in September a conference of the Powers interested was held at Nyon to consider the question of appropriate action. Italy was to have been present, but she foolishly allowed herself to become the victim of a Russian manœuvre. Stalin felt that something must be done to restore Soviet prestige, reduced as it was almost to vanishing-point by the repeated executions of his opponents, and the readiest method seemed to be to convert the Nyon Conference into a court-martial on Italy, whose submarines were suspected in many quarters to be guilty of the acts of piracy in question. The first thing to do was to prevent Italy's attendance, and this was achieved by the presentation at Rome of two insulting notes: the Italians very stupidly played into the Russian hands, and stayed away, which was exactly what Moscow wanted. However, the British Government had no intention of becoming a partner in the Franco-Soviet Pact, which was the Russian manœuvre, and its representative made no reference to general politics, but confined himself to the subject for which the conference had been summoned, namely the suppression of piracy in the Mediterranean. The upshot was that Great Britain and France decided to patrol specific areas of that sea, and Italy soon associated herself with them: any submarine encountered in suspicious circumstances by the warships of any of the Powers represented at the conference was to be attacked immediately.

By this time the attitude of Berlin towards the Spanish struggle had become extremely equivocal. Hitler had recognised Franco, and was apparently giving him every assistance to procure an early victory, but as the year 1937 drew to a close the question began to be asked whether German diplomacy was not in fact being directed towards a prolongation of the contest. It was remembered that tension in the Mediterranean had always suited the German book since the French occupation of Tunis had thrown Italy into the arms of Bismarck; therefore credence was given to the growing rumours that German relations with Russia were resuming something of their old cordiality, and that Berlin was supplying arms to Franco's opponents as well as to the Nationalists. It was, too, Germany which put pressure on Italy to cease co-operation in the naval cordon which prevented contraband from reaching Spain, and the abolition of this form of control was, in the existing military situation, not in the interests of Franco. Of course, the ideologists on both sides resolutely shut their eyes to these developments, but they were straws to show which way the wind was beginning to blow, as was proved two years later when the conclusion of the Russo-German Pact was announced.

As the war progressed without victory inclining to either side, both the Nationalists and the Government were increasingly affected by the course which it was taking. It was soon apparent that Franco's followers had widely different aims. The *requetes*, who were among the best of the Nationalist troops, and whose main recruiting-ground was Navarre, were the heirs of Carlism, and were inspired by its religious and political ideals. Then there were the Alfonsists: it is true that only a minority of them wished for the restoration of Don Alfonso XIII, but they all supported his branch of the House of Bourbon, and looked forward to the reign of his son, Juan, with Franco as a second Primo de Rivera. Lastly, there were the Phalangists, who had no use for a monarchy at all, but who desired the establishment of a totalitarian state on the model of the Third Reich. In these circumstances, and with victory still postponed, it is hardly surprising that in the spring of 1937 there should have been conspiracies against Franco both in Málaga and in Morocco. They were easily crushed, but the Generalissimo did not neglect the warning, and he endeavoured to make the best of the three worlds of his supporters by combining them in one organisation called the *Falange Española Tradicionalista y de las Juntas de Ofensiva Nacional Sindicalista*. In January, 1938, a further step was taken, and Franco set up a regular Cabinet, consisting of three generals and eight civilians, presided over by himself. At the Interior was his brother-in-law, Serrano Suñer, a convinced Phalangist and a zealous partisan of the closest co-operation with Germany and Italy. In view of the assistance which the Nationalist movement was receiving from these two Powers, some approximation to their ideological standpoint was inevitable, but the events of the Second World War were to show that it was nothing like so close as was generally believed by foreigners. At no time, for instance, was Franco prepared to consider the bartering of Spanish territory for foreign help.

A not dissimilar situation developed among the followers of the Government, with Negrín as a far more powerful Serrano Suñer. Although the extreme Left was by now in effective control, Russia had to move more cautiously than Germany and Italy, not only for the geographical reasons to which allusion has already been made, but also because many of the Spanish Communists looked to Trotsky rather than to Stalin, while a not inconsiderable number of the Government's supporters were Anarchists. Accordingly, Moscow, to use a phrase of Madariaga, "always kept the Spanish Revolutionists on short commons so as to have them well in hand", though she by no means neglected her own material interests, for as early as the autumn of 1936, while Negrín was Minister of Finance, about fifteen hundred millions of pesetas in gold were transferred from Spain to Russia. Gradually Azaña and Largo Caballero receded into the background, and by the summer of 1938 all real power on the Government side was in the hands of Negrín. The hold of Russia increased, too, as French support dwindled: it had become clear that the Spanish Government's aims were actually Communist, whatever might be alleged to the contrary, and this in no way appealed to the vast majority of the French people, whose gaze in any case, as the whole international horizon grew steadily darker, was directed across the Rhine rather than across the Pyrenees.

By this time the conflict had already proved itself to be the most bitter and the most bloody of all the civil wars ever fought in the Peninsula. It was not that the fighting was at any time on the scale which characterised the American Civil War, but rather that, as the Nationalist forces advanced, the evidence of the atrocities committed by the more extreme supporters of the Government accumulated rapidly until it amounted to a tale of horror which the outside world long found it difficult to credit. In particular, the Church was subjected to a persecution without parallel for several centuries. From the beginning of the war it had been the object of relentless severity, and between fourteen and sixteen thousand priests were murdered in the territory controlled by the Government. No Catholic worship was allowed there, and many a church and cathedral was used as a market or as a thoroughfare for animal-drawn vehicles. Nor did the few Protestants fare any better, and all the Church of England chaplaincies in republican Spain were closed at the beginning of the war, and they remained in that condition until it came to an end. In this connection it is not without significance that when the Deans of Rochester and Chichester visited Barcelona in 1937 they did not dare to appear in the streets in clerical garb. Yet by Article 27 of the constitution, liberty of conscience and freedom of worship were guaranteed.

Prisons were only too often a synonym for torture-chambers, and the Gestapo had nothing to teach those responsible for the revolting crimes perpetrated in such cities as Barcelona upon all suspected of Nationalist sympathies. Exact figures are impossible to ascertain, but in 1943 the Minister of Justice estimated that the cases of murder actually investigated amounted to 85,940, and it is probable that the number of those slaughtered in cold blood reached at least a quarter of a million. In Nationalist Spain, on the other hand, where the ordinary courts of law continued to function, there is no evidence of execution without proper trial according to the law. This does not, of course, mean that all administration of justice was perfect in the territory controlled by the Nationalists, for feeling naturally ran high, especially among people whose friends and relatives had been murdered, but in this case the judges were trained lawyers and professional men: in the Government area men and women were sent to their death by self-constituted tribunals drawn from the dregs of the population.

In these circumstances it is in no way surprising that the conduct of the war in the field should also have deteriorated. Contemporaries, little knowing what was to be common practice on both sides during the Second World War, were particularly horrified at the bombing of the civilian population from the air. This was begun at Toledo by Largo Caballero, and in December, 1938, the Duke of Alba presented a note to the British Foreign Office stating that in the first two years of the war Government planes had, in two thousand raids, caused 18,985 deaths, mostly among the civilian population. The German allies of the Nationalists, however, soon proved more expert at this form of warfare than the Government supporters; indeed, to what extent a good deal of this bombing was carried out by foreign airmen in defiance of Spanish wishes is not easy to determine, and Valladolid was unquestionably raided by the Communists in January, 1937, in opposition to the orders of the Air Minister, Indalecio Prieto.

The opening of the year 1938 found the issue of the war still in doubt, in spite of the foreign assistance which was reaching both sides. It began with an offensive on the part of the Government forces, who successfully attacked at Teruel, which formed the spearhead of a dangerous salient into their eastern lines: the Nationalists, however, soon launched a counter-offensive, and Teruel was recaptured in the last week of February. In the following month there took place the attack which Franco had long been preparing, in fact ever since the defeat of his Italian allies at Guadalajara had opened his eyes to the fact that he must chiefly depend upon his own right arm. Once the offensive in Aragon had been commenced it pro-

gressed rapidly: Caspe was captured on March 17, and the Nationalists then turned North, occupying Lérida at the beginning of April.
A few days later they reached the Mediterranean, with the result that
the territory still in Government hands was cut in two. As in the
autumn of 1936, for a brief space it looked as if the Nationalists had
final victory within their grasp, but their opponents counter-attacked
on the Ebro, and Franco's advance on Valencia was held up. For the
rest of the year there was in this theatre some of the fiercest fighting
of the war, and it was not until November that the Government
troops were driven from their last bridge-head on the Ebro. Losses
were heavy on both sides, and the Nationalist General Staff announced
that on this sector they had killed thirteen thousand of the enemy,
captured twenty thousand, and shot down some three hundred
aeroplanes.

Franco had long ago decided not to make another frontal attack
on Madrid, partly because of the casualties which would be involved,
and partly because he did not wish to damage the city. In any case,
it was no longer the enemy capital, for this had been moved first to
Valencia and then to Barcelona. In these circumstances everything
pointed to an offensive against Catalonia. For this purpose the
Nationalists could now put into the field an army of 350,000 men, of
whom 16,000 were Italians, and the attack began on December 23,
1938, along the rivers Segre and Noguera Palloresa. Artesa fell on
January 4, 1939, and although the Italians were held up at Borgas
Blancas for a few days, the place was taken when the Navarrese came
to their assistance. On January 25 the city of Tarragona was occupied, and on the following day the *requetes* and the Moorish troops
entered Barcelona, closely followed by the Foreign Legion and the
Arrow Mixed Division, which consisted both of Italians and
Spaniards. By this time both the Catalan and Spanish Governments
had fled north.

The war had by now been won by the Nationalists, but it had still
two months to run. The supporters of Negrín, for it would be absurd to describe them any longer as Government forces, were still in
possession of a considerable part of the country from Sagunto to
Almaden, and they held Madrid: they also had several thousand men
in arms, and they had disposal of a certain amount of war material.
On the other hand, they had lost Catalonia with seventy per cent of
their industrial resources and a large proportion of their armed
forces, while they no longer possessed any land communication with
the rest of Europe. All the same they decided to fight on, for reasons
which have been well stated by Madariaga: "Dr. Negrín was not
free. He was attached to Moscow by a chain of gold. . . . One thing
is certain: at that moment, none but Dr. Negrín and the Communists
were for fighting. It is obvious that the Communists had instructions
to carry on the war and to hold fast to Dr. Negrín."

Events began to move with considerable rapidity. On February 27 the British and French Governments officially acknowledged Franco, and on the following day Azaña, who had fled to France, announced that he had resigned the Presidency of the Spanish Republic. Meanwhile, the Nationalist armies began to gather in force round Madrid, and watched the intensive conflict which broke out in the ranks of their opponents. After sharp fighting and a number of atrocities the Communists in the capital were crushed, and negotiations for peace were initiated by the victorious Council of Defence. Franco's terms proved to be complete surrender combined with promises of generosity and pardon to those not guilty of any crime. On March 29 the city surrendered, and the date is held to mark the end of the Civil War.

MODERN SPAIN

Showing the provinces and the old regions and including the Balearic and Canary Islands.

CHAPTER XLV

Spain and the Second World War (1939–1945)

WHEN the termination of the Civil War gave Franco and his colleagues leisure to regard the international scene, they saw Europe divided into two armed camps, and events were to prove that an early clash between them was inevitable. Spain was utterly exhausted, and it was the primary task of her new rulers to take care that she did not become involved in any conflict which might break out. The difficulties were not inconsiderable. The Nationalists owed a great deal to the German and Italian dictators, and there was a strong body of Phalangist opinion which admired the existing order in Berlin and Rome; on the other hand, the Church, whose support meant much to Franco, regarded the Third Reich with disapproval and Fascism with suspicion, while the Army and the monarchists could be relied upon to take a side opposed to the Phalangists in any dispute which might arise.

The complications, however, were not only of Spanish origin. In two of the three major wars of the previous centuries Spain had been a battle-field, and it behoved Franco to walk extremely warily if he was to avoid that false step which might so easily have completed the ruin of his country, worn out as she was by her long internal struggle. The possession of the Peninsula would be of the greatest importance to either group of combatants, but if that was out of the question Spain had a number of overseas territories, such as Spanish Morocco and the Balearic and Canary Islands, which might well tempt the appetite of one of the combatants.

Fortunately all the foreign troops had left the country by the time that the Second World War began in September, 1939. In this connection it may be pointed out that, in spite of innumerable prophecies to the contrary, not an inch of Spanish territory was ceded to Berlin or Rome in return for services rendered, and the archives of the German Foreign Office prove that at no time were the Nationalists prepared to give way on this point. It is true that in April, 1939, Spain signed the Anti-Comintern Pact, but in the light of the history of the previous three years it is difficult to express surprise at her action. On the other hand, there can be no doubt that when war did come the task of the Spanish Government in preserving the country's neutrality was rendered a great deal easier by the conclusion of the Russo-German agreement, which had a profound effect upon public opinion all over Spain, for Spanish hatred of Communism was not unnaturally far stronger than Spanish gratitude to Germany.

For Spain, as for the rest of the world, the war fell into several sharply defined periods. As soon as it began the Spanish Government issued a declaration of neutrality, but Spanish diplomacy was by no means inactive during what was termed the "phoney war": every effort was made to second the Pope's attempts to secure a negotiated peace, while the country's views of Germany's Communist ally were clearly revealed by the assistance given by the Spanish Red Cross to Finland, both in supplies and volunteers during the war between Finland and Russia. In March, 1940, an Anglo-Spanish trade agreement was signed covering the settlement of outstanding debts and balances by Spain, and granting to her credits in London for four million pounds. A few months earlier a Franco-Spanish trade agreement had been signed, and the two events were evidence of an increasing cordiality in the relations between Madrid and the Western Powers.

Then in May there came the German invasion of Holland, Belgium, and France, followed, with lightning rapidity, by the collapse of France and the entry of Italy into the war. This last event caused the Spanish Government to change its official attitude to one of "non-belligerency": this was widely interpreted as foreshadowing Spain's appearance in the field on the side of the Axis, but it proved to have no meaning at all. In any event Spanish neutrality was in the gravest danger. At any moment Hitler might demand a passage for his armoured divisions through the Peninsula to Gibraltar and North Africa, while in preparation for just such an eventuality Great Britain began to assemble an expeditionary force to seize the Canary Islands. The parallel with the events of 1807-9 was ominously close. Nor was this all, for, as on previous occasions, there was no inconsiderable body of opinion in Spain itself which inclined to Germany as against the Western Powers, and in the present instance this was reflected in the attitude of the Phalangists, upon whose support the Franco regime so largely depended.

Franco himself made no secret of his belief that a German victory was inevitable, but he was determined to remain neutral at all costs. Whether he would be allowed to do so was another matter, and Sir Samuel Hoare, who was at this time appointed British ambassador to Spain, had an aeroplane continually standing by in case of need. In pursuit of his policy of neutrality Franco had to gain time at all costs, and to prevent any precipitate act on the part of Hitler; this implied the appeasement of Germany on a considerable scale. In September the Führer presented Franco with a high German decoration, and in reply the Caudillo referred to the friendship which existed between the two nations and their strife against the common enemy of Communism. The moving spirit on the Spanish side in the appeasement of Germany was Serrano Suñer, and he paid personal visits at this time both to Hitler and to Mussolini when he made flattering speeches about the identity of aim of Spain and the Axis.

Mr. Churchill was indeed right when he said that Spain "seemed to hang in the balance between peace and war", and also when he wrote that Franco "only thought about keeping his blood-drained people out of another war". The result of the battle of Britain in the late summer did not make the situation any easier where Spain was concerned. Hitler had failed in his direct attack upon his main enemy it is true, but he was now devising other methods of getting at her. Franco hastened to bow to the storm. At the end of October not only did Himmler visit Madrid but Suñer replaced Beigbeder as Foreign Minister, and on the 23rd of the month there was a meeting between the Führer and Franco at Hendaye. Great pressure was put upon the Caudillo to allow the German army a passage through the country, but he refused, and Spain remained neutral. This was by no means to the liking of the German Government, and in November the Führer summoned Suñer to Berchtesgaden, where he expressed his annoyance at the failure of Franco to enter the war, while three weeks later Admiral Canaris, the Chief of the German Secret Service, was sent to Madrid to make the final arrangements. Still Franco made excuses, and at the beginning of February, 1941, the Führer wrote in the strongest possible terms to urge immediate intervention. One man, however, was certainly not deceived by the attitude of the Spanish Government, namely Ribbentrop, and he told Hitler that he was convinced Franco had no intention of fighting. The Führer seems to have held the same opinion, for he said of the Hendaye meeting, "We shall get nothing out of that man."

The relations between Spain and Germany continued on this somewhat uneasy basis during the first six months of the year 1941. Hitler, contrary to general expectation, contented himself with vague threats, possibly because he was already committed to the invasion of Russia, and mindful of the fate of Napoleon he did not wish to have a Peninsular campaign on his hands, for he had been left in no doubt by Franco that Spain would resist invasion from whatever quarter it came. Then, in June, came the German attack on Russia. This event gave a great impetus to the influence of the Reich, for the pro-German element was able to forget the Russo-German agreement of two years before, and to acclaim Hitler as the champion of civilisation against Communism. Suñer, in particular, distinguished himself by a number of violent speeches in favour of Germany, and in disparagement of Great Britain and the United States. Evidence of the strength of pro-German feeling was further afforded by the recruitment and despatch to Russia of the "Blue Division", which was composed of volunteers from the ex-combatants of the Civil War, under General Muñoz Grande. This was clearly a violation of Spanish neutrality, but there was a recent precedent in the International Brigade, which had intervened against the Nationalists in 1936. Fuel was added to the fire in the middle of July by Franco himself in a speech to the Spanish Phalanx, when he restated his hatred of Russia and Communism, and declared that Great Britain had already lost the war.

This was probably the point in the Second World War when the situation between Spain and the Western Powers was most critical.

The German invasion of Russia had naturally roused the greatest enthusiasm in a country which had recently had so much experience of Communist violence, and the early successes of the German armies there and in North Africa were generally regarded as presaging final victory for the Reich. Still, however, it is to be noted that Franco did not take the decisive step of bringing his country into the war on the side of the Axis. Certainly Suñer did nothing to improve Spanish relations with the West, but it was otherwise with the ambassadors, and to them must go most of the credit for the fact that there was no open breach. Especially was this the case with the Duke of Alba, the Spanish ambassador in London, and it was largely due to his wisdom and untiring efforts that Spain did not, like Italy, espouse the losing cause: her debt to him is very great indeed. A like service was performed by Professor Carlton J. H. Hayes, who represented the United States in Madrid, and by the British ambassador there, Sir Samuel Hoare, in spite, it may be added, of what he subsequently wrote.

The danger of a conflict with the Western Powers at this time was enhanced by the fact that they were themselves making preparations for extensive operations in the Mediterranean, and were therefore watching the attitude of Spain more carefully than ever. Once again the Spanish Government became fearful for the Canaries, more particularly in view of the declaration of President Roosevelt that the Azores were in the sphere of American interests. At the end of August, 1942, however, the tension was eased by the replacement at the Ministry of Foreign Affairs of Suñer by General Count Jordana, and when, in November of the same year, British and American troops landed in North Africa, he was notified by Sir Samuel Hoare that "the operations in no way threaten Spanish territory, metropolitan or oversea". The worst was over, and Spain could breathe more freely than at any time since the fall of France.

There was, however, one cause of friction with the West, and that was the position in Tangier. That port had, as has been shown on an earlier page, not been included in either the French or the Spanish Zone by the settlement of 1912, and it had since then been subject to an international regime. During the First World War it appeared more than once likely to pass into Spanish hands, but in actual fact that conflict came to an end without any change taking place in its status. On June 14, 1940, Spanish troops occupied Tangier, and the Spanish Government declared that the occupation was of a temporary nature with the object of guaranteeing the neutrality of the town. It is probable that the step was taken to forestall a similar act on the part of Great Britain. In November matters were taken a stage farther, for Colonel Yuste somewhat unexpectedly assumed the governorship of Tangier in the name of the Spanish Government, and abolished the existing legislative assembly and committee of control. This action was in direct violation of international settlements, and protests were made by London and Washington. As a result, a temporary arrangement was reached in February, 1941, by which British rights and interests in Tangier were safeguarded, and an undertaking was given that the zone would not be fortified: the whole question was to be reviewed at the end of the war.

Hardly was the ink dry on this document than, in the following month, the Sultan's representative in Tangier was ejected, and his residence was handed over to Germany for use as a consulate. In January, 1943, it was announced that Tangier had been incorporated in the Spanish Zone, and this was met by a reminder from the British Government that it refused to recognise any unilateral act on the part of Madrid. Soon afterwards the military situation in the Mediterranean changed to the disadvantage of the Axis, and in September, 1944, the German consulate in Tangier was closed. It only remains to add in this connection that in August, 1945, an international conference on the problem was convened at Paris, to which Spain was not invited, and the old international regime was restored with some modifications: the Spanish Government accepted this settlement under protest.

This, however, is to anticipate. Nothing succeeds like success, and it was only natural that the progress of Allied arms in the Mediterranean should have impressed Spanish opinion, and should have diminished greatly the influence of the pro-German element in the Peninsula. At the same time it was not easy for a Spaniard to become enthusiastic for an alliance which included Soviet Russia among its more important members. The fall of Mussolini at the end of July, 1943, caused alarm in Phalangist circles, and this was not greatly lessened by Franco's argument that there was all the difference in the world between the Spanish Phalanx and Italian Fascism. Then the virtual imprisonment of the Pope by the Germans created a final revulsion of feeling, and affected still further the relative sympathies of the Spanish people towards the belligerents. Lastly, came the collapse of the Third Reich as the British and Americans drove across France in the latter part of 1944, and every Spaniard had to realise that his country must henceforth conciliate London and Washington.

Not unnaturally, as the Western Powers came nearer to final victory their attitude stiffened towards what they considered to be Spanish infractions of neutrality, and the culmination of their pressure was reached by the application to Spain of sanctions in the form of the cessation of oil shipments.

Of the main points at issue during the last phase of the Second World War, two turned on the vexed question of the interpretation of a neutral's rights. The first problem was that of wolfram supplies to Germany, which Spain was perfectly justified in sending, but which the Western Powers were equally justified in endeavouring to stop. The second was concerned with some eleven Italian men-of-war and merchant ships which had taken refuge in Spanish ports for one reason or another at the time of the surrender of Italy. The Spanish Government alleged its obligation as a neutral to intern any warship which remained more than a specified time in its harbours, while it laid claim to the merchantmen as compensation for Spanish ships previously sunk by Italian submarines. Great Britain and the United States, on the other hand, claimed the ships on the ground that they had been surrendered to them by Italy. The third problem was of a different nature, for it concerned the Blue Division, which, with the open approval of the Spanish Government, was fighting for the Germans against the Russian ally of the Western Powers. A fourth cause of friction was the question of German activities in Tangier, which has already been discussed.

After extensive negotiations through the regular diplomatic channels a settlement was reached in May, 1944, of the outstanding questions at issue. Wolfram supplies to Germany, except for a small monthly token shipment, ceased; the Italian merchant ships were to be released with the exception of two, and the fate of the men-of-war was to be settled by arbitration; while as regards the Blue Division it was announced that this had now been withdrawn. On the other side, the renewal of oil shipments to Spain was granted.

Such was the position when the Second World War came to an end twelve months later. Franco had kept his country out of the war, but to what extent this state of affairs was due to his patriotism or his cynicism, to his ability or his luck, is likely to remain a matter of opinion.

CHAPTER XLVI

The Past and the Future

WHAT strikes us especially, in course of the study, is the slowness of Spain to achieve her political unity: a unity always precarious, and often called in question. The separatist tendency is to some degree congenital in Spain, and anarchist and revolutionary movements are certainly more frequent there than in the other countries of Europe.

There is in this a curious survival of mediaeval and Arab–Berber mentality, of the *taifas* of the South, and the little Christian kingdoms of the North, of the Peninsula. The particularist spirit which so long kept Spain in a condition of dispersion and internal division is still alive. While this spirit manifests itself in Catalonia, in Navarre, and in the Basque Provinces, as well as in the Provinces of the South, it seems that Socialist and Communist tendencies are more peculiar to Andalusia and the old kingdom of Valencia, that is to say in the regions which were most profoundly affected by Islam.

These tendencies in the agricultural masses have been explained by the persistence of great landed estates, a legacy of the *latifundios* of the Visigoth and Roman period: the serf attached to the soil has only one ambition, which is to possess himself of his lord's land. But one may also see here the old spirit of *sof*, brought to Andalusia by the African Berbers, *i.e.* the land as the indivisible property of the tribe. This is Socialism in its rudimentary and barbarous form. Far from being modern, or as is improperly said "advanced", these tendencies are, on the contrary, as retrogade as they can possibly be, and represent a return to the Arab mentality of the Middle Ages.

Be that as it may, it is another fact no less striking that the political unity of Spain, in a more or less ephemeral form, was never realised except by foreign dynasties: first by the Visigoth kings, then by the Arab caliphs, next by the princes of the House of Habsburg, and finally by the Bourbons. The Catholic Sovereigns, Ferdinand and Isabel, while they paved the way for this unity, still maintained the division of the Peninsula into two great kingdoms, Aragón and Castile.

Spain seems, therefore, refractory to the idea of centralisation, under any regime. The regionalist idea is extremely popular there, despite all the dangers which regionalism involves, especially in a country where the political education of the masses remains to be accomplished. The most apparent of these dangers is anarchy, and it is a re-assuring fact that of late years the vigorous individualism of the nation has triumphed over Socialist and Communist tyrannies, whose rules of life are, for that matter, absolutely contrary to the temperament of the Latin peoples and especially of the Spanish people.

Moreover, to conjure away the peril of national dissolution through excess of individualism and regionalism, any government can depend upon that sense of Race which is so strong throughout the Iberian world. During the reign of Alfonso XIII this racial solidarity developed in the most extraordinary fashion, thanks to the rebirth of Americanism. This Americanism has marched step by step with the progressive industrialism of the country during the last half-century.

Once more the Spaniards have acquired the habit of turning towards Latin America, towards their old Empire of the Indies, not merely to find markets there, but also to restore the moral and intellectual unity of the Race. In solemn festivals, of a highly national character, the immortal Race has been glorified as a divinity. Together with the ties of blood, the spiritual ties that unite America to the old metropolis have been recalled. An effort has been made to re-establish the fraternal relationship of Spain with the lands of the *Conquistadores*.

There is here, as it were, the sketch of another Latinity, a Latinity wider than the French. In vain do the French appeal to these Latins in the name of a problematic consanguinity. These Latins are Westerners, whose eyes are turned elsewhere: elsewhere than towards our little Europe. Separated from France by their mountains, at the extremity of the European continent, they look towards the West, beyond the Ocean. One might think that they were seeking to raise the lost Atlantis by renewing Pan-Iberian solidarity with the Western Indies.

In any case, the mentality of these Occidental Latins is not that of the French, or even that of the more imperialist Italians. The Race, of which they are the living consciousness, has no need to be warlike or conquering. It concerns itself neither with literature, nor with aesthetics, nor with ideology, nor with humanitarianism to be propagated. It knows only that it exists; that it covers two continents; and that it manifests itself in a very specialised human type, who regards himself more or less openly as superior to all others, and, whatever happens, and despite all unfavourable hazards, is persuaded that he will survive them, and that he cannot die.

Pride of blood, even among the most humble; an obscure consciousness of a whole heroic past, of a great role once played in the world, of Christendom and Western civilisation saved by their ancestors, of a world immensely enlarged by the audacity of their navigators and their conquerors; consciousness also of having been a people of masters and aristocrats in a Europe subject to Spanish hegemony, and of having created, through generations of artists, dramatists, novelists and poets, a whole world of plastic forms and ideal figures—these feelings live in the depths of all Spanish souls.

Relying upon them, and upon the proud individualism of her people, a Spain united under a regime of authority and liberty, and at the same time of social foresight, may once more be ready tomorrow for a great destiny.

BIBLIOGRAPHY

Abd el Wahid El Merrakeshi: *Histoire des Almohades,* translation by Fagnan, Algiers, 1893.
Altamira y Crevea, R.: *Historia de España y de la Civilización Española,* 4 vols., Barcelona, 1902.
Armstrong, E.: *Elisabeth Farnese,* London, 1892.
Armstrong, E.: *The Emperor Charles V,* 2 vols., London, 1902.
Ballesteros y Beretta, Antonio: *Historia de España y su Influencia en la Historia Universal,* Salvat, Barcelona, 1918, etc.
Baró, T.: *Historia de España,* Barcelona, 1911.
Baudin, Louis: *L'Empire socialiste des Inkas,* Paris, 1928.
Baudrillart, Mgr.: *Philippe V et la Cour de France,* 5 vols., Paris, 1890-1901.
Bertrand, Louis: *Sainte-Thérèse,* Paris, 1926.
Bertrand, Louis: *Philippe II: Une ténébreuse affaire,* Paris, 1929.
Bertrand, Louis: *Philippe II à l'Escorial,* Paris, 1929.
Bratli: *Philippe II,* Paris, 1912.
Brown, V. L.: *Studies of the History of Spain in the Second Half of the Eighteenth Century,* Northampton, Mass., 1929.
Burke, M. R.: *History of Spain to the death of Ferdinand the Catholic,* 2 vols., London, 1900.
Calvert, A. F.: *Moorish Remains in Spain,* London and New York (John Lane).
Cappa, Ricardo: *Estudios críticos acerca de la dominación española en América,* 1889-1891.
Chapman, Charles E.: *A History of Spain,* New York, 1919.
Circourt, A. de: *Histoire des Maures Mudejares et des Morisques, ou des Arabes d'Espagne sous la domination des Chrétiens,* Paris, 1848.
Davies, R. T.: *The Golden Century of Spain,* 1501-1621, London, 1937.
Diaz, Bernal: *Véridique histoire de la Conquête de la Nouvelle Espagne,* translation by J.-M. de Heredia, 4 vols., Paris, 1887.
Dozy, R.: *Histoire des Musulmans d'Espagne jusqu'à la Conquête de l'Andalousie par les Almoravides,* 4 vols., Leyden, 1861.
Dozy, R.: *Recherches sur l'histoire et de la littérature de l'Espagne pendant le moyen âge,* 2 vols., Leyden, 1860.
Edrisi: *Descripción de España,* translation by Antonio Blázquez, Madrid, 1901.
Ellis, Havelock: *The Soul of Spain,* London (Constable), New York (Houghton Mifflin), 1915.
Ford, J. D. M.: *Main Currents of Spanish Literature,* New York (Holt), 1919.
Forneron, H.: *Histoire de Philippe II,* 2 vols., Paris, 1881-1882.
García Mercadal, J.: *Cisneros,* 1436-1517, Zaragoza, 1939.
Gossart, E.: *Espagnols et Flamands au XVIe siècle,* 2 vol., Brussels, 1905-1906.
Gossart E.: *Charles-Quint, roi d'Espagne,* Brussels, 1910.
Grandmaison, Geoffrey de: *L'Espagne et Napoléon,* 2 vols., Paris.
Griffin, C. C.: *The United States and the Disruption of the Spanish Empire,* 1810-1822, New York, 1937.
Guyot, Yves: *L'Evolution politique et sociale en Espagne,* Paris, 1899.
Hale, E. E. and S.: *Spain,* New York (Putnam), 1886.
Hannay, D.: *Don Emilio Castelar,* London, 1896.
Hannay, D.: *Spain* (The Nations' Histories), London, 1917.
Herrera, Antonio de: *Historia general de los hechos de los castellanos en las islas y Tierrafirme del Mar Oceano,* Madrid, 1924.
Houghton, A.: *Les Origines de la Restauration des Bourbons en Espagne,* Paris, 1890.
Howells, W. D.: *Familiar Spanish Travels,* New York (Harper), 1913.
Hume, Martin: *History of Modern Spain,* 1788-1918, London, 1923.
Hume, Martin: *Spain, its Greatness and Decay,* Cambridge, New York (Putnam), 1924.
Hume, Martin: *Philip II of Spain,* London, 1938.
Hume, Martin: *The Court of Philip IV and the Decadence of Spain,* New York, 1907.
Hume, Martin: *The Spanish People,* New York (Appleton), 1900.
Ibn Adhari: *Al Bayan' ol Moghreb,* translation by Fagnan, Algiers, 1901.
Ibn el Athir: *Annales du Moghreb et de l'Espagne,* translated by Fagnan, Algiers, 1901.
Irving, Washington: *The Alhambra,* London and New York (Macmillan).
Jacobs, J.: *Inquiry into the Sources of the History of the Jews in Spain,* London, 1894.
Lecquerq, Dom: *L'Espagne chrétienne,* Paris, 1906.

Lema, Marqués de: *Spain since 1815*, Cambridge, 1921.
León, Cieza de: *Cronica de las guerras civiles del Peru.*
Loveday, A. F.: Spain, 1923–1948, London, 1949.
Lummis, Charles F.: *The Spanish Pioneers*, New York (McClurg), 1914.
Madariaga, S. de: *The Rise of the Spanish American Empire*, London, 1947.
Madariaga, S. de: *The Fall of the Spanish American Empire*, London, 1947.
Marçais, G.: *Manuel d'art musulman*, 2 vols., Paris, 1926–1927.
Mariéjol, J. H.: *L'Espagne sous Ferdinand et Isabelle*, Paris, 1892.
Marmol Carvajal, Luis del: *Historia del Rebelión y Castigo de los Moriscos del Reyno de Granada*, Malaga, 1600.
Marvaud, Angel: *L'Espagne au XXe Siècle. Etude politique et économique*, Paris, 1913.
Maura Gamazo, Gabriel: *Carlos II y su Corte*, Madrid, 1911.
Maura Gamazo, Gabriel: *Historia crítica del Reinado de D. Alfonso XIII*, Barcelona, 1925.
Mendoza, Diego Hurtado de: *Guerra de Granada que hizo el rey D. Felipe II contra los Moriscos de aquel reyno*, Valencia, 1776.
Menéndez Pidal, Ramón: *La España del Cid*, 2 vols., Madrid, 1929.
Merriman, R. B.: *The Rise of the Spanish Empire in the Old World and in the New*, 2 vols., New York (Macmillan), 1918).
Mignet, F. M. A.: *Rivalité de François Ier et de Charles-Quint*, Paris, 1875, 2 vols.
Parry, E. J.: *The Spanish Marriage*, 1841–1846, London, 1936.
Peers, E. A.: *The Spanish Tragedy*, 1930–1936, London, 1936.
Peers, E. A.: *The Church in Spain*, 1737–1937, London, 1938.
Pereyra, Carlos: *Historia de la América española*, Madrid, 1920–1924.
Pereyra, Carlos: *La obra de España en América*, Madrid, 1924.
Pizarro, Pedro: *Relación del Descubrimiento de los reinos del Peru*, Unpublished Documents, Vol. V.
Prescott, W.: *History of the Conquest of Peru.*
Rousseau, F.: *Règne de Charles III d'Espagne*, 2 vols., Paris, 1907.
Rubio, Ortega: *Los Visigodos en España*, Madrid, 1903.
Sedgwick, H. D.: *Spain: A Short History of its Politics, Literature and Art*, London, 1926.
Sencourt, R.: *Spain's Uncertain Crown*, London, 1932.
Sencourt, R.: *King Alfonso, A Biography*, London, 1942.
Shepherd, N. R.: *Latin America*, New York (Henry Holt), 1919.
Simonet, Xavier: *Descripción del reyno de Granada bajo la dominacion de los Naseritas*, Madrid, 1860.
Templewood, Vincent: *Ambassador on Special Mission*, London, 1946.
Trend, J. B.: *A Picture of Modern Spain, Men and Music*, London, 1921.
Vega, Garcilaso de la: *Histoire des Incas, roys du Pérou*, translation by L. Baudoin, Paris, 1633.
Vignaud, Henry: *Histoire critique de la grande entreprise de Christophe Colomb*, 2 vols.
Villar, E. H. del: *El Valor Geográfico de España*, Madrid, 1922.
Walsh, W. T.: *Isabella of Spain*, London, 1931.
Walsh, W. T.: *Philip II*, London, 1938.

PRINCIPAL EVENTS IN THE HISTORY OF SPAIN

711.   Spain conquered by the Arabs
718.   Battle of Cavadonga
755.   Arrival of Abd er Rhaman I
929.   Caliphate established at Cordova by Abd er Rhaman III
997.   Sack of Compostela by El Mansour
1031. Abolition of the Caliphate
1043. Birth of Rodrigo Diaz de Vivar, the Cid Campeador (d. 1099)
1085. Conquest of Toledo by Alfonso VI
1094. Conquest of Valencia by the Cid Campeador
1118. Conquest of Zaragoza by Alfonso I (el Batallador)
1195. Battle of Alarcos
1212. Battle of Las Navas de Tolosa
1236. Conquest of Cordova
1238. Reconquest of Valencia by James I
1248. Conquest of Seville by Ferdinand III (el Santo)
1478. Inquisition introduced into Castile
1492. Conquest of Granada by Ferdinand and Isabella
1492. Expulsion of the Jews from Spain
1492. Discovery of America by Christopher Columbus
1494. Naples conquered by Gonzalo de Córdova
1519. Charles V elected Emperor
1519. Hernan Cortes begins conquest of Mexico
1524. Discovery of Peru by Francisco Pizarro
1525. Battle of Pavia
1535. Conquest of Tunis
1557. Battle of Saint Quentin
1559. Treaty of Cateau-Cambrésis
1563. Foundation of the Monastery of the Escuríal by Philip II
1572. Battle of Lepanto
1581. Annexion of Portugal
1588. Expedition of the Invincible Armada
1599. Birth of Velazquez (d. 1660)
1605. First edition of *Don Quixote*
1609. Expulsion of the Moriscos
1643. Battle of Rocroi
1648. Peace of Westphalia
1659. Treaty of the Pyrenees
1668. Independence of Portugal
1701. War of Succession: Formation of the Grand Alliance
1713. Treaty of Utrecht
1763. Treaty of Paris
1767. Expulsion of the Jesuits
1796. Alliance with France against England
1805. Battle of Trafalgar
1808. War of Independence
1808. Battle of Bailen
1812. Constitution promulgated at Cádiz
1820. Revolt of Riego

PRINCIPAL EVENTS IN THE HISTORY OF SPAIN

1823. French army enters Spain under the Duke of Angoulême
1824. Battle of Ayacucho
1834. First Carlist War
1859. Tetuan taken by General O'Donnell
1865. War against Chile and Peru
1868. Outbreak of revolution; Isabella II leaves Spain
1871. Amadeo of Savoy becomes King of Spain
1873. King Amadeo leaves Madrid; first Republic proclaimed
1874. Cortes dissolved by General Pavia
1874. Proclamation of Alfonso XII by General Mártinez Campos
1876. End of third Carlist War
1898. War with the United States; loss of Cuba and the Philippines
1909. Hostilities break out in Morocco
1921. Disaster of Anual
1923. General Primo de Rivera forms a Military Directory
1925. Spanish forces land at Alhucemas
1925. Civil Directory formed under General Primo de Rivera
1926. End of hostilities in Morocco
1930. End of Dictatorship under Primo de Rivera
1931. Second Republic proclaimed in Spain
1936. Civil War begins
1939. Civil War ends; Second World War begins
1941. Death of Alfonso XIII
1945. Second World War ends

CHRONOLOGICAL LIST OF THE SOVEREIGNS OF SPAIN

I. MUSULMAN SPAIN

Principal Rulers only

EMIRS OF CORDOVA

	A.D.
Abd er Rhaman I	756
Hisham I	788
Hakam I	799
Abd er Rhaman II	822
Mohammed I	852
Mondhir	886
Abdallah	888

CALIPHS OF CORDOVA

	A.D.
Abd er Rhaman III	912
Hakam II	961
Hisham II	976
Mohammed II	1008
Soleyman	1009
Hisham II (second time)	1010
Soleyman (second time)	1012
Ali ben Hamoud	1017
Abd er Rhaman IV	1021
Alcasim	1022
Abd er Rhaman V	1022
Mohammed III	1023
Yahya ben Ali	1024
Hisham III	1027

ALMORAVID SULTANS

	A.D.
Yousouf ben Teshoufin	1067
Ali ben Yousouf	1107
Teshoufin ben Ali	1144

ALMOHADE SULTANS

	A.D.
Abd el Moulmin	1147
Yousouf abou Yacoub	1163

ALMOHADE SULTANS (*continued*)

	A.D.
Yacoub ben Yousouf	1178
Mohammed ben Yacoub	1199
Abou Yacoub	1213
Abou Malik	1223
Mamoun	1225

KINGS OF GRANADA

	A.D.
Mahommed I	1238
Mahommed II	1273
Mahommed III	1303
Nazar	1309
Ismail I	1312
Mahommed IV	1325
Youcef I	1333
Mahommed V	1354
Ismail II	1359
Abou-Said	1361
Mahommed V (second time)	1362
Youcef II	1391
Mahommed VI	1396
Youcef III	1408
Mahommed VII	1425
Mahommed VIII	1427
Mahommed VII (second time)	1429
Ebn Alhamar	1431
Mahommed VII (third time)	1432
Ebn Ostman	1445
Ebn Ismail	1454
Muley Hacen	1456
Abou Abdilehi (Boabdil)	1482

II. CHRISTIAN SPAIN

Principal Rulers only

KINGS OF ASTURIAS

	A.D.
Pelayo	718
Favila	738
Alfonso I	739

KINGS OF ASTURIAS (*continued*)

	A.D.
Fruela I	756
Aurelio	768

	A.D.
Silo	774
Mauregato	783
Bermudo I	789
Alfonso II	791
Ramiro I	842
Ordoño I	850
Alfonso III	866

KINGS OF LEÓN

	A.D.
García	909
Ordoño II	914
Fruela II	924
Alfonso IV	925
Ramiro II	930
Ordoño III	950
Sancho I	955
Ramiro III	967
Bermudo II	982
Alfonso V	999
Bermudo III	1027

KINGS OF LEÓN AND CASTILE

	A.D.
Ferdinand I	1037
Sancho II	1065
Alfonso VI	1072
Doña Urraca	1109
Alfonso VII	1126

KINGS OF LEÓN

	A.D.
Ferdinand II	1157
Alfonso IX	1188

KINGS OF CASTILE

	A.D.
Sancho III	1157
Alfonso VIII	1158
Henry I	1214
Doña Berenguela	1217

KINGS OF LEÓN AND CASTILE

	A.D.
Ferdinand III	1217
Alfonso X	1252
Sancho IV	1284
Ferdinand IV	1295
Alfonso XI	1312
Pedro I	1350
Henry II	1369
John I	1379
Henry III	1390
John II	1406
Henry IV	1454

KINGS OF NAVARRE

	A.D.
Sancho Garces	905
García Sánchez I	925
Sancho Abarca	970
García Sánchez II	994
Sancho the Great	1000
García Sánchez	1035
Sancho V	1054
García Ramírez IV	1134
Sancho VII	1150
Sancho VIII	1194
Teobaldo I	1234
Teobaldo II	1253
Henry I	1270
Juana I	1274
Luis Hutín	1305
Philip	1316
Charles I	1322
Juana II	1328
Charles II	1349
Charles III	1387
Doña Blanca and Don John	1425
Doña Leonor	1479
Francisco Febo	1479
Catalina and Don John of Aragón	1481

KINGS OF ARAGÓN

	A.D.
Ramiro I	1035
Sancho Ramírez	1065
Pedro I	1094
Alfonso I	1104
Ramiro II	1134
Doña Petronila	1137
Alfonso II	1162
Pedro II	1196
James I the Conqueror	1213
Pedro III	1276
Alfonso III	1285
James II	1291
Alfonso IV	1327
Pedro IV	1336
John I	1387
Martín I	1395
Ferdinand I	1410
Alfonso V	1416
John II	1458
Ferdinand II	1479

KINGS OF SPAIN

	A.D.
Isabel I and Ferdinand V	1474
Philip I and Doña Juana	1504
Ferdinand V (as Regent)	1506
Cardinal Cisneros (as Regent)	1516

House of Austria

	A.D.
Charles I	1517
Philip II	1556
Philip III	1598
Philip IV	1621
Charles II	1665

House of Bourbon

	A.D.
Philip V	1701
Luis I	1724
Philip V (again)	1724

KINGS OF SPAIN (*continued*)

	A.D.
Ferdinand VI	1746
Charles III	1759
Charles IV	1788
Ferdinand VII	1808
Joseph Bonaparte	1808
Ferdinand VII (again)	1814
Isabel II	1833
Provisional Government	1868
Amadeo I	1871
First Republic	1873
Alfonso XII	1874
Maria Cristina (as Regent)	1886
Alfonso XIII	1886
Second Republic	1931
Franco regime	1936

INDEPENDENT COUNTS OF BARCELONA

	A.D.
Wifredo the Hairy	874
Borrel y Suniario	989
Borrel y Mirón	954
Ramón Borrell III	992
Berenguer Ramón I	1018

	A.D.
Ramón Berenguer I	1035
Ramón Berenguer II	1076
Ramón Berenguer II	1082
Ramón Berenguer III	1096
Ramón Berenguer IV	1131

KINGS OF MAJORCA

	A.D.
James I (the Conqueror)	1231
James II	1276

	A.D.
Sancho I	1311
James III	1324

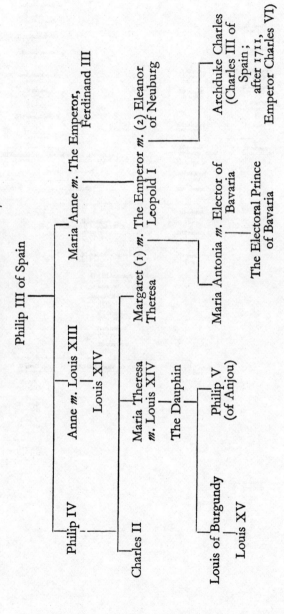

SPANISH SUCCESSION 1700

Philip III of Spain

Philip IV — Anne *m.* Louis XIII — Maria Anne *m.* The Emperor, Ferdinand III

Louis XIV

Charles II — Maria Theresa *m.* Louis XIV — Margaret (1) *m.* The Emperor *m.* (2) Eleanor of Neuburg

The Dauphin

Leopold I

Philip V (of Anjou) — Maria Antonia *m.* Elector of Bavaria — Archduke Charles (Charles III of Spain; after 1711, Emperor Charles VI)

Louis of Burgundy

The Electoral Prince of Bavaria

Louis XV

GENEALOGICAL TABLE OF THE

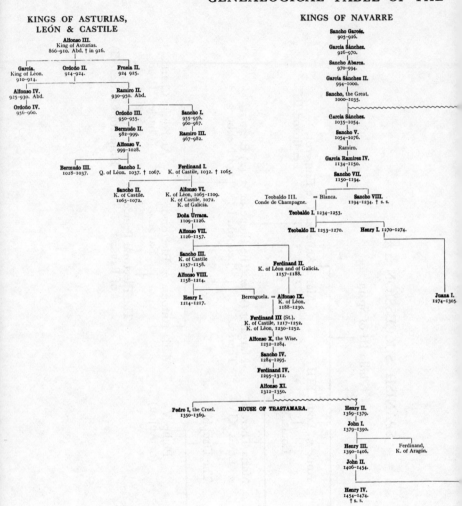

KINGS OF ASTURIAS, LEÓN & CASTILE

Alfonso III. King of Asturias. 866–910. Abd. † in 916.

García. King of Léon. 910–914.

Ordoño II. 914–924.

Fruela II. 924–925.

Alfonso IV. 925–930. Abd.

Ramiro II. 930–950. Abd.

Ordoño IV. 950–960.

Ordoño III. 950–955.

Sancho I. 955–956. 960–967.

Bermudo II. 982–999.

Ramiro III. 967–982.

Alfonso V. 999–1028.

Bermudo III. 1028–1037.

Sancho I. Q. of Léon. 1037. † 1067.

Ferdinand I. K. of Castile, 1032. † 1065.

Sancho II. K. of Castile. 1065–1072.

Alfonso VI. K. of Léon, 1065–1109. K. of Castile, 1072. K. of Galicia.

Doña Urraca. 1109–1126.

Alfonso VII. 1126–1157.

Sancho III. K. of Castile 1157–1158.

Alfonso VIII. 1158–1214.

Ferdinand II. K. of Léon and of Galicia. 1157–1188.

Henry I. 1214–1217.

Berenguela. = **Alfonso IX.** K. of Léon. 1188–1230.

Ferdinand III (St.). K. of Castile, 1217–1252. K. of Léon, 1230–1252.

Alfonso X, the Wise. 1252–1284.

Sancho IV. 1284–1295.

Ferdinand IV. 1295–1312.

Alfonso XI. 1312–1350.

Pedro I, the Cruel. 1350–1369.

HOUSE OF TRASTAMARA.

KINGS OF NAVARRE

Sancho García. 905–926.

García Sánchez. 926–970.

Sancho Abarca. 970–994.

García Sánchez II. 994–1000.

Sancho, the Great. 1000–1035.

García Sánchez. 1035–1054.

Sancho V. 1054–1076.

Ramiro.

García Ramirez IV. 1134–1150.

Sancho VII. 1150–1194.

Teobaldo III. = Blanca. **Sancho VIII.** Conde de Champagne. 1194–1234. † s. s.

Teobaldo I. 1234–1253.

Teobaldo II. 1253–1270.

Henry I. 1270–1274.

Juana I. 1274–1305.

Henry II. 1369–1379.

John I. 1379–1390.

Henry III. 1390–1406.

Ferdinand, K. of Aragón.

John II. 1406–1454.

Henry IV. 1454–1474. † s. s.

NOTE.—The Spanish ruling sovereigns are printed in **black type.** Abd. = Abdicated. † = Died.

CHRISTIAN KINGS OF SPAIN

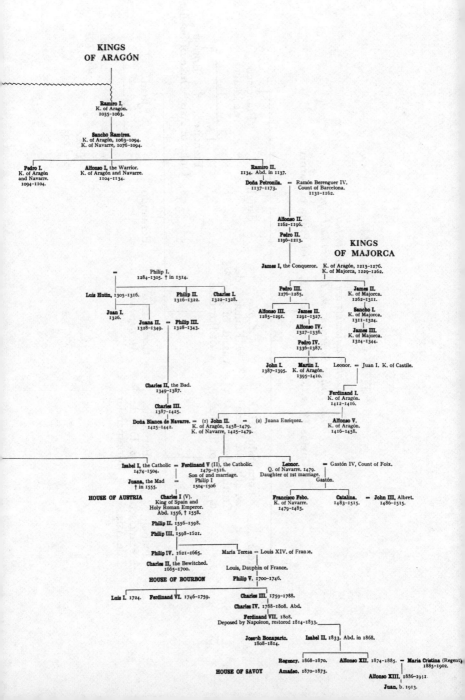

THE CARLIST CLAIM

The Carlist claimants are shown in italics
The Ruling Sovereigns are shown in bold type

Carlos IV *m.* Maria Luisa Teresa, d. of Philip of Parma

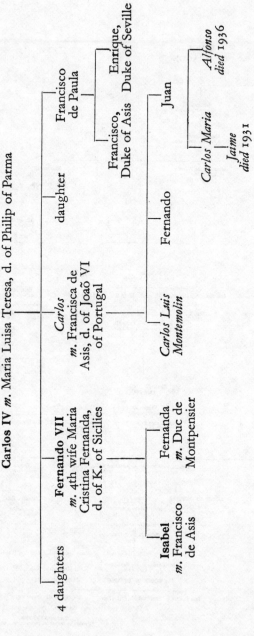

INDEX

413